New Governance and the European Employment Strategy

In recent years new or experimental approaches to governance in the EU, namely the Open Method of Co-ordination (OMC), have attracted great interest and controversy. This book examines the European Employment Strategy (EES) and its implementation through the OMC, exploring the promises and limitations of the EES for EU social law and policy and for the safeguard of social rights. This significant and timely work offers new insights and fresh perspectives into the operation of New Governance and its relationship with both European and national law and constitutionalism.

This book will be of great interest to academics, researchers and postgraduate students working in European law – specifically in the field of EU employment law and gender equality – and European governance studies in general.

Dr Samantha Velluti is Senior Lecturer in Law at Lincoln Law School. She has researched extensively in the area of EU governance and constitutionalism and the Open Method of Co-ordination in the context of employment, gender equality and migration. Her current research focuses on the relationship between New Governance and EU constitutionalism and law, gender mainstreaming, gender equality and migration. Recent publications include: *Gender and the Open Method of Coordination: Perspectives on Law, Governance and Equality in the EU* (Ashgate, 2008) co-edited with Professor Fiona Beveridge, Liverpool Law School and *Gender and Migration in 21st Century Europe* (Ashgate 2009) co-edited with Dr Helen Stalford and Dr Samantha Currie, Liverpool Law School.

Routledge Research in EU Law

Available titles in this series include:

Centralised Enforcement, Legitimacy and Good Governance in the EU
Melanie Smith

Forthcoming titles in this series include:

Criminal Law and Policy in the European Union
Samuli Miettinen

Human Rights and Minority Rights in the European Union
Kirsten Shoraka

The Evolving EU Counter-terrorism Legal Framework
Maria O'Neill

EU External Relations and Systems of Governance
The CFSP, Euro-Mediterranean Partnership and migration
Paul James Cardwell

Local Government in Europe
The 'Fourth Level' in the EU Multi-Layered System of Governance
Carlo Panara and Michael R. Varney

New Governance and the European Employment Strategy

Samantha Velluti

LONDON AND NEW YORK

First published 2010
by Routledge
2 Park Square, Milton Park, Abingdon, Oxon OX14 4RN

Simultaneously published in the USA and Canada
by Routledge
270 Madison Avenue, New York, NY 10016

Routledge is an imprint of the Taylor & Francis Group, an informa business

Typeset in BaskervilleMT by
RefineCatch Limited, Bungay, Suffolk
Printed and bound in Great Britain by
CPI Antony Rowe, Chippenham, Wiltshire

British Library Cataloguing in Publication Data
A catalogue record for this book is available
from the British Library

Library of Congress Cataloging-in-Publication Data
Velluti, Samantha.
  New governance and the European employment strategy / Samantha
  Velluti.
    p. cm.
  Includes bibliographical references.
  1. Manpower policy—European Union countries.   2. Labor laws and
  legislation—European Union countries.   3. Constitutional law—
  European Union countries.   I. Title.
  KJE3195.V45 2010
  344.2401—dc22   2009035805

ISBN10: 0–415–46779–9 (hbk)
ISBN10: 0–203–85646–5 (ebk)

ISBN13: 978–0–415–46779–7 (hbk)
ISBN13: 978–0–203–85646–8 (ebk)

In memory of Bart Burgess
and his living spirit

Contents

List of illustrations

Preface

EC social policy has attracted the attention of a large community of lawyers, policy makers and scholars, in particular, because it presents the European Union (EU) with a difficult regulatory task which is explained by, *inter alia*, opposing views about its function, scope and objectives. Recent actions and strategies by the EU institutions in the area of social policy reveal an increase in the use of complementary or rather experimental modes of regulation which draw upon multi-tiered and "loose" forms of regulation.

The introduction in 1997 of a new strategy at European level for fighting high levels of unemployment, the European Employment Strategy (EES), ratified a regulatory technique based on co-ordination of action – later to be named Open Method of Co-ordination (OMC) – which was already applied in the context of Economic and Monetary Union (EMU). It also paved the way for Community intervention in the field of employment while, at the same time, enabling the accommodation of national diversity and respect for the autonomy of the Member States. In particular, at European level the EES entailed a shift from social law and legislative intervention towards the use of soft law measures: soft law has rapidly become the principal legal instrument for "coercing" Member States to adopt employment-related measures in line with European objectives. At national level Member States may implement European *soft* policies through the adoption of *hard* law measures.

The heart of this book is a legal study blended with social, political and economic analyses of the genesis, implementation and further development of the EES and its implementation through a "new" mode of EU governance, the OMC, from its origins to the adoption of the Lisbon Strategy and post-Lisbon, spanning chiefly the period of 1997–2005. The book, belated as it is in entering into the debate on New Governance and experimentalism and, more specifically, on the effectiveness of the EES and (since the year 2000) also the Lisbon Strategy, has the benefit of some hindsight.[1] As such it builds on the copious literature on New Governance, and specifically on the EES which has identified their main limitations and intrinsic weaknesses.

The starting point of the book is that New Governance, law and constitutionalism form part of the same *corpus unicum*, each performing a specific role in ensuring the effective functioning of the EU by compensating each other's regulatory deficiencies. On this premise, the book develops a hybrid model of governance which seeks to overcome the limitations of both traditional modes of regulation and experimental governance processes and techniques by revisiting extant conceptualizations of law and constitutionalism.

---

1 I have borrowed this expression from Hatzopoulos (2007: 310).

Many of the ideas in the book were first explored in my doctoral thesis which I completed in 2004 under the supervision of Erika Szyszczak and then Tamara Hervey. I am indebted to both of them for their guidance, insights and encouragement during the writing of the thesis and I would like to extend my warmest thanks to them. I would also like to take this opportunity to record my gratitude to my examiners, Jeffrey Kenner and Kenneth Armstrong for the many useful observations they made on how to enhance the quality of my work and Jo Shaw who acted as my academic mentor while at Manchester Law School, for her intellectual rigour and for instilling in me a sense of critical reflection. My thanks go to Ken Hurry for his assistance with improving the quality of the written text and to Khanam Virjee and Katie Carpenter at Routledge and the anonymous referees. I am also grateful to the interviewees at the European Commission, DG Employment, Social Affairs and Equal Opportunities, the Employment Committee (EMCO), the Danish and Italian trade unions' representatives at ETUC, the researchers at ETUI, the functionaries of the Bank of Italy and officials of the Czech Ministry of Labour for accepting to contribute to this book with their expertise and availability in answering my questions on the EES.

Since completing the doctoral thesis, my ideas have been subject to what Weiler defines a "process of mutation" which by pure coincidence (and somewhat ironically) mirrors the many paths of evolution, stagnation and rebirth of EC social and employment policy, broadly the topic of this book. This accomplishment could not have been possible without all those who have assisted and encouraged me in the course of researching and writing this book. In particular, I would like to extend my warmest thanks to Fiona Beveridge who has helped me at different times to disentangle the intricate filaments of my thought and thus explain more clearly and coherently my line of thinking and argumentation. I would also like to thank Dora Kostakopoulou for her continued intellectual help and support. Michael Dougan and Gareth Davies deserve special mention for their invaluable comments and feedback on Chapter 2 – a key part of the book – and with whom I also had the great pleasure and privilege of discussing some of the ideas put forward in that chapter. I am also particularly grateful to my friends Giulia Andreoli, Dalila Bihrouchen, Martin Brook, Gianfilippo De Astis, Nina Learner, Mara Parpaglioni and Gabriel Zagni for their sense of humour *così vicini, sebbene così lontani*. Lastly, I would like to express my endless thanks to mum and dad to whom I owe everything in a very fundamental way and my family for their love and continued support and, in particular, to Marcello for putting up with what seemed to be a never-ending project and to my two little gems Sarah and Gaia who are the main drive behind this project. I would like to conclude with a famous adage from the play *The Three Sisters* by Anton Chekhov: *feci quod potui, faciant meliora potentes*.

S.V.

July 2009

Please note that the new numbering of Treaty Articles further to the Treaty of Lisbon is not included in all parts of the book as it was being published at the time of entry into force of the Treaty of Lisbon. For the same reason the book contains references to the European Community without specifying that it ceased to exist as of 1 December 2009.

Routledge Editorial Team

Acknowledgments

I am very grateful to the following copyright holders for permission to reproduce either extracts or figures and tables from previously published material:

Meyer, C., Linsenmann and Wessels, W. (2007), 'Evolution Towards a European Economic Government? Research Design and Theoretical Expectations' in Linsenmann, I., Meyer, C. and Wessels, W. (eds) *Economic Government of the EU. A Balance Sheet of New Modes of Policy Co-ordination* (Basingstoke: Palgrave Macmillan), pp. 11–36

Velluti, S. (2008), 'Gender Equality and Mainstreaming in the Re-articulation of Labour Market Policies in Denmark and Italy' in Beveridge, F. and Velluti, S. (eds) *Gender and the Open Method of Co-ordination. Perspectives on Law, Governance and Equality in the EU* (Aldershot: Ashgate), pp. 141–168

Velluti, S. (2007), 'What European Union Strategy for Integrating Migrants? The Role of OMC Soft Mechanisms in the Development of an EU Immigration Policy', *European Journal of Migration and Law* 9: 53–82

Wallace, H. (1996), 'Politics and Policy in the EU: the Challenge of Governance' in Wallace, H. and Wallace, W. (eds) *Policy-making in the European Union* (Oxford: Oxford University Press), pp. 3–36

Table of cases

Opinions of the European Court of Justice

Advocate General Opinions

Court of First Instance

Table of EU material

Treaties

European Economic Community Treaty, 1957 (EEC) *(Treaty of Rome)*

European Community Treaty (EC) (as amended by the Treaty on European Union, Treaty of Amsterdam and the Treaty of Nice)

Treaty on European Union, 1992 (TEU) (OJ C191 of 29 July 1992)

Treaty of Amsterdam, 1997, amending the Treaty on European Union, the Treaties Establishing the European Communities and certain Related Acts (97/C 340/01)

Treaty of Nice amending the Treaty on European Union, the Treaties establishing the European Communities and certain Related Acts (2001/C 80/01)

Treaty Establishing a Constitution for Europe, OJ C 310/1, 16 December 2004

Treaty of Lisbon amending the Treaty on European Union and the Treaty establishing the European Community, OJ C 306/50, 17 December 2007

Treaty on European Union

Treaty on the Functioning of the European Union

Community Charter of Fundamental Social Rights of Workers 1989 (Luxembourg: OPEC, 1990)

Charter of Fundamental Rights of the European Union, OJ 364/01, 18 December 2000

Council of the European Union

European Parliament

European Parliament and Council of the European Union

European Commission

European Council

European Central Bank

Committee of the Regions

Economic and Social Committee

Monetary Committee

Documents on the Future of Europe

EuroStat

EU Bulletins

Web sites

List of abbreviations

ALMP	Active Labour Market Policy
APR	Annual Progress Report
ARF	Danish Federation of County Councils
ARI	Implementation Assessment Report
ASP	Agreement on Social Policy
BEPGs	Broad Economic Policy Guidelines
CEC	Confédération Européenne des Cadres
CEDAW	Convention on the Elimination of all Forms of Discrimination against Women
CEEC	Central East European Country
CEEP	European Centre of Employers and Enterprises providing Public services
CFI	Court of First Instance
CFSP	Common Foreign and Security Policy
CFU	Danish central federation of state employees
CGIL	Confederazione Italiana Generale del Lavoro
CISL	Confederazione Italiana dei Sindacati Lavoratori
CMKOS	Czech–Moravian Chamber of Trade Unions
COCOCA	Commission-initiated and Council-implemented collective agreement
COPA	Committee of Agricultural Organizations in the EC
COREPER	Committee of Permanent Representatives of the Member States
COSICA	Commission-initiated but self-implemented collective agreement
CT	Constitutional Treaty
DA	Danish employers' confederation
DG	Directorate General
EAGGF	European Agriculture Guidance and Guarantee Fund
EC	European Community
ECB	European Central Bank
ECHR	European Convention of Human Rights
ECJ	European Court of Justice
ECOFIN	Economic and Finance
ECOSOC	Economic and Social Committee
ECSC	European Coal and Steel Community
ECU	European Currency Unit
EDF	European Development Fund
EDRC	Economic and Development Review Committee

EEA	European Economic Area
EEC	European Economic Community
EEI	European Employment Initiative
EEP	European Employment Pact
EES	European Employment Strategy
EFC	Economic and Financial Committee
EFTA	European Free Trade Area
EGTC	European Grouping of Territorial Co-operation
EIB	European Investment Bank
EMA	European Monetary Agreement
EMCC	European Monitoring Centre on Change
EMCO	Employment Committee
EMI	European Monetary Institute
EMS	European Monetary System
EMU	Economic and Monetary Union
EP	European Parliament
EPG	Employment Policy Guidelines
EPSCO	Employment, Social Policy, Health and Consumer Affairs
EPU	European Payment Union
ERDF	European Regional Development Fund
ESCB	European System of Central Banks
ESF	European Social Fund
ETUC	European Trade Union Confederation
EU	European Union
EUA	European Unit of Account
EUROCADRES	Council of European Professional and Managerial Staff
EUROCOMMERCE	Retail, Wholesale and International Trade Representation to the European Union
EWC	European Works Council
FRA	Fundamental Rights Agency
GDP	Gross domestic product
IAP	Individual Action Plan
IGC	Intergovernmental Conference
ILO	International Labour Organization
IMF	International Monetary Fund
IRES	Istituto di Ricerche Economiche e Sociali
JAP	Joint Assessment Papers
JER	Joint Employment Report
KL	Danish national association of local authorities
KTO	Danish association of local government employees' organizations
LAP	Local Action Plan
LO	Danish federation of trade unions
MC	Monetary Committee
MEP	Member of Parliament
MNC	Multinational company/corporation
NAIRU	Non-accelerating inflation rate of employment
NAPs	National Action Plans for Employment
NCB	National central bank
NEP	National Employment Plans (of the Czech Republic)

NGO	Non-governmental organization
NOG	New/Old Governance
NRP	National Reform Programme
OECD	Organization for Economic Co-operation and Development
OLAF	European Anti-fraud Office
OMC	Open Method of Co-ordination
PES	Public Employment Services
QMV	Qualified Majority Voting
RAP	Regional Action Plan
SAP	Social Action Programme
SEA	Single European Act
SGP	Stability and Growth Pact
SICOCA	Self-initiated but Council-implemented Collective Agreement
SIL	Italian Employment Information System
SISICA	Self-initiated and self-implemented Collective Agreement
SMEs	Small to Medium-size-Enterprises
SPA	Social Policy Agreement
SPP	Social Policy Protocol
TCN	Third-country National
TEPs	Territorial Employment Pacts
TEU	Treaty of Maastricht
TFEU	Treaty on the Functioning of the European Union
ToA	Treaty of Amsterdam
ToN	Treaty of Nice
UEAPME	European Association of Craft, Small and Medium-size Enterprises
UIL	Unione Italiana del Lavoro
UNICE	Union of Industrial and Employers' Confederations of Europe
USSR	Union of Soviet Socialist Republics
WFD	Water Framework Directive

1 Introduction

A sixth phase in EU social policy and the European Employment Strategy

1 Introduction

Since the foundational period and the minimalist and non-interventionist approach of the Community in the social field which relied heavily on the Ohlin and Spaak reports that argued that the functioning of the market would ensure conditions close to levels of Pareto optimality, EU labour law and policy have undergone different paths of evolution and involution which highlight its fragmented structure.

With regard to the study of EU social law it has become customary among labour lawyers to systematize its paroxysmal development into various phases. Following this hermeneutic approach we may argue that the social dimension of the European Union has entered a new distinct sixth phase which started with the Amsterdam European Council, further reinforced by the Lisbon Strategy and, more recently, by the Barcelona and the Brussels European Council meetings. This phase is characterized by a tendency for negative forms of integration, the establishment of a set of goals rather than the pursuit of harmonization by way of Directives and their achievement through processes, strategies and action programmes and, more broadly, new typology of acts, new institutions, actors and, as posited by Ashiagbor (2005), by a displacement of employment and economic discourses over social policy and social law.

The new scenario also explains why at European level the focus has shifted from "government" to the broader notion of "governance" encompassing economic, technological and knowledge-based processes as well as the political and legal as well as including both formal and institutionalized procedures and informal and non-institutionalized ones. The shift towards the experimentation of new methodologies in European socio-economic regulation is, at the same time, a means *for* and a consequence *of* the furthering of the Europeanization process.

By focusing on this sixth phase of the European Union's social dimension, the book provides a detailed analysis of the emergence of the Open Method of Co-ordination (OMC) in the field of employment and it throws fresh light on the role of this New Governance technique in EU social governance and, more broadly, in the Community legal system and its relationship with both European and national law from the perspective of effectiveness and legitimacy of Community social intervention. The book is thus a timely contribution to the burgeoning literature on New Governance processes and practices, their function and effectiveness in the EU system. "New Governance" is an umbrella term which broadly refers to:

a wide range of processes and practices that have a norm-setting or regulatory dimension but do not operate primarily or at all through the conventional mechanisms of command-and-control type legal institutions. The term "new", therefore, does not necessarily entail a claim of originality or temporality, but is used to refer to the increasingly widespread, deliberate and explicit use of such forms of governance in the place of more traditional legal and regulatory techniques.

(de Búrca: 2008)[1]

In so doing, the book explores what the implications may be for the roles of law and constitutionalism of the development of new modes of governance in the European Union and in turn what role New Governance has or may have within the more well-defined structures of law and constitutionalism at both European and national levels.

The Treaty of Amsterdam marked a significant turning point in the development of EU labour law and social policy by introducing a new Title on Employment, Title VIII, and by incorporating the provisions of the Social Policy Agreement (SPA) on the European Social Dialogue in the Treaty with the amendment of old Title VIII, now Title XI. Furthermore, the Luxembourg Extraordinary European Council Meeting on Employment fast-tracked the EES envisaged in Title VIII. At the Lisbon European Council, followed by subsequent European Councils, the European Employment Strategy (EES) has been defined as a regulatory tool to be included in the OMC. The two processes have greatly contributed to the further development of a European social and employment policy.

This investigation, therefore, focuses on the European Union's employment policy processes, considering the scope and dynamics of EU social policy development, and it shows how EU employment policy has gradually taken on an independent identity since the beginning of the 1990s. In contrast, social policy has been mainly related to the regulation of the labour market, and stemmed from European values of social democracy, as well as from the right of free movement of labour sanctioned in the Treaty. Employment policy, as the focus here, is mainly a product of the "1990s values" of free markets and competitiveness. The main objectives of EU employment policy are job creation and vocational training, with the aim of striking a balance between a free labour market and the protection of the worker's interests. These objectives accord well with the current process of reconceptualization of the notion of "social".

The EES clearly exemplifies these changes in policy making. The book, therefore, starts by looking at the variety of determining factors explaining the genesis and further development of the EES, and it analyzes the evolution of social policy in the European Union. In addition, the investigation focuses on the Economic and Monetary Union (EMU) and the Lisbon Strategy, which have acted as catalysts for an emphasis on regulatory approaches to social policy. As Amitsis *et al.* (2003: 33) maintain:

> Today, EU social policy is no longer the "stepchild" of European integration. The completion of the Internal Market and the EMU made it increasingly difficult to exclude employment and social concerns from the European policy agenda. To be

---

1 There are currently a plethora of exhaustive literature reviews of governance and New Governance studies and analyses, which explain the omission in this chapter (although see Chapter 2). On governance see Treib *et al.* (2005), Kohler-Koch and Rittberger (2006); on New Governance see Citi and Rhodes (2007), Armstrong and Kilpatrick (2007), de la Porte (2008: 18–29).

sure, claims with respect to the emancipation of "Social Europe" should not be exaggerated. By and large, the Europeanization of the employment and social policy agenda is the result of "spill over" effects arising from the dynamic of Single Market and monetary integration, complementing rather than replacing entrenched national social policy repertoires.[2]

This analysis is important because it helps us to understand the extent to which the EES departs from the classical Community Method. This study is necessary because the genesis and further implementation of the EES must also be understood against the backdrop of economic processes taking place in the European Union, particularly the economic policy co-ordination process in the context of which the Council, through the formulation of Broad Economic Policy Guidelines (BEPGs), establishes specific policy objectives that aim at achieving an adequate policy mix for the Member States. Moreover, it also tells us how the problem with strategies pursuing different political and socio-economic objectives or underpinned by opposing discourses (a deregulatory agenda or neo-liberal versus social democratic; social justice and social protection versus flexibility) such as the EES and the Lisbon Strategy is that they have inherent paradoxes that may be difficult to overcome and which might, ultimately, undermine the effectiveness of their overall process.

After analysing the variety of determining factors explaining the launch and further implementation of the EES, the book examines the evolution of EU labour law and how EU employment policy has taken on an independent identity as well as exploring the elements of continuity and break from previous legal and policy instruments in order to identify and assess the main strengths and limitations of this New Governance process. In this context the analysis focuses on the use of "soft" law to manage social policy pluralism, to overcome the underlying tension within the discussion of the roles for social policy and law and to "smoothly" coerce Member States to tackle labour market regulation in accordance with European objectives and policies. The use and status of soft law may be defined in many different ways. The definition adopted in this book is the one elaborated by Snyder (1995) and refined by Ştefan (2008) according to which soft law instruments are rules of conduct that, in principle, have no legally binding force but which nevertheless may have practical effects and also legal effects.[3] The study then considers the effectiveness of the EES and its regulatory tool, the OMC, as a non-binding co-ordination method and its impact on the constitutional and institutional structures of the Member States, by jointly assessing macroeconomic, labour market and employment policies at national level on the basis of empirical findings and comparative case studies. Effectiveness in this book is not intended in the narrow and standard meaning of measuring Member States' compliance with the Employment Guidelines, that is, of attempting to trace a direct link between national employment measures and the EES, but rather in the broader sense of identifying

---

2 I am not arguing that the spill-over effects of EMU and the Single Market project constitute the sole explanation for the development of EU social policy. As I go on to show in subsequent chapters, there are other factors which need to be considered for a full understanding of its development. We also need to take into account the power struggle between the Commission and the Member States and their respective interests in expanding the social dimension of the European integration process.

3 For a detailed analysis of the effects of soft law in the Community legal system, see Borchardt and Wellens (1989: 24–30).

the influence of the EES on the *discourse* within Member States over employment and labour market policies. In this context, the book considers both the implementation stage, that is, the EES as a policy instrument capable, *inter alia*, of promoting participatory forms of democracy, and the enforcement stage, that is, the EES as a normative tool capable of ensuring policy transfer and policy learning.

In the Commission's (2007) own evaluation of ten years of the EES Vladimír Špidla, Commissioner for Employment, Social Affairs and Equal Opportunities, stated *sic et simpliciter* that the Employment Strategy ten years after its launch has become a benchmark for the further development of EU social governance and, more broadly, one of the key successes of the European Union. To what extent, however, do the EES and the OMC enable European social policy to reconstruct its own architecture on the basis of social citizenship, social justice and social solidarity discourses, rights and quality of jobs, in addition to fostering experimental regulatory techniques in the social field? As will be shown later in the book, the peculiarity of the EES is that it eschews the well-established individual rights-based model, and, in particular, rather than providing for specific rights, such as, for instance, the right to work, it is proactive and collective as it places a positive duty on public authorities to identify the causes of unemployment and to remedy them. Even though it does not provide for enforceable individual rights it may nevertheless be said to produce normative effects in that it creates a duty to act which the state and, more broadly, all public authorities must undertake.

The study of the EES and its implementation through the OMC is pivotal to fully understanding EU social governance in that its further development has determined the future direction and agenda of EU social policy, which in turn has focused Community and national debates on the creation and strengthening of a "European social model" and the definition of a new paradigm for social governance in the European Union. Moreover, the analysis of the Employment Strategy is also important for its salience in relation to legitimacy discourses of EU social policy as one of the reasons explaining the launch of the EES is its legitimizing function of Community social intervention and, more broadly, of EU action. Critically, the aim is to examine what the implications of the aforementioned displacement of social policy and social law may be for EC social rights in view of the absence of a rule of law approach in the EES and, linked to this, in light of its lack of a system of accountability and judicial scrutiny and also in consideration of the fact that the EES as in the case of other modes of New Governance tends to focus on process rather than substance.

2 Challenging legal thought and revisiting approaches to the understanding of law and constitutionalism in the European Union

The EES is characterized by a constellation of legal, institutional and political factors. As a new form of soft law[4] based on the co-ordination of policies, peer pressure and exchanges of best practice, lacking a system of legal sanctions and enforcement procedures, and,

---

4 "New" in this context is not used to refer to the EES as being an alternative to the Community Method but rather to emphasize the fact that it relies on the use of soft law in a different way in comparison with how soft law instruments had been used before the 1992 Treaty of Maastricht. This is explained in more detail in Chapter 4.

more broadly, as an iterative and multi-level process, the EES constitutes a challenge for legal theory. Roberts and Springer (2001: 51–52) maintain that 'policy has changed from a legislative agenda to a program agenda, while the main action has moved from legislative chambers to meeting rooms'. Moreover, the EES can be neither economically determined nor exclusively built in accordance with political objectives. On the contrary, it is the result of a combination of both economic realism and political requirement and it exemplifies the continuous tension between the intergovernmental and the supranational elements of the European decision-making process. The reason is the multi-faceted nature of the factors determining the EES process and the iterative nature of the overall process whereby the policy input comes from different levels of decision making. The new typology of acts, the new institutions and actors, and the new processes and outcomes that the Strategy has brought to social policy thinking add further challenges to the traditional understanding that lawyers have of the legal and constitutional processes and structures of the European Union. The central claim of the book, however, is that the EES is neither entirely new nor old. As explained in more detail throughout the book, in terms of decision-making processes at EU level the OMC presents elements of continuity with existing EU modes of governance in the sense that it represents one of the means of intense dialectical exchanges between centre and periphery. Moreover, co-ordination and networking are not new in the EU system. Hence, from this point of view, New Governance is nothing radically new and may be said to exemplify what Sabel and Zeitlin (2003) have termed "pragmatic constitutionalism". On the level of normative constitutionalism,[5] however, there are stark differences between the classical Community Method based on hard law, legal sanctions enforceable EU rights and the involvement of mainly public or quasi-public institutions and bodies and the OMC, which is structured around the participation of an array of stakeholders (both public and private actors), is built on the blurred definition of targets (apart from the more well-defined social indicators of the EES) and relies on the use of soft sanctions. In this context, the true novelty of the OMC lies in its democratic participatory element, although a significant number of studies show that the EES as it stands at present remains far from the standard democratic narrative of representative democracy and from the democratic ideal of directly deliberative polyarchy.

The book puts forward an approach to the understanding of law and constitutionalism which is procedural, relational and dialogic (Shaw 2000), that is, one which enables them to accommodate and interact with New Governance. It is posited that such a relationship could then provide the conditions for identifying a more workable resolution of intractable problems about the European Union's democracy, legitimacy and efficiency gaps. A strong hybridized system of co-regulation could also reduce the putative weakness of New Governance for its lacking of accountability and judicial scrutiny. In particular, with regard to the field of employment, by strengthening the relationship between New Governance and EU constitutionalism social rights and labour standards could be built into the EES in order to counterbalance that weakness, creating the basis for the justiciability of enacted measures. In this way a space for national diversity and experimentation would be preserved and the open method would be maintained intact without incorporating it into the "command and control" regulatory model of EU constitutionalism.

The study of the EES and its further implementation through the OMC, therefore, provides the hermeneutical tools to better understand New Governance processes in the

---

5 See further in Chapter 2.

wider context of the EU system, its relationship with the Community Method as well as the manifold role of law which may be said to perform three broad functions: first, it subsumes and institutionalizes values, principles and paradigms developed in the new processes; second, it acts as a "proceduralizer" in that it systematizes and defines new modes of governance; and, third, it has a pivotal role at the implementation and enforcement stages in ensuring policy transfer which may be defined as a 'process whereby knowledge about policies, administrative arrangements, institutions, ideas, and so on are used across time and/or space in the development of policies, institutions, and so on elsewhere' (Bomberg and Peterson 2000: 10). The book, therefore, sets out to examine the various roles performed by law in new regulatory processes, for example, the capacity of law in systematizing change, and analyzes the extent to which law is capable of encapsulating the variety of norms, paradigms and ideas that shape the patterns of European employment policy through the iterative process of the EES.

More specifically, the significance of this book lies chiefly in subjecting the theoretical assumptions of how the EES operates (for example, distribution of competence between the European Union and the Member States and, within the state, between the central government and the regional and local policy makers) to further empirical research and in elaborating a model of governance which may help overcome the regulatory problems besetting both New Governance and EU constitutionalism.

3 The European Employment Strategy and European integration theories: is there a "grand" theory of New Governance?

The book employs Marshall's (1975: 15) broad notion of EU social policy, defined as the 'political power to supersede, supplement or modify operations of the economic system in order to achieve results which the economic system would not achieve on its own'. The difficulty in embarking on the study of the EES and the OMC is increased by the fact that the analytical and hermeneutical methodology must go beyond historical contingency that sees national labour markets and industrial relations systems within the equation: regulatory systems of employment = nation-state.

The post-Fordist transnational processes of labour market transformation and the attempts to establish a supranational system of employment regulation are phenomena that cannot be fully understood by adopting concepts and notions of labour market studies undertaken in the context of the above equation. Moreover, the Supiot Report (1999) highlighted the common pitfalls that labour lawyers must avoid when analysing the transformation of work, employment relationships and their overall regulation. These are: either overestimating or underestimating differences between Member States; the use of law for the rationalization of socio-economic changes or, conversely, to preclude the use of law in the analysis of social and economic change; and finally, to overestimate or, on the contrary, underestimate the degree of transformation resulting from a global economy.

The EES, therefore, requires a rethinking of analytical methods and concepts for understanding the impact of the overall process and the new dynamics and mechanisms taking place in national labour market systems. This new analytical approach is made even more compelling in view of the dichotomy of ideology and targets within the Employment Strategy which has been further exacerbated by the Lisbon Programme: on the one hand, the strategies are inspired by neo-liberal theories, which refer to the creation of a competitive and dynamic knowledge-based society and thus the objectives of high and now full employment and creation of an efficient entrepreneurship system. On the other hand, they are inspired by social democratic and socialist ideologies and thus the objectives of sustainable economic growth in tandem with the achievement of social cohesion and qualitatively better jobs.

One innovative aspect of the book is thus the methodological approach of study: rather than applying a pre-existing theoretical assumption to the analysis of EU governance and focusing the study only on formal institutions, formalized modes of operation and policy outcomes, the investigation also takes into consideration the political, economic and legal dimension of the EES and embraces a wider notion of institution as defined by new institutionalism. The book, therefore, takes into account a variety of different actors as well as ideas, practices and paradigms that inform institutions and decision-making processes within the European Union (Armstrong and Bulmer 1998).

Neo-functionalism, rationalism and intergovernmentalism as single narratives of how European integration evolves are analytical approaches that cannot fully explain the complexity of the multi-tiered and polycontextual policy-making process taking place within the European Union. Hence, by drawing on the combined tenets of meta-constitutionalism, reflexive law, directly deliberative polyarchy theories and critical constructivist approaches to law, the book proceeds to reconsider accepted and fixed understandings of law and constitutionalism that have led to a static and limited juxtaposition of the former and New Governance, failing to grasp their multidimensional meaning and role in the wider European integration process. It then develops a model of governance that enables law, constitutionalism and New Governance processes and prac-tices to interact with one another and operate in tandem. This model is aspirational in nature, that is, it represents an ideal model of governance that the European Union should aspire to. There is no "one-size-fits-all" solution to the challenges facing the European Union. Under the current conditions of transnationalization legal institutions themselves need to be multiple and diverse, particularly as the regulatory practices of modern constitutionalism are increasingly moved out of their territorialized social contexts.

In order to meet its research objectives, the book employs a diachronic approach con-cerned with the historical development of the Employment Strategy and covering a time frame that spans the 1997–2005 period. The study examines a series of documents, papers and reports. In particular, official documentation of the EU Institutions, which includes, *inter alia*: Protocols annexed to the Treaty, Presidency Conclusions of the European Council, reports of the Convention on the Future of Europe and its Working Groups, documents of the European Central Bank (ECB), Communications, Green and White Papers of the Commission, Decisions, Directives, Recommendations and Resolutions of the Council of Ministers and European Parliament, BEPGs and documents included in the Employment Package and, within the Lisbon Strategy, the Guidelines Package, as well as working papers of *ad hoc* groups created under the auspices of the Commission and reports of the Employment Committee (EMCO). The investigation also examines documents produced by individual Member States such as National Action Plans for Employment (NAPs) now replaced by National Reform Programmes (NRPs), other reports and working papers especially of the Treasury and the Ministries of Labour and Finance as well as primary and secondary legislation. Other documentation used in the book includes texts of both the European and national social partners, non-governmental organizations and other inter-national organizations, chiefly the Organization for Economic Co-operation and Devel-opment (OECD). Part of the empirical data has been collected through interviews with representatives of the Commission, governments and social partners.

4 Organization of the book

The structure of the book is as follows. Chapter 2 provides an analytical and evaluative framework for the research puzzle of the book, situating the study of the EES in the context of New Governance and constitutionalism debates. In particular, by setting aside the conventional binary approach to the understanding of law, constitutionalism and New Governance, it examines to what extent and in what way legal instruments and processes as well as constitutional values and norms are or may be involved in the operation of "new" modes of governance and what role new approaches to regulation have or may have within the more well defined structures of law and constitutionalism. The chapter presents a hybrid governance model which enables law and constitutionalism to accommodate and interact with New Governance by overcoming the limitations of both traditional modes of regulation and experimental governance processes and techniques.

Chapter 3 proceeds as follows. First, from a policy perspective it unravels and examines the economic reasons that have propelled a drive towards the development of a "European social dimension" which has gathered momentum since the 1990s and why employment and growth have become top priority on the Community agenda. More precisely, it examines why European Institutions are seemingly at the forefront of efforts to overcome the extant constitutional asymmetry between market efficiency and market-correcting policies. Second, from a governance perspective the chapter seeks to explain the rebirth of soft law instruments, the economic rationale of and increase in the use of policy co-ordination. In a narrower sense, it examines how the idea of launching the EES came about within the overarching aim of the completion of the Single Market, which the EMU may be said to be part of. The purpose of these analyzes is to provide a basis on which we can subsequently consider the different components which make up the Employment Strategy in order to discern the elements of continuity with pre-existing forms of regulation from those which may be said to be new. The analysis focuses on globalization, market integration and EMU as the main determining factors for a reconceptualization of the roles of law and the state and for the search of alternative solutions or modes of policy making within the European Union.

Chapter 4 provides an examination of the evolution of social policy in the European Union from the Treaty of Rome to the Treaty of Amsterdam, which marked the beginning of a sixth phase in the development of EU social policy.

In order to maintain the logical coherence of the critical analysis of the EES in the context of the developments in EU social policy post-Amsterdam, the full examination of the sixth phase is provided in Chapter 5. While essentially descriptive, this chapter serves an important purpose for the research questions of the book. The aim is to identify and unravel the reasons for such developments and understand why and in what way EU employment policy has taken on an independent identity from EU labour law. In this context, the chapter also explores the different rationales for EU intervention in domestic labour law which in turn explains the conflicting objectives that it has been said to pursue. The study employs a chronological narrative concerned with the historical development of EC social policy. However, rather than a beginning-to-end chronology, the story line is systematically subdivided into specific periods so as to provide a clearer framework of study. Chapter 5 examines the origins and further development of the EES during a time frame that spans the 1997–2005 period, unfolding the reasons for its creation and exploring its significance in the context of the sixth phase of EU social policy. In this context, the chapter also provides a thorough examination of its main mode of operation, namely, the OMC. The purpose of this chapter is twofold. First, it aims at analyzing the elements of continuity and break with previous regulatory instruments in the field of social policy and, in particular, it seeks to explain why and how employment policy has taken on an independent identity from the beginning of the 1990s and, more precisely, the reasons for the displacement of employment and economic discourses over social policy and social law. The second aim of this chapter is to provide a preliminary evaluation of the functioning of the EES. The term "preliminary" is employed to refer to the fact that a more detailed assessment of the EES is given in Chapter 7 on the basis of the cross-country case studies conducted in Chapter 6.

Chapter 6 provides an empirical study of the main research questions of the book on the basis of a comparative case study by focusing on gender equality and mainstreaming in national labour markets. The countries selected for the case study are Italy, Denmark and the Czech Republic, representing Southern European, Scandinavian and Central Eastern European social policy systems. The chapter is concerned with the EES's ability to bring about changes in the way in which gender equality objectives and measures are articulated in the context of the modernization of labour market organization. The significance of this chapter lies chiefly in subjecting the theoretical assumptions of how the EES operates (for example, distribution of competence between the European Union and the Member States and within the state between the central government and the regional and local policy makers), to further empirical research and, in particular, to evaluate how, and the extent to which, the objectives and goals of the EES become integrated into domestic policies and institutional structures in the context of different welfare state models, chiefly from the viewpoint of policy learning, policy convergence, national institutional capabilities and broad participation.

In Chapter 7 the empirical findings of Chapter 6 are used together with the theoretical conclusions of Chapter 5 to evaluate critically the effectiveness of the EES in the wider context of EU social governance. This study is particularly important following the 2004 and 2007 waves of EU enlargement because it evaluated whether the OMC is capable of managing successfully such a wide spectrum of diversity in social policy. In particular, the chapter examines the main strengths and weaknesses of the EES and its implementation through the OMC. In order to meet its aim it proposes to utilize the governance model elaborated in Chapter 2, which may help overcome the EES regulatory deficiencies without reverting to more classical modes of governance within the Community Method.

Chapter 8, the concluding chapter of the book, draws together the main arguments of the study and findings from the core chapters of the book. In so doing it refocuses attention on the need to develop an approach to law and constitutionalism which is procedural, relational, dialogic – that is, one which enables them to accommodate and interact with New Governance. It is posited that such a relationship could then provide the conditions for strengthening the "European social model" and, more generally, for ensuring a more effective EU employment policy with positive "spill-over" effects for EU social governance as a whole.

2 Conceptualizing "New" EU Governance

Revisiting law and constitutionalism in an evolving European Union

1 Introduction

The central aim of this chapter is to provide an analytical and evaluative framework for the research puzzle of the book situating the study of the EES in the context of New Governance and constitutionalism debates. In particular, by setting aside the traditionally perceived divide between "soft" and "hard" law, it seeks to question to what extent and in what way legal instruments and processes as well as constitutional values and norms are or may be involved in the operation of "new" modes of governance and what role new approaches to regulation have or may have within the more well-defined structures of law and constitutionalism.

The investigation takes place on two levels of enquiry. The first line of enquiry focuses on the relationship between New Governance and law intended both as a set of legal norms and a legal system. The aim is, on the one hand, to understand the role(s) performed by law in the context of New Governance processes and, on the other, to explore what the contribution of New Governance methods and instruments may be to the adoption and implementation of law and to the effective functioning of a legal system. The second line of enquiry concentrates on the relationship between New Governance and constitutionalism intended both as limited collective (self-)government under the rule of law[1] and as a set of fundamental constitutional values, norms, processes and structures forming part of a given polity.[2] Both aspects of the enquiry are equally important if the governance model I here propose is to carry any conviction.

The chapter does not seek to convey any (re)conceptualization of New Governance, law and constitutionalism for mere lexical or taxonomical purposes but rather the objective is to develop a dynamic theorization of these three objects of study, more apt at capturing the evolving nature of the European Union and thus more appropriate to serve

---

1 For a thorough study of the rule of law in the EU, see Pech (2009); for the social significance of the rule of law, see Walker (2009).

2 More specifically, constitutionalism is linked to a series of substantive institutional values such as democracy, accountability, equality, the separation of powers, the rule of law and fundamental rights which act as a basis for the exercise of individual freedom within an overarching framework of collective action and protection. At procedural level, constitutionalism is linked to the idea that the 'institutional specification, interpretation and balanced application of these values as an exercise in practical reasoning is a matter of contestation and should accordingly be solved through forms of deliberation and decision (Constitutional Conventions, referenda, constitutional courts, etc.) which satisfy those involved in or otherwise affected by their legitimacy' (Walker 2003: 33–34); see also Rosenfeld (1994).

as the basis for establishing a dialogical relationship between new and experimentalist modes of regulation, law and constitutionalism. Their intrinsic differences notwithstanding, the chapter postulates that New Governance, law and constitutionalism form part of the same *corpus unicum*, each performing a specific role in ensuring the effective functioning of the European Union by compensating each other's regulatory deficiencies. In the context of socio-economic and employment policies, Hatzopoulos (2005: 1633) maintains that:

> the Lisbon objectives and recourse to the OMC – considered to be the paradigm of New Governance – constitute the supplement, in the form of (soft) positive integration, to the (hard) negative integration already achieved by the Community judiciary. . . . Seen from this perspective, the lack of legitimacy and the absence of judicial control of the Lisbon process, appears far less dramatic.

Thus, by drawing on the combined tenets of meta-constitutionalism (Walker 1999),[3] reflexive law (Teubner 1993)[4] and directly deliberative polyarchy theories (Cohen and Sabel 1997)[5] and critical constructivist approaches to law (Kingsbury 1998; Slaughter *et al.* 1998),

---

3 Meta-constitutionalism is explored in detail in the penultimate section of this chapter. Briefly, metaconstitutional law is open-textured and it is used to consider the dynamic and multi-faceted nature of the EU system. It takes the current post-Westphalian system as a point of departure in which the state is no longer the sole political authority and in which national constitutional law and traditional international public law, both of which constitute the legal and judicial pillars of the Westphalian order that had its point of origin in the 1648 Treaty of Westphalia, cease to be the central sources of EU public law *lato sensu*.

4 Reflexive law is a legal theory which proposes a procedural approach to questions of governance. It is primarily concerned with the nature of law and its role and effectiveness in a functionally differentiated society. Its main tenet is that society is structured on the basis of various subsystems (the economic, the social, etc.) which are self-referential, and the law's role is to foster mechanisms that systematically further the development of "reflexion" structures within other subsystems. In particular, its normative concern is on how law should be structured in order to be effective. It holds that the conditions under which a deliberative process may succeed may be identified and, once identified, must be affirmatively created rather than be considered pre-constituted. The kind of institutional constructivism required is one which will make it possible for the actors to reflect upon their understanding of a given problem to be overcome and their interests, both of which may be redefined through a process of deliberation and collective learning, by arriving at a new perception of the problem they are seeking to resolve. These interests and this perception are shaped by the context in which the actors are located, and any renewed understanding of that context will result in the actors concerned redefining their positions.

5 The idea of directly deliberative polyarchy is premised on the acceptance of (rather than resistance to) the current postmodern, plural and heterogeneous society, disconnecting the democracy principle from the political institutions of the nation-state. In a directly deliberative polyarchy the local and, more broadly, lower-level actors are granted autonomy to experiment with solutions of their own devising within broadly defined areas of public policy to ensure the flow and the pooling of information within and between deliberative units and to strengthen direct participation of citizens in policy formation and decision making. A central feature of this vision of democracy is that democratic self-government is not thwarted by, but rather benefits from, multiplicity of sites, the heterogeneity of participants and different voices therein. On this basis the guiding idea is to associate the concept of radical democracy, its properties of deliberativeness and of direct participation with functionally specified problem-solving units and capacities. Moreover, in this democracy model the normative infrastructure of political discourse is based on the equal weight of constitutional reason and policy reason, thus ensuring both substantive and procedural due process.

the aim is to reconsider the accepted and fixed understandings of law and constitutionalism that have led to a static and limited juxtaposition of the former and New Governance, and a failing to grasp their multidimensional meaning and role in the wider European integration process. While their basic differences cannot be denied 'differences in historically shaped "cultural" conditions should not be reified into irremovable obstacles' (Nelken 2008: 306).

The chapter, therefore, puts forward an approach to the understanding of law and constitutionalism which is procedural, relational and dialogic (Shaw 2000), that is, one enabling them to accommodate and interact with New Governance. It is posited that such a relationship would then provide the conditions for identifying a more workable resolution of intractable problems about the European Union's democracy, legitimacy and efficiency gaps. A strong hybridized system of co-regulation would also reduce the putative weakness of New Governance for its lacking of accountability and judicial scrutiny. In particular, with regard to the field of employment, by strengthening the relationship between New Governance and EU constitutionalism social rights and labour standards could be built into the EES in order to counterbalance that weakness by creating the basis for the justiciability of enacted measures. In this way a space for national diversity and experimentation would be preserved and the open method would be maintained intact without incorporating it into the "command and control" regulatory model of EU constitutionalism. Andronico and Lo Faro (2005) identify one main reason for coupling the OMC with fundamental rights. They maintain that while the OMC is said to guarantee diversity, fundamental rights are meant to ensure unity. In other words, 'fundamental rights constitute the element of indispensable hierarchy which corrects the unsustainable heterarchy of an otherwise excessively "open" method of co-ordination'.

The challenge attendant upon such enterprise is acknowledged from the outset. Law and constitutionalism are impacted by an idea of "stateness" (Shaw and Wiener 2000) not found in New Governance processes. There are also a series of other inherent, intertwined and cumulative paradoxes and problems besetting the European Union and its present and future existence. Each of these encapsulates a weakness or limitation of the European integration process, and can also be found in part of the copious literature on New Governance. This makes it all the more difficult to establish a relationship between these different modes of regulation and to identify appropriate normative standards against which to assess the operation and efficacy of new and experimentalist modes of regulation in the wider context of EU social governance. It also explains why, as Weiler and Wind (2003: 3) have put it elsewhere, this chapter is 'not a contribution as to how to do it, but as to how to think about it'.

The chapter proceeds as follows. The first section starts by explaining the emergence of new or experimental forms of regulation in the European Union and the New Governance turn in the literature on European integration. In so doing, it examines the reasons why legal scholars, chiefly constitutional and administrative lawyers, have generally shown either some resistance or reluctance towards the idea of accepting the phenomenon of New Governance. In this context, it looks closely at issues of democratic legitimacy and accountability and puts forward a renewed understanding of them which may be more appropriate to pluralist and multi-tiered legal systems like the European Union and New Governance structures and processes. The first section also analyzes the distinction between soft law and hard law and examines how the European courts have interpreted the legal effects of non-binding legal instruments. This analysis is important because it will help us to a better understanding and assessment of the legal effects of soft law instruments employed in the context of the EES. The second section explores some of the most salient problems and paradoxes of the European Union as a post-national and multi-tiered polity and how they affect our understanding of the role and significance of New Governance in the EU system. The third section presents a hybrid model of governance which seeks to overcome the limitations of both traditional modes of regulation and experimental governance processes and techniques by revisiting extant conceptualizations of law and constitutionalism. The model developed in this chapter will serve as a "benchmark" for evaluating the governance of the EES in Chapters 5–7 of the book. One caveat: some parts are developed in a rather schematic manner as they will form the object of further and more thorough examination in subsequent chapters of the book.

2 The rise of New Governance: a phenomenon lawyers can no longer disregard

2.1 Putting New Governance in context

In the current post-modern and post-national era and in the context of the EU constitutional reform process, New Governance practices and processes have reached a period of consolidation, some obtaining full recognition with the insertion of new provisions in the Treaty.[6] Abstract questions have become practical questions which can no longer be avoided, given the prominence that New Governance has gained over the last decade in European regulation. Although the ToA has provided a legal basis for the development of a uniform regulation of social policy at European level, questions concerning implementation and compliance have arisen as a consequence of the greater reliance on forms of New Governance which need to be taken into consideration in order to understand what role they perform in the EU system. An analogy may be drawn between this situation and Vervaele's (1999: 361) metaphor that 'once the house is ready and house rules have been determined, it becomes more and more important that those rules are complied with and that the house will not be undermined by inferior upkeep or operations that endanger the structure'.

---

6 See e.g. Articles 2(3), 2(5), 5 and 6 TFEU regarding employment and economic policy co-ordination and supporting, co-ordinating and supplementing measures to the actions of the Member States. The Treaty of Lisbon, following the EU Constitution, has a separate category of competence for economic, employment and social matters, Craig (2008: 148; see also Craig 2004: 334–340) observes that the existence of this category was controversial in the Convention on the Future of Europe, with some calling for these areas to come within shared competence while others argued for the inclusion of employment and social policy as well as economic policy within this separate category. This second solution prevailed, mainly for political reasons. If these matters had been placed within shared competence, then the general rules of pre-emption would have been applicable, and this was regarded as being unacceptable by many. Craig (2008: 148) argues that there may be boundary problems between this category and that of shared competence (compare provisions of Article 4 TFEU and Article 5 TFEU), and that it should be recognized that, while this head of competence is framed largely in terms of coordination, the detailed Treaty provisions concerning economic policy nonetheless accord the EU powers to take dispositive and peremptory action in certain circumstances.

The emergence of new or experimentalist approaches to EU governance[7] may be first explained as a manifestation of wider international processes and phenomena. As global trends dismantle barriers, bring about destabilization and in certain ways impose changes at domestic level – which will eventually lead to social, economic and cultural similarities transnationally – this will bring pressure on law to follow suit. As with globalization, so with Europeanization, it makes less and less sense to think of "domestic" norms as forming part of distinct national jurisdictions that subsequently interact with transnational norms (Nelken 2008: 307).[8] Legal fields are increasingly internationalized, even if this process does not affect all fields to the same extent and varies by different areas of legal and social regulation. The "denationalization" of rule making means that transnational public and semi-public networks replace, to an increasing extent, national fora (Nelken 2008: 307).

As a consequence the state and public bodies have started to "mimic" the practices of private organizational models and to apply market-based management theories to achieve the same degree of efficiency as the private sector. Under the heterogeneous and complex realities of globally rapid advancements, states have come to realize that the more flexible and adaptable structure of the private sector should be configured into their legal system. In particular, new modes of governance have already started relying on the use of private-sector techniques such as information pooling, learning by self-monitoring and peer review, knowledge networks and benchmarks for best practices. Lobel (2004: 366) notes that 'in many contexts, the interconnections between the object of regulation (the economy) and the strategy by which it is regulated (law) motivate the push for renewal through the adoption of market practices in the public sphere'. This overarching change has established a link between contemporary problems in the organization of the economy and innovative legal theory on regulation and governance to react to increasing heterogeneity. For Cotterell (2007: 147):

> law is faced with representing or managing difference in legal aspirations no less than with promoting similarity in legal experience. Questions about national sentiment and diversity of cultural allegiances are also becoming legally significant, (as matters bearing on law's practical claims to authority) in a far more obvious way than in past decades. In a culturally complex world, allegiances (to law as to most other embodiments of authority), become complex and multiple.

Hence rule formulation and settlement increasingly take place within new forms of transnational governance. It follows that the governance paradigm is a natural successor to the classic regulatory model. Lobel (2004: 365) explains that the reason for this is that the governance model 'addresses the changes in both the goals and capabilities of legal regulation, and avoids the central deficiencies of substantive law. [It] fundamentally transforms legal control into a dynamic, reflexive, and flexible regime'. This in turn has led to a scenario whereby not only have legal techniques become outmoded and the need for change become conspicuous but, significantly, the aspirations of law and policy have themselves also undergone transformation (Lobel 2004: 364).

Moreover, the European Union forms an integral part of a postmodern trend in

---

7 See also Symposium on UCLA Law Review (2002) and Lobel (2004) for comment and analysis of new approaches to governance in the United States, which shows that there are evident similarities between the European Union and the United States.

8 See further Chapter 3.

international capitalism which has reduced the traditional framework of government, increasing processes of privatization of the law and promoting a stronger legal culture of contract. In this context, the European Union has acquired a unique role, acting, on the one hand, as a liberalizing force for international capitalism and, on the other, as a regulator of capitalist economic forces. It has therefore followed the tendency for transnational systems of governance to experiment with new, less prescriptive and less hierarchical ways of regulating. In this context, New Governance should therefore be seen as a product of the contingencies of history and transnationalism, with multiple overlapping and conflicting juridiscapes (Appadurai 1996). The blurring of the public–private divide within New Governance has significant implications in relation to the question of the European Union's polity identity as it raises questions on whether government is public, private or a combination of the two. In this broad and fluid "fusion zone" the public sector becomes more open to the dynamics, techniques and language of the market, whereas private actors have to deal with conditions set by public authority or integrate broader citizen concerns on their own initiative and to improve their market position, often under the banner of corporate social responsibility (Smismans 2007: 619–620). In this context, Peters (2005) argues that 'in the era of globalization, a constitutionalist reconstruction is a desirable reaction to the visible deconstitutionalization on the domestic level'.

These systemic changes have significant implications for regulation in the European Union and the way we study it. They highlight the fact that positivistic images of law based on the unity of the nation-state say little about the multi-faceted processes by which EU law is formed or the actors involved in decision and policy making. It follows that regulation in the European Union can no longer be reduced to mere dichotomies between a supranational and a domestic level of rule making, but should be constructed and analyzed as being differentiated and multi-level. As Armstrong (1998: 169–170) aptly puts it, 'this more complex picture of governance raises practical and normative problems for law in constitutional and administrative law terms. In short, as governance evolves and as actors within different governance regimes or networks seek to recast their conflicts in legal terms, how ought law, as an institution, to approach such issues?'

Within the EU context, some of the specific reasons for the way in which New Governance has emerged and spread can be related to features of the European Union's economic constitutional framework and the rigidities of traditional constitutionalism (de Búrca 2003). With its series of enlargements the European Union can no longer 'sustain the degree of homogeneity, commonality and unity of purpose and method which seemed to characterise the earlier Community' (de Búrca and Scott 2000: 2). Further, the initial model and ideal of European integration, aimed at developing a uniform and harmonized legal system, has gradually started to exhibit vulnerability as it has exacerbated and polarized differences between Member States, resulting in various degrees of disintegration (Shaw 1996). The constitutionalization of differentiated integration[9] with the Treaty of Maastricht and the manifold path to integration that it has fostered rather than leading to a "Europe of bits and pieces" (Curtin 1993) has strengthened rather than weakened the ability of the European Union to evolve constantly in response to changing pressures and new priorities.

More specifically, New Governance is part of the ongoing search for new forms and

---

9 Differentiated integration is a term which encompasses 'variations in the application of European policies or variations in the level and intensity of participation in European policy regimes' (Wallace 1998: 137).

methodologies of integrative policy making and rule setting (Dorf and Sabel 1998; Lobel 2004; Sabel and Zeitlin 2008) and, in broader terms, it represents one of the many answers to external and internal challenges that the European Union is confronted with and the outcome of a complex mix of strategic and sectoral politics.[10] Borrowing a phrase by Walker (2000: 12) in relation to flexibility, New Governance may be described as being 'an ubiquitous device which can serve quite different – even diametrically opposed – end games'. In some ways, New Governance may be seen as the offspring of all the contradictory urges and pains of the Europeanization process and of the European Union's constitutional self-understanding. In this sense, de Búrca (2003: 814) talks about the paradoxical nature of the European Union's constitutional system: a fundamental tension between EU constitutionalism based on limited EU powers, clarity in the division of competences between states and the European Union, on the one hand, and on the other, the reality of a highly reflexive and pragmatic form of governance entailing the expansion of EU activity into virtually all policy fields (which critics define as "creeping competences" or "Europeanization by stealth"), a profound degree of competence and power sharing between levels and sites of decision making on the other.

In particular, the birth of New Governance processes and practices may be explained by several reasons which can be summarized as follows (de Búrca 2003; Sabel and Zeitlin 2003):[11] the reluctance of Member States to grant the Union further powers or, similarly, to concede powers in very narrow terms. Linked to this, various simultaneous economic pressures brought about by globalization, together with the constraints of the EMU and the Internal Market projects have led Member States to rely more heavily on the use of co-ordination in sensitive policy areas where they wanted to maintain their independent decision-making powers. Thus New Governance appears to provide pragmatic solutions to common and complex socio-economic problems by depoliticizing them and by side-stepping obstacles at national level represented by domestic constitutional structures and methods.

It is also important to emphasize the different functions that European law has had within the fifty years of existence of the European Community. In the 1950s, since European law was conceived chiefly as a means of attaining largely economic objectives, the law was viewed as 'law that *emerged from* the Community's legislative, administrative and judicial processes rather than law that *accounted for* and *explained* those processes' (Bermann 2001). European law has since then gradually evolved into being more than merely instrumental to the pursuit of the Internal Market and to Europeanization and is increasingly seen as exemplifying the various processes and phases of European integration and governance. Post-Maastricht, the legal debates have focused mainly on constitutionalism issues, democratic deficit, European citizenship, transparency, subsidiarity and human rights. What is striking about recent enlargements (and chiefly the 2004 enlargement) is that the very same factors, political, economic and social, which make it in many ways unprecedented, have not only refocused attention on debates over the European Union's constitutional project but also emphasized law as an institution with an important capacity-building function, thus reassigning a renewed instrumental role to European law in order to enable it to perform problem-solving tasks and to shape the European Union's rule-making processes rather than being merely a positivistic manifestation of formal legitimacy.

---

10 For an overview of the competing representations of the New Governance phenomenon in the EU (with a specific focus on the OMC), see Andronico and Lo Faro (2005: 44–51).

11 These factors are examined more thoroughly in Chapters 3–5.

Recourse to a single process of integration, based on a single structure, has been made untenable by several waves of enlargement and the typology of new competences which have required an increase in the diversity and flexibility of both policy and legal responses.

The reasons for its emergence offer sustenance to the view that the term "New Governance" is a misnomer[12] and, rather than constituting an alternative process to the Common Market "core", it operates within the "constitutional embrace" of the Treaties.[13] The provisions on enhanced co-operation inserted by the TEU and the ToN[14] and much earlier scholarly notions such as that of "Europe of concentric circles", "variable geometry Europe", "multi-speed Europe" or "Europe *à la carte*",[15] all refer to the idea of a non-uniform form of European integration and implicitly recognize the limitations of classic European government. Recourse to minimum standards and harmonization, framework legislation and mutual recognition has proved to be an effective method of accommodating diversity among Member States and has had a key role in the completion of the Single Market. Dougan (2006: 873–874) posits that the growth of alternatives to total harmonization while being a clear indication of a growing resistance to centralization are 'all phenomena which have grown from within the "Community Method", and represent equally valid manifestations of it, rather than evidencing its outright rejection or innate weakness'. In particular, the revolutionary and "avant-garde" principle of mutual recognition – an ingenious creation of the ECJ's judicial activism and device to promote European legal (negative) integration – are clear examples of alternative forms of regulation to the classic Community Method. According to Schmidt (2007) mutual recognition embodies many of the claimed benefits of New Governance as it allows for more voluntary acts by the Member States than other forms of hard law, more flexibility, decentralization and increased public–private horizontal forms of co-operation. Hence, as in the case of New Governance, mutual recognition responds to the limits of hierarchical government and facilitates an accommodation of national diversity, while respecting the institutional integrity and political autonomy of its Member States in all matters where uniformity and centralization are not necessary or not possible (Scharpf 2001: 13).

> Mutual recognition often leads to ex-post harmonization and what changes is not so much the degree of sovereignty transferred but more how it is transferred . . . in a decentralized manner by regulatory competition . . . [Mutual recognition] could perhaps be better identified as a form of horizontal deliberation.
>
> (Poiares Maduro: 2007: 819; see also Armstrong 2002a)

The European Union is constantly searching for new ideas on how to "re-dress" its own political identity and image, and New Governance may be said to represent one of the answers to the European Union's democratic deficit/legitimacy crisis. And yet the practices, processes and tools that are part of New Governance, the *way* they operate and the *extent* to which they may be said to be effective and, if so, *in what way* and *in relation to what*

---

12 Scott and Trubek (2002) look at different modes of regulation pre-dating New Governance such as Comitology and the institutionalization of the European Social Dialogue.

13 Both expressions are borrowed from de Búrca (2000).

14 See Title VII TEU, Articles 11 and 11a EC.

15 For some examples of the use of flexibility in the social field, see Barnard (2000) and Sciarra (2005); see also Chapter 4.

are still far from being settled issues. New Governance, therefore, forces European scholars to rethink the concept(s) and the role(s) of law, the theories and models of EU constitutionalism, their relationship with "new" modes of regulation and, *a fortiori*, to re-examine the way the EU system operates and the way Europeanization is being pursued.

Despite the growing importance of the New Governance phenomenon in the European Union, as the focus in the last decade of a considerable volume of investigation and analysis (see for example the NEWGOV and CONNEX projects and the database of the European Centre of Excellence of the University of Wisconsin on the OMC),[16] the legal dimension remains partially under-explored, having been examined more thoroughly and in a more structured manner only in the last few years (see, for example, Barbera 2006; Deakin and De Schutter 2005; de Búrca and Scott 2006; de Búrca and Scott 2007). Reduced interest in the legal literature can be explained *prima facie* by the fact that most legal scholars *sic et simpliciter* fail to recognize the relevance of New Governance in the Community's legal and judicial system. This is the object of the ensuing analysis.

2.2 Soft law and hard law: two worlds apart or two sides of the same coin?

One reason explaining this narrow approach may be the fact that New Governance practices and processes are simplistically and narrowly equated to soft law instruments[17] and thus, in line with legal positivism, they are considered as not being "legally" relevant. Within this frame lawyers consider soft law not to be law and thus they consider it to be either irrelevant to the Community legal system or a redundant concept (Klabbers 1996). Soft law instruments – particularly before the entry into force of the Treaty of Maastricht – have acted mainly as addenda or as instruments of interpretation of hard law instruments and overall they have not formed part of a regulatory process beside the Community Method or pertained to a governance subsystem within the broader Community Method as they have now become.

Moreover, there is a well-ensconced tendency in the legal arena to view the world of regulation and New Governance in dichotomous terms and to rely on the so-called "binary" logic which considers the equation of soft law to hard law an obvious *non sequitur*. By drawing on this approach, most lawyers identify these experimental modes of regulation as "non-law" and thus primarily by comparison to what they are not and by contrast with traditional regulatory approaches which are considered more capable of achieving the desideratum of "good governance" (de Búrca and Scott 2006).[18] In this context, law is intended as formally encompassing legally binding and enforceable instruments, and

---

16 More information about these projects is available at <http://www.eu-newgov.org> and <http://www.connex-network.org>; <http://eucenter.wisc.edu/OMC>.

17 In subsequent chapters of the book I explain why this is a very limited view, as it does not take into account the different layers of policy and decision making in the European Union and that within New Governance processes there is often a combined use of soft and hard law instruments. The heavier reliance on one mode of regulation than the other is dependent on the level of regulation taken into consideration (domestic and/or European) as well as the policy area concerned and the targeted objectives; see further Trubek and Trubek (2007) and Sabel and Zeitlin (2008).

18 Good governance is a form of governance that embodies eight specific characteristics, and can be seen as an ideal of governance. Good governance embodies processes that are 'participatory, consensus oriented, accountable, transparent, responsive, effective and efficient, equitable and inclusive, and [which follow] the rule of law' (UNESCAP 2009); see also the European Commission (2001: 10) definition of good governance.

constitutionalism as connoting, in narrow terms, a self-limiting government and, in broader terms, a set of constitutional features of a given polity encapsulated by the rule of law.

This limited view recalls the equally narrow concept of "surface law". Surface law is a metaphor applied in comparative legal studies suggesting that what lies beneath the surface may be different from what is observable on top. In this context, legal rules expressed in legal texts are surface law: below this surface are the practices of law. As Twining (2008: 178–182) argues, the notion of surface law may be misleading. It presupposes an opposition between "appearance" and "reality" in law: law in the books and law in action; paper rules and real rules; rules and results (outcomes), and so on. These dichotomies put too much emphasis on the separation between the "bare text" on the one hand and the underlying problems, principles, policies and rationale on the other (*ibid.*: 181). Treating these familiar formalist/realist contrasts as binary suggest that the two poles of each dichotomy may even be unrelated alternatives (*ibid.*: 181). Consequently, there may be a temptation to focus attention on one branch of the dichotomy and to neglect the other. While it is true that informal legal and normative orders may sometimes proceed independently and without reference to official or state law, in the majority of cases there is some form of "interlegality", be it competition, coexistence, complementarity or subordination. As de Sousa Santos (2002: 437) argues, 'our legal life is constituted by an intersection of different legal orders. Interlegality is the phenomenological counterpart of legal plurality, and a key concept in an oppositional post-modern conception of law.'[19] With regard to New Governance, Armstrong posits that new forms of governance pose a challenge to EU constitutionalism because they occupy an unsettled constitutional space. This space is characterized by a range of possible encounters between constitutionalism and governance. Armstrong 'characterize[s] these as involving "accommodation" – an ability of one to coexist with the other without change to either – "adaptation" – an encounter which alters in a limited manner one and/or the other – and "transformation" – a more fundamental change to either governance or constitutionalism – as well as "antagonism" – manifested as either incompatibility or irritation' (Armstrong 2008: 416).

In order to use surface law as a valuable and meaningful analytical concept we need to separate it from the recurring pitfalls of this binary approach. In particular, we may only have proper accounts of surface law if we combine the legal text with its practices: legal rules are not self-enacting, self-interpreting, self-applying or self-implementing (Twining 2008). The bare legal text on its own is rather uninformative and not useful to an understanding, interpretation, use and enforcement of the provisions of legal norms and when trying to assess their effects. If we apply this line of reasoning to new modes of governance and to their role within the Community legal system it may be possible to hold to the view that they provide a common cognitive framework for understanding domestic legal problems affecting several Member States and for identifying workable legal measures which will be more apt to take into consideration differences between Member States' socio-legal and economic systems and thus reduce actual or potential inconsistencies between Community law and national constitutional and legal systems. The reduced friction between European and national levels may also provide a solid ground for better implementation and enforcement of EC law.

Linked to this, we should also avoid conceiving of surface law necessarily as being either hard or soft for it be a meaningful concept. An example which illustrates the limitation

---

19 See also Barber (2006); Pernice (1999).

of scholarly distinctions such as that between soft and hard law is the operation of the EES: while technically a purely soft co-ordination process at European level it may nevertheless introduce "hard" legal harmonization at national level. In particular, this may happen because Member States enact new employment legislation in accordance with the guidelines of the EES (which are now part of the Lisbon Strategy's Integrated Guidelines). This also explains why it is challenging *per se* to understand and define its multi-tiered and iterative stages of policy formation and implementation. Its core components, soft and hard, supranational and intergovernmental, are strictly intertwined and equally important to the outcomes and results of the overall process of the Strategy. The hard impact of the open method's soft co-ordination does not merely consist of exerting political pressure on Member States to comply with centrally designed policies. To argue this would be to maintain that the EES is essentially supranational and that Member States have to "obey" what is basically decided and enforced by the triptych made up of the European Council, Council of Ministers and Commission without any concrete decision making input in the adoption of the Employment Guidelines. As I will go on to show in the chapters that follow, on the contrary Member States have a rather strong and powerful decision-making role in the design of the guidelines (either via the European Council or the Council of Ministers) which embody objectives which most Member States want to achieve (at their own pace) in circumstances where there is no unanimous consensus either in respect to the definition of the objectives or the way of achieving them in the hard law realm. Problems may arise when the Commission attempts to promote certain policy measures at a time or in a manner which goes against the will of the Member States. For instance, the initial proposals by the Commission for the first set of Employment Guidelines containing specific quantitative targets and timetable were subsequently watered down by the Council and the final draft of these guidelines did not contain the specifications suggested by the Commission.

If we were to embrace the view that surface law is only hard in nature, then soft law may be of aid towards a better understanding and better effecting of legal prescriptions. Once again the EES is suggestive. It provides a common cognitive framework for understanding and describing shared problems in national labour markets and for identifying workable solutions that are adaptable to the different socio-economic structure of different welfare systems. Thus concepts and categories developed in the context of the iterative process of the EES are increasingly used in national labour market policy discourse and have had at least a symbolic impact nationally. The cognitive framework created through the EES may serve as a basis for a better understanding and thus implementation of EC law by the Member States (particularly those countries that have recently joined and are still learning the legal methodologies and substantive law of the European Union), namely Directives in the field of employment or gender equality.

Moving to the legal effects of soft law instruments, we need to reconsider the definition of soft law outlined in Chapter 1. Soft law instruments are rules of conduct which, in principle, have no legally binding force but which nevertheless may have practical effects and also legal effects (Snyder 1995; Ştefan 2008). It follows from this definition of soft law that the notions of legally binding force and legal effects do not always have the same meaning. Indeed, soft law instruments may produce various legal effects such as, *inter alia*, 'creating legitimate expectations for the individuals, clarifying the content of certain hard law provisions, or structuring the discretion of certain institutions' whilst not having any legally binding force (Ştefan 2008: 756).

A careful reading of the European courts' rulings in the field of competition law seems to confirm this. The courts make a clear distinction between soft and hard law but in so doing they do not deny the legal effects of soft law instruments.[20] In *BASF* a decision of the Commission was considered to be "vitiated of illegality"[21] because of the misapplication of Section B(e) of the Leniency Notice. This case would seem to suggest that soft law instruments may be used as standards for reviewing the legality of an act of secondary (hard) legislation, such as decisions of the Commission. In other cases the courts seem to suggest that soft law provisions adopted by the Commission "bind" it to its own actions[22] and that taking into consideration soft law instruments may lead to their juridification[23] granting them legally binding force (*ibid.* 768–769).[24] However, a further examination of the mechanisms through which legal effects are recognized as soft law instruments shows that this is not a correct interpretation of the courts' approach to soft law, particularly when reading the above rulings in the context of and in combination with other decisions.[25] What transpires from these decisions is that the obligation to "abide by" soft law provisions does not have its source in their binding nature but in the general principles of law such as the respect of legal certainty, legitimate expectations or equality. For instance, the Guidelines on Fines may produce legal effects in that legal certainty requires the Commission to apply them, creating a legitimate expectation for undertakings that the Commission will do so in cases of non-compliance. Advocate General Tizzano argued that for the above reasons they could in principle become the object of an Article 241 EC objection.[26]

A similar approach has been adopted by the ECJ in *Mangold*,[27] a case concerning a horizontal dispute on age discrimination, where it held that the Employment Framework Directive (Council of the European Union 2000b) embodied among others the principle of non-discrimination on grounds of age which should be regarded as a general principle of Community law derived from international instruments and the constitutional traditions common to the Member States. In this way the Court once again sidestepped the rather piquant issue of the horizontal direct effect of unimplemented Directives and enabled the German court to enforce this general principle of Community law embodied by the Directive in question.[28] In particular, by adopting a teleological approach, the Court held that there is a prohibition to discriminate on grounds of age as a general principle of Community law independently of the Employment Framework Directive which constitutes a part of the general principle of equal treatment as a fundamental right under Community law. The Court seemed to be assuming that general principles of law are directly effective, advancing the proposition that they are capable of conferring substantive rights and imposing substantive obligations in legal relations between individuals. In particular, with *Mangold* the Court seems to have recognized that the constitutional principle of equal treatment on grounds of age may have legal effects of its own. There are two consequences

20 Joined Cases C-189, 202, 205, 208 and 213/02, *O Rørindustri and others v. Commission* [2005] ECR I-05425.
21 Case T-15/02, *BASF v. Commission* [2006] ECR II-497, para. 541.
22 E.g. Case C-3/06, *Groupe Danone v.* Commission [2007] ECR I-1331; Joined Cases T-71/03, T-74/03, T-87/03 and T-91/03 *Tokai Carbon Co. Ltd v. Commission of the European Communities* [2005] ECR II-10.
23 For a meaning of juridification, see Blichner and Molander (2008).
24 See also Case C-393/92, *Municipality of Almelo* [1994] ECR I-01477.
25 See Joined Cases C-189, 202, 205, 208 and 213/02, *O Rørindustri and others v. Commission* [2005] ECR I-05425, Case C-76/06P, *Britannia Alloys & Chemicals v. Commission* [2007] ECR I-4405, Case T-16/99, *Lögstor Rör (Deutschland) v. Commission* [2002] ECR II-01633, Case T-224/00, *Archer Daniels Midland Company and Archer Daniels Midland Ingredients v. Commission* [2003] ECR II-2597.
26 Opinion of AG Tizzano in Joined Cases C-189, 202, 205, 208 and 213/2002 *O Rørindustri and others v. Commission* [2005] ECR I-05425, paras 54 and 236.
27 Case C-144/04, *Werner Mangold v. Rüdiger Helm* [2005] ECR I-9981.
28 For further comments and critique, see Schiek (2006); Editorial (2006); Muir (2006).

of this ruling worthy of mention (Schiek 2006: 339). First, in relation to the scope of application of the non-discrimination clauses as constitutional principles, the Member States and their courts are now under an obligation not to apply contravening national legislation, administrative orders and even case law principles independently of whether they apply to public bodies or concern horizontal relations. Second, the decision enhances the incidental direct effect of both Directives and general principles of Community law.

While it is difficult to predict what type of impact or influence *Mangold* will exert on how we conjure the legal effects of soft law in the wider context of enforcement of Community hard law measures, at the same time it cannot be denied that its implications for the interpretation of soft law by the ECJ may be very significant because this case tells us how far the ECJ is willing to go to ensure the respect of a general principle of constitutional value and essentially a fundamental right against the respect of other general principles of EC law, namely legal certainty and legitimate expectations. Thus, in the light of *Mangold*, the proposition that nothing could stop the ECJ in the future from ruling that a given Employment Guideline enshrines a general principle of constitutional value or a fundamental right on the basis of a combined reading of, for example, Article 13 EC and Article 21 or Article 23 of the Charter while probably difficult to effect in practice cannot be completely ruled out. It would also be a way of solving the question raised by the horizontal provisions of the Charter as to whether measures adopted by the Member States in the context of OMC processes may be considered as implementing measures of EU law.

Turning back to the legal effects of soft law, the ECJ seems to be treating soft law as being part of the body of European norms to be used for interpretation when deciding a case; in particular, it considers it as an important point of reference and interpretative tool, for example to reinforce an argument[29] or to describe more accurately a given legal framework.[30] The Court therefore considers soft law as being an integral part of European law *lato sensu*. The way the courts have been using soft law instruments in such competition law cases shows that the courts are willing to recognize the legal effects of non-binding legal instruments whenever they facilitate the enforcement of certain general principles of law common to both European and national legal orders.[31]

In *Grimaldi*[32] and *Deutsche Shell*[33] the ECJ held that even though soft law may have no binding effect, it does not preclude the European Court from ruling on its interpretation in proceedings for a preliminary ruling under Article 177 EC (now 234 EC) and added that, although soft law measures cannot confer upon individuals rights which they may enforce before national courts, the latter are nevertheless obliged to take them into consideration in resolving disputes submitted to them. In particular, soft law measures will be of relevance in cases where they cast light on the interpretation of national measures adopted in order to implement them or where they are designed to supplement binding Community

---

29 Case C-393/92, *Municipality of Almelo* [1994] ECR I-01477; Case T-201/04, *Microsoft Corporation v. Commission* [2007] ECR II-3601.

30 Case C-301/04, *Commission v. SGL Carbon* [2006] ECR I-5915.

31 See Klabbers (1994:1004–1016) for a critical analysis of the ECJ's case law on the legal effects of Community soft law instruments. This analysis together with the one by Ştefan (2008) illustrates how in the period between the 1970s and the first years of the twenty-first century there has been continuity in the legal reasoning of the Court.

32 Case C-322/88, *Grimaldi v. Fonds des Maladie professionnelles* [1989] ECR 4407; see also Case 90/76, *Van Ameyde v. UCI* [1977] ECR 1091.

33 C-188/91, *Deutsche Shell v. Hauptzollamt Hamburg-Harburg* [1993] ECR I-363.

provisions and may thus be included in the "acts" under Article 177(1)b EC. This line of thinking of the European Court has been said to be 'reminiscent of *Von Colson*'[34] (Arnull 1990: 318), recalling ideas of a duty of consistent interpretation for non-binding legal instruments, while others consider that the European Court is introducing a mandatory interpretation aid for national courts (Senden 2004: 387–393). Thus the principle of duty of consistent interpretation may be a vehicle through which general principles of Community law might become directly enforceable in the implementation of Union law.

Independently of how we may conceive of the legal effects of soft law instruments, their symbolic value may be of great significance. The EU Charter is illustrative. While the Charter is soft in the sense that it is not legally binding, nevertheless it has been very influential and of great symbolic significance.[35] The inclusion of the so-called "horizontal provisions" in the Charter (Articles 51–54) are evidence of the anxiety and concern Member States have of the potential effects, whether normative or practical in nature, of the Charter itself. In the *BECTU* case – one of the first cases where reference to the EU Charter was made – Advocate General Tizzano in addressing the Charter's status said that because it incorporates provisions reaffirming rights enshrined in other international instruments 'in proceedings concerned with the nature and scope of a fundamental right, the relevant statements of the Charter cannot be ignored; in particular, we cannot ignore its clear purpose of serving, where its provisions so allow, as a substantive point of reference for all those involved, Member States, institutions, natural and legal persons, in the Community context'.[36] This view was embraced by the ECJ in the *Parliament v. Council* case.[37] Since 2006 the European Court has conferred an indirect legal status upon the Charter by referring to it as another valid source of inspiration for its own case law on fundamental human rights (Dougan 2008; Syrpis 2008), similar to a consolidating document which breathes new life into pre-existing principles and rights sanctioned in other constitutional documents.[38] In particular, the European Court appears to have adopted the view that the Charter is one of a range of sources it may use to identify general principles of law and not to create new rights, but rather and in line with the wording of the Preamble of the Charter and the horizontal provisions (as well as the current political climate), reaffirm rights as they result from various other sources.

In sum, recurring dichotomies such as that between soft law and hard law may be of some significance analytically, but they generally reflect different underlying concerns of how to achieve a more effective and democratic legal system. While governance

---

34 Case C-14/83 *Von Colson and Kamann v. Land Nordrhein-Westfälen* [1984] ECR I-1891.

35 If the Lisbon Treaty enters into force the EU Charter will cease to be a soft law instrument and will acquire the same legal status as the EU Treaties and thus become a primary and binding source of EU law; see Article 6(1) TEU.

36 See Opinion of Tizzano AG delivered on 8 February 2001 in Case C-173/99 *Broadcasting, Entertainment, Cinematographic and Theatre Union (BECTU) v. Secretary of State for Trade and Industry* [2001] ECR I-4881 paras. 27–28; see also paras. 22–28. See Case T-54/99 *Max.mobil v. Commission* [2002] ECR II-313, paras 48 and 57 (Articles 41 and 47 of the Charter); Case T-198/01R *Technische Glaswerke Ilmenau* [2002] ECR II-2153, para. 85 (Article 41 of the Charter), and Case T-177/01 *Jégo-Quéré & Cie v. Commission*, [2002] ECR II-2365, para. 47 (Article 47 of the Charter).

37 Case C-540/03, [2006] ECR I-5769. See also Case C-432/05, *Unibet*, [2007] ECR I-2271; Case C-303/05, *Advocaten voor der Wereld*, [2007] ECR I-3633; Case C-438/05, *International Transport Workers' Federation, Finnish Seamen's Union v. Viking Line, OÜ Viking Line Eesti*, [2007] ECR I-10779; Case C-341/05, *Laval & Partneri v. Svenska Byggnadsarbetareförbundet, Svenska Byggnadsarbetareförbundets avd. 1, Byggettan, Svenska Elektrikerförbundet*, [2007] ECR I-11767.

38 For a critique of the Court's approach to the EU Charter, see Drywood (2007).

encompasses broader processes of varying nature such as political, economic, techno-logical and knowledge-based affecting decision and policy making in the European Union, whether in a structured or unstructured setting, law and constitutionalism are mainly concerned with the government or regulation of the European Union. The foregoing distinction, therefore, should not be overemphasized.

2.3 New Governance as a threat to the founding pillars of the Community Method

Another reason which may explain why placing greater reliance on the processes and practices of New Governance is objectionable to many lawyers is a more or less explicit concern that "new" or experimentalist approaches to regulation based on horizontal forms of co-operative or collaborative governance may undermine the foundations of the Community Method[39] in that they operate in the shadow of the law and its hierarchy, evading the democratic controls of parliamentary and judicial scrutiny. In particular, the perceived perniciousness of New Governance would result in a reduction of the 'capacity of law to steer, to inform the normative direction of policy, and to secure accountability in governance . . . by virtue of the mismatch between the fundamental premises of law and the premises of New Governance' (de Búrca and Scott, 2006: 5; Walker 2000: 12). In this sense, Sbragia (2002) says that governance in the European Union may be described as "government minus". Such concerns have led to demands by the Commission (2001) that the OMC should not be used when legislative action under the Community Method is possible and to explicitly state that it should be used as a complement of the latter. In many ways this comes as no surprise as it is easily noticeable how New Governance practices and processes (combined with interrogatory post-nationalism discourses of the European Union) erode the comfortable relationship between law, constitutionalism and European integration. This "orthodoxy of hostility"[40] towards New Governance propounded by those who envisage only a form of integration through law based on the "solid ground" of traditional constitutionalism[41] may be associated with the fear that experimentalism may circumvent pivotal political commitments and constitutional safe-guards given that it eschews traditional legal mechanisms of accountability, alongside transparency, its *alter ego* which could further alienate an already disinterested and distrust-ful populace. Moreover, there is a concern that there may be a trade-off between demo-cratic accountability and policy efficiency (the input–output dilemma) (Papadopoulos 2007: 484). However, as stressed by Weiler (1995: 232), democracy and legitimacy are not "coterminous". Legitimacy may be preserved by values other than representative dem-ocracy and by substantive policy outcomes rather than process (Scott 1998: 176). On this point, Esty (2006: 1515–1523) explores various types of legitimacy aside from democratic legitimacy – results-based, order-derived, systemic, deliberative and procedural – which may equally guarantee a legitimate government or, more precisely, provide a logic for the

---

39 In a similar vein, see Klabbers (1998) on the undesirability of soft law. He maintains that: 'By creating uncertainty at the edges of legal thinking, the concept of soft law contributes to the crumbling of the entire legal system. Once political or moral concerns are allowed to creep back into the law, the law loses its relative autonomy from politics or morality, and therewith becomes nothing else but a fig leaf for power' (at p. 391).

40 I have borrowed this term from Shaw (2000: 339).

41 Constitutionalism in this context is seen as an ideal closely related to a formalized notion of the rule of law which offers an overarching goal which many scholars and commentators are willing to accept that 'the EU *should* aspire to in so far as it represents a common endeavor of a collectivity of liberal states' (Shaw and Wiener 2000).

acceptance of political authority, including supranational policy making, even though any democratic underpinnings may be absent. Moreover, the sources of legitimacy interact in complex ways, reinforcing and substituting each other and at other times being in tension.

It should also be noted that from a management point of view the European Union has grown too fast. As Harlow (2002: 171) posits, the peculiar problems of welding together a transnational bureaucracy have made it hard to develop an ethos of management appropriate to the Community Method and, more broadly, to the multi-tiered policy-making system of the European Union.[42] By the same token Everson (1998: 196, 201; 214–215) argues that operating under peculiar EU conditions of constitutional and political uncertainty administrative law's traditional role of ensuring the accountability and fidelity of delegated legislation is obsolete: accountable to whom, faithful to what? Under present conditions EU administrative law is forced to reassess its underlying constitutional logic and long-standing normative reference points. In particular, it must explicitly move away from its idealized view of "legitimate" administration, predicated upon a narrow vision of current world politics and on the existence of a pre-existing and unitary political will (of the state). In turn, this requires the development of a new set of administrative rules and structures that are sensitive to the complex realities of the pluralist and composite European system, reflecting a general phenomenon, that is, the crumbling away of the central state at national level and the involvement of a multiplicity of both public and private actors.[43] More broadly, Poiares Maduro (1998: 175, 2003) argues 'that European integration not only challenges national constitutions . . . it challenges constitutional law itself. It assumes a constitution without a traditional political community defined and proposed by that constitution. . . . European integration also challenges the legal monopoly of states and the hierarchical organization of the law (in which constitutional law is still conceived of as the "higher law").'[44]

A quick glance at the present European Union will suffice to see that within the European Community and precisely in the context of the Community Method there are different levels or layers of accountability, be it *ex ante* or *ex post*, and different degrees of judicial scrutiny both at European and national levels. This system of accountability and judicial scrutiny is far from being perfect. The scope of the Commission's relationships with advisory committees and the role the latter play in national governance are already problematic because informal interplay and influence between Commission staff and national civil servants or experts are much harder to regulate or control. Similarly, the way the Committee of Permanent Representatives of the Member States (COREPER) operates has also been the subject of much debate in terms of transparency, particularly given that most decisions are actually taken by the COREPER before they even reach ministerial level. In addition, the Council is not subject to any real form of political *ex ante* accountability at European level but only to *ex post* judicial accountability, for example through actions for annulment brought before the ECJ under Article 230 EC. Although it may be said that the Council is in some way responsible to the European Parliament, which arises out of the co-decision procedure (Article 251 EC), no such form of accountability may be said to exist in relation to pillars two and three. In addition, even though members of the

---

42 More generally Grant and Keohane (2005: 30) posit that in the international context 'even the minimal types of constraints [on power] found in domestic governments are absent'.

43 See also Esty (2006: 1537), who identifies parallels between supranational and domestic administrative law structures.

44 See also Shaw (1999: 591).

Council may be politically accountable to their national parliaments the Council itself is not accountable in the same way that the Commission is to the European Parliament, whose supervisory functions have increased significantly over the years (Articles 192–193 EC, 197 EC, 200–201 EC, 214 EC). Moreover, the comitology process under Article 202 EC, through which highly technical and complex implementing measures concerning the Internal Market are agreed in specialist committees composed of technocrat representatives from Member States and chaired by a Commission official, has been the subject of much controversy for its lack of transparency and accountability (Brandsma *et al.* 2008). As co-legislator it has been rather difficult for the European Parliament to accept implementing measures decided on in a Council–Commission setting only. Hence, further to the introduction of the 'regulatory procedure with scrutiny' (Council of the European Union 2006d), the European Parliament may oppose the adoption of a Commission decision prepared in committee where it is felt that the matter should be dealt with through co-decision (Schusterschitz and Kotz 2007).

It follows that if it is difficult to achieve an efficient system of accountability within the more traditional mode of regulation, it becomes even more challenging to develop a model of accountability, be it legal or political, that is appropriate to the less formal and less structured processes of New Governance. On accountability, Mulgan (2000: 555) notes, 'the word crops up everywhere performing all manner of analytical and rhetorical tasks and carrying most of the burdens of democratic "governance" ' (see also Bovens 2007). It is invariably equated with a strong system of judicial review, the mechanics of law enforcement or the principles of procedural due process (legal accountability) and set of procedures of governments' public control and censure through elected institutions (political accountability) – all elements which seem to be absent in New Governance. The Commission's response to public concern over the extensive and growing use of soft law instruments has been to promote democratic self-management in the rule-making and standard-setting processes, delegating wherever possible to agencies, committees or social partners so that the rules are made either by those directly interested or by representatives of civil society by way of delegation. The delegation of power to various independent bodies and agencies ("agencification") has been justified by the need to ensure the credibility of those entrusted with decision making, and this credibility is deemed to be primarily safeguarded through independence and expertise according to the "fiduciary" principle (Majone 2002). The main criticism voiced by many lawyers is that it adds confusion as to who should be held accountable as well as raising doubts about its participatory democracy aspect, given the limited and piecemeal involvement of certain actors and stakeholders of civil society. These new actors are, for the most part, excluded from the decision-making sphere and are given a more important role in the implementation side of policy making. In this sense, these actors may clearly be seen as being regulatory and legitimacy resources of the European Union.

While the Commission together with the European Economic and Social Committee has been an advocate and promoter of developing a discourse on participation in European policy making beyond the traditional route of parliamentary politics, a careful reading of the Commission's White Paper *European Governance* (2001) and its follow-up initiatives shows that there is a focus on participation through functional intermediaries and an absence of the concept of citizenship (Smismans 2007). In particular, in the White Paper, participatory governance has mainly been defined in relation to the Community Method, thus confirming the view that civil society consultation is used only in so far as it acts as a form of legitimacy token to strengthen the Commission's institutional position (Armstrong 2002), as well as the claim that the Commission is clearly restricting the scope of action and intervention of participatory "new" governance (Velluti 2003). Moreover, these top-down deliberative modes of governance promoted by the Commission have been criticized for reducing associative pluralism and intra-organizational diversity, either by imposing an official policy paradigm or by failing to co-opt in governance actors who do not comply or fit with it (Wälti and Kübler 2003). An additional criticism of participation has been its association with a narrow conceptualization of Union citizenship. Since its introduction by the Maastricht Treaty, the participatory dimension of EU citizenship has mainly been thought of in terms of electoral participation. Further, while subsequent Treaty reforms have highlighted the nature of participation as a constitutional practice, it seems more apt to talk about "activated citizenship" in the sense that European decision makers are trying to activate civil society top-down to sell the product, rather than with real active citizenship (Smismans 2007: 600–601).

In relation to the EES, Smismans (2005: 116–117) observes that the EES both in its constitutional and institutional set-up and in its actual working is far from the standard democratic narrative of representative democracy as well as from the democratic ideal of directly deliberative polyarchy (Cohen and Sabel 1997; Gerstenberg 1997). In particular, 'it does not provide the coherent institutional framework that can encourage decentralized self-regulation in an accountable and democratic way and that can ensure interaction between subsystems without subordination of one to the other' (Smismans 2005: 135).

While these concerns cannot be brushed aside, the issues identified should be viewed in the light of the fact that paradoxically a national polity may represent a limit to democracy and constitutionalism. As Poiares Maduro (2003: 82–83) aptly notes:

> participation in national democracies is not granted to all those affected by the decisions of the national political process but only to those affected who are considered as 'citizens of the national polity' or as legally resident in the host country. Hence the dependence of democracy and constitutionalism on the narrow premises of nationality or legal residence is 'in contradiction with the founding principles of constitutional democracies which aim at full representation and participation'.
>
> *(Ibid.*, 83)

This diminished inclusiveness is further aggravated by the fact that 'the borders of national democracy no longer correspond to the scope of action of the "modern citizen" ' (*ibid.*). By the same token, Davies (2005) points out that because residence has become an alternative to nationality as the criterion for membership of society and rights to benefits, the distinction is not so much between a "national" and a "foreigner" as between "resident" and "non-resident". National democracies seem to have become incapable of coping with nationals' transnational affinities to European common or shared values or rights. Second, states do not always recognize other polities and their institutions, procedures and processes precisely because of a taken-for-granted primacy of national constitutionalism over any "other" constitutionalism.

Moreover, the aforementioned concerns over the limitations of new modes of governance are not insuperable, particularly if the aim is not that of achieving fully fledged democratic legitimacy but, more modestly, better functioning supranational global governance bodies with improved legitimacy (Esty 2006: 1537). Indeed, notwithstanding these limitations to experimentalist modes of regulation, it is posited here that the extent to which the departure from the procedures of legal and political accountability may represent a serious weakness of New Governance will be determined by the extent to which classical modes of accountability are considered as being necessary elements of "new" modes of governance and, more broadly, of a given transnational polity. The answer to this is necessarily linked to a personal vision as to what constitutes adequate democratic governance in the context of European integration and how we conceive of the European Union, which remains an unsettled and vexed issue. In discussing the international rule of law, Peerenboom (2009: 4–5) neatly summarizes the nature of the problem and the pitfalls to be avoided. He observes that:

> most attempts to conceptualize international rule of law are based on an analogy to domestic rule of law. Given the many differences between sovereign nation states and the international legal order, the results have been fairly disappointing. . . . Rather than trying to fit square pegs into round holes, it may be better to try a radically different approach that does not begin with domestic rule of law as the model. . . . It may provide a more realistic framework for pursuing the possibilities and limits of international rule of law.

The statal approach would tempt us to prioritize traditional, statal forms of account-ability through traditional representative parliamentary institutions and *ex post* control by the courts (Harlow 2002: 3). Conversely, the post-national approach would lead us to consider the European Union as being chiefly a system of transnational governance and thus one with "multi-polar" systems of accountability coexisting within the European Union (Hood 1986; Scott, 2000: 50). This is not to say that actors involved in governance networks are not accountable at all. They are subject to peer or professional accountability, to reputational and market accountability, to fiscal/financial, administrative or legal accountability. There is no guarantee, however, that such diffuse or composite control mechanisms can be effective, as they operate in a fragmentary and uncoordinated way without forming a coherent system. Also, the problem of a lack of political and democratic accountability remains: only some network actors are subject to it, and control over them can be merely indirect or partial.

In this model of accountability forms of institutional balance are less closely rooted in the institutional arrangements of a nation-state which the Community Method partially conforms to. According to Scott's "interdependence model" the actors are 'dependent on each other in their actions because of the dispersal of key resources of authority (formal and informal), information, expertise, and capacity to bestow legitimacy such that each of the principal actors has constantly to account for at least some of its actions to others within the space, as a precondition for action' (Scott 2000: 50). However, the problem with this model, as mentioned earlier, is that it relies too heavily on behavioural pressures (for example, through moral commitments and social or peer pressure) as a substitute for classical accountability (Harlow and Rawlings 2007: 545). This is because mutual account-ability networks tend to be more concerned with policy input and long-term relationships than retrospective evaluation, rendering accountability difficult.

If we combine mutual accountability with classical democratic and political account-ability it may be possible to develop a notion of accountability which may improve the democratic accountability of the European Union's multi-level system.[45] For instance,

---

45 See also Kingsbury *et al.* (2005) and Krisch and Kingsbury (2006), who develop the notions of "global adminis-trative space" and "global administrative law". The first term refers to a multiplicity of actors, including international institutions and transnational networks, as well as domestic administrative bodies that operate within international regimes or cause transboundary regulatory effects. In this transnationalized context "global

Benz and Papadopoulos (2006) and Benz (2007), respectively, have elaborated a decisional pattern characterized by a functional separation of power between policy formulation in networks, and by constituent and veto power dedicated to institutions that are authorized and accountable to citizens. Formally authorized institutions could first set the "meta-governance" (the governance of governance networks) procedural rules and administrative tools that provide checks and balances ensuring *inter alia* fair participation and account-ability in network forms of governance such as for example conflict of interest rules, monitoring and audits and lobbying disclosure to avoid clusters of authority (see further Esty 2006: 1524–1537). Although the formalization of networks (provisions about selection of participants, modes of operation, etc.) may be questionable to some, assigning the design function explicitly to the democratically authorized institutions may reinforce at the same time neo-Weberian expertise-based legitimacy, Habermasian deliberation and Fullerian principles of legality.

Hence formally authorized institutions could also have the final say on policy outcomes and outputs, by being an effective locus of critical scrutiny over proposals formulated by governance networks, which have for their part the advantage of pooling expertise and of facilitating acceptance by stakeholders. What is being put forward is nothing new and we can already find this pattern at both national and EU level. Benz and Papadopoulos (2006) suggest increasing the availability of resources in terms of legal instruments as well as time, information intelligence and organization. Hence, at national and regional levels, constitu-ent and veto functions could be performed by national parliaments or elected governments. Actors participating in New Governance processes would then have to convince veto players about their policy proposals, while veto players would be forced to supervise participation and policy making in governance effectively.

Within this meta-governance frame we could include what Everson (1998: 214) defines as a 'rule of reasons provision' which could serve as a basis for judicial review. In particular, European administrative law *lato sensu* could be built upon Article 253 EC, which provides decision making to be well reasoned. This provision could require all committees, agencies, private standardization bodies and fixed actors within more informal regulatory networks, to maintain and make public detailed records of the processes of decision making and give access to information and documents, thus ensuring transparency. In turn, judicial review proceedings could be triggered by the standing of impartial bodies such as parliamentary committees rather than merely by individual *locus standi* (which would be less likely to succeed, given the multi-level and heterarchical setting of the EU system).[46]

This renewed notion of accountability could ensure a loose coupling of New Governance with democratically legitimate representative structures, creating interfaces that can be beneficial for mutual learning. Hence, while departing from the classical con-cept of accountability, it would nevertheless enable the more nebulous New Governance

---

administrative law" refers to the legal mechanisms, principles and practices, along with the supporting social understandings, that promote or otherwise affect the accountability of global administrative bodies, in particular by ensuring those bodies meet adequate standards of transparency, consultation, participation, rationality and legality, and by providing effective review of the rules and decisions these bodies make. This is described as "global" rather than "international" to emphasize that this is not part of the accepted existing law (*lex lata*), and to include informal institutional arrangements and other normative practices and sources that are not encompassed within standard conceptions of "international law". Both notions mark a departure from orthodox understandings of international law, in which the "international" is largely conceived as being intergovernmental, and there is a strict separation of the domestic and the international.

46 See also Ladeur (1997).

practices and processes to operate in a way which may be held more democratically accountable and responsive while ensuring governability, policy efficiency and remaining more representative of public needs and values (Benz and Papadopoulos 2006; Benz 2007; see also Everson 1998). Moreover, this notion of accountability would not entail a return to the same substantive regulatory rationality of "command and control" of the classical forms of regulation. On the contrary, it would preserve and strengthen the structure and mechanisms of both classical and experimental forms of governance.

In this context law would retain an important and renewed role. As Walker (2000: 12) observes, 'the very circumstances that challenge and dilute the problem-solving capacity and symbolic authority of law guarantee that it remains a precious currency. The problems of co-ordination and legitimacy of the new flexible order are on such a scale that law, with its traditionally vast regulatory potential, will inevitably continue to be invoked as a means of containing and resolving crises. Moreover, as a deeply-layered and richly-resourced repository of traditional and cultural meanings, the legal form retains a "legitimacy credit" and a versatility even in the face of new and apparently discontinuous contexts of political organization and regulation'. In a similar vein, Röben (2003) maintains that the Union's constitutionalism is stable even if its positive constitutional manifestations are not. This is achieved through a specific constitutionalism of the European Union as a three-level system of government that works through an inverse hierarchy between centre and periphery. The state is placed both at the lowest and at the highest level of this system, with the Union/Communities at the middle level of government. In the first process, the Union forms a hierarchical centre, with the Member States acting at the "lowest level", to the extent the Community enacts policies in areas such as the Internal Market and the Member States carry them out. But the periphery also inverts this hierarchy, with the Member States acting at the "highest level" to the extent that they inspire and determine the action of the centre. At this level of the hierarchy, the Member States act through the Heads of States and governments assembled in the European Council, the national constitutional courts and national parliaments in their treaty-making capacity, while at the "lowest" level they act through their executive organs and their courts. According to Röben this three-level system of government ensures that EU constitutionalism may be more capable of resolving the paradox of the deliberate choice for a union of constitutional nations states rather than a federal state.

Röben's model is exemplified by the operation of the OMC and, in particular, the EES. The Member States' legitimacy to act is bestowed upon them by the European Institutions, chiefly the European Council, the Council and the Commission via the adoption of Employment Guidelines, and Member States have to account for their actions (or inaction) to them upon receipt of the Commission's recommendations. Governments may also have to give account for measures adopted pursuant to the EES to their national parliaments. Moreover, empirical studies show that OMC processes, and namely the EES, return the responsibility for any adopted measure to the Member States. The process of (legal) harmonization or convergence takes place at national level rather than at supranational or European level, even though the Commission clearly acts as a propeller. This is a rather different scenario from the one depicted by the Commission, which places much emphasis on the alleged association of accountability with citizenship and participatory democracy whereby accountability is part of a continual process of "giving an account" to an informed and active civic society. Democratic accountability of this type and more broadly participatory democracy within the EES has been said to be designed to control policy outcomes, being prospective in character rather than solely retrospective. However, as the book goes on to show, thus far the EES has been rather disappointing in relation to its much acclaimed "bottom-to-top" participatory democracy and democratic accountability. If we conceive of the EES as being largely intergovernmental as opposed to supranational, we may argue *a fortiori* that Member States may be held accountable (that is, within the framework of classical legal and political accountability) for measures taken pursuant to the Employment Guidelines by their parliaments, irrespective of whether EC law is "soft" in nature. In other words, national measures adopted in the context of the EES would have a life of their own and become justiciable through domestic judicial procedures.

2.4 The relationship between rights and New Governance[47]

One further question concerns New Governance and, chiefly, the OMC and its relationship with constitutionalism: what is the place of fundamental rights in such processes that eschew traditional forms of regulation which have clearly defined mechanisms for their respect and safeguard? For instance, in the context of the EES – given that Title VIII of the EC Treaty provides a legal framework whereby the soft law discourse may be translated into binding normative rules at national level, what are the implications that these experimental and non-binding regulatory techniques may have for social rights? Or, more simply, what should their relationship be? This question gravitates around the underlying issue of identifying which locus, supranational or domestic, is appropriate to carry out the balancing exercise between conflicting values concerning the protection of human rights (Spaventa 2009). In particular, the fundamental rights discourse in the European Union reflects the evolution of, and the tensions inherent in, the Union's constitutional process. As pointed out by Spaventa (*ibid.*: 343–344) the debate about fundamental rights protection mirrors the tension between federalization and centralization and also reflects the existence of two conflicting forces, centripetal and centrifugal, in relation to fundamental rights protection. The centripetal force attracts the fundamental rights discourse within the European Union whereas the centrifugal force, by contrast, pulls the fundamental rights discourse away from the European Union.

One of the virtues of the OMC is its apparent flexibility and non-rigidity. In other words, rather than prescribing outcomes or defining specific results and setting them in law, it is essentially a process: through the procedures of information exchange, identification of best practices, reporting, monitoring and iteration, it is anticipated that learning will take place, and that satisfactory policy outcomes will emerge over time (Velluti 2003). However, one of the fears expressed is that there is no mechanism for checking against the dangers either of a race to the bottom, or an undesirable slippage of protection, in respect of certain fundamental values.

This concern has led to the need of establishing a relationship between co-ordination processes and fundamental rights. But what kind of relationship? Human rights and labour lawyers (De Schutter 2005; Ashiagbor 2005) have pointed out that co-ordination processes such as the OMC need to be underpinned by a European-level core of fundamental rights and principles to counterbalance the dominance of the economic policy rationale over discourses of social justice and solidarity. The question is therefore whether there is a way for fundamental rights and values to be respected within OMC-type processes other than as flexible policy standards which may be subject to revision (de Búrca 2003: 833–835; de Schutter 2005: 334–343).

---

47   The issues and problems briefly examined in this section (analyzed by Andronico and Lo Faro 2005: 93–96 but see also De Schutter 2005) will be the object of further and more detailed analysis in Chapter 7.

One can view this relationship either as one where fundamental social rights, conceived as substantive rights, have a corrective or limitative function in relation to New Governance or, following a more Habermasian approach which considers fundamental social rights as procedural or participatory rights, as one in which New Governance and, in particular, the OMC becomes a means to implement fundamental social rights.

In this context it has also been suggested that the OMC could be used to develop an EU fundamental rights policy (de Búrca 2003; De Schutter 2005; Sciarra 2005; Smismans 2005a). In particular, de Búrca (2003) and De Schutter (2005) have put forward a proposal for combining the OMC method with the more familiar constitutional instrument in the form of the Charter of Fundamental Rights. Within the traditional model of EU constitutionalism, fundamental rights have generally been presented as judicially enforceable, negative constraints on EU action. However, the EU Charter could also be more broadly regarded as an expression of the fundamental values which underpin the Union, and which ought to be integrated within all of its policies (de Búrca 2003). In particular, the idea would be to depart from the court-centric approach towards the Charter and to enable OMC processes to become suitable vehicles for ensuring the general and abstract guarantees of the Charter in specific settings and policies. In turn the rights protected under the Charter could operate as ideal norms in relation to which the outcome of the process would be appraised and which could be used to stimulate reform or revision of the standards that emerge when the outcomes are considered substantively unsatisfactory.[48] In this context, notwithstanding the problems identified and examined by Andronico and Lo Faro (2005: 55–61) and De Schutter (2005)[49] such as the limited scope of the Charter[50] and the artificial distinction made by the Charter between (enforceable) rights and (non-enforceable) principles, the Fundamental Rights Agency (FRA) could play an important role with its reports and opinions. In particular, the FRA could play an active role in promoting initiatives aimed at developing exchanges of information and best practices, providing comparative analysis and advice as well as promoting innovative approaches and evaluating experiences. In addition, the FRA could analyze and comment on Member States' national plans concerning measures which directly or indirectly or potentially may affect the level of protection of fundamental rights. This proposal would bode well with the functions and objectives of the Agency envisioned in the Founding Regulation (Council of the European Union 2007).[51]

According to this Regulation, the Agency's objective is to provide assistance and

---

48 See also EU NIEFR (2002: 25).

49 The coupling of the OMC and fundamental rights while being a very attractive proposition (as fundamental rights would be acting as barriers against excessive deregulation or a race to the bottom) is not devoid of institutional and conceptual problems particularly because of the so-called horizontal clauses in the Charter which on close analysis would make it difficult to couple the OMC and fundamental rights. For example, can the decisions and measures taken by the Member States in the context of the OMC be considered as an implementation of Community law? It's not easy to answer this question because of the OMC's iterative process in which there is no clear distinction between the shaping/formation and implementation of measures. The exclusion of binding measures imposed on Member States would seem to indicate that there are no implementing measures of Union law at national level. See further Andronico and Lo Faro (2005: 54–61).

50 As De Schutter (2005) observes, the problem of the EU Charter is also linked to the fact that fundamental rights in the EU have never influenced the allocation of powers and competences between Member States and the EU. In other words, the EU has not been attributed a clear competence to fulfil fundamental rights; the distribution of competences between the levels has been devised without the debate having been influenced by the need to ensure an effective protection of fundamental rights in the EU; the shape of the evolution of market freedoms has not been seen as having to be influenced by the need to promote fundamental rights effectively.

51 For an example of how this could be applied to a specific OMC process see Velluti (2007).

expertise in the field of fundamental rights to bodies of the Community as well as to Member States. In particular, the Agency is to support them 'to fully respect fundamental rights' within their respective fields of competence (*ibid.*: Article 2). Moreover, Article 4(1a/b) of the Founding Regulation enables the Agency to collect, analyze and disseminate relevant, objective and comparable information and data in the field of fundamental rights and to develop methods and standards to improve the comparability, objectivity and reliability of such data at European level. The FRA may also carry out and encourage scientific research, surveys and studies on its own initiative or at the request of the European Parliament, the Council or the Commission (*ibid.*: Article 4(1c)). Another politically significant task of the FRA is the formulation and publication of conclusions and opinions on specific thematic topics, for the Union Institutions and the Member States when implementing Community law, either on its own initiative or at the request of the European Parliament, the Council or the Commission (*ibid.*: Article 4(1d)). A further important reporting task of the Agency is the delivery of the annual report on fundamental rights issues in which examples of good practice may be highlighted (*ibid.*: Article 4(1e)). Finally, particularly worthy of mention is the fact that the Founding Regulation (*ibid.*: Article 4(1h)) also entrusts the FRA with developing a communication strategy and promoting dialogue with civil society, in order to raise public awareness of fundamental rights and actively disseminate information about its work. To this end a Fundamental Rights Platform has also been set up to ensure close co-operation with all relevant stakeholders of civil society (*ibid.*: Article 10).

As de Búrca (2003) suggests, it could also be possible to envisage a role of the ECJ in monitoring the self-compliance of European Institutions and actors to guidelines which they have been themselves involved in outlining and implementing without undermining the flexibility of the OMC. The ECJ has already ruled in this sense in other areas of law. In various competition law cases[52] the Court has ruled that, even though guidelines are not formally legally binding, they nevertheless produce important legal effects such as legitimate expectations and the decision maker has to show that they are taken into account and adequate reasons have been given where a departure from the criteria for guidance has been laid down. In the different context of the Charter and the OMC, the judicial role could at least involve imposing a public-reason type of obligation to demonstrate that the rights specified in the Charter have been taken into account within the OMC process, to indicate how this was done, and to explain in what way the outcome was considered to satisfy the normative requirements of the right in question (de Búrca 2003).

2.5 Concluding remarks

This section has showed that New Governance presents significant practical and conceptual challenges for the Community legal order, for our understanding of law and legal processes and ideas such as that of democracy and self-government which are embedded in the concept of constitutionalism. The very existence of these problems explains why New Governance is a phenomenon that can no longer be disregarded by legal scholars who are called to rethink in a meaningful way the roles of law and constitutionalism in the wider EU context.

---

52 See above in this chapter. Outside the field of competition law see, for example, Case C-378/00, *Commission v. Parliament and Council* [2003] ECR I-937.

3 Problems and paradoxes of European legal integration

3.1 European legal integration as a set of dynamic and contradictory processes

The challenges described above are accentuated by the existence of a series of inherent, intertwined and cumulative paradoxes and problems besetting the European Union and its present and future existence. Each of these encapsulates a weakness or limitation of the European integration process, and can be found in part of the copious literature on New Governance. Depending on the "lens" we use to analyze and interpret them and on the "solution" employed to resolve these tensions and problems we may have different understandings of the strengths, limitations and role of experimentalist forms of governance in the European Union. As posited by Andronico and Lo Faro (2005: 91) the 'first phase of regulation consists of an identification of the problem and, therefore, of choosing possible solutions. . . . The possibility of a rule being truly inscribed into social reality depends on the manner in which the problem to which the rule intends to respond has previously been constructed.'

The underlying claim is that 'the complexity of European legal integration processes can be understood neither by static concepts and descriptions nor by simply following the prescriptions offered by the legal categorizations of Europe issuing from the ever-changing political agenda of European integration' (Madsen *et al.* 2008: 1). This is even more compelling when we think about the dramatic expansion of competences of the EU Institutions through the dynamic and expansive approach of the ECJ and of the Commission towards Articles 28 and 30 EC.

I therefore suggest rethinking European legal integration as a set of dynamic and even somewhat contradictory processes or put simply as being paradox laden. Paradoxes may be defined as a set of tensions or conflicting forces which are important drivers in the making of the European Union (*ibid.*). In this section I address some of the main tensions and problems besetting the European Union, the understanding of which may explain some of the contradictions found in European integration. While this may only provide an unfinished picture, it is inevitable and necessarily so, given that European integration is itself a perpetual ongoing and evolving process and new paradoxes and problems may arise in the future.

3.2 Understanding European legal integration: legal cultures, harmonization and compliance

The ECJ has always construed the development of the principles of direct effect, indirect effect and supremacy of EC law as the building blocks of a cohesive, uniform and effective EC legal system. In particular, the rhetoric of the European Court has focused upon the integrative, unifying and cohesive force of the legal order. However, the reality of the European Union has shown quite a different scenario. In practice, as the European legal system has evolved it has tolerated, embodied and (in some cases) promoted certain elements of disintegration, differentiation and disruption (Shaw 1996). For instance, EU constitutionalism has shifted from the so-called constitutionalization of the Treaties by the ECJ to the reconceptualization of the post-Maastricht European Union as a constitutional order.

The objective here is to go beyond a narrow focus on harmonization and diversity in order to better understand and assess implementation of and compliance with EU law. The first step in studying the processes by which law produces integration is to break the question down into a number of distinct enquiries (Petersen *et al.* 2008). For example, what are we studying when we explore legal culture as an object, vector or outcome of integration? Legal culture, in its most general meaning, can be defined as 'one way of describing relatively stable patterns of legally oriented social behaviour and attitudes' (Nelken 2004). The specific legal culture embraces the body of laws, jurisprudence, principles and values, procedures and practices of a given polity. Legal culture should be analyzed in the context of national and transnational processes and it is the result of particular historical trajectories (Merry 2003). Moreover, as a form of culture it is marked by hybridity and creolization rather than uniformity or consistency. It follows that legal culture is a concept *in fieri* (Friedman 1975).

Having considered legal culture, we may now turn to integration and address another set of questions. What is being integrated, by whom, in what way, for which reasons and to achieve which results? It is also necessary to distinguish between national and transnational jurisdictions and common and civil law traditions. Further, what type of changes does integration (both as a means and as an end in itself) entail? And who or what does it affect? To what extent do institutions, constitutions, codes, principles and values, procedures, norms and practices change? How do we evaluate the degree of change? It is also interesting to note that differences between legal cultures are considered either as being irreducible or on the contrary not particularly deep but contingent on practice or a given situation and that they may consequently change. In this latter context, some are of the view that legal cultures are discursively constructed or imagined and used only as a convenient excuse for avoiding changes in the way law is practised within domestic legal systems (Nelken 2008: 300). At this juncture it is important to note that the boundaries of law do not coincide with national jurisdictions and therefore laws will be contingent and vary on the basis of variations in the wider culture. Equally, the degree of legal integration will depend on what is being integrated and the reasons for such harmonization. In this context, much of the literature has centred mainly on the implementation of European Directives or Decisions. The focus of analysis has been squarely on compliance in terms of new legislative or administrative measures or lack of them at domestic level and chiefly from the perspective of the European Commission. Within this framework Member States have been categorized and subdivided into different groups depending on the degree of compliance with EU law.

However, as argued by Nelken (2008: 302), integration is not always the result of deliberate design on the part of the European Commission, a Member State or any other agent. Moreover, just as efforts by design can succeed or fail, other processes that proceed independently, or even in opposition to these efforts, can have varying or unexpected outcomes. The language of "implementation" and "compliance" is likely to be less conceptually adequate for tracing such processes. Other terms or metaphors therefore such as "interaction", "collision", "dialogue conflicts", "convergence" or "diffusion" may be more apt to describe larger and more various processes taking place between law and other "sites". In referring to the complex relationship between law and other subsystems such as economics and politics Teubner (1998) talks about "irritation" to describe the difficulty law has in communicating with the practices of these other subsystems of society and he argues that law may "irritate" them into unpredictable changes. In addition, with regard to the implementation of and compliance with soft modes of governance, methodological problems arise in assessing compliance and, in particular, in evaluating whether there is a causal link between the adoption of domestic measures and European soft law.

In the light of this complex picture it seems unrealistic first to claim that legal systems merely represent a coherent set of formal legal norms and second to assume that state, group or individual behaviour could ever completely conform to international commitments, especially as global pressures are ongoing and changeable. Indeed, we may cite Henkin's (1968) classic observation: 'almost all nations observe almost all principles of international law and almost all of their obligations almost all of the time'. Further, we also need to bear in mind that there can be disagreement about what is meant by and who should define integration and compliance and thus it may be difficult or even inappropriate to theorize a generalized model of either harmonization or compliance. There would always have to be a certain degree of relativity and flexibility in measuring conformity and again take into account what is being integrated and for what purpose. In particular, outside the economic sphere of the European integration project, and in situations where Member States see the requirements of integration as challenging features of their sovereignty or identity, they are going to be less prone to accept change. For example, candidate countries have been more willing to accept the terms of "conditionality" and tolerate diversity. But this then raises the further difficult question of what sort of diversity the European Union is pursuing.

Finally, a prominent place in European integration is what may be defined as "symbolic" change. At times it may receive wide acceptance provided it remains what it is, that is, symbolic, and does not encroach upon the constitutional values and principles of the Member States and, more broadly, upon the beliefs and lives of citizens. At other times it is precisely the symbolic nature of the changes being proposed that is being rejected – which may explain why the proposed defunct European Constitutional Treaty or European Constitution failed and why a "European Treaty",[53] that is, the Lisbon Treaty, has been more acceptable. The latter is a much less ambitious document in this sense and it has 'been stripped of many elements that gave the former a "constitutional" flavour' (Cooper 2009); it also represents 'a climb-down from lofty constitutional aspiration to mere institutional tinkering' (*ibid.*). This "deconstitutionalization" of the Treaty is reflected in the change of language used in the Lisbon Treaty. In particular, many terms have been removed which may have implied or made reference to the idea of the European Union as a state-like entity. In addition, the document has been drafted in a way that strengthens safeguards against further encroachment by EU law into the realm of national law.[54]

3.3 The touch of "stateness"

The literature on European integration contains a plethora of definitions of the European Union such as "supranational federation" (von Bogdandy 1999), "layered international organisation" (Curtin and Dekker 1999), "European Commonwealth" (MacCormick 1999), system of "multilevel constitutionalism" (Pernice 1999) and "multilevel governance" (Hooghe and Marks 2001). All these terms to a different degree effectively capture the *sui generis* nature of the European Union as an ever-changing, dynamic, multi-tiered and hybrid post-national polity and its paradoxical relationship with the state. The European Union is simultaneously both "near-state" and antithetical to "stateness" (Shaw and Wiener, 2000; see also Craig 1997); the Union is clearly less than a state but also clearly more than

---

53 For a critique on the symbolism of the European Constitutional Treaty, see Ladeur (2008).
54 For further analysis, see Cooper (2009).

a classical international organization (Weiler 1995). It follows that EU law cannot be fully analyzed using the tools of either international law or national law, but only with a combination of the two. As Shaw and Wiener (2000) illustrate EU law reflects this "betweenness":[55] while "the letter of the law" has never made explicit reference to the concept of stateness, the "spirit of the law" which has guided the generation of the leading constitutional principles of "direct effect" and supremacy of EU law is shaped by it. In addition, as Nicolaïdis (2007: 683) eloquently puts it: the 'European Union is built on the quicksand of archetypes, the construct of lawyers and political scientists fighting the twin perils of a postmodern Napoleonic vision of a harmonized continent and a Westphalian nostalgia for absolute sovereign autonomy'. This makes a fuller understanding of European governance precisely because of 'the continuous *revival* of the idea of stateness, whether that takes the form of *resistance* against or *reform* towards the establishment of state-like patterns. It lies in studying a non-state polity within the frame of stateness, with all its theoretical and methodological implications' (Shaw and Wiener 2000). In this context, it is interesting to note that while there is almost unanimous agreement on not wanting the European Union to become a "state", the structures, institutions and principles of the state are often used as the key comparator or benchmark to assess and vet the European Union's legal and political system.

Similarly, Ladeur (2008: 159) notes that while the concept of "supranationality" has been conceived as open ended and entailing experimentalism it has gradually been revisited in a more "state-centred perspective" 'on a kind of "super-state" in spite of the fact that this runs counter to the new relational logic of societal self-organization and its open dynamic of self-transformation'. Member States too have been witnessing profound changes in their systems of governance taking into consideration diversity. And yet it seems that the 'European Union is associated with more centralization, more hierarchy and more harmonization'. Ladeur uses the example of subsidiarity as illustrating this state of affairs: rather than being a principle for preserving Member States' sovereignty it is used as an instrument for ensuring the efficiency of problem-solving strategies. Hence for him 'new "constitutionalism" returns to the traditional state logic of the nineteenth century'.[56]

The "betweenness" adverted to above translates into further complex conundrums. In this register, should legitimacy, democracy, accountability and equality (which feature prominently in the EU legal system) be given an autonomous European meaning with unique features as regards their meaning, scope of application and normative effect? Autonomous meaning, however, should not imply unprecedented meaning. National understandings of these constitutive elements in reality do and should necessarily inform EU understanding. In this sense it is possible to talk about a genealogical link between national and European concepts,[57] hence the challenge of constructing and applying a European concept. Democracy is illustrative. In exploring the meaning of democracy, Dahl (1982: 5) observes that the term today 'is like an ancient kitchen midden packed with

---

55 See also Bellamy and Castiglione (1997); MacCormick (1999).

56 See also the critique of the White Paper on European Governance by Joerges, Mény and Weiler (2001); for a similar critique on the principle of subsidiarity see Davies (2006).

57 Walker (2003) defines this problem as one of "constitutional translation" from the state to the post-state context. In particular, the challenge is to show that there are elements of state constitutionalism such as the ethical value of responsible self-government which are worthy of preservation and of applying to the non-state context of the European Union, providing, as in the national context, a source of legitimation.

assorted leftovers from twenty-five hundred years of nearly continuous usage'. In turn, the complexity of the meaning of democracy in plural legal systems like the European Union leads us to the strictly related and open question of the European Union's democratic deficit. 'The varying attitudes towards the existence or not of a democracy deficit will depend on the type of democracy which the observer believes does and should operate in the Community' (Craig 1997: 129) and the alleged lack of democracy put forward in some quarters may be read as the expression of a more explicit will to re-establish a vision of *res publica* and separation of powers in the tradition of the nation-state. Shaw and Wiener (2000) suggest that the language of "deficit" indicates a predilection for relying on the political form of the state as a comparative entity or polity rather than international organizations and most importantly it also forces a normative response to overcome the deficit (Wiener and Della Sala 1997).

In this context, the rigorous implication of the "No Demos" thesis[58] – which postulates that in the absence of a European "Volk" and nationhood there can be no European identity and thus the Union and its Institutions can have neither the authority nor the legitimacy of a democratic state – is that in the absence of a "European demos", there cannot, by definition, be a democracy or democratization at European level.[59] Hence, even the modest gains in the power of the European Parliament over the decisional process cannot contribute to resolving the democratic dilemma since in the absence of a "European Demos" the European Parliament cannot enjoy full independent authority or legitimacy as a rule-making body in the EU system. In this strict sense, the 'fundamental paradox of constitutionalism is that a constituting "demos" is needed in order to produce a constitution that will in turn consolidate (if not create) the constituted "demos" ' (Philippopoulos-Mihalopoulos 2008: 32, 40; see also Weiler 2002).

However, as Weiler (1995) points out in the EU "demos" should not be equated exclusively to "Volk", nor should the European Union be considered as some statal form as expressed by the terms *Staat* and *Staatentruct*, or that it is a state in the making. Weiler (1995) invites us to rethink the analytical tools for studying the European Union in order to depart from the organic cultural homogeneous terms of the unity of "Volk–Nation–State–Citizenship" and consider other understandings of "demos" which may lead to different conceptualizations and potentialities for the European Union, envisioning a "European civic, value-driven demos" coexisting with a national organic-cultural one.

'It would be more than ironic if a polity set up as a means to counter the excesses of statism ended up coming round full circle and transforming itself into a (super)state. It would be equally ironic if the ethos which rejected the boundary abuse of the nation-state, gave birth to a polity with the same potential for abuse. The problem with this "Unity vision" is that its very realization entails its negation' (Weiler 1995):

> Further, decoupling *Volk* from demos and *Demos* from state, in whole or in part, does not entail the rejection of the values of nationality. The decoupling of nationality and citizenship opens the possibility, rather, of thinking of coexisting "multiple demoi" enabling people to aspire and live both as nationals of a Member State and European

---

58 For a critique of the "No *demos*" thesis within a constitutional law discourse, see Poiares Maduro (2003).

59 This is because the *Volk*, the nation, understood in this national, ethno-cultural sense is the basis for the modern state. A parliament is, on this view, an institution of democracy not only because it provides a mechanism for representation and majority voting, but because it represents the *Volk*, the nation, the *demos* from which the authority and legitimacy of its decisions derive; see Weiler (1995) for further comment and analysis.

citizens, particularly in cases where there are affinities to shared values which transcend the ethno-national diversity and have a more European dimension.

(Weiler 1995)[60]

Shaw (2000: 343) effectively captures the nature of this paradox concerning European democracy when arguing that it is 'unhappily positioned between sometimes over-idealized visions of national democracies within the states and the conventions of diplomatic practice between states which admit of little or no conception of representation and direct popular accountability'. Linked to this there is also another problem concerning the increase in power of the European Parliament. Members of the European Parliament are directly elected in their Member States, and large Member States are represented by more members than small Member States. Therefore, from the point of view of the European Union taken as a whole, more power to the European Parliament does seem to be a step in a more democratic direction. However, from a national perspective, at least when it comes to the smaller Member States, increased power to the European Parliament might not be seen as a democratic development.

Because of the potency of the political threat that the democratic deficit problem represents for the European Union, it has been addressed in different ways by the European Institutions: (1) with the setting up and further development of co-ordination processes such as the EES (thus focusing on more putatively deliberative forms of democracy), (2) with the so-called "citizens' initiative" provided for by the defunct Constitutional Treaty (Article I-47(4) CT) and maintained by the Reform Treaty (Article 11(4) TEU and Article 24 TFEU) (introducing a form of direct democracy at European level), (3) and with the setting up of an "Early Warning System" (Article I-11 CT and Protocols 1 and 2; Article 5 TEU; Article 12(1b) TEU and Protocols 1 and 2),[61] which gives an important role to national parliaments in the rule-making process of the European Union (supposedly strengthening representative democracy).[62] The citizens' initiative and the early warning system could bring a breath of fresh air into the democratic quality of the way the European Union operates. However, it is unclear what their "added value" may be as the Reform Treaty provisions do not offer much clarity in terms of their operation in practice and some commentators have already emphasized the type of problems which we may be faced with (Ippolito 2007; Dougan 2008). The European Court could also play a crucial role in defining the political and democratic implications of these new provisions. 'Judicial engagement with the novelty of direct democracy within the Union might well build new synergies in the Court's conceptions of participation and citizenship – and thereby enrich

---

60 In another paper Weiler, Haltern and Mayer (1995) have advanced the thesis that there may be different models of democracy which best capture the essence of democracy in EU governance: the international sphere may be explained through a "consociational model", the supranational sphere through a combination of "pluralist democracy" and Schumpeterian "elite democracy" and the infranational elements through a "neo-corporatist model".

61 Protocol on the Role of National Parliaments in the European Union and Protocol on the Application of the Principles of Subsidiarity and Proportionality.

62 Under the Lisbon Treaty, national parliaments have been given an important role in the safeguarding of the subsidiarity principle and have been involved in the EU's decision-making process when draft legislative proposals concern areas of shared competence. National parliaments may receive draft legislative proposals directly from EU Institutions and, if an infringement of subsidiarity is detected, they may send a "reasoned opinion" to the Commission, the European Parliament or the Council. This triggers the "Early Warning Mechanism" aimed at the review of such a proposal. If ultimately circumvented, a national parliament or its chamber may initiate proceedings before the ECJ.

its own distinctive contribution to the ongoing debate about how to enhance the Union's frail popular legitimacy' (Editorial 2008: 940).

The democratic deficit of the European Union remains a moot point among scholars and commentators. One should take cognizance of the fact that we find such "democratic imbalance" even at national level, where major national institutions may be exempt from immediate democratic scrutiny. Moreover, the increase in the use of private sector instruments and tools in the public sphere has made accountability more difficult. Hence, while the risk of the emergence of new forms of governance that escape from control and accountability cannot be denied, it is limited by the reciprocal transnational interdependences that block the preponderance of national special interests (Ladeur 2008: 165).

3.4 When differentiation and experimentalism may lead to fragmentation

In focusing on the impact of Europeanization (and the different modes for effecting it) on the Member States, Majone (2008) argues that 'as long as resources and preferences are fairly similar across countries, the advantages of harmonization are likely to exceed the welfare losses, but when heterogeneity exceeds a certain threshold, the reverse will be true'. This line of thinking can also be applied to the advantages of differentiation and experimentalism for heterogeneity in socio-economic structures and the philosophy under-pinning them makes it difficult to achieve policy learning and convergence. In particular, if a certain threshold of experimentalism is exceeded, the result may entail conflicting centrifugal forces. The risk, therefore, may be a dispersion of energy, input and informa-tion and the maintenance of the *status quo* and/or of a fragmented or fractured polity. The OMC, for example, being largely under the control of national executives, is used in areas where it is in harmony with domestic priorities. The application (or, better, the misimple-mentation) of the OMC to the field of immigration is illustrative: the failure of the Council to adopt the Commission's proposals for an OMC in immigration and the subsequent patchy implementation of OMC soft mechanisms in this area mirror the fragmented legislative framework in the field of immigration (see further Velluti 2007).

The paradoxes inherent in mutual recognition identified by Poiares Maduro (2007) may be said to be found also in New Governance practices and processes. For example, mutual recognition is defined as being a conflict rule and, in particular, as an instrument to promote integration while preserving diversity and Member States' regulatory autonomy. However, at the same time, mutual recognition has an important impact on Member States' sovereignty. Moreover, any effective operation of mutual recognition also requires a certain degree of mutual trust between countries. For this to happen there has to be a certain degree of common identity, as only this can provide the grounds for establishing a positive relationship between mutual trust and mutual recognition. Further, 'the problem is that the same variable that pushes for mutual recognition (the difficulty to achieve political consensus on common rules) also makes it more difficult to enforce it (because of the lack of sufficient mutual trust)' (Poiares Maduro 2007: 823). This paradox of mutual recognition can also be presented from a normative perspective: the greater the level of policy or systemic divergence between Member States, the greater the need for implementing mutual recognition as an instrument for economic and political integration. Such divergence creates regulatory and political obstacles to the pursuit of other legitimate goals within the European integration process: it is precisely in these instances that the information and transaction costs arising from national treatment will be higher (*ibid.*) due also to the resistance of some countries towards furthering Europeanization.

3.5 What do we mean by "new"? An attempt to disentangle the "truth" from the "myth"

There is little dispute that (a hybridized toolkit of) governance beyond the nation-state complementing the Community Method has become a *conditio sine qua non* for the existence of the European Union. In this context, the newness of New Governance as an alternative to the Community Method is often highlighted in the literature, but how appropriate is it? As explained at length above, procedures, practices and processes under the umbrella term "New Governance" have always existed (Scott and Trubek 2002) and represent the inherent ability of the EU system to constantly reinvent itself as part of an evolutionary process of political and economic survival (Szyszczak 2006). The OMC, in particular, has already been implemented in the context of the economic co-ordination process of EMU even before its formal recognition at the 2000 Lisbon European Council meeting.[63] The success of the Community Method may be said to have been the creation of a *sui generis* constitutional order intertwined with flexibility and differentiation, even within the Common Market "core" (de Búrca 2000).

The empirical research carried out for some of the EU-funded projects on New Governance[64] confirms what is being said and casts doubt on the accuracy and usefulness of the term "New Governance". Lobel (2004: 450) comes closest to describing what happens in the early stages of theorizing a new genre or model of legal thought (as is the case of the New Governance literature):

> when advancing a new model of law, there is some tendency to insist too much on its newness. The old is easily dismissed as conventional, its approaches antiquated. This tendency often results in aligning old approaches to law with our critical understandings of power, legality, action, and change [. . .] In such cases, *power* is framed as a characteristic of the regulatory model, while *empowerment* is the promise of governance.

By the same token, classical forms of regulation are considered to pertain exclusively to certain settings or spheres of law in action while other policy areas or activities are considered as being outside the traditional legal arena. The risk with these approaches is that of instigating 'contemporary bias that universally aligns the regulatory model with conservative commitments, and the governance model with transformative politics' (*ibid.*). Further, the problem is that these tendencies, rather than attempting to overcome the limitations of the overall EU system with a regulatory model which may have the in-built capacity to adapt and constantly renew itself, end up maintaining the European Union's regulatory deficiencies by merely putting forward a shift from one regime (with a set of given rules, processes, procedures), considered obsolete, to another model of regulation deemed more workable and efficient.

An accurate assessment of the New Governance phenomenon and, in particular, the

63 See Chapter 5.
64 See above, note 16.

OMC should read as follows. From the perspective of decisional supranationalism[65] the OMC presents elements of continuity with existing EU modes of governance in the sense that it represents one of the means of intense dialectical exchanges between centre and periphery. Moreover, co-ordination and networking are not new in the EU system. Hence, from this point of view New Governance is in no way radically new and may be said to exemplify what Sabel and Zeitlin (2003) have termed "pragmatic constitutionalism". On the level of normative constitutionalism,[66] however, there are stark differences between the classical Community Method based on hard law, legal sanctions, enforceable EU rights and the involvement of mainly public or quasi-public institutions and bodies and the OMC structured around the participation of an array of stakeholders (both public and private actors), which is built on a blurred definition of targets (apart from the better-defined social indicators of the EES) and relies on the use of soft sanctions. In this context, the true novelty of the OMC lies in its democratic participatory element. However, as explained briefly above[67] and more thoroughly in Chapters 5 and 7 of the book, as it stands at present the OMC remains far from the standard democratic narrative of representative democracy and from the democratic ideal of directly deliberative polyarchy. This is because the OMC fails from a legitimacy perspective to provide the communicative presuppositions and procedural conditions of democratic opinion and will formation. In other words, the OMC thus far has failed to be a process of self-determination of the actors involved (and chiefly of those representing the lower levels of policy making) and remains trapped in a conception of procedure according to which the law or the "command-and-control" type of vertical regulation is still deemed the best means for the pursuit of Community objectives. Part of the problem has been a tendency of 'solving the question of the effectiveness of governance by reducing it to a question of justification, thereby confusing the degree of "practical" acceptance with that of "rational" acceptance' (Andronico and Lo Faro 2005: 90). Critics of the OMC have called into question precisely this: merely involving the addressees of a given measure, be it legislative or non-legislative,[68] cannot be reduced to an instrumentalist function of input/output legitimacy purposes in the process of policy formation, nor equally can it be used to claim the latter's effectiveness. What is essential is the provision of an institutional mechanism showing that true communication and deliberation is taking place in a way that ensures the construction of interests by the individual actors involved or, more precisely, that the intended addressees consider themselves also as the authors of a measure adopted rather than merely the recipients. This, in turn, will ensure better and more effective implementation.

3.6　Is the communitarization of the OMC the right desideratum for good governance in the European Union?

Even though the OMC was largely ignored during the constitutional debate on the European Convention it may be argued that it has nevertheless been communitarianized,

---

65　According to Weiler (1981: 267) decisional supranationalism relates to 'the institutional framework and decision-making processes by which Community policies and measures are, in the first place, initiated, debated and formulated, then promulgated and finally executed'.

66　According to Weiler (*ibid.*) normative supranationalism is concerned with the relationship and hierarchy that exist between Community policies and legal measures on the one hand and competing policies and legal measures of the Member States on the other.

67　See above, p. 27.

68　In any case we would still need to see what type of involvement it is and the degree of such participation.

becoming an invaluable policy instrument in its own right within the Community Method, following its ratification with the adoption of the Lisbon Strategy to the point that we now have a series of different OMC processes with variations in structure and participation of the actors and institutions involved. Moreover, while there is no explicit reference to the OMC, both the defunct Constitutional Treaty and the Reform Treaty have included co-ordination among existing competences in the European Union. In particular, forms of governance based on policy co-ordination processes have risen significantly in importance in the European Union and have been given formal recognition in recent constitutional reforms of the Union. The defunct Constitutional Treaty recognized a new category of 'supporting, co-ordinating and complementary' competence (Part III, Title III, Chapter V), although this was expressed as supplementary to the specific competence to co-ordinate economic and employment policies (Article III-179 CT and Article III-206 CT). Similarly, the Reform Treaty includes these two categories of policy co-ordination and distinguishes between economic and employment policy co-ordination as a category of competence rather than a competence to 'support, co-ordinate or supplement' the actions of Member States (Articles 2D and 2E TFEU). While this "ratification" is a recognition of the OMC as a workable tool for achieving European integration, it remains to be seen what effects it will have on the functioning and operation of the OMC. Calls for better definition and regulation of the OMC have often been put forward by commentators and scholars, following fears that it may be simply a window-dressing exercise or the propeller for the adoption of measures and initiatives at national level without ensuring any convergence of results but rather resulting in more nationally distinct and diverse policies, ultimately inducing greater diversity rather than convergence. In addition, the greater openness and vagueness of the way the OMC operates has not only entailed a greater lack of transparency and accountability, but has also raised further concerns that OMC processes may become entangled in the trappings of certain elites or lobby/interest groups. However, at the same time, a better-defined operational framework which reduces the openness of the OMC may alter its nature and lead to a rigid structure with a risk of returning to the same substantive regulatory rationality of "command and control" or hard law from which the OMC is said to be departing from. The challenge attendant upon us, therefore, is to find a middle ground which enables us to improve the operation of the OMC without undermining its distinctive nature and way of functioning. The model proposed in section 4 addresses this problem and will be used for a critical analysis of the EES in subsequent chapters of the book.[69]

3.7 The (inherent) problems concerning EU constitutionalism are mirrored by the (inherent) weaknesses/limitations of New Governance

As Walker (2006) posits, despite its diversity and internal divisions, constitutional discourse remains constrained by the legacy of an "old paradigm" (as explained in detail throughout this chapter). There are various significant consequences of this limitation, one being that there is a strict correlation between Europe's constitutional problems and national constitutional limits. Indeed, as Poiares Maduro (2003) fully demonstrates current European constitutional problems are not entirely unique to the EU polity but rather

---

69 See Chapters 5–7.

reflect constitutional problems that already exist in the context of national constitutional-ism. Similarly, New Governance analysis risks being excessively dependent on the "new-ness" of this experimental mode of governance despite the fact that umbrella term New Governance encompasses rather different processes and forms of governance. From this we can infer that problems of policy making and implementation are not merely a procedural issue: they are evidence of deeper problems relating to internal contradictions and tensions within specific policy areas and spheres of law, as the field of gender equality illustrates. In addition, both are tied up with normative political positions as to what the status of the European integration project currently is and where it should go in the future (its "finality") (Shaw 2000).

In this context de Búrca (2003) argues that OMC processes replicate the original (im)balance in the EC's economic constitution. In particular, she argues that the hier-archical relationship between the Treaty's Internal Market provisions and the softer powers in the social field can also be found in the operation of the OMC. In a similar vein Barnard (2009) distinguishes between the European Union's economic and *not so* economic constitu-tion to highlight in a rather nuanced but equally suggestive way the primacy given to the Union's economic objectives over its social ones.[70] There is real concern that rather than representing a challenge to this hierarchy OMC processes end up mirroring the same situation that exists in classical forms of regulation. Such a hierarchy may weaken the commitment of the OMC to policy learning and may hinder the achievement of social objectives being pursued within it. Economic policy co-ordination (Article 99 EC) is the most powerful of the existing OMC processes. Moreover, other OMC processes, including the EES (Article 125 EC), must be "consistent with" the BEPGs, which seems to indicate a subordination of the former to the latter (Chalmers and Lodge 2003: 2). Moreover, while the European Council has specifically said that the BEPGs must take into account the results of the other policy processes, this OMC process has mostly failed to do so. The streamlining and synchronizing of the OMCs in the field of employment and economic policy have not directly addressed the question of the perceived hierarchy of the economic policy co-ordination process, the main focus being on better efficiency and regulation. In turn the combination of the existing imbalance/hierarchy with the simplification of the EES (reducing the number of guidelines) has reduced the visibility of gender equality objectives within the Employment Strategy, with Member States limiting their measures to those gender equality objectives that may be associated with labour market policies,[71] as opposed to those objectives which are more social in nature and tackle structural forms of inequality, for example measures aiming at reconciling work with family life.

The current dominance of the economic over the social is problematic in different ways. There is the risk that pairing proliferated participation with the pervasiveness of economic language and objectives may lead to the colonization of governance by economic models (Lobel 2004). In turn, this may entail a shift in the allocation of power and decision making in the Union in favour of technocratic or financial elites rather than through open and democratic debate. This explains why in some quarters there is the perception that New Governance practices and instruments constitute mere technocratic processes intended

---

70 Emphasis added.

71 In particular, the objectives are either quantitative in nature – for instance, focusing on reaching certain employ-ment levels – or are already addressed by extant Directives such as that on equal pay and thus "easier" and "less problematic" to regulate also from a political point of view, given that these objectives may be subsumed under the overarching economic objective of the Lisbon Strategy.

to depoliticize issues in a way which will only favour the interests of a minority of people, namely the rich and powerful (Lobel 2004: 455–456).

4 New Governance, law and constitutionalism in a "metaconstitutional" frame: when uni(formi)ty meets diversity

> The future of the law in the twenty-first century lies in the mutant forms and experiments which prove to be fittest and survive the demands of tomorrow.[72]

In this section I focus on developing a model that draws on the combined theories of metaconstitutionalism, reflexive law, directly deliberative polyarchy[73] and critical constructivist approaches to law. This hybrid model[74] aims at bridging the gaps between New Governance and EU constitutionalism and enables them to build on one another's strengths in order to enable the European Union, as a highly complex, multi-tiered and post-national site, to provide new answers to the new collective action problems posed by further EU enlargements and by ever-increasing transnationalized and globalized markets that have blurred the divide between public and private spheres of regulation. Attempts to model processes of legitimation premised upon nation-states thus far have failed to recognize the elements of discontinuity as well as continuity within nation-states. What is needed, rather, is to develop processes of legitimacy which are appropriate to the nature of EU governance (Armstrong 1998: 169). In particular, the model's objective is to establish new bonds of association and political configuration in which New Governance and EU constitutionalism can happily coexist, thereby identifying the conditions necessary to assure and optimize effective voice and participation as well as ensuring the preservation and application of the rule of law and due process (as defined in the previous section).

In this context, constitutionalism, rather than representing a fixed legal framework, provides the ground for a process of continuous renewal and dialogue in relation to a polity

---

72 Lobel (2004: 361).

73 I use the term "model" more for practical reasons than for normative purposes. As pointed out by de Munck and Lenoble (2001: 29) the current crisis in politics is itself a crisis of the idea of models itself. Applied to social regulation, this means that the crisis concerns not so much the various models of social regulation that have been used thus far but the very idea that social regulation may be solved by recourse to a model. I do not intend, therefore, merely to put forward a model which I see as being fit for the European Union but rather my objective here is to develop a conceptual frame which enables New Governance and EU constitutionalism to meet one another in a more dialogical way and to rely on each other's strengths. This also explains precisely why in this chapter I call for a reconceptualization of law and constitutionalism, because the aim is not to graft New Governance onto the terrain of the classical Community Method (which would seem to suggest that New Governance is somewhat subservient to the ideologies, path dependences and structures of the Community Method) but rather to revisit law and constitutionalism with a new order of discourse where – it is acknowledged – there are still many aspects *in fieri*. A new manner of conceiving them has become prevalent as a consequence of globalization and transnationalization processes: the "grammar" used to describe and implement law and constitutionalism has inevitably and irreversibly changed, and failing to grasp this pivotal change would be equal to a failure to understand current trends in world politics and international relations.

74 In this section I refer to my model as being both hybrid and transformative. I am aware that this does not strictly follow the scholarly distinction between hybridity and transformation theses made by de Búrca and Scott (2006: 6–10) in the Introduction to their edited collection. The combined use of these two terms does not denote a superficial use of them but rather, following the aforementioned distinction, it conceives of developmental hybridity and transformative theses as being linked to one another in a natural and progressive (although not necessarily linear) way.

– the European Union – that is always in the course of negotiation and renegotiation. Law in turn acquires an important renewed and transformative role aside from its more traditional instrumental and prescriptive function. If we also consider law as an institution, we can see that in the European Union it has carried with it a specific normative vision about the relationship between the Union and its Member States, the ECJ and the other European Institutions, and between law and other subsystems such as the social, the political and the economic spheres (Armstrong 1998). In particular, with regard to the latter, law has traditionally subsumed and transformed them into categories of rights so that citizens can exercise their right to have rights. However, in doing so the problem has been the subjection of these rights to law's narrow normative vision. In this register, 'law projects itself upon the individual as object, while claiming to recognize the individual as a subject of the Community legal patrimony' (*ibid.* 166). Another problem associated with classic conceptions of law has been the maintenance of a static vision of political and legal systems. In this frame, law's temporal structure is limited to the construction of the future of a political order through the maintenance of past meanings, and the classic concept of the rule of law has been employed to ensure its own continuation, stability and predictability (Haltern 2002: 8). In sum, law has been instrumental in maintaining the *status quo*. This explains why the law conceived in this narrow and traditional way has been unable to act as a bridge between the citizen and the process of European integration (*ibid.*).

Insights about state and market failure confirm the need to move beyond existing patterns of law making. It is necessary, therefore, as a first step, to eschew one-directional, positivist and statist approaches to law and constitutionalism based on unity and hierarchy. In particular, we should start from the premise that new modes of governance reflect a deep transformation of the nation-state, a shift towards a post-national era in which the European Union has emerged as the nation-states' changing self (Lobel 2004). Ladeur (1997: 43) argues that conceptions of hierarchical, centralized and unitary states ignore the extent to which processes of differentiation and pluralization in decision making have transformed the "state from within". There is a need to develop a model of regulation that takes into account the peculiarities and realities of the EU system.

The model presented, therefore, aims at being a reconstructive project both in its experimentalism and theoretical linkages. It also necessarily incorporates a high degree of flexibility and resilience, given the heterogeneity of the European Union, and it is aspirational in nature in that it represents an ideal model of governance that the European Union should aspire to. There is no "one-size-fits-all" solution to the challenges facing the European Union. Under the current conditions of transnationalization legal institutions themselves need to be multiple and diverse, particularly as the regulatory practices of modern constitutionalism are increasingly removed from their territorialized social contexts. In turn, interpretation and implementation of the principles and legal norms depend increasingly on lower-level-based cultural, social and legal practices (Wiener 2007: 2). In the highly diversified system and governance of the European Union this translates into contestation of the meaning and implementation of norms being expected and enhanced given that, as social constructs, norms are contested by default. From a normative and legitimacy perspective this means that contestation is a necessary condition for norm validity and, therefore, norms must in principle be contestable. The democratic inclusiveness and legitimacy of the European Union will depend on the level of access to participation and public contestation and on continuous "democratic communicative action" (Tully 2002: 20–22). In sum, 'if democratic processes require contestation as a necessary element in order to generate and maintain legitimacy of legal norms, contestation needs to be integrated in supranational institutional settings as a common procedure' (Wiener 2007: 6). This means that justiciability of rights by individuals alone does not suffice to confer legitimacy upon the European Union, because of the narrow normative vision which EU law encapsulates (as explained above) and because of the absence of an inter-institutional system that enables active participation and deliberation by citizens (Armstrong 1998). Moreover, the narrow approach of the ECJ to the standing of non-privileged applicants in actions for annulment shows that moves towards the decentralization of EU action and active Union citizenship still belong to the realm of political rhetoric even in the light of the changes introduced by the Lisbon Treaty, promoting greater involvement by national parliaments in EU decision making and direct democracy. These changes represent a response to concerns over the Union's alleged democratic deficit and, therefore, remain premised on a state-centric understanding of democracy which does not take into account the complex and pluralist policy and legal system of the European Union. The lack of any real judicial standing of non-privileged applicants shows unwillingness on the part of the ECJ to take cognizance of the new actors involved in the decision and policy-making system of the Union and the new collective action problems facing the European Union, while its narrow stance ends up inhibiting the full exercise of rights at European level.[75]

Another key feature of this model of governance, therefore, is that it embraces a broad notion of democracy transcending any conceptual dichotomy and combining direct, representative, participatory and deliberative forms of democracy. Central to this broad notion of democracy is partnership, as it 'does not involve the parcelling out of limited pockets of sovereignty to different tiers of government, but a genuine pooling of sovereignty that demands intense interaction between the different tiers within a single, undivided, policy sphere' (Scott 1998: 182). In addition, this model is based on an *empowerment* paradigm in which there is an active participation in the political sphere rather than mere *enablement*, in which there is only technical participation to reach the objectives of a given policy. At the same time, it promises to reconcile the objectives of efficiency of New Governance with those of democratic legitimacy and accountability of EU constitutionalism.

In this context, meta-constitutionalism (Walker 1999 and 2000) enables us to assign law with a renewed role. This theoretical approach is particularly apt for addressing the challenges that the European Union is faced with because rather than seeing state constitutionalism and postnational constitutionalism as entirely separate, it seeks to unfold their genealogical link: while the premises on which they are based may vary in many different and important ways at the same time one (the post-national) derives from the other (the statal).[76] Specifically, on the one hand, this governance model acknowledges the importance of state constitutionalism rather than transcending it. On the other hand, it acknowledges the challenges to the constitutional state as the primary unit of political authority and accepts the existence of a more heterarchical order. Within these currencies it also acknowledges 'the continuities and discontinuities between the public law discourses of the state sphere and the non-state sphere' (Walker 2000: 24) which it seeks to address. On this

---

75 It is possible to trace a continuum between the *Plaumann* case (Case 25/62 *Plaumann v. Commission* [1963] ECR 95) when it first developed the stringent test for individual concern for non-privileged applicants and the *UPA* (C-50/00 *Union de Pequeños Agricultores v. Council of the European Union* [2002] ECR I-6677) and the *Jego Quéré* (C-263/02 *Commission v. Jego Quéré* [2004] ECR 1-3425) cases, in which it applied the same narrow criteria of the *Plaumann* test and refused to acknowledge that in so doing it was depriving the applicants of effective judicial protection.

76 See also Hirst (1994, 1997).

point Armstrong (1998) rightly posits that law has generally been conceived of as being mainly instrumentalist, particularly as a medium by which the ECJ has pursued a pro-integrationist agenda. 'Allied to this instrumentalist image of law is an assumption of law's ability to deliver integration both in terms of the integration of the national and the Community legal orders and in respect of law's ability to deliver social, political and economic integration' (*ibid.*: 156). The most enduring manifestation of this view has been the image of the "constitutionalized Treaty".[77] It is therefore necessary to revisit the concept of law in order to combine the use of law as a "medium" with that of law as an "institution" encompassing the organizational, procedural, substantive and normative elements of law. As observed earlier, law retains an important problem-solving capacity and symbolic authority and the problems of co-ordination and legitimacy of the current multifarious and multi-tiered EU system are on such a scale that law, with its traditionally vast regulatory potential, continues to be an invaluable means of containing and resolving crises (Walker 2000: 12). Hence law's function is not solely prescriptive but also becomes facilitative and reconstitutive (Stewart 1986), providing for a set of rules about the procedure, organization and constitution of other social fields and subsystems. In this sense law should enable a "harmonious fit" between institutional structures and social structures rather than influence the social structures themselves (Teubner 1988). Law, therefore, continues to play a significant role through its capacity to co-ordinate different social institutions (e.g. political, economic, etc.) but it is no longer based on the narrow and traditional conception of law as top-down, prescriptive, fixed and universal. Law's co-ordinating function is based on its retained *Kompetenz–Kompetenz* role ("competence competency"), that is, the competence to determine other actors' competences. The legal system discerns the capacities of different actors, arenas and subsystems, defines and allocates responsibilities among them and their self-regulatory institutional processes. Its jurisdictional role should be seen in this reconstitutive context, one which also gives voice to the different actors who actively participate in the multi-tiered system of the European Union. This approach would also bring representation and participation closer to one another, giving a renewed and strengthened value to Union citizenship. The hybrid model of governance broadly outlined here follows a very similar theoretical pattern to the one that Poiares Maduro (2003) has termed as "counterpunctual law" which aims at preserving the identity of national legal orders while at the same time promoting their inclusiveness within the EU system.

At present there are many instances where we can see New Governance practices and processes and law operating in the same policy domain.[78] In certain configurations they are not only complementary but they are also integrated into a single system in which the functioning of each element is necessary for the successful operation of the other. In these scenarios law is in effect transformed by its relationship with New Governance. Trubek and Trubek (2007) have identified four types of such transformation. First, it may be associated with a shift to legal proceduralism in which law mainly provides procedural rules for conflict resolution and problem solving; second, to configurations in which New Governance practices and processes have been added to areas which were initially covered by traditional forms of legal regulation and rights-based structures are retained to provide

---

77 See the language used by the ECJ in Case 294/83, *Parti Ecologiste 'Les Verts' v. European Parliament* [1986] ECR 1339; Opinion 1/91, Draft Agreement on a European Economic Area [1991] ECR I-6084.

78 For examples of such coexistence with comment and analysis, see Sabel and Zeitlin (2008); de Búrca and Scott (2006); de Búrca and Scott (2007).

a kind of "safety net"; third, to situations whereby law sets minimum standards and New Governance may be used for exceeding those standards through self-regulation and self-monitoring; fourth, to instances in which legal regulation provides general norms and New Governance is used to help them become more specific (*ibid.*).[79]

While this model has clear advantages from the perspective of regulation and democracy, the growth in legal pluralism and experimental approaches to EU governance, however, has destabilizing effects and creates a series of problems to law as an institution. National and European courts are forced to adjudicate conflicts between a broader range of actors engaged in rule-making processes. In this context, the role of the judiciary is a complex one, given that New Governance processes often operate beyond formal structures (Scott and Sturm 2007). *In primis*, courts have an important monitoring function as deliberative problem-solving units and, in particular, they have a process-perfecting function by ensuring that the decision makers themselves make policy with explicit reference to constitutional reasons and to policy reasons.[80] The increase in decentralized, heterarchical and dispersed sites of policy and decision making raises the issue of how and which substantive and procedural safeguards need to be imposed to limit the risk of abuse in power relationships. My argument is that while the definition of these safeguards needs to be elaborated through enabling mechanisms of deliberative democracy and structures of participation for policy formation (so that all those affected have a voice or have given their consensus in shaping it following a process of reflexivity) the respect of these safeguards should be assured by the courts acting both in their more traditional role as norm enforcers and in their renewed role as catalysts facilitating the creation of 'process values and legitimacy principles by the institutional actors responsible for norm elaboration within New Governance . . . providing an incentive structure for participation, transparency, principled decision-making, and accountability which in turn shapes, directly and indirectly, the political and deliberative process' (Scott and Sturm 2007: 565).

In this way we reconcile what at first sight appear to be opposing rationales and aims of apparently divergent forms of regulation, namely, EU constitutionalism and New Governance. In particular, a way of democratizing New Governance, providing the necessary safeguards for preventing abuse or concentration of power while, at the same time, ensuring efficiency of regulation, could be the design of guidelines or rules to ensure decentralization and participation of different actors with the involvement of European and national parliaments within New Governance processes and practices. Both European and national parliaments could have a key role in setting a meta-governance frame (as outlined above in the second section) defining objectives and procedures, monitoring progress towards agreed goals and revising the processes in light of the results achieved. Their involvement in New Governance, however, would require a transformation of their traditional role as legislators by passing framework legislation containing commitments to a broad set of goals such as OMC objectives, establishing administrative infrastructures to stimulate decentralized experimentation, monitor the efforts of local units to improve their performance against them, pool resulting information and set provisional standards in light of what they have learned; reviewing the results and revising framework objectives and

---

79 The Water Framework Directive (European Parliament and Council of the European Union 2000a) provides for a number of informal and horizontal processes and at the same time it provides for more detailed legislation. It is considered by some scholars as a prime example of how a hybrid system may create a new type of law (Holder and Scott 2006; Sabel and Zeitlin 2008: 54–56).

80 The ebb and flow of reason giving is the political process of directly deliberative polyarchy (Dorf and Sabel 1998).

administrative procedures accordingly (Zeitlin 2005: 224–225). This renewed role may give national legislators access to insights and tools for producing better legislation and provides them with grounds for criticizing governmental legislative and administrative measures[81] (Duina and Raunio 2007; de Ruiter 2009). Moreover, this could generate what Sabel and Zeitlin (2008) have termed a "democratizing destabilization effect" and could also help to remove the primacy given to executive federalism which has empowered the governments and marginalized the European and national parliaments.

In practice, the involvement of national parliaments in OMC processes such as the OMC is not easy to ensure in practice because of the intergovernmental nature of the process and because national parliamentarians may find it difficult to follow the iterative process of the OMC. In addition, as noted by Benz (2007), national parliaments have to rely on information provided by the governments which could be manipulated. He claims that a way to ensure the involvement of national parliaments in OMC processes is by increasing cross-national policy comparisons on a more competitive basis. More broadly, the level and type of involvement of national parliaments will vary depending on the institutional structure of the country's democratic system.

That said, in the context of the OMC it is worth pointing out that the mid-term review of the Lisbon Strategy in 2005 and its relaunch as Lisbon II, while not bringing about major substantive policy revision, provided an opportunity to refocus priorities and re-evaluate the governance structure of the OMC, drawing on reports by the High Level Group chaired by former Dutch PM Wim Kok (Kok 2004) and the "New Start" report issued by the European Commission (2005).

The revamped strategy emphasized the need to generate support for the implementation of the Lisbon Strategy by bringing it closer to EU citizens. It called for greater "ownership" of the Strategy by national institutions, particularly national parliaments, and greater participation by civil society and social partners at national and sub-national levels. The Commission's 2005 report also called upon the European Parliament to become more involved in the process by providing input on the Commission's strategic annual report to be taken into account by the Council (COM 2005). In addition the Kok report proposed that the European Parliament should acquire an active role in scrutinizing the role of the Commission in the context of the Lisbon Strategy (Kok 2004: 41–42). As regards to national parliaments, the Bruegel Policy Brief (Pisani-Ferry and Sapir 2006) provided comparative data on their involvement in the design and adoption of the NRPs and showed that there is still very little involvement. The report suggests establishing minimum standards for national parliament involvement in the NRPs to address the uneven engagement of national parliaments.

The European Parliament, however, seems to have been taking on a more active role in the Lisbon process and in so doing it has also helped to increase the involvement of national parliaments. In 2004 the Conference of Presidents of the European Parliament established a group of thirty-three members of the European Parliament drawn from all the European Parliament's standing committees dealing with issues relevant to the Lisbon Agenda (the so-called G-33 group). The main task of the G-33 group is to establish the position of the European Parliament in relation to the operation, objectives and results of the Lisbon Strategy, submit recommendations to the Conference of Presidents of the European Parliament Political Groups and organize fora with, among others, the national

---

81 Some argue that governments used the marginalization of national parliaments from OMC processes to prevent criticism of national policies voiced at EU level coming via domestic parliaments (Raunio 2006; Tsakatika 2007).

parliaments. On the basis of these recommendations a resolution is drawn up annually. The resolution is debated and approved by the European Parliament in plenary session and then sent as input for the deliberations of the Spring Council (European Parliament 2007). Before the resolution is sent to the Spring Council, the European Parliament holds an annual meeting with representatives of the national parliaments on the main priorities to be discussed in the Spring Council with working groups co-chaired and made up of members of national parliaments and of the European Parliament to discuss and report on each priority area.[82] Importantly, the Presidents of the Commission and the Council, representatives of other EU Institutions, civil society and the social partners also attend these meetings. Through the G-33 group and the annual joint meeting European political parties and party coalitions are able to develop examples of good practice facilitating mutual cross-country learning. In addition, such new configurations could trigger political confrontation and realignments through public deliberation and be justified on the basis of either constitutional or policy reasons in the context of a more comprehensive framework.

The quests for the recognition of practices and processes taking place outside or beside the classic Community Method brings back to surface the issue of standing before the ECJ in actions of annulment of Community legislation. As posited by Scott and Sturm (2007: 566) courts represent an apposite location where New Governance and law may be reconciled: because of their role as norm elaborators and enforcers they are in an ideal position to grasp changes in society and to understand the emergence of new practices and processes and within them to see the participation of new actors in policy shaping. In addition, the 'judiciary does not operate in a vacuum: courts have a dynamic relationship with other institutions involved in normative practice and are actively constructing and being influenced by those practices' (*ibid.*: 570). It should also be noted that each stage of a judicial process provides an opportunity for bringing together involved stakeholders to deliberate and to act upon what they have learnt from that conflict resolution. Each phase, therefore, also constitutes a communicative and discursive process (*ibid.*: 572). Hence, 'courts themselves participate in deliberations about the meaning and scope of norms as a necessary part of reaching other decisions less directly tied to coercive imposition of rules and liability' (*ibid.*: 573). In the context of judicial review, courts have always been aware of the political nature of a case as well as the involvement of different and less traditional actors. Indeed, judicial review is an area of judicial intervention where the objective is not just that of enforcing *ipso facto* legal norms but also, and perhaps most important, of verifying the legality of the way measures which may affect citizens are adopted and implemented against specific benchmarks or criteria which on closer inspection may be said to be departing from the narrow idea of law understood according to the more canonical dictates of legal positivism.[83] Ely (1980) posits that judicial review is concerned with questions of participation designed to ensure the appropriate functioning of pluralist politics. In this register, it may be posited that judicial review fosters a certain degree of reflexivity (in the sense that the various stages of the proceedings and not only the decision of the judges will give space to a phase of reflection of the stakeholders involved) and dynamic interaction between the judicial and non-judicial phases by introducing rule-of-law values and principles to deliberations by non-judicial actors. Scott and Sturm (2007)[84]

---

82   Three such meetings were held in 2005, 2006 and 2007.
83   Procedural impropriety just to give one example follows the principles of natural law.
84   In their article Scott and Sturm analyze some key cases of the ECJ to illustrate and explain the catalyst (albeit limited) role of the European courts; see in particular Part II.

show how this renewed catalyst role of the courts has already been in place at EU level for some time but the courts have not been sufficiently aware or willing to define their judicial intervention in such terms and thus, ultimately, they have been unable to fully accommodate New Governance processes and practices or give the necessary standing to less traditional or non-privileged actors because of their incapability to conceptualize and internalize these processes outside a rights-based sphere.[85] In the future the ECJ may need to adapt or develop procedural rules on legal standing and constitutional norms in respect of representation to deal with these problems.[86] Hence, once again, the ECJ is forced to confront the evolving political realities of EU governance (Armstrong 1998: 171).

5 Conclusion

The aim of this chapter has been to provide an analytical and evaluative framework for understanding and examining the EES in the context of New Governance and constitutionalism debates. The underlying rationale throughout has been that the Union is not going to develop along the lines of the nation-state even though national constitutionalism plays an important part in post-national constitutionalism. 'Supranational differentiation[87] heralds the maturity of the integration project in so far as it transcends the emphasis on unity building principles during the first decades of integration and accommodates divergent national views on the substantive reach and political orientation of European policies with the European majority will' (Thym 2006: 794).

From the outset, the explicit aim has been to revisit and problematize the traditional meanings and languages of law and constitutionalism in the European Union by questioning narrow understandings of accountability, democracy, transparency, the place of fundamental rights and the role of institutions and non-state actors in the post-national and postmodern system of the Union as well as the traditionally perceived dichotomy between soft law and hard law. On this basis, it has then been possible for the chapter to explore in what way legal instruments, processes and institutions as well as constitutional values and norms are or may be involved in the operation of "new" modes of governance and what role new approaches to regulation have or may have within the better-defined structures of law and constitutionalism. In this context the chapter has shown that the teleological and one-directional approach to European integration fiercely promoted by the ECJ is artificial. As Armstrong (1998: 172) puts it, this approach has the effect of 'smoothing out blemishes, blurring the nuances and concealing the complexities of EU governance'. In addition, the analysis of the legal and practical effects of non-binding legal instruments and the case law of the European Courts has demonstrated that through their "judicial engineering" soft law may have significant legal effects aside from

---

85   This explains why in cases where non-privileged applicants have participated in the processes leading to the adoption of the contested decision (e.g. Case T-122/96 *Federolio v. Commission* [1997] ECR II-1559) or where the applicant's participation in the process leading to the adoption of the contested Directive would have ensured an adequate level of collective representativity (e.g. Case T-135/96 *UEAPME v. Council* [1998] ECR II-2335) the European Courts have been more willing to engage with New Governance.

86   In part this has already been addressed by including the Committee of the Regions among the applicants who have the standing to bring an action for annulment under Article 263 TFEU. However, as the ECJ case law in relation to the standing of non-privileged applicants shows very clearly, the inclusion of this committee is far from being enough to ensure that it will be given a strong voice in challenges against EU legislative measures of general application.

87   My argument is that the New Governance phenomenon should be included in supranational differentiation.

its more widely accepted practical effects such as peer, political or moral pressure and symbolic value.

In this chapter I have taken a deliberately critical stance towards classical and traditional understandings of law and constitutionalism because they appear to be in a position of denial, in that they fail to acknowledge the importance of the (at times informal) processes of socialization and social norms and practices that may both precede the adoption of legal norms and participate in their implementation. As will be shown in subsequent chapters of the book, social norms play an important role in the formation of legally binding norms as well as in rule compliance. We have seen that this position of denial may be explained by the so-called "touch of stateness" and the associated pitfall of the "deficit" argument and, more generally, by centripetal and centrifugal forces which underscore quests for and against further Europeanization. Besides explaining the consequences of adopting either a statist or a post-national approach to an understanding of the European Union and the European integration process I have also attempted to show that key to the resolution of any problem and paradox is their perception and understanding as social meanings that are discursively constructed.

At the same time, the approach has also been purely descriptive showing that New Governance processes and practices are not entirely new and that like other phenomena they may be explained as the result of – as well as the answer to – concomitant interacting processes, such as globalization and transnationalization processes on the international plane, regulatory and democratic legitimacy problems of the European Union and limitations and crisis of national constitutionalism. Illustrating this was important not only to remind critics of the New Governance phenomenon that the latter is intrinsically and necessarily linked to historical contingencies but also, and significantly, to show that the widely voiced criticism that the informal and soft procedures of New Governance may represent a threat to the classic Community Method is premised on a wrong understanding of the former and, more broadly, of the different objectives that governance and government aim at achieving. Particularly in relation to the OMC, there has been concern that the use of soft law instruments may displace the use of hard law instruments even when the European Union already has the competence to legislate. However, this concern seems to miss the point both theoretically and empirically. OMC processes have been introduced or suggested in policy fields where the European Union has limited competence, where there is insufficient consensus among Member States to adopt hard law measures or in instances where cross-country diversity impedes harmonization *tout court*, this being the case of the EES. Moreover, we have seen that in a wide range of areas there is increased complementarity between EU Directives and OMC tools and techniques, and in some configurations there have also been instances of transformation of the law. Hence 'the OMC can be seen as one element in a larger emergent system of experimental governance within the European Union that blurs the distinction between hard and soft law, including growing reliance on Framework Directives, comitology, networked administrative agencies, and a commitment to transparency as a procedural safeguard' (Zeitlin 2005: 221). One of the main advantages of the OMC is that it provides the ground for a continuous and open dialogue between the objectives of the European Union and the measures of the Member States. Moreover, we have seen that OMC-type processes may act as vehicles ensuring the guarantees of the EU Charter. In turn, the rights protected under the Charter may act as standards for appraising policy outcomes of the OMC. Experimental forms of governance such as the OMC, therefore, may ensure renewal rather than replacement of the Community Method (*ibid.*: 223). However, the chapter has also shown how the main limitation of the OMC at present is a failure to ensure effective forms of accountability and participatory democracy while giving primacy to elitism and executive federalism.

Hence, the final section of the chapter presents a governance model that aims at being reconstitutive and reconstructive, overcoming the limitations of New Governance and EU constitutionalism and providing a meta-governance frame in which law retains an important and central integrating role by facilitating an open-ended dialogue between New Governance and EU constitutionalism.[88] This model will be used to examine critically the functioning and results of the EES in subsequent chapters of the book.

---

88 For a thought-provoking debate on the relationship between New Governance, law and constitutionalism, and on transformation and hybridity theories, see Sabel and Simon (2006).

3 The impact of globalization, market integration and EMU on EU social governance

1 Introduction

The aim of this chapter is twofold. First, from a policy perspective it seeks to unravel and examine the economic reasons that have propelled a drive towards the development of a "European social dimension" which has gathered momentum in the last decade, and why employment and growth have become top priority on the Community agenda. In this context, it examines why European Institutions are seemingly at the forefront of efforts to overcome the extant constitutional asymmetry between market efficiency and market-correcting policies. Second, from a governance perspective the chapter seeks to explain the rebirth of soft law instruments, the economic rationale of and increase in the use of policy co-ordination. In a narrower sense, it examines how the idea of launching the EES came about within the overarching aim of the completion of the Single Market which the EMU may be said to be part of.

The purpose of these analyses is to provide a basis on which we can subsequently consider the different components which make up the Employment Strategy in order to discern the elements of continuity with pre-existing forms of regulation from those which may be said to be new. The analysis focuses on globalization, market integration and EMU as the main determining factors for a reconceptualization of the roles of law and the state and for the search of alternative solutions or modes of policy making within the European Union.

The investigation is based on the following hypothetical question: given that globalization has generated new political, economic and social transnational processes, which require in turn a rearticulation and reconceptualization of law, the state, structures, institutions and modes of governance, how are we to systematize these changes? More precisely, to what extent are recent developments in the Europeanization of social policy a product of globalization and the EMU? In this context, what is the relationship between these two major economic processes and would the definition of this relationship have any relevance for understanding the development of the European social dimension and for a shift in emphasis towards policy co-ordination?

In this chapter, therefore, the study also examines the way EMU, chiefly the Stability and Growth (SGP) and the BEPGs co-ordination process, has been the main source of inspiration for recent developments in the regulation of social policy and has fostered the gradual separation of EU employment policies from EU social law and policy by creating an independent identity of the former.[1]

---

1 The evolution of European labour law and the development of EU employment policy are examined in detail in Chapter 4.

This analysis sets out the factors that foster and, at the same time, constrain the adoption and implementation of social policy measures and thus explain the creation of the EES. This helps us to understand to what extent the Employment Strategy is a product of and, at the same time, a response to globalization, market integration and EMU.

2 The roles of the state, law and EU (social) governance in the global context

EC social and labour law, both from the perspective of primary and secondary law, as well as in the ECJ case law, has developed in the framework of what has been defined as differentiated integration, namely a unification characterized by a strong differentiation between European countries, which has arisen due to the continuing tensions between the nation-state, Community-state and government-state theories that underlie Member States' attitudes and policies, but which also originates from the particular intrinsic nature, structure and evolution of the European Community.[2] The discourse on flexibility is pivotal with regard to the understanding of the European integration process. It may be argued that the whole Europeanization process is permeated by differentiation. The various areas and policies of EU law may be considered as being individual *tesserae* of a bigger mosaic, namely the differentiated European integration process or, to use another expression, single microcosms of the wider universe. In this context Barnard (2000: 197) argues that 'social policy represents a microcosm of the flexibility debate in the European Union'.

What follows is a brief analysis of the EU system from a governance perspective that helps us to understand how the EES is composed of both the intergovernmental and supranational elements of the European Union. The EU system, which represents a supra-system *sui generis*, can be subdivided into two systems, intergovernmental co-operation and an EU/EC Institution–institutionalized system. In this regard, Pernice (1999) argues that, despite their formal distinction, Member States' constitutions and the EU founding treaties constitute a unity in substance. In referring to the concept of "divided sovereignty" between Member States and the EC Institutions, Pernice also claims that the EU system represents a coherent institutional system, within which public authority or, more precisely, the power to exercise sovereign rights, is distributed among two or more levels (*ibid.*). This basic dual structure of the EU system has always characterized its conceptualization. The two major subsystems mentioned above are linked to other different subsystems, not necessarily interrelated to one another, but which might be overlapping in what may be defined a "polycontextual dimension". Sciarra (2000) refers to a 'polycentric approach to European integration' describing it as a 'flow of messages between centre and periphery, with the constant reassessment of global, supra-national standards against the re-evaluation of national needs'.[3] Similarly, Weiler (1993) argues that the political institutions of the European Union, the Member States and the new actors which participate in the EU policy-making process are 'all partners to a dialogue,' which he defines as "multilogue".

In the context of this polycontextual dimension of the European Union, there are various subsystems. In the first place, there are a series of "processes" which are a form of intergovernmental co-operation (Szyszczak 2001), for example, the Luxembourg, Cardiff, Cologne Lisbon, Nice and, more recently, the Barcelona and Brussels Summits. In particular, these processes may be defined as meetings or fora in the context of which the main

2 For a full account of the concept of *differentiated integration*, see Walker (1998).
3 See also Jachtenfuchs (1995).

actors decide the general policy framework or direction of Community action, with the aim of defining and co-ordinating the Commission's activities in the short or long term. Second, we have the decision-making processes at EU level which fall within the broad category of the Community Method. The Community Method is the expression used for the institutional operating mode set up in the first pillar of the European Union, the supranational pillar of the Union, which corresponds to the European Community. It has the following salient features:

- Commission monopoly of the right of legislative initiative.
- Widespread use of qualified majority voting in the Council.
- An active role for the European Parliament.
- Direct effect of Community law and the right of private litigants to challenge national law.
- Uniform interpretation of Community law by the Court of Justice.

It contrasts with the intergovernmental method of operation used in the second and third pillars, which proceeds from an intergovernmental logic of co-operation and has the following salient features:

- The Commission's right of initiative is shared with the Member States or confined to specific areas of activity.
- The Council generally acts unanimously.
- The European Parliament has a purely consultative role.
- The Court of Justice plays only a minor role.

Third, there are the interrelationships between Member States and within each Member State, between the government and the regional and local authorities (European Commission 1996). Finally, there is the participation, whether direct or indirect, of experts, firms, non-governmental organizations (NGOs) and interest groups. Figure 3.1 illustrates the dynamics between the various subsystems. It is within this broader framework of subsystems that the EES has taken shape, which sees the participation of government representatives, the Commission and the social partners.

European Union

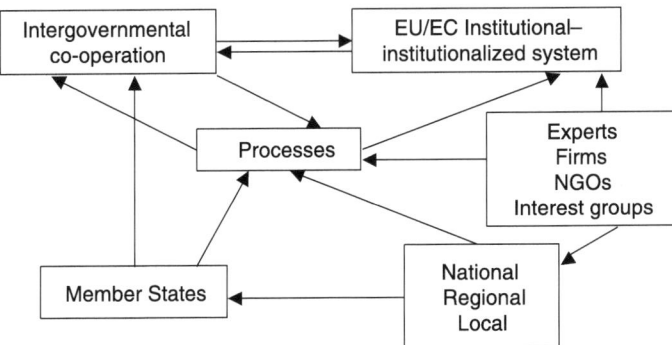

Figure 3.1 The polycontextual dimension of the European Union.

The multidimensional system of the European Union should be seen in the framework of globalization. Globalization is an ongoing process, with multi-faceted aspects, and it comprises a series of processes which reinforce the tendency for economic and political relations to become more global in character over time. It is certainly not a new phenomenon. It goes back many years, both in terms of economic development and labour achievements. However, the "products" that globalization has generated such as new social and economic rights, diverse and heterarchical forms of interrelationships, horizontal and vertical networks of governance with new political actors,[4] have indeed materialized in the last couple of decades and may therefore be said to be new.

Globalization has also decentralized the central vision of the state in the making of law and politics that the German notion of *Staatsrecht* aptly summarizes,[5] fostering the creation of "bottom-to-top" processes in which decision making is not exclusively a prerogative of the state and the locus of policy making is no longer the central government but also includes regional and local authorities (Pernice 1999).[6] In addition to this fragmenting tendency, globalization has also integrated the different levels of policy making, namely supranational, national and regional, creating a transnational multi-level form of governance (Marks, Hooghe and Blank 1996).

Rosenau (1999) refers to "fragmigration" to describe how globalization fosters at the same time a tendency towards integration and fragmentation. Furthermore, Wallace (1996: 12–15) effectively illustrates the effects of globalization on the European Union with what she defines as the 'pendulum of policy-making or co-operation' represented in Figure 3.2. The pendulum represents EU governance, which oscillates between two magnetic areas: national and transnational. The latter includes European integration and other international fora. Depending on the power exerted by either field, there will be a propensity for transnational policies at some times and, at other times, for national ones. The term pendulum is a metaphor for the movement in the process of European integration. The model is based on three interrelated premises:

- The West European State is politically inadequate.
- Globalization has a significant impact.
- The West European region has specific features.

De Búrca (1999: 2, 6) gives us a clear definition of this new form of governance in analysing the evolution of the principle of subsidiarity after the Treaty of Amsterdam. De Búrca describes transnational forms of governance as being an 'increasingly interlocking and interdependent world' and, more precisely, as 'part of a language, which attempts to articulate and to mediate some of the fundamental questions of political and legal authority, government and governance within a complex and multiple-layered polity' (*ibid.*: 2, 4 and 6). However, the term "transnational" is to be used with caution, since this new form of polity is still gradually taking shape and mainly concerns the economic and political activities at international level. De Búrca argues that this form of internationalization has not

---

4 E.g. private, public or mixed public–private bodies, such as multinational firms, non-governmental organizations and social movements. See further Chapter 2.

5 According to this concept the law is adopted exclusively by the state and is at the same time at the exclusive service of the state. See Mayer (1895).

6 Pernice argues that the concept of "multi-level constitutionalism" leads to a notion of constitution which is not bound to a rigid concept of the state; see also Sand (1998: 270–273).

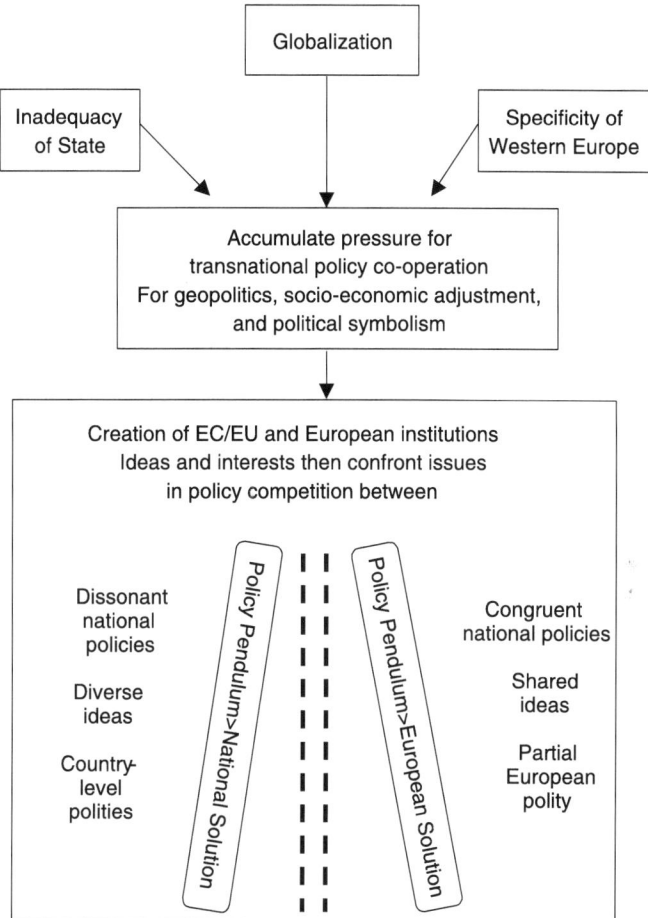

Figure 3.2 The pendulum of policy making.

been 'accompanied by the development of a transnational political and social community in any real sense: national-level politics and citizen identification remain compelling' (*ibid.* 12).

Nevertheless, it cannot be denied that this "bottom-to-top" mobilization is important, since it broadens the scope of current EU policies by including local government problems within common policy issues (Mastronardi 1998: 37–41; Garonna 1998: 4–8). In the framework of a global economy, cities and regions have grown as a result of international networking. Cities and regions represent the locus where the main economic and financial processes take place. This explains the increased presence of local authorities in the EU decision-making fora. In the "euro era" of fiscal policy restraint and simplification of public administrations, Member States can delegate the responsibility for economic and employment policies both "downwards" to local authorities and "upwards" to the European Institutions.

The Commission has taken cognizance of the importance of the local level for the Europeanization process and since the late 1990s it has continuously interacted with local authorities (European Commission 1995; European Commission 1996a). Since the White Paper *Growth, Competitiveness and Employment* (European Commission 1993) various Directorates General of the Commission have focused on local employment and development projects. In addition, the EC Commission Forward Studies Unit, which reports direct to the President, has co-ordinated much of the work on local initiatives. In the *European Strategy for Encouraging Local Development and Employment Initiatives* report (European Commission 1995) it is stated that the local economy enhances the creation of new jobs, thereby diminishing the level of long-term unemployment. Moreover, in two further Communications, the EC Commission has stressed the importance of strengthening the local dimension of the EES (European Commission 2001; European Commission 2000).

In 2006 the European Grouping of Territorial Co-operation (EGTC) (European Parliament and Council of the European Union 2006) was set up to establish a legal instrument capable of providing a strong legal foundation for cross-border co-operation. The instrument aims to simplify administration, co-operation and financial control of territorial co-operation in Europe. The EGTC represents an alternative to the rather technocratic approach to governance that used to typify EU cohesion policy, taking into account multi-tiered levels of governance and territorial stratification within the Member States. In so doing, this legal instrument increases the involvement of different actors in policy planning and implementation, the horizontal integration between different policy sectors and the integration of different government hierarchies (vertical integration) and the decentralization of competences. Thus far the integration of regional and sub-regional actors has been rather unsatisfying from the perspective of multi-level governance. Hence the EGTC is particularly attractive for regional and sub-regional actors as it provides an additional interface to take part on equal terms in the implementation of territorial co-operation measures (Committee of the Regions 2008). Several factors may hinder such co-operation in practice, for example different political interests and linkages, the amount and scope of co-funding available and constitutional structures of the Member States.

Moreover, the Community Cohesion Policy Strategic Guidelines for 2007–2013 (European Commission 2005) call for the integration of growth strategies at European, regional and local levels by taking into account regional specificities and based on reinforced multi-level governance. At regional level, partnerships for Structural Funds have to be entwined with other economic and social networks of partners, thus strengthening the link between EU cohesion and structural policy and, more broadly, from a governance perspective, the integrated approach to policy formation. The Guidelines stress that EU cohesion policy also contributes to better governance at all levels by improving responsibility and ownership of the Lisbon Strategy. In addition, the Lisbon Treaty has included territorial cohesion as an EU objective (Article 3(3) TEU).

The EC Commission has also identified various areas of local development, which may generate significant employment in the future.[7] European labour market and macro-economic policies have, therefore, been broadened to include also the regional and sub-regional levels.[8] This is confirmed by regional (RAPs) and local action plans (LAPs)

---

7 The areas of local development are precisely seventeen, regarding day-to-day services to improve the quality of life, leisure, cultural and environmental services.
8 See also former President of the European Commission Jacques Santer's speech on the importance of the local level for ensuring growth and employment (Santer 1996).

emerging in some Member States (European Commission 1996a).[9] With regard to sub-regional actors, cities are now being represented at European level through various associations among which Eurocities is one of the most influential in Brussels.[10] These associations together with the representative and lobby groups mentioned above are to be seen in the framework of wider "bottom-to-top" processes based on the agreement between local administration, social partners and other economic operators, public and private, for the promotion of development initiatives in disadvantaged regions.

Over the last few years, EU policies have been implemented in such a way as to take into consideration the urban dimension. The DG Employment, Social Affairs and Equal Opportunities launched a series of networks focusing on the integration of ethnic minorities at local level.[11] Likewise, a unit of the DG for the Environment working on the urban environment launched the "Sustainable Cities and Towns" campaign,[12] which seeks to support local governments in their local action towards local sustainability. The DG Research launched the action programme "The City of Tomorrow" for improving urban planning and design in the field of research technologies under the Fifth Framework Programme for Research and Development.[13] The DG Information Society and Media established a European network of cities known as Telecities for the introduction of information and knowledge-based technology at local level, ensuring also that the position of European cities is reflected in European policy development.[14] Finally, the DG Education and Culture introduced intercultural and educational action programmes among various cities (European Commission 1997).

The EC Commission has also launched Territorial Employment Pacts (TEPs) aimed at creating new forms of employment at local and regional levels (European Commission 1998). The idea of TEPs was first introduced by Commission President Santer in his Communication *A Confidence Pact for Employment* (European Commission 1996a). The concept of TEPs is based on the idea that the creation of new forms of jobs must be based on confidence-inspiring economic measures. Santer argued that these measures should be adopted through concerted action and with the involvement of different actors in the economic, social and political spheres in order to establish a co-ordinated employment strategy. Territorial concertation or pacts are based on formal agreements between local authorities, social partners and other important local actors, aimed at promoting economic development and employment creation.[15] Partnerships between public and private actors for the promotion of local development are not a novel idea. What is new, however, is their regulation at European level, thus creating more stable conditions for their launch and further implementation. At the Florence Summit of June 1996 the European Council (1996) decided to implement the TEPs project and entrusted the Commission with the task of selecting various cities or areas for evaluating the effectiveness of the project. By the year 2000 the number of TEPs amounted to

9   RAPs have been adopted in Finland, Portugal and the United Kingdom, whereas LAPs have been adopted in Greece, France, Ireland and Sweden; see European Commission (2001).

10 The association of Eurocities represents ninety-seven major cities from twenty-six European countries. Its web site provides information on its activity, networks and programmes, <http://www.eurocities.org>.

11 See further, Velluti (2007).

12 Further information is available at <http://www.sustainable-cities.eu/>.

13 Further information is available at <http://cordis.europa.eu/eesd/ka4/home.html>.

14 Further information is available at <http://www.majorcities.org/pics/medien/1_1102506953/BETUING.pdf>.

15 For a detailed analysis, see Regalia (2003).

ninety[16] and since the 2000–2006 Structural Funds programmes the TEPs no longer exist as a separate instrument but have been integrated in the European Union's structural policy.

The importance of these "bottom-to-top" processes has been highlighted by Swyngedouw (1992), who has merged the words "globalization" and "local" into "glocalization" in order to show how the effects of globalization on the territorial level are gradually creating a new form of governance and more precisely a multi-tiered form of governance. In addition, civil society and social partners are called upon to play an important part in 'shaping and delivering EU policy' (European Commission 2001: 3) at national level.[17]

As seen in Chapter 2, the European Union is searching for new ideas on how to overcome its structural regulatory inadequacy to the new transnational processes and reboot its own political identity and image. The main challenge with which the Union is confronted lies in bridging the gap between these transnational forms of policy making and its democratic deficit/legitimacy crisis (Joerges and Vos 1999: 79–80). Participatory democracy and deliberative supranationalism as opposed to representative democracy and democratic supranationalism 'potentially address the problem of how to deal with diversity in the Community and attempts to find a *modus vivendi* between the various actors at all levels' (*ibid.*: 87).[18] And yet, despite representing the link between the European Union and its citizens, problems arise as to what constitutes the concept of "organized civil society" at both levels of policy making, as well as its boundaries with social dialogue. Moreover, the ambiguity of the concept increases the confusion surrounding the already highly complex distribution of competence in the European Union and augments the dispersion and fragmentation of the decision-making system.

Transnational governance, therefore, not only poses a threat to Member States' sovereignty but, at the same time, it also represents a challenge to the Community Method (Liebfried and Pierson 1995). Hence what we are witnessing is a contraposition between two opposing forces, namely a resilient tendency towards adaptability to these new forms of diversity and flexibility versus the maintenance of a traditional conception of law (Velluti 2003).

This may explain why the White Paper *EU Governance* (European Commission 2001: 21–22) appears to be concerned more with limiting the sphere of action of these new processes than with fostering them and why these new actors are, for the most part, excluded from the decision-making sphere, and are given a more important role in the implementation side of policy making. In this sense, these actors may clearly be seen as being regulatory and legitimacy resources of the European Union. Scott and Trubek (2002: 2–5) aptly describe this current state of affairs by introducing a distinction between "New/Old governance" (NOG), namely, Framework Directives, Comitology and civil society, which do not represent "fully fledged alternatives" to the Community Method and "New Governance," that is, partnership, social dialogue and the OMC, which, on the contrary, represent a departure from the Community Method.

Hence the various forms of transnational or transborder co-operation are in the process of being attributed legal value. This can be seen in the development of processes at European level, where clear objectives and targets for Community action are decided and

---

16 Further information is available at: <http://ec.europa.eu/regional_policy/innovation/innovating/pacts/en/index.html>.

17 On civil society, see Armstrong (2002).

18 See also Joerges (2002); De Schutter (2002).

in the context of which we can see the participation of new actors such as the social partners and regional and local authorities. From a policy and governance perspective, this can be seen in the wealth of soft law instruments and co-ordination strategies. From a substantive perspective, this is visible in the creation of new forms of contracts which adapt more easily to the rearticulation or rationalization processes currently implemented in most national labour markets. Contractual agreements, being more flexible, have what may be termed an "intrinsic self-organizing effect" as they go in tandem with society's economic evolution and swiftly adapt to new forms of regulation. In particular, collective bargaining at EU level may generate new forms of binding legal instruments, since they also integrate institutional elements, thus guaranteeing in a systematic way the inclusion of different sets of interests which vary between the private and the public field.[19] In this context, as explained in Chapter 2, law is led into the role of "proceduralizer" and "organizer" rather than "coercer". More precisely, law has the role of systematizing the new processes generated by globalization by way of creating new rules and procedures and, more broadly, new modes of policy making.

Moreover, recent actions and strategies by the EU Institutions in the area of social policy reveal an increase in the use of complementary or rather alternative methods of regulation that enhance diversity and pave the way towards transnational modes of governance and deliberative forms of democracy. These developments also illustrate the continuous tension between a tendency towards supranationalization of social policy and a tendency towards entrenchment of state sovereignty, the orientation towards forms of proceduralization of standards and common values (Barnard 2000: 211) and the preference for "management by objectives" rather than "management by regulation" (Biagi 2000).

These new forms of governance do not signify a return to the minimal or *laissez-faire* state nor a complete shift from the public to the private sphere of intervention or regulation. Szyszczak (2002a) argues that the decrease in state intervention in the market has been accompanied by 'experimentation with legal tools to allow the state to retain some control over privatized companies, especially where the supply of goods and services in sensitive sectors is involved'.

The new institutional dynamics involved in the constitutionalization of new forms of governance in the European Union have fuelled debates on constitutionalism (Everson 1998).[20] In this register, Pernice (1999) has developed two interrelated concepts: "European multi-level constitutionalism" and "European multi-level constitution". The first concept defines the European Union as a divided power system, in which each level of government, regional (or *Länder*), national (state) and supranational (European), reflects one of two or more possible political identities of the citizens concerned and thus different levels of society (*ibid.*: 707). The second concept includes the sum of the constitutions of the Member States linked to one another through the supranational constitutional norms of the European Treaties (*Verfassungsverbund*) and which 'bridges the apparent conflict between European constitutionalism and the constitutionalism of the Member States' (*ibid.*). The European integration process is, therefore, multi-level constitutionalism in the making. Pernice (1999: 727) maintains that:

> the development of the European Union is an open and dynamic constitutional process of (re)allocation and (re)definition of powers in a multi-level system of

---

19 This is discussed in detail in Chapter 4.
20 See in more detail Chapter 2.

political governance. The goal is not a "super-state". The goal is rather to open statehood and complete it by supra- and, possibly, global structures of public policy and action according to the real needs of citizens.

The constitutionalization process mentioned above is exemplified by the birth of a collective body of EC rules in the area of employment policy and social protection.[21] In this context, questions arise as to whether the instruments of soft law devoid of any legal sanction can effectively lead to a sea change in the implementation of employment policies within the Member States and what this may mean for social rights.[22] Sciarra (1999a: 501) argues that:

> a renewed and stronger legitimacy of supranational associations, whose representativity should be ascertained following the criteria established in soft law, would also entitle them to new rights, such as introducing collective complaints when social rights are infringed by Member States, as well as when insufficient action is taken to permit the correct exercise of the rights themselves.

Moreover, Community intervention in social and employment policies remains a moot point to date (Cullen and Campbell 1999) and, as the next chapter goes on to show, soft law at times has been used to hinder any expansion of Community social competence, particularly in periods of economic crisis and social stagnation.

To recap, globalization and the shift towards "bottom-to-top" and transnational forms of regulation have called into play new actors, namely, regional and local authorities and organized forms of civil society. In addition, this process of change has led to a reconceptualization of the roles of the state and law and to the gradual establishment of alternative forms of decision-making procedures and mechanisms which complement the Community Method. In particular, in the area of EU social policy, this can be seen in the wealth of soft law instruments that eschew traditional modes of regulation, such as, for example, the EES and its implementation through the OMC.

In the subsequent sections, the study shows how these new forms of governance within the EU context have been shaped and further developed in accordance with the objectives of EU integration, and chiefly pursuant to market integration and EMU.

3   Social and labour market policies in the framework of market integration, EMU and the Lisbon Strategy

Globalization has entailed a high degree of fragmentation, severely undermining the traditional power of the state to regulate while, at the same time, it has not provided for a supranational order or for a fully integrated world economy. The European Union, as a supranational order, has an important role in the realm of globalization. In particular, it promotes the adoption of new regulatory tools, which ensure an effective systematization of these new transnational processes by providing the new actors with a specific role in the policy-making process, it fosters the strengthening of the protection of economic and social rights and assigns a role of "guarantor" and "organizer" to national legislation. In this sense, the furthering of the European integration process represents a counter-tendency to globalization.

---

21   See, further, Chapters 4 and 5.
22   This question was explored in part in Chapter 2; see, further, Chapters 5 and 7.

However, the constraints posed by the Single Market project and EMU on Member States have led to a situation whereby national labour market policies have become dependent on and conditioned by supranational decisions (Sciarra 1995). As Sciarra aptly says, not only do European labour lawyers have to 'think in terms of reinterpreting their own constitutional traditions in the light of a new and distinct legal system, but they must do so having in mind that Europeanization is the outcome of separate open processes and is an open process in itself' (Sciarra 2000: 275). Pieterse (1995) argues that the European Union is a form of globalization leading to 'both supranational and sub-national regionalism'. In addition, domestic policy areas have become increasingly subject to European policy-making to the point that EU political and economic dynamics have reoriented the direction and shape of national decision-making processes, becoming part of the organizational logic of national politics (Ladrech 1994). Various lawyers have developed ideas on the discourse of a "re-nationalization or re-regulation process of law" (Sciarra 2000; Szyszczak 2001; Lafoucrière 2000: 7) referring to the readjustment to supranational standards and re-evaluation of national needs (Sciarra 2000: 288) in order to propose valid policy solutions.

Hence there is a dialectical relationship between globalization and the European integration process, which are strictly linked to one another and to a great extent overlapping but often conflicting forces. This can be seen in the context of the European Union's economic projects, exemplified in particular by the Single Market, EMU and the various economic processes such as the Luxembourg process (Employment) Cardiff process (Structural Reform) and the Cologne process (Macroeconomic Dialogue), which were "capped" by the broader Lisbon Strategy adopted in 2000 (European Council 2000). The Lisbon Strategy is an all-European effort to meet the challenges identified above, namely the strengthening and the co-ordination of the new regulatory tools alongside the Community Method and the identification of viable policy solutions which increase the European Union's competitiveness by way of bolstering, at the same time, both the economic and social dimension of the Community. The Special European Council Summit focused on the strict link between economic growth, employment and social cohesion in the new framework of a knowledge-based economy and society and restored structural reforms at the heart of the European Union's policy priorities. Unlike previous European Councils, which relaunched economic reforms, the Lisbon Council did not introduce a new process. The accent was instead placed on rationalizing the existing framework and establishing a new open method of co-ordination (Rodrigues João 2001).

The integration of the European economies, therefore, has become an irreversible and self-sustaining process which has gradually influenced other areas such as the political, the social and, more generally, Member States' own historical and traditional culture. In particular, the implementation of EMU has major effects on other EC policies, specifically on EC labour market and employment policies. In theory, joining the euro is not an irreversible process because every country has the possibility to back up and to abandon the EMU project. When asked this question, Jacques Delors, former President of the EU Commission, said that talking about joining the EMU as being an irreversible process was wrong, since the TEU allows any Member State to withdraw from participation in the euro (see also the voluntary withdrawal clause introduced by the Lisbon Treaty, Article 50 TEU). However, in practice, it seems highly improbable that a participating Member State would withdraw. Since 1 January 2002 not only have euro banknotes and coins started to circulate but, as from that date, new public debts are issued in euros. In addition, since 1 July 2002 national banknotes have ceased to be legal tender. This means that a participating Member State which withdrew would find itself in serious difficulties.

The focus of analysis, therefore, is on the EMU, particularly because of its impact on

Member States' fiscal, employment and labour market policies. Since its launch it has been a catalyst for an emphasis on the regulation of social policy in two ways. First, from a policy perspective, the creation of a centralized European monetary policy, with the impossibility for Member States to have recourse to interest rates as a tool of macroeconomic policy and the constraints on fiscal and budgetary policies, has shifted attention to other supply-side policy measures, for example the EES. Second, from a governance perspective, the OMC has its origins in the "hard" fiscal provisions and "soft" economic provisions of the EMU. This analysis, therefore, helps us to understand the genesis and further development of the EES and it enables us to separate the elements of continuity from those of "newness" of the strategy, both from a governance and a policy perspective.

3.1 The EMU and its impact on Member States' economic constitutions

European Monetary Union[23] applies to sixteen of the twenty-seven Member States of the European Union[24] and it represents a form of differentiated integration or flexibility.[25] Monetary union may be defined either as an area within which there are several currencies set at irrevocably fixed exchange rates, or an area within which there is a single currency controlled by a single central bank (Padoa-Schioppa 1994). Monetary union *stricto sensu*, as it is conceived in EMU, embraces both meanings. In the economic field, it has been decided to make macroeconomic and budgetary rules and procedures binding, whereas, in the monetary field, the decision fell on the irrevocable locking of exchange rates and the transition to a single monetary policy, with the transfer of the responsibility for the formulation and implementation of monetary policy to the European System of Central Banks (ESCB). The EMU project should not be considered as the end result of the current EC strategic economic, monetary and fiscal policies. The Treaties do not describe EMU as an end in itself but as a policy contributing to "economic and social progress" and "price stability".[26] The inception of the EMU dates back to the late 1960s and it represents the end of a process which started even before the founding Treaties came into force.[27] It was consolidated in the Maastricht Treaty and left virtually untouched by the Treaty of Amsterdam.[28]

The system established with the EMU (Council of the European Union 1997, 1998) is based on three interrelated elements which ensure, *inter alia*, economic soundness within each participating Member State. These are:

---

23 See Articles 109j(3) third indent EC (now Article 121(3) third indent) and 109j(4) EC (now Article 121(4)EC).
24 The euro zone comprises the following countries: Austria, Belgium, Finland, France, Germany, Ireland, Italy, Luxembourg, the Netherlands, Portugal, Spain and Greece. Among the new Member States, Slovenia adopted the euro in 2007, Cyprus and Malta in 2008 and Slovakia in 2009. Three European micro-states – Monaco, San Marino and the Vatican – have concluded agreements with the European Union permitting them to use the euro as their official currency and mint coins, but they are neither formally part of the euro zone nor represented on the board of the ECB. Several other countries have officially adopted the euro as their sole currency, such as Andorra, Kosovo and Montenegro, without signing any official agreement with the European Union. These states are not considered part of the official euro zone by the ECB; however, in some usage the term "euro zone" is applied to all such states and territories that have adopted the euro as their sole currency. On the impact of EMU in an enlarged European Union and in Central Europe, see Altomonte and Nava (2005 and Schadler *et al.* (2005).
25 On the EMU and flexibility, see Tuytschaever (2000).
26 See Preamble to the TEU and Article B ToA; see also Article 2 EC (same numbering) and 3a EC (now Article 4 EC).
27 See European Court of Justice *Opinion 1/91* [1991] ECR I-6079.
28 For a historical account of the EMU, see Della Posta (2008).

- Price stability as the primary objective.[29]
- Fiscal discipline.
- A central bank system detached from political bargaining.[30]

Following the TEU,[31] the EC Treaty provides that monetary and exchange rate policy is transferred to the European Community, the design and implementation of which is the preserve of the ESCB,[32] encompassing the European Central Bank (ECB),[33] which makes monetary policy decisions,[34] and the national central banks (NCBs), which are primarily responsible for implementing those decisions.[35]

The EMU raises issues of sovereignty and it represents a significant expansion of central powers within the "euro zone", since it entails the transfer of powers until now exercised exclusively by governments, including the right to authorize issues of currency, to an independent ECB.[36] Not only have participating Member States handed over their monetary independence to the ECB both politically and practically, but the EMU also brings constraints on the conduct of fiscal policy, which remains with the Member States. According to Baroncelli (2008: 121) the two key elements of the European Union's monetary policy, namely price stability and independence of the ECB, have led to the 'legitimation of an institutional architecture which is different from that of the Community Method, characterized by a singular subtle link between the ECB and the Community Institutions, with the effect of excluding the ECB from a full-blown system of checks and balances'. The independence of the ECB has been clearly defined by the ECJ in a case brought by the Commission against the ECB's decision not to abide by an EC regulation aimed at fighting financial fraud. In *Commission v. ECB*[37] the ECB tried to promote its special independent

---

29 See Article 105(1) EC (same numbering).

30 See Article 108 EC (former Article 107 EC).

31 See Preamble of the Treaty of Maastricht, Articles 2 (same numbering), 3a(2) (now Article 4a(2) EC), 4aEC (now Article 8 EC) and Part Three, Title VI, Articles 102a–109m EC (now Title VII, Articles 98–124 EC), supplemented by the Protocol on the Statute of the ESCB and the ECB, the Protocol on the Statute of the EMI, the Protocol on the Excessive Deficit Procedure, the Protocol on the Convergence Criteria referred to in Article 109j EC, the Protocol on the Transition to the Third Stage of EMU, and the Protocols on Certain Provisions relating to the United Kingdom and Denmark.

32 See Article 8 EC (former Article 4a EC), Article 105 EC (same numbering), Article 107(1) EC (former Article 106(1) EC), Article 110 EC (former Article 108a EC), Article 111 EC (former Article 109 EC), Article 123(1) EC (former Article 109(l) EC); Articles 1–6 of the Protocol on the Statute of the ESCB and ECB.

33 See Article 8 EC (former Article 4a EC), Article 107(1) EC (former Article 106(1) EC); Protocol on the Statute of the ESCB and ECB, Articles 1, 9 and 10, Article 109l(1) and (2) EC (now Article 123(1) and (2) EC), Article 23(1) of the EMI Statute, with regard to the liquidation of the former EMI at the commencement of Stage Three of EMU.

34 See Article 105 EC (same numbering) and Article 106 EC (former Article 105a EC), Article 110 EC (former Article 108a EC), Article 111 EC (former Article 109 EC), Article 113(3) EC (former Article 109b(3) EC), Article 123 EC (former Article 109 EC), Protocol on the Statute of the ESCB and ECB, Articles 12, 15–25, 34–35, 44–47.

35 See Article 107(1) EC (former Article 106(1) EC), Protocol on the Statute of the ESCB and ECB, Article 14.

36 See Article 105a EC (now Article 106 EC). The independence of the ECB as a legal entity is an innovative concept and it was almost unknown to the legal traditions of most Member States. Most countries used to assign monetary policy decisions to governmental Ministers who were politically responsible to their parliaments. The impact of this concept has been twofold (Baroncelli 2008: 122). On the one hand, the independence of the ECB represents a challenge to the classical theory of parliamentarism. On the other hand, the notion has a direct impact on the economies of the Member States who traditionally had sole decision-making powers in this field.

37 See Case C-11/00, *Commission v. European Central Bank* [2003] ECR I-7147.

status in order to justify its decision not to abide by the regulation which set up the European Anti-fraud Office (OLAF) (European Parliament and Council of the European Union 1999). The ECB (1999) sought to create its own anti-fraud committee through a decision detailing its functioning.[38] The ECJ agreed with the Commission and forced the ECB to accept the control exercised by OLAF because according to Treaty provisions the ECB's tasks fall within the Community's framework. In its ruling the European Court construed a notion of independence under Article 108 EC in functional terms.[39] According to the ECJ the independence of the ECB is strictly linked to the pursuit of the objectives set out in the Treaty and the ESCB Statute, namely price stability and sound fiscal policies. Its independence, therefore, is limited to ensuring that in performing its tasks it is not subject to political interference or external pressures.[40] The independence of the bank should not be considered as an all-purpose notion but should be seen in the context of the EC system and general objectives as laid down in Article 2 EC. Tasks undertaken in fields falling outside monetary policy, therefore, are not covered by the guarantee of independence unless the ECB can demonstrate that they interfere with the performance of the tasks assigned to it by the Treaty and the ESCB Statute.

The EC Treaty as amended by the TEU[41] forces national fiscal policy not to exceed budget deficits of more than 3 per cent of GDP and government debt at less than 60 per cent of GDP, except for cases of severe recession. The EC Treaty is supplemented by the SGP (European Council 1997: 1). This system calls for the close co-ordination of economic and fiscal policies and an effective surveillance of government spending (European Council 1998; Council of the European Union 1998). By focusing on budget balance, the SGP has contributed to strengthening a so-called "stability culture" based on stable money and sound public finances (Sapir *et al.* 2004). Although the SGP mainly aims at guaranteeing that the "ins", that is, the Member States joining the euro, fulfil the convergence criteria; at the same time it also aims at ensuring that the policies of the "outs", that is, the Member States which have opted out of EMU, are implemented in tandem with those of the ins, in order for the Council to examine effectively whether the outs are orienting their economic and financial policies in a way so as to meet the conditions for joining the euro and, if necessary, to make recommendations (which can also be made public) to the Member State concerned to take any adjustment or corrective measures needed. This explains why the outs are to submit yearly updated convergence programmes just as the ins are to submit yearly updated stability programmes. These reports are analyzed in detail in the next section. Their object-ive is to strengthen the relationship between the ins and the outs (Council of the European Union 1997a; Monetary Committee 1998).[42]

Hence the three components mentioned above, namely price stability, fiscal discipline and a central bank system detached from political bargaining, represent the pivotal con-stituents of the transfer of monetary sovereignty to the European Community. As key elements of the EC economic constitution they touch the very foundation of the European

---

38 This decision was adopted by the Governing Council of the ECB on the basis of Article 12.3 of the ESCB Statute.

39 *Ibid.*, para. 92.

40 *Ibid.*, para. 134.

41 See Articles 103(5) EC (now Article 99(3) EC), 104c EC (now Article 104 EC), 109e(4) EC (now Article 116(4) EC); Council of the European Union (1993); the Protocol on the Excessive Deficit Procedure, Article 1, first indent; Council of the European Union (1997a: 1); Council of the European Union (1997b: 6).

42 The Commission, at the ECOFIN's request, has also analyzed the possibility of reinforcing the procedures concerning the convergence programmes, see Commission (1997a: 4).

Union, since they entail great changes to the Member States' constitutional structure, internally,[43] *inter se*, and in their relationship with the European Union.

EMU, however, does not change the allocation of responsibility for policies other than monetary and exchange rate policies. Fiscal and labour market policies remain mostly a matter of Member States' concern, although they are subject to surveillance by EC Institutions.[44] The SGP, agreed in June 1997, established the procedures for surveillance of national fiscal policies, in addition to the provisions of the Treaty. Budgetary discipline was inserted because a certain level of fiscal discipline was deemed the appropriate instrument to reduce Member States' fiscal disorder and to ensure the stability of monetary union.

The decision to include this element in EMU, however, was based on political more than economic grounds (Chalmers and Szyszczak 1998: 244), which were not fully considered, as the implementation of the EMU project has been undertaken with the objective of fostering European political integration (de Grauwe 2002: 693). In this register, Tsoukalis (1996: 280) argues that EMU 'can be seen as a dialectical process between wider political objectives and market realities'. The economic aspects of monetary union were instrumental, therefore, in the creation of the EMU rather than being the reason for having EMU (de Grauwe 1997: 210).

Certainly, on political grounds, sound budgetary policies were seen as a precondition for an efficient monetary union since consensus on monetary union would have been very difficult to achieve without reassuring public opinion that it would be built on strict fiscal policies (Padoa-Schioppa 1994: 199; Chalmers and Szyszczak 1998: 244). Furthermore, fiscal discipline is also desirable for a number of different reasons, one of which is that it guarantees the better functioning and implementation of national budgetary policies.

3.2 The Stability and Growth Pact and the Broad Economic Policy Guidelines

Articles 98–104 EC and 121 EC,[45] together with the Protocol on the Excessive Deficit Procedure, the Protocol on the Convergence Criteria and the SGP (European Council 1997; Council of the European Union 1997a, b) have introduced basic rules for budgetary soundness and established procedures for the surveillance of national fiscal policies. Member States have agreed to meet certain convergence criteria in the form of benchmarks, namely a sound government budgetary position with budget deficits that should not exceed 3 per cent of GDP and a public debt ratio of no more than 60 per cent of GDP.[46] In the event of non-compliance with the SGP the Council can make a recommendation and issue a formal sanction in cases of infringement of the SGP. More specifically, the SGP consists of a "preventive arm" and a "dissuasive arm". Under the provisions of the preventive arm, the euro countries have to submit annual stability programmes (whereas the countries outside the euro area have to submit convergence programmes) in which they set out their strategy and budgetary aims for the next three years. As explained further below, the preventive arm includes two policy instruments. First, the Council, on the basis of a

---

43 In Italy, for example, the Treasury created an *ad hoc* committee, Comitato Euro, on 12 September 1996, entrusted with similar tasks of the EMI and in particular to guarantee the smooth transition to the euro, <http://www.tesoro.it/Euro/comitato.htm>.

44 See Articles 103 EC (now Article 99 EC), 104c EC (now Article 104 EC), 109j EC (now Article 121 EC) and Protocol on the Excessive Deficit Procedure and Protocol on the Convergence Criteria.

45 Ex-Articles 102a to 104c and 109j EC.

46 See Article 2 of the Protocol on the Convergence Criteria.

proposal of the Commission, can address an early warning to prevent the occurrence of an excessive deficit. Second, using the policy advice, the Commission can address policy recommendations to a Member State as regards the broad implications of its fiscal policies. Stability programmes must include the following information:

- A medium-term objective for the budgetary position of close to balance or in surplus, the adjustment path and the expected path of the general government debt ratio.[47]
- The main assumptions about expected economic developments (growth, employment, inflation and other important economic variables).
- A description of budgetary and other economic policy measures being taken and/or proposed to achieve the objectives of the programme.
- An analysis of how changes in the main economic assumptions would affect the budgetary and debt position.

On the basis of assessments by the Commission and the Economic and Financial Committee, the Council examines:

- Whether the medium-term budget objective in the stability programme provides for a safety margin to ensure the avoidance of an excessive deficit.
- Whether the economic assumptions on which the programme is based are realistic.
- Whether the measures being taken and/or proposed are sufficient to achieve the medium-term budgetary objective.

The Council will also examine whether the content of the stability programme facilitates the closer co-ordination of economic policies and whether the economic policies of the Member States concerned are consistent with the BEPGs. On a recommendation from the Commission, and after consulting the Economic and Financial Committee, the Council submits the programmes for peer review and publishes its opinion. Where it considers that the objectives and content of a programme should be strengthened the Council can invite the Member State concerned to adjust it. Updated stability programmes will be examined by the Economic and Financial Committee on the basis of assessments by the Commission and, if necessary, the Council. As part of multilateral surveillance, the Council will monitor the implementation of stability programmes on the basis of information provided by the Member States and of assessments by the Commission and the Economic and Financial Committee.

The dissuasive part of the SGP governs the excessive deficit procedure. In particular, if the Council identifies significant divergence of the budgetary position from the medium-term budgetary objective, it will, with a view to preventing the occurrence of an excessive deficit, address a recommendation to the Member State concerned to take the necessary adjustment measures and give a time frame for doing so. If subsequent monitoring shows that the divergence is persisting or worsening, the Council will make a recommendation to the Member State concerned to take corrective measures. This recommendation may be made public. Non-compliance with the recommendations may trigger further steps in the procedures, including for "euro-area" Member States the possibility of sanctions. Moreover, in order to ensure closer co-ordination of economic policies and sustained convergence of

---

47   Convergence programmes also have to present information on the medium-term monetary policy objectives and the relation of those objectives to price and exchange rate stability.

the economic performances of the Member States, the Council will, on the basis of reports submitted by the Commission, regularly carry out an overall assessment of the economic situation in each of the Member States and in the Community.

This regulatory structure combines hard and soft law measures at each stage with the first measure adopted by a European Council Resolution setting the scene for the more legalized co-ordination that follows and providing firm political guidance for Member States, the Commission and the Council on the operation of the Pact. Furthermore, the absence of a deadline in the Pact for achievement of the medium-term budget rule softens multilateral surveillance. Hence this combination of binding but, nevertheless, not legally enforceable obligations allows for gradual policy incorporation with a more medium-term approach that also takes into account Member States' social and economic differences. In most Member States the SGP has led to institutional changes which have reinforced the control of central governments over the overall developments of public finances in their own country (Le Cacheux and Touya 2007: 81). In addition, the centrality of fiscal deficits has also reinforced the position of Finance Ministers within national governments (*ibid.*: 81–82). The "naming and shaming" mechanism overall has also made large deficits politically more costly in domestic public discourse as the media have used non-compliance with European rules as a stick to beat national governments.[48]

One of the most conspicuous limitations of the SGP has been its inconsistent application and weak enforceability. The credibility of the SGP has been undermined by the rather inefficient operation of both the preventive and the dissuasive arms of the Pact. The conflict between the Council and the Commission on the application of the excessive deficit is a case in point.[49] On 24–25 November 2003 the ECOFIN Council rejected the Commission's recommendation on French and German fiscal policies and failed to apply sanctions against France and Germany, despite legal proceedings being started when dealing with Portugal in 2002 and Greece in 2005 (though fines were never imposed). The Commission decided, therefore, to bring an action for annulment against the Council's decision to place the excessive deficit procedure in abeyance for France and Germany. The ECJ's ruling *de facto* only partially supported the Commission. The European Court said that the Council's decision to depart from the rules laid down by the Treaty or those which it sets for itself was unlawful. However, the European Court rejected the Commission's other claim, that the Council's decision not to adopt the Commission's recommendations pursuant to Article 104(8) and (9) EC was a decision that should be annulled. It said that the responsibility for making Member States observe budgetary discipline lay essentially with the Council and that if the necessary majority within the Council to approve the recommendations of the Commission was not secured there was no decision that could be reviewed under Article 230 EC.[50] The Pact, therefore, has proved not to be enforceable against big countries such as France and Germany which, ironically, were its strongest advocates when it was created. These countries have run excessive deficits under the Pact definition for some years. The reasons for this may be explained by several factors, *inter alia*

---

48   For further analysis, see Meyer and Kunstein (2007).

49   See Case C-27/04, *Commission of the European Communities v. Council of the European Union* [2004 ECR I-6649]. For analysis and comment, see Baroncelli (2008: 139–143).

50   The decision was also important because the European Court applied the so-called "ERTA principle" according to which 'an action for annulment must be available in the case of all measures adopted by the institutions, whatever their nature or form, which are intended to have legal effects.' In so doing, the Court rejected the Council's argument that its conclusions were texts of a political nature which did not entail any legal effects. See Case 22/70, *Commission of the European Communities v. Council of the European Union* [1971] ECR 263.

their influence and large number of votes in the Council, which must approve sanctions (Le Cacheux and Touya 2007: 88); their greater resistance to "naming and shaming" tactics, since their electorates tend to be less concerned by their perceptions in the European Union; their comparatively weak commitment to the euro as compared to smaller states; the relatively greater role of government spending in their larger and more enclosed economies.

The SGP and the weaknesses in the extant procedures have been subject to heated controversy since the adoption of the SGP which was agreed in return for the German acceptance of swapping the stable Deutschmark for the euro. Debates over its effectiveness and validity have increased since 2002 under the influence of fiscal developments in various Member States that have joined the "euro zone" and following the flouting of the system by some Member States, as seen above (Navarro 2001; Le Cacheux and Touya 2007). Moreover, the "Renault–Vilvoorde" case,[51] concerning the breach of the right of information and consultation of the workers on behalf of a Renault plant in Belgium, which announced the temporary discharge of workers, had a great impact on the political arena and it fostered the introduction of employment issues in the SGP (European Council 1997: 1). In March 2005 the Council (2005: Annex II) adopted a reform of the SGP as a response to concerns that the financial system in the European Union was excessively pro-cyclical because of the Pact's stringent rules,[52] unnecessarily amplifying swings in the real economy to reduce the risk of financial instability and attendant macroeconomic costs. It is, therefore, supposed to remedy some of its major weaknesses, *inter alia* its pro-cyclical character as mentioned above and its insufficient flexibility in order to better take country-specific circumstances into account (Le Cacheux and Touya 2007: 72). In addition, the reform is meant to take into account the challenge that Member States face in ensuring the long-term sustainability of public finances owing to the impending impact of population ageing. To this end, common long-term budgetary projections are established at European level and the individual Member States' situations assessed and monitored. On 27 June 2005 the Pact was complemented by two additional Regulations amending the 1997 Regulations (Council of the European Union 2005a, b). The result of these changes has been to soften and render more discretionary the multilateral surveillance and excessive deficit procedures, thereby rendering it less likely that soft or hard sanctions will be imposed.[53] According to Martin (2004) the SGP would pose much less of a problem if the ECB's monetary policy were not so restrictive. By keeping economic growth too low and thus unemployment levels too high the ECB has also slowed down the growth of revenue as well as adding social policy burdens because of increased pressures on welfare financing, making it much harder for governments to meet the SGP requirements.

Le Cacheux and Touya (2007: 72) maintain that 'although this reform may be deemed an improvement from a strictly economic point of view, it is not clear that it will make the SGP easier for countries to obey'.[54] Moreover, even though there is agreement on the objectives of the Lisbon Strategy, namely on promoting growth and competitiveness, there is no common or even co-ordinated strategy to deliver on the objectives (*ibid.*: 83).

In addition to stability and convergence programmes, Member States have to submit

---

51 For further analysis, see further Chapter 4.
52 In economic policy this term refers to any aspect of economic policy that could magnify economic or financial fluctuations.
53 For further analysis, see Maher (2004).
54 See also Louis (2006).

national reports on their economic situation in accordance with the BEPGs which constitute the main instrument of economic co-ordination. Policy co-ordination is a process through which Member States agree to meet common European concerns and objectives while fully preserving their competences to legislate in the respective policy areas. Policy co-ordination is not a new regulatory tool. Pre-Maastricht, it was used to achieve a certain level of convergence under conditions of unanimity voting. However, it was only with the TEU that a series of co-ordination processes were formalized in the EC Treaty.[55] The need for co-ordination (Le Cacheux 2007) arises in contexts characterized by interdependences, due either to collective goods or to externalities. In economic theory, decentralized decision making in the absence of co-ordination mechanisms may lead to sub-optimal, non-co-operative equilibrium because each player will act without taking into account the consequences of his/her actions for the other players. In the context of the Single Market project the abolition of barriers may lead to an increase in spill-over effects which result from the use of national economic policy tools such as fiscal policies. This situation combined with the creation of the EMU in which Member States share a single currency and uniform nominal variables requires monetary and financial stability which becomes, therefore, a collective good in so far as joint action or co-ordination is necessary to reduce unwanted consequences. In this respect the BEPGs, discussed below, represent a positive attempt to provide a macroeconomic environment for structural reforms and the increased flexibility of the labour markets.

The ECOFIN Council is empowered to formulate and adopt the BEPGs. The BEPGs have two functions: to provide guidelines for national economic policies and to formalize a common analysis of economic prospects, the aims to be achieved and the best measures by which to achieve them. The main policy goal of the BEPGs is sustainable and co-ordinated socio-economic policy making. The guidelines are qualitative in nature but, depending on the policy area, they also set quantitative targets which Member States have to meet and report on in their national plans. There are no legal sanctions and the whole process is based on peer pressure and negative publicity through individual recommendations and rankings. The Commission has a supervisory role through the ECOFIN DG and the EU Parliament has an *ex post* right to be informed about the BEPGs and compliance with the guidelines. There is no direct involvement of non-governmental actors, although indirectly they are involved through the so-called "Macroeconomic Dialogue".

The "Macroeconomic Dialogue", launched at the Cologne Summit in 1999 (European Council 1999: Annex I, Part IV), aims at improving the interaction between wage developments and fiscal and monetary policies via regular biannual meetings where representatives of the ECOFIN and Social Affairs Council, the Commission, the ECB and the social partners meet to exchange information and to better co-ordinate their policies, in particular, fiscal and wage policies in order to achieve sustainable non-inflationary growth and employment.[56] The soft co-ordination process of the BEPGs constitutes the main precedent of the EES, the main differences being the participation (which is indirect only in the BEPGs) of the social partners and the absence in the Employment Strategy of any

---

55 For a historical account of the BEPGs, see Linsenmann (2007: 145–147).

56 At political level, a regular dialogue – two meetings a year – takes place in the framework of the ECOFIN Council, in co-operation with the Social Affairs Council and the participation of representatives of the Commission, the ECB and the social partners. At a technical level, this dialogue is organized as a working group in the framework of the Economic Policy Committee, in liaison with the Employment and Labour Market Committee (now Employment Committee) and with the participation of representatives of both Committees, the ECB and the Macroeconomic Group of the Social Partners.

role for the EU Parliament. What follows is a more detailed examination of the BEPGs process.

Economic co-ordination, as set out in the Treaty,[57] starts with the Council setting out policy objectives for the European Union as a whole with specific recommendations for each Member State in the BEPGs. In particular, the Commission prepares a recommendation which is to be presented to the ECOFIN Council. The latter then adopts the BEPGs on the basis of this recommendation and the European Council subsequently approves them. The Treaty also established a system for the multilateral surveillance of economic policies, based on the BEPGs. The ECOFIN Council monitors the compliance of Member States' policies with the BEPGs on the basis of reports submitted by the Commission. When particular policies implemented by a given Member State have the potential of jeopardizing the proper functioning of the EMU or fail to comply with the BEPGs the Council makes recommendations to the Member State concerned and may also choose to make these recommendations public. This happened for the first time with Ireland in February 2001.[58] The content of the BEPGs has changed significantly since their first issue in 1993. During the early years they focused primarily on reducing public deficits and monetary stability. Since 1998, and following two European Council resolutions (European Council 1998; European Council 1998a), the emphasis is more on structural policies. The text of BEPG reports has thus gradually adopted a more general approach and since the launch of the third phase of EMU it has been divided into two parts: general recommendations and recommendations addressed specifically to each Member State. There is empirical evidence (e.g. GOVECOR 2004) showing that the implementation of BEPGs has led to institutional change with inter-ministerial or interdepartmental co-ordination between domestic Ministries. However, procedural innovation has not been particularly significant. According to Linsenmann (2007: 155), the BEPGs have not become an important document for parliaments when adopting the annual budget or, more broadly, for discussing macroeconomic measures. Moreover, national administrative bodies already entrusted with European affairs tasks have been deployed for ensuring the implementation of the BEPGs without the creation of any *ad hoc* or new committee or body. On the policy implementation side official EU documents of the Commission and the Council shows that there hasn't been any real implementation of the guidelines. The Lisbon Strategy has not really altered this situation and because of the highly political nature of macroeconomic measures the absence of the European and national parliaments in this policy co-ordination process represents a significant limitation for its effective implementation.

In 2002 the BEPGs process was subject to review with the Commission's Communication *Streamlining the Annual Economic and Employment Policy Co-ordination Cycles*, which aimed at placing more emphasis on the social dimension of economic policies (European Commission 2002). This streamlining process[59] entails the adoption in January of an annual "Implementation Package" which comprises the implementation reports on the BEPGs, the Joint Employment Report, the economic reform process (Cardiff process), the Macroeconomic Dialogue (see below) and other reports. The Implementation Package supports the Commission's spring report to be submitted to the European Council. On the basis of the Presidency Conclusions of the spring European Council the Commission will adopt a "Guidelines Package" in April with a medium-term focus which includes drafts

---

57   See Article 99 EC.
58   For a detailed account of the Irish case, see Navarro (2001).
59   See Appendix 4.

of the BEPGs, with both general and country-specific policy recommendations, the Employment Guidelines and the employment recommendations to Member States. The Internal Market Strategy also forms part of this Guidelines Package. The adoption of the BEPGs and the employment guidelines then takes place after the June European Council meeting by the various Council formations. This overall timetable brings other policy co-ordination processes in line with the pre-existing timetable of the BEPGs and, therefore, does not significantly affect the BEPG procedure. In addition, the Guidelines have become less detailed and more strategic, with a clearer indication of the various policy instruments that can be employed, and they are reviewed only once every three years, with the possibility of introducing changes in the medium term. In 2003, the first year of the synchronized timetable, the Commission had difficulty in adopting coherent recommendations because of divergent views of the DG Employment, Social Affairs and Equal Opportunities and the DG Economic and Financial Affairs on the content of the recommendations emphasizing a conflict between different socio-economic rationales and perspectives. The streamlining of existing co-ordination processes has not entailed a greater role for the European Parliament. While the BEPGs envisage *ex post* information rights of the European Parliament the other OMC processes in the socio-economic policy fields do not assign any role to the European Parliament other than – in some instances – mere *ex ante* consultation. Similarly, the European Parliament is not involved in the run-up to the spring European Council meeting. According to Linsenmann (2007: 153) the 'tighter timetable before and after the spring European Council has further reduced opportunities for the Parliament to table suggestions for the Guidelines Package'. The role of the European Parliament, therefore, is reduced to making comments on various policy documents produced within a given policy cycle. While the European Parliament put forward specific changes to the BEPGs for 2002, only a few proposals were taken into consideration by the Commission (*ibid.*). Moreover, it has tried strengthening co-operation with national parliaments but with limited success (*ibid.*).

3.3 EMU and real convergence

The adoption at European level of new policy instruments aside the Community Method to co-ordinate Member States' policies in the context of EMU signifies the concerns that European Institutions have of the repercussions that economic integration has on national social and economic structures.

The main concern with regard to political economy and the reallocation of power which the EMU involves is the effectiveness of existing policy instruments to deal with structural change at national level and, more precisely, to ensure real convergence, namely long-term productivity and employment growth as well as a reasonable correlation of the business cycle among the EMU participants. The main objective that Member States have had to pursue in order to join the EMU has been the achievement of a sufficient degree of monetary convergence, which is measured with reference to the exchange rates, inflation rates, interest rates, fiscal deficit and debt terms. One of the strongest criticisms of the Treaty provisions is that, besides nominal economic variables, they do not take into account real economic variables such as employment and output.[60] The Treaty only has one provision which refers to real convergence, Article 121(1), sub-para. 3 EC (ex-Article 109j

---

60 Output in economics is the total value of all of the goods and services produced in an entity's economy. It is a concept used in macroeconomics or in the study of the economic transactions of broad groups such as countries.

(1), 3 sub-para. EC),[61] where it is stated that in their reports on convergence the EU Commission and the EMI 'shall also take into account the results of the integration of markets, the situation and development of the balances of payments on current account and an examination of the development of unit labour costs and other price indices'. However, no mention is made of economic growth or unemployment. As we have seen, following the Renault–Vilvoorde case, employment issues were inserted in the SGP and Member States must submit information on the main assumptions about expected economic developments in their stability or convergence programmes. However, the focus is clearly on Member States' budgetary positions, with budget deficits that should not exceed 3 per cent of GDP and a public debt ratio of no more than 60 per cent of GDP. Moreover, with the exception of budgetary policy, other economic policy areas are not subject to the provisions regarding monetary union. Neither have Member States lost their decision-making power over these other areas.

As a consequence of this unbalance between economic policy and monetary union, there is the risk of a dysfunction between the way Member States implement their economic policies and the way the ECB implements monetary policy. Lastra (1992) talks about "friction losses", which "result from unco-ordinated monetary and fiscal policy". Lastra, however, also points out that although price stability remains the primary objective of the ESCB, Article 105(1) EC also provides that 'the ESCB shall support the general economic policies in the Community with a view to contributing to the achievement of the objectives of the Community as laid down in Article 2'. Hence the ESCB must adopt monetary policy decisions which also take into account the objectives of economic policy (*ibid.*). Furthermore, the provision laid out in Article 99 EC (ex-Article 103 EC) providing for economic co-ordination is a means to provide a strong macroeconomic environment (Chalmers and Szyszczak 1998: 259).

Hence, it may be argued that the EMU reinforces the effects of globalization which may be categorized under various headings:

- The adoption of a deflationary monetary policy to ensure price stability rather than to increase the employment rate.
- A decrease in labour demand (in particular a shortage of demand for low-skill workers in the long term).
- The higher mobility of firms.
- The new technology, which has a strong and immediate destabilizing effect on the economy in the short run and which slows down the adaptation of the labour market to the economic change in the long run.
- Changes in the social and sociological structure of society (particularly growth in female labour market participation, ageing of the population, highly qualified labour skills).
- Changes in the national social security systems.
- Demand shortage in the product market with a parallel inadequate demand for investment.

One of the areas of national policy making which has certainly been affected is "Social Europe", which encompasses, *inter alia*, the welfare state, collective bargaining and more specifically labour market regulations (Teague 1998). The convergence criteria do not

---

61　Now Article 121, third sub-para. EC.

contain any index on (un)employment. Member States, therefore, have tackled unemployment with various employment-related measures. In addition, the strict convergence criteria, which do not take into consideration real economic variables, have compelled Member States to adopt rigid retrenchment policies which entail cuts in welfare and social expenditure. Cutbacks in labour costs have often been interpreted as ensuring improvements in individual well-being through new economic growth. Likewise, deflationary policies are considered to lead automatically to positive social trends. However, cuts in costs have overlooked and, at the same time, underestimated the costs of cuts, namely, increase of unemployment, social exclusion and poverty: when structural reforms decrease social protection[62] they automatically increase the number of people in poverty. This is confirmed *a contrario* by the fact that states which have the highest expenditure on social protection also have the lowest levels of inequality. Unemployment sets a vicious circle in which it simultaneously increases demand for benefits and reduces total income and social contributions, forcing a small working population to support an increasing financial burden. Moreover, because of globalization and the Single Market firms demand increasingly skilled employees. This produces higher levels of unemployment and sets in train a de-skilling process of the long-term unemployed. In broader terms, in order to maintain the SGP targets, governments are not only forced to cut social expenditure but also forced to implement new social policies in order to counterbalance the negative effects of EMU.

An OECD (1997) report on the employment outlook argues that the competition from low-wage countries does not have positive effects on the European economy and the outcome could be social dumping within the "euro area", namely, unfair/distorted competition based on access to artificially cheap or (undervalued) labour (Blanpain 1998) which may be reinforced by the split between the Member States that joined EMU and those that have not and also by the recent waves of enlargements. What may happen is that a direct effect on unemployment is increased by an indirect effect: firms not wanting to relocate attempt to increase productivity through the automation of the production process. At the same time, firms try to increase technological progress, which may increase redundancies and unemployment. The migration that may follow will weaken the negotiating power of the trade unions.

Now that the unemployment rate has become a major concern of most euro countries, and the EC labour market has become far too rigid, the need for real convergence has increased. Most fiscal policies oriented towards economic growth and employment in the EC are currently made at national level but in the absence of the possibility to resort to substantial public spending tax policy is insufficient. Hence the risk is that if both labour market and fiscal measures prove ineffective the EMU could indeed increase the existing economic divergences among the participating states.[63]

This situation presents two major problems that are closely connected. On the one hand there is the danger that the existing political and legal structures may not be adequate or appropriate for performing the necessary economic functions, since the EMU does not create the basis for a sufficiently strong fiscal policy owing to the weak sanctions provided by Article 103EC (now Article 99 EC) and to the absence of effective co-ordination of different national fiscal policies in the framework of the single currency (Inman and

---

62 In particular, social protection for low-skilled workers such as those on social benefits and minimum wages.

63 Article 104c (11), second indent, EC (now Article 104 EC) provides a Member States with an excessive deficit may be required to publish additional information, to be specified by the Council before issuing bonds and securities.

Rubinfield (1994). On the other hand, this situation raises doubts as to whether the European Union is an "optimal currency area," which is based on the idea that economic convergence is a precondition for any monetary union.[64] This notion refers to an area in which the response to a shock, be it political or economic, external or internal, or even both, can be pursued either through the change in the value of its currency against other currencies or through capital or labour mobility. After the removal of capital controls in the Community,[65] capital has undoubtedly become a highly mobile factor of production. However, because of cultural and language differences, labour mobility across EC Member States is still very low (Puhani 1999). Hence for the European Union to represent an "optimal currency area" there has to be a strong convergence of long-term growth and fewer country-specific or asymmetric exogenous economic shocks affecting individual Member States than in a region with high labour mobility. At present, however, the European Union is far from having achieved these conditions. The alternative would be a very high degree of wage flexibility but decisions regarding wages are still within the national domain and thus differences between Member States remain high (Taylor 1995: 70). A partial although insufficient solution has been the decision to streamline the BEPGs and the EPGs co-ordination processes by taking into consideration a more medium and long-term approach. Hence due to the low degree of real convergence the European Union can hardly be defined as being an "optimal currency area" (Chalmers and Szyszczak 1998: 237; Barrell 1992: 221–222).

From the above considerations, it may be argued that the Maastricht entry conditions to EMU have brought about a rather uneven economic development in favour of the more dynamic areas within Europe and they, therefore, increase local inequality. Moreover, the various criteria are more substitutive than complementary and fixed for every Member State. Employment, therefore, has become the only flexible economic variable for market adjustment, with the consequence that the levels of unemployment may increase at each recession because all other important economic variables remain fixed.

This situation has forced Member States to implement new national and/or European employment policies by co-ordinating their labour and employment policies and by establishing a convergence of targets to foster employment in the European Union. This explains why the EES which was formalized with the Treaty of Amsterdam has been fast-tracked by the Luxembourg Summit before the entry into force of this treaty: precisely because of the urgency with which the European Union was called to solve the unemployment problem affecting most Member States.

Hence, it may be argued that the EES as an alternative supply-side policy represents a response to the negative impact of the EMU on both national macroeconomic and employment policies. The SGP has severely limited the margin of manoeuvre in the area of fiscal policy as a tool for economic adjustment. In addition, the Pact has an inherent imbalance between the regulation of Member States' public deficits and the absence of any rules on public surpluses which has led to an asymmetry between long-term growth and short-term policies. Member States, however, still have to maintain stability-oriented macroeconomic policies in order to foster economic growth and employment creation. Hence, faced with the impossibility of having recourse to interest rates as a response to economic shocks or fluctuations and the lack of a common taxation policy, it was necessary

---

64   For an analysis of the different aspects of the theory of an optimal currency area, see Mundell (1961); McKinnon (1963); Johnson (1996: 98–102).
65   See Article 56 EC (former Article 73b EC).

to focus on other measures of political economy. Among the various policy options, the Amsterdam European Council agreed to adopt a specific supply-side policy and the choice fell on the EES.

4 Conclusion

This chapter showed how Member States are legally and economically constrained by the creation of the Internal Market, the realization of the EMU and the impact of global economy. In particular, it showed how both globalization and the economic integration process within the European Union have both caused, albeit at different levels and degrees, the gradual erosion of Member States' traditional legal authority and regulatory capacity as summarized by the German notion of *Staatrecht*, with the assignment of a new role to the state: from "interventionist" to "guarantor" of minimum standards and human rights.

Consequently, the roles of law which have always been conceptualized in relation to territoriality have gradually begun to change in order to dovetail with the transnational economic system created by globalization. Law is thus led into the role of "proceduralizer" and "organizer" rather than "coercer". The new scenario also explains why at European level the focus has shifted from "government" to the broader notion of "governance" encompassing economic, technological and knowledge-based processes as well as the political and legal ones.

With regard to the EMU, we have seen that important instruments of macroeconomic policy such as monetary policy and the management of debt and deficits have been transferred to the European Union. However, the political responsibility for the results of the decisions taken in these fields is still vested with the Member States which creates a tension that is bound to be resolved in favour of the Member States (de Grauwe 2008: 277) as the *Excessive Deficit* case illustrated. Furthermore, the incapacity of the European Union and, in particular of the "euro zone", to be an "optimal currency area" combined with the lack of a system of redistribution that can compensate countries hit by negative shocks undermine the sustainability of the monetary union (*ibid.*) This situation represents a barrier to ensuring co-ordination between national social policy systems and to achieving common results. Martin and Ross (2004: 3) argue that 'the intergovernmental politics of monetary integration has channelled EMU in a direction that is more likely to threaten the European Social Model's viability than to facilitate its rejuvenation'. In particular, extended periods of disinflation should be followed by a period of economic growth to ensure, *inter alia*, higher levels of employment. However, the macroeconomic policy orientation promoted by the ECB does not favour such a growth spurt its focus being rather on labour market flexibility measures (Sbragia 2004: 61–63). Moreover, as we shall see in the next chapter, efforts to adopt a "European" social policy are impeded by the diversity of national welfare states, differing not only in levels of economic development but also in their normative and institutional structures. As Siedentopf and Hauschild (1988: 78) maintain, 'if policy making is a collective action by the Member States, policy implementation is an individual action by them, and that action is coloured by each country's own culture and legal system'.

Two internally competing and overlapping discourses have underlined the European integration process: on the one hand, an economic policy discourse which represents the rationale for EC economic governance and, on the other hand, a social policy discourse, which underlies the extant modernization of the "European social model".[66] Particularly

---

66 For a definition of the "European social model", see Chapter 4.

since the Lisbon Strategy, these two contested discourses have been streamlined to fit in with the wider overarching project of EU economic competitiveness and convergence. It is against this background that a "European" employment policy which relies heavily on the interaction between both of these two discourses has been developed.

The chapter also revealed more about the roles of law. In particular, law has become instrumental to the achievement of Community goals and thus law ensures the enforcement of substantive and procedural norms but also institutionalizes values or principles, articulates processes and brings about domestic change.

However, having understood the *quomodo* we still need to understand the *quid*, namely, the developments in the field of EU social policy (particularly the increased use of measures that eschew traditional forms of legislation) from an endogenous perspective, in order to see how and to what extent the employment co-ordination process differs from the BEPGs and other co-ordination processes and which elements of the Employment Strategy may be considered to depart from traditional modes of regulation.

4 The evolution of European labour law

From "employment law" to "employment policy"

1 Introduction

European intervention in the social sphere – and annexed questions such as why, to what extent and in what way – has long been a *vexata quaestio*. It has attracted the attention of a large community of lawyers, policy makers and scholars mainly because it presents the European Union with a difficult regulatory task, the reason for this being the coexistence of different national welfare regimes, differing not only in levels of economic development, but also in their normative and socio-philosophical aspirations and institutional structures (Scharpf 2002). The different understandings of the "social" also explain the uneasy – at times conflictual – relationship it has always had with the "economic", the uncertain place of social rights in the completion of the Single Market and, more generally, the lack of coherence at legislative and policy levels. Periods of "embedded liberalism" have been followed by years of social activism which in turn have been followed by phases of "re-embedded liberalism".[1] As Lord Wedderburn (1995: 391) suggestively puts it, 'the social can of course contribute to competitiveness, but when it conflicts with the economic, whatever the rhetoric, it has few friends'.

European labour law developed its bone structure originally from the focus on the creation of the Single Market and later on the establishment of the EMU and, accordingly, has mainly concerned labour market measures and employment-related matters which were directly linked to them. This explains why Community social policy has traditionally lacked the same general scope as national social policy which typically embraces areas such as regional, structural, cultural, education and health policies (Weatherill and Beaumont 1999: 613; Marshsall 1975: 7; Majone 1993).

The main purpose of this chapter is to explain how EU social regulation has developed into two distinct branches: on the one hand, employment law linked to the Internal Market, the focus being on, *inter alia*, the free movement of workers, working conditions of labour, employment protection and health and safety at work and, on the other hand, policies aimed at employment creation that eschew the use of traditional legal instruments. The study employs a chronological narrative concerned with the historical development of EU labour law and employment policy. However, rather than a beginning-to-end chronology, the story line is systematically subdivided into specific periods, providing a clearer framework of study. In particular, the chapter charts the main developments of EU labour

---

1 For a distinction of the phases of EU social policy in "embedded liberalism" and "re-embedded liberalism", see Giubboni (2006).

law and employment policy, from the Treaty of Rome to the Treaty of Amsterdam which marked the beginning of a so-called "sixth phase" in the development of EU social policy. In order to maintain the logical coherence of the critical analysis of the EES in the context of the developments of EU employment policy post-Amsterdam, the full examination of the sixth phase is provided in Chapter 5. In this context, the chapter also compares the operation of the EES with that of the OECD Jobs Strategy first adopted in 1992 with which it shares certain common objectives and characteristics.

While essentially descriptive, this chapter serves an important purpose for the research questions of the book. By tracing key phases in the evolution of the European Union's social dimension it does not seek to provide a detailed analysis of EU social law and policy, which has already been done exhaustively elsewhere (Barnard 2006; Bercusson 2009; Hervey 1998; Kenner 2003; Nielsen and Szyszczak 1997; Szyszczak 2000). The aim instead is to identify and unravel the reasons for such developments and understand why and in what way EU employment policy has taken on an independent identity from EU labour law. In this context, the chapter also explores the rationales for EU intervention in domestic labour law (namely, the integrationist, the economic and the social)[2] and in so doing it helps to fathom the different, even conflicting, objectives which it has been said to serve.[3] Moreover, by looking at the different phases of EU intervention in the social sphere it is possible to look closely at the various legal structures and mechanisms developed thus far. In particular, it is possible to examine the use of soft law within a fifty-year time frame and how the latter's role has changed in quite a significant way, from a mere instrument or technique complementing regulations and Directives to an important mode of social governance in its own right. More generally, from a governance perspective, the diachronic approach adopted here is a particularly useful focus of study given the array of traditional and new approaches to governance which have been deployed, from harmonization through Framework Directives to the OMC, as well as the range of actors participating therein. Thus the chapter also looks at the European Social Dialogue as exemplifying a new approach to EU governance which differs quite significantly from the Classic Community Method on the input side while leading to similar results on the output side (Scott and Trubek 2002: 4). This study is important since the social partners both at European and national levels have been given an important role within the EES.[4]

2 According to Syrpis (2007: 12, 53, 61 and 68) the "integrationist rationale" refers to situations where the European Institutions act with the aim of establishing, or improving the functioning of, the European market; the "economic rationale" refers to situations where European Institutions intervene in order to improve the performance of the European economy, for example by encouraging growth, reducing unemployment, enhancing efficiency, investing in infrastructure and improving Europe's international competitiveness; the "social rationale" is concerned with the distribution of the benefits derived from improved economic performance and ensuring the values associated with the "European social model", such as solidarity, cohesion and distributive justice.

3 For a detailed analysis of the various forms of social regulation in the European Union and models of the European economic constitution which have influenced the former, see Giubboni (2006: Chapter 4).

4 The High Level Group on Industrial Relations (2002) has suggested the introduction of OMC-like methods of benchmarking and follow-up reporting in the social partners' negotiated text. In line with this proposal the European social partners therefore have negotiated a new typology of framework agreements in which they make recommendations to their national member organizations and undertake to follow them up by regular reporting on implementation at national level.

2 A short history of EU labour law and employment policy

When the European Community was first created in the late 1950s, domestic social regulation was not conceived within an EC perspective and the adoption and implementation of social measures were considered to be largely, if not exclusively, part of the national legal realm. However, as the European integration process evolved and, in particular, as EU labour law and social policy developed, albeit in a non-coherent manner, they gradually began to have an impact on national legislation (Bercusson 1996: 5). Furthermore, as the Community developed into a quasi-state polity with the pursuit of a broader scope of objectives other than economic, the national and European decision-making processes in the area of social law became more intertwined and reciprocally influenced each other.

The analysis from a historical perspective is thus required to emphasize how the development of EC social policy is characterized, on the one hand, by the imbalanced influence of the intergovernmental and supranational elements on decision making as well as negative as opposed to positive forms of integration, and, on the other hand, by the particular conceptualization of the "social" in a given moment of the European integration process. In addition, this analysis is important to unpack and assess the different elements that make up the EES to discern the ones that may be said to be new from the ones that may be said to embody continuity with previous measures.

A major premise in understanding EU labour law and employment policy is to consider its *sui generis* nature, which also explains the lack of consistency and coherence as opposed to other spheres of EU governance and regulation. Furthermore, attempts to advance social intervention at European level have often been met with political opposition by many Member States. Despite the opposition to Community intervention, a range of social matters have been covered by EU legislation, such as worker mobility, health and safety at work, education, equal treatment, youth training and vocational training. The focus has been primarily on employment law and labour market policy due to the constraints imposed initially by the EC Treaty.

It was during the 1990s with the leadership of the Delors Commission that the social dimension of European integration was given renewed emphasis. In its Green Paper *European Policy Options for the Future* the European Commission (1993) set out a medium-term strategy which 'recognized that an economic community cannot survive without some social ground rules', that economic growth and social justice are interdependent, and that the social crisis cannot be met by a single European state acting alone (*ibid.*: 33). The major objectives included 'properly directed social instruments' which contribute to stable growth of output and jobs and to social and political stability; economic measures which respect social goals, such as equality and solidarity; a new balance between public, private and individual welfare provisions; and a minimum level of income for those in distress. The means suggested included convergence and co-operation policies, financial support, social partners' agreement at European level and legislation. The Green Paper correctly took cognizance of the fact that there was a need for social regulation (whatever form this would take) and not simply one pertaining to labour relations. The 'old model of labour and welfare legislation, which saw everyone solely from the perspective of work, as a future, present, or past worker, had to be replaced by one whose point of departure was the *European citizen*, a person whose social standards have to be guaranteed even if never in work' (Hepple 1994: 181–182). To address the social dimension from the narrow perspective of employment law would be equal to widening 'the gulf between an elite core of full-time (mainly male) permanent workers, and unemployed or part-time and casual (mainly female) workers' (*ibid.*: 182). In the White Paper *European Social Policy* (European Commission 1994), published at about the same time as the Green Paper, the Commission linked social rights to competitiveness and high labour standards to high levels of productivity, thus awarding a new revitalized function to social policy. Most importantly, emphasis was given to a "European social model"[5] and to the social dimension of the European Community, omitting any reference to the EMU project. Despite the ambiguity of these two terms and, in particular, of the notion of "social dimension", which may encompass a range of different, even conflicting, policy objectives the point of relevance in this context is the reconceptualization of the "social" at the beginning of the 1990s. As explained throughout this chapter the creation and further development of the Single Market added to calls for a complementary emphasis on social issues. The course of European integration from the 1950s onward generated a fundamental asymmetry between market efficiency and market-correcting policies due to the communitarization of economic policies which reached its apex with the creation of the EMU while, at the same time, social and labour policies remained the domain of national decision making (Scharpf 2002: 646). Prior to the SPA annexed to the EC Treaty in 1992, there was no firm legal basis for EU social policy proposals and thus no clear scope of Community intervention in this area. Further, the Maastricht Treaty with its emphasis on economic convergence and controls on the recourse Member States could have to fiscal, monetary or exchange rate policies, strengthened such arguments as the creation of a "euro zone", entailed a reconfiguration of macro-economic policy instruments available to Member States and forced a rethinking and rationalization of national social security systems (Begg 2002) and demands to recreate a "level playing field" by Europeanizing social policies as well (Scharpf 2002). The origins of the EES may be traced back to the immediate post-Maastricht period. Although concerns over high unemployment levels throughout the European Union already existed towards the end of the 1980s and proposals for having some degree of EU competence in the social arena had already been put forward, it was during the early 1990s that high employment and job creation became top priority on the Community agenda.

In turn this leads us to question why this change has occurred, to what extent it has determined a radical rethinking of social regulation and, linked to this, whether this reconceptualization has entailed a complete separation of social policy from the economic objectives of the European Union. The answers to these questions provide us with the necessary information to understand the creation of various modes of policy making in EU social governance and, chiefly for the purposes of this book, the launch and further implementation of the EES. The next sections address this set of questions by way of looking at the various phases of EU social policy and within each phase the main rationales and objectives.

2.1 The different phases of EU social regulation

With regard to the study of EU social law and policy, it has become customary among labour lawyers to systematize its paroxysmal development into various phases (Barnard 2006; Cullen and Campbell 1999; Giubboni 2006; Hervey 1998; Kenner 2003; Nielsen and Szyszczak 1997). Following this hermeneutic approach, we may argue that the

---

5 The "European social model" concept is reflected through three basic principles: (*a*) the recognition of social justice as a policy target; (*b*) the acceptance of the productive role of social policy and its contribution to economic efficiency; and (*c*) the development of a process of high-level bargaining between the social partners. For further analysis and comment, see Jepsen and Pascual (2005: 231).

evolution of Community social policy can be subdivided into six phases. These phases are the following:

- A period of neo-liberalism (1957–1972).
- A period of social action (1972–1980).
- A period of stagnation or crisis (1980–1986).
- A period of optimism (1986–1993).
- A period of consolidation of the social dimension of the European Union (1993–1997).
- A period in which a new paradigm for EU social law and policy is established (1997 to the present).

Each of these phases is characterized by a gradual expansion of Community intervention, with a pivotal role played by the ECJ in shaping and enforcing socio-economic rights at a time when the Community had limited decision-making powers in the social field (Ball 1996: 314; Sciarra 2001), that is, roughly until the mid/end of the 1980s. The European Court's case law has been particularly significant in developing and strengthening the Community provisions on equality between men and women[6] and, chiefly, Article 119 EEC on the principle of equal pay (now replaced by Article 141 EC) and the Equal Pay (Council of the European Union 1975)[7] and Equal Treatment Directives (Council of the European Union 1976; European Parliament and Council of the European Union 2002; Council of the European Union 1979; Council of the European Union 1986).[8] However, as posited by Luciani (2000: 530), what the Community (and the Member States) are committed to are social interests presented in the form of objectives (employment, social protection, social dialogue, etc.) and it is these which are protected by the Treaty (which is still the basic law of the Community). Social rights *per se*, however, remain in the background and the opportunity of invoking them is linked to the need to achieve the social objectives stated. In short they boil down to their status as *Reflexrechte*.[9]

The *Albany* case[10] illustrates the limitations of a reference to fundamental social rights that remains tied to the notion of being purely instrumental to the pursuit of social objectives (Giubboni 2006: 104). While the European Court carried out a balancing operation between social policy and competition law objectives, it refused to consider collective

6 For a critique of the role of the Court in gender equality, see Shaw (2001).

7 This Directive has been repealed by the "Recast" Equal Treatment Directive (European Parliament and Council of the European Union 2006a). For comment and analysis of the Recast Directive, see Burrows and Robinson (2007).

8 Most of these Directives have been repealed by the "Recast" Equal Treatment Directive (European Parliament and Council of the European Union 2006) with the exception of the Directive on equal treatment in matters of social security (Council of the European Union 1979) and the Directive on equal treatment for the self-employed (Council of the European Union 1986a).

9 For a similar line of criticism of an instrumental use of fundamental rights, although not specifically in relation to fundamental social rights, see Spaventa's (2009) critique of the *Schmidberger* case, Case C-112/00 *Schmidberger* [2003] ECR I-5659. In particular, she argues that 'the problem with this line of reasoning is that it suggests the demotion of fundamental rights from "individual" rights to public policy reasons; from fundamental rights to legitimate *interests*, albeit interests which might prevail *even* over the free movement of goods. Furthermore, while at first sight it might seem that the Court either altogether rejects a hierarchy of rights or privileges fundamental rights over Treaty rights, its analysis leads to the opposite conclusion, giving the impression of a hierarchical superiority of the Treaty rights over fundamental rights' (356); see also Coppel and O'Neill (1992: 669), who argue that 'the high rhetoric of human rights protection can be seen as no more than a vehicle for the Court to extend the scope and impact of European law'.

10 Case C-67/96 *Albany International v. Stichting Bedrijfspensioenfonds Textielindustrie* [1999] ECR I-5751.

bargaining as the exercise of a fundamental social right 'forming part, as such, of the nucleus of minimum preconditions for an autonomous labour law system' (*ibid.*). Moreover, in the *Viking*,[11] *Laval*,[12] *Rüffert*[13] and *Commission v. Luxembourg*[14] cases the Court, using the market access approach, said that the collective and governmental action in these cases constituted "restriction" on free movement and so breached Articles 43 and 49 EC even though in *Viking* and *Laval* it recognized that the right to strike was a fundamental right which formed an integral part of the general principles of Community law. It also seemed to suggest that the fundamental economic freedoms of the Treaty are not just meant to prevent protectionist discrimination against foreign suppliers but more broadly to provide a bulwark against any government or trade union measures that might, in some way, impede the exercise of those freedoms. These rulings may therefore have devastating effects on national employment law (Barnard 2009).[15] There remains an obvious asymmetry between the status of fundamental social rights and the fundamental economic freedoms that the EC Treaty guarantees to individuals.

Moreover, while social rights have gradually been given formal recognition by being admitted into the *acquis communautaire*, this recognition has taken place with very unequal degrees of force and effectiveness (Craig and de Búrca 2003: Chapter 8). In this context the ECJ has had an important role in striking a more even balance between the social values and economic values of the Union.[16] At times, however, the 'Court's own legitimacy has been eroded by some poorly reasoned judgments and a lack of consistency' (Barnard 2006: 35). For example in *ex parte Sutton*[17] the European Court undermined the effectiveness of its earlier ruling in *Marshall (No. 2)*[18] on the value of compensation (*ibid.*; Dougan 2004: 303). In *Marshall (No. 2)* the European Court held that effective protection for the victim of a discriminatory dismissal from employment requires that domestic rules must provide for full compensation, including the payment of interest. The European Court, therefore, intervened directly in the domestic legal order of the United Kingdom because its rules on remedies were considered to fall below the standards of effective judicial protection required under Community law. However, in *ex parte Sutton* the European Court held that the effective protection for the victim of a discriminatory refusal to provide social security benefits did not require the national courts to award interest. The European Court recommended the claimant to bring a supplementary state liability action against the United Kingdom on grounds of substantive breach of Community law and seeking damages for losses suffered. This ruling was problematic for a number of reasons. Specifically, the unwillingness of the European Court to intervene directly to remove the inadequate

11 Case C-438/05 *International Transport Workers' Federation, Finnish Seamen's Union v. Viking Line ABP, OÜ Viking Line Eesti* [2007] ECR I-10779.

12 Case C-341/05 *Laval & Partneri v. Svenska Byggnadsarbetareförbundet, Svenska Byggnadsarbetareförbundets avd. 1, Byggettan, Svenska Elektrikerförbundet* [2007] ECR I-11767.

13 Case C 346/06 *Rüffert v. Land Niedersachsen* [2008] ECR I-1989.

14 Case C-319/06, *Commission v. Luxembourg* [2008] ECR I-4323.

15 For comment and analysis on the *Viking* and *Laval* cases, see Blanpain and Swiatkowski (2009); Dashwood (2007–2008); Deakin (2007–2008); Novitz (2007–2008); Rönnmar (2007–2008); Sciarra (2007–2008).

16 E.g. Case C-50/96 *Deutsche Telekom v. Schröder* [2000] ECR I-743. In this case the European Court said that the economic aims pursued by Article 119 EEC (now Article 141 EC), namely the elimination of distortions of competition between undertakings established in different Member States, is secondary to the social aim pursued by the same provision, which constitutes the expression of a fundamental human right.

17 Case C-66/95 *R v. Secretary of State for Social Security, ex parte Sutton* [1997] ECR I-2163.

18 Case C-271/91 *Marshall v. Southampton and South West Hampshire Area Health Authority (Teaching) (No. 2)* [1993] ECR I-4367.

domestic remedy forces the claimant to go through two separate actions to exercise and protect his/her Community rights.[19] Moreover, as Dougan posits (*ibid.*), 'the Court is sometimes more concerned to ease the financial consequences for the Member State of its own unlawful conduct than with ensuring the effective judicial protection of individuals attempting to enforce their Community law rights'. Another example showing lack of consistency on the part of the European Court is the *Danfoss* case,[20] in which it held that:

> since length of service goes hand in hand with experience, and since experience generally enables the employee to perform his duties better, the employer is free to reward it without having to establish the importance it has in the performance of specific tasks entrusted to the employees.

The Court's ruling seemed to depart from two basic requirements of its previously established two-stage approach. These are, first, the shift of the burden of proof to the employer at the justification stage and, second, the need of any justification for compliance with the principle of proportionality (Beck 2007).[21] Hence, as mentioned above, there remains an asymmetry between the status of social rights and the fundamental economic freedoms. In addition, while the European Court may be said to have been willing to strengthen the substantive protection provided by social legislation, some of its rulings have been criticized by many commentators for being conceptually flawed. Space does not permit a more thorough examination of the European Court's case law.[22]

The focus of this chapter is mainly on the process of Europeanization in the social sphere which has manifested itself both in the form of hard law via the adoption of Regulations and Directives (labour market policies) or soft law with a predilection for co-ordination and co-operation as opposed to the Community Method (social policy). The other main focus of the chapter is on the gradual involvement of new actors (both public and private) and the adoption of a new typology of acts, with greater reliance on horizontal forms of subsidiarity,[23] proximity and decentralized modes of operation.

2.2 From the Treaty of Rome to the Declaration of Paris

When the European Economic Community (EEC) was founded, few provisions on social policy were inserted in the 1957 Treaty. The Community was established with the central aim of creating a Common Market centred on the free movement of products (goods and services) and production factors (labour and capital). This prime objective explains why the founders of the Community adopted a minimalist approach to social regulation. The period between 1957 and 1972 was a period of economic neo-liberalism and, particularly

---

19 Cf. Opinion of Advocate General Tesauro in Cases C-192-218/95 *Comateb* [1997] ECR I-165.

20 Case C-109/88 *Danfoss* [1989] ECR 3199.

21 Recently the Court confirmed these findings in the *Cadman* case, Case C-17/05 *Cadman* [2006] ECR I-9583. This decision seems to contradict its post-*Danfoss* case law on the burden of proof at the justification stage as well as the Directive on the burden of proof (Council of the European Union 1997).

22 Some key social policy cases in which the Court took the opportunity to develop principles ensuring the effectiveness and enforcement of EU law will be explored later in the chapter. However, for an extensive analysis of the case law, see Sciarra (2001), Blanpain (2001), Giubboni (2006), and specifically on gender equality see Ellis (2005), Schiek *et al.* (2007).

23 The concept of horizontal subsidiarity is explained in detail later in this chapter, in the context of the European Social Dialogue.

in the 1950s, the prevailing perspective was that the proper and effective functioning of the Common Market would not require Community intervention in the social field.

The Spaak Report (1956: 19–20 and 60–61), drawn up by the Foreign Ministers of the founding Member States, signed prior to the signing of the Treaty of Rome, embraced the view that only limited action in the social field would ensure the functioning of the Common Market and in particular that free movement of labour would ensure social prosperity. It did not consider harmonization necessary as it was thought at the time that any harmonization might be the result of, rather than a condition necessary prior to, the creation of the Common Market (Barnard 2006: 5). In this register, co-ordination of the common efforts of the Member States was all that was required of the EU Institutions (Hervey 1998: 8). However, even though the Spaak Report opposed general intervention in the social field, it did envisage that action would be necessary in certain areas, such as the relationship between salaries of men and women, working time, overtime and paid holidays, as well as measures concerning credit, to eliminate or correct the effects of specific distortions which might advantage or disadvantage certain branches of activity.

The Spaak Report was based on the Ohlin Report, drafted by a Committee of Experts of the International Labour Organization (ILO: 1956), which pursuant to the economic theory of comparative advantage maintained that countries adopting labour market measures on the basis of ILO standards did not have to harmonize social legislation transnationally in order to prevent unfair or distorted competition, the only exception being equal pay. According to Ohlin the system of national exchange rates would cancel out the apparent advantage of low-wage states, so avoiding a "race to the bottom".[24] Moreover, higher costs tended to go alongside higher productivity levels and thus differences between countries were not as significant as they seemed. In short, the market itself would ensure that conditions of competition were not distorted. This explained why there was no need for transnational harmonization.

The underlying theory of the creation and operation of the Common Market, therefore, was that economic integration would ensure an optimum allocation of resources, which in turn would guarantee an optimum rate of economic and thus social prosperity. In particular, the EC Treaty by guaranteeing the gradual integration of the Member States' economies was presumed to favour the effective protection of both economic and social rights in that it fostered the 'dynamics of material development which constitute the essential precondition for the fulfilment, in particular, of social redistribution rights' (Giubboni 2006: 98). Hence any recognition of fundamental rights in the Treaty of Rome was considered superfluous, and from a political perspective it would have been rather pernicious to do so because, at a time when the Community was still predominantly intergovernmental, a formal recognition of fundamental rights as such would have been perceived as a move towards centralized competence of the Community to the detriment of Member States' sovereignty (*ibid.*: 99). This also explains why the language of fundamental rights that gradually evolved and was articulated in the European Court's case law in a frequent dialogue with the national courts focused on social rights only marginally (de Búrca 1995). It essentially concerned first-generation rights (civil and political rights) the only exception being equal treatment between men and women and equal pay. The emergence of the Community social dimension developed outside the language of fundamental

---

24 This is a phenomenon whereby standards of social protection are lowered (or at least prevented from rising) in states with higher standards by increased competition from states with substantially lower social standards.

rights *stricto sensu*. Giubboni (2006: 100) argues that this asymmetrical protection of social rights *vis-à-vis* economic rights has been aggravated by the European Court's case law by 'exposing the social rights recognized by the Member States' legal systems more directly to the pressures of transnational economic liberalization, amplified by the tendency to accord fundamental rights status solely to economic freedoms, to a degree unknown to many national constitutions'.

Because of the link between EC social policy and the creation of the Common Market, in particular through the free movement of workers, EC social policy has been generally conceptualized with a focus on employment. As posited by Hervey (1998: 5) 'the most obvious justifications for taking social policy measures on a European level is to enhance labour mobility, and create a level playing field of competition for employers with the Member States'. She also presents two illuminating variations of this neo-liberal model (*ibid.*: 7–8). The first one may be found in the view that there is no need for European social intervention because high social standards are a "reward" for economic efficiency, not a rigidity imposed on the market. The second one may be found in the argument that EC social policy is detrimental to the long-term interests of the European Union, especially to the poorer Member States. In particular, EC social policy is seen as a form of protection for the richer Member States (Barnard 1996: 153–154). This may occur because the imposition of high social protection standards on poorer Member States may remove their competitive advantage in the Internal Market. This advantage derives from their comparatively low labour costs, which might provide an incentive for investment in those Member States. This incentive, however, might cease to exist if high social standards via European social regulation require higher wages or higher contributions to social security benefits. Furthermore, there was a strong conviction at the time that the existing ILO Conventions together with those adopted under the Council of Europe would ensure the protection and safeguard of both individual and collective social rights (Kenner 2003: 3).

Consequently, Articles 48–51 EEC (now Articles 39–42 EC; see also Article 3c EEC, now Article 3c EC) were inserted in the Treaty to secure the free movement of workers within the Community. In addition, Article 123 EEC (now Article 146 EC) provided for the establishment of a European Social Fund (ESF) with the aim of ensuring the mobility of labour and the adaptation of workers to industrial change, in particular, through vocational training and retraining (see also Article 3i EEC, now Article 3j EC). Because of the limited funds available and limited legal basis for setting up EEC structural policies, the ESF focused mainly on re-employment, retraining of redundant workers and their resettlement to areas where there was employment.

In line with the then prevailing economic neo-liberal approach, the social chapter of the Treaty, Title III (Articles 117–127 EEC, now Title XI, Articles 136–151 EC), contained for the most part exhortatory and programmatic social provisions, the only exception being Article 119 EEC (now Article 141 EC) on equal pay, due to the important role it had in facilitating the free movement of labour. Social policy measures, therefore, were mainly adopted under Article 100 EEC (Article 94 EC) and 235 EEC (Article 308 EC), which were the original Treaty provisions empowering the Council either to issue harmonization Directives in connection with the establishment of the Common Market or to adopt 'appropriate measures' where 'action by the Community should prove necessary to attain (within the completion of the Common Market) one of the objectives of the Community' and the Treaty had not provided the necessary powers.

Article 117 EEC merely repeated the aims laid out in the Preamble of the Treaty and it did not provide a legal basis for adopting social policy measures but made reference to approximation measures and this could be considered as an implicit reference to Article

100 EEC. Article 118 EEC instead contained a more specific provision and charged the Commission with the task of promoting close co-operation between Member States in certain areas of labour law and social policy such as employment and working conditions, basic and advanced vocational training, social security, prevention of occupational accidents and diseases, occupational hygiene, the right of association and collective bargaining between management and labour.

With regard to secondary legislation, a series of Regulations and Directives were adopted in order to promote the free movement of labour: Directive on the co-ordination of special measures concerning the movement and residence of foreign nationals which are justified on grounds of public policy, public security or public health (Council of the European Union 1964),[25] Directive on the harmonization of health and safety (Council of the European Union 1967), Regulation 1612/68 on the free movement of workers and their families (Council of the European Union 1968),[26] Directive 68/360 on the rights of residence (Council of the European 1968a)[27] and Regulation on the co-ordination of social security (Council of the European Union 1971).[28]

2.3 From social minimalism to social action, 1972–1980

Towards the end of the 1960s, the *laissez-faire* approach to social regulation came to an end due to growing dissatisfaction with the European integration project and social unrest across the Member States. It was recognized that the Community could no longer pursue exclusively economic objectives but should also focus on the social dimension of the European integration process.

The 1972 Declaration of the Heads of State and Government who met in Paris is considered to be the first important official document which signifies a shift towards social action at European level. In particular, in the Declaration it was stressed that Member States were committed to vigorous action in the social field as much as they were to the achievement of EMU and that the social partners should be involved in the economic and social decisions of the Community (EC Bulletin 1972: paras. 6, 19). This change of approach was due to the social unrest of 1968 and also to the economic recession caused by the oil shocks of the 1970s. It was felt at the time that the Community needed to show its "human face" and that it also aimed at tackling social problems as well as (and not only) pursuing the objectives of the Common Market. During the early 1970s it was realized that the 'neoliberal ideology of the European Economic Community was not actually delivering on its promises' (Barnard 2006: 9; Hervey 1998: 16–17) and that it was also necessary to develop the social dimension of the European integration project.

The first Social Action Programme for 1974–1976 (SAP) (Council of the European Union 1974) confirmed the Community's stronger commitment to social action. The SAP set out ambitious objectives such as full and better employment, the improvement of living and working conditions and a more favourable attitude towards industrial action. In this context, a European Regional Development Fund (ERDF) (Council of the European

---

25   This Directive has been repealed by the Citizenship Directive (Council of the European Union 2004).
26   This Regulation has been amended by Citizenship Directive (Council of the European Union 2004).
27   This Directive has been repealed by Citizenship Directive (Council of the European Union 2004).
28   Last amended in 2008 (European Parliament and the Council of the European Union 2008). See also Implementing Regulation on the application of social security schemes (Council of the European Union 1972) and the Regulation on the co-ordination of social security systems (European Parliament and the Council of the European Union 2004).

Union 1975a)[29] was established to address social and economic cohesion in the Community, and a number of employment protection Directives were enacted:[30] a Directive on the acquired rights of workers on the transfer of undertakings (Council of the European Union 1977),[31] a Directive on collective redundancies (Council of the European Union 1975a)[32] and a Directive protecting the rights of the workers on insolvency (Council of the European Union 1980). Kenner (2003: 31) posits that by relying on the use of Directives the European Institutions were able to provide a flexible set of standards acceptable to all the Member States. The partial harmonization and flexible approach to implementation helped to provide 'a more coherent rationale for introducing Community social policy' (*ibid.*). 'As integrationist tools the three Directives combined the technique of partial harmonization with flexible "forms" and "methods" of implementation implied in Article 189 EEC' (*ibid.*: 40).

In addition, a series of Directives were adopted in the area of sex discrimination such as equal pay (Council of the European Union 1975), equal treatment (Council of the European Union 1976), equality in social security (Council of the European Union 1979). The principle of equality was given new emphasis as a consequence of the ruling in *Defrenne v. Sabena (No. 2)*.[33] In this case the European Court gave horizontal direct effect to Article 119 EEC (now Article 141 EC) the consequence being that the equal pay right could be claimed not only against public authorities but also against other private parties. Kenner (2003: 46) argues that Article 119 EEC, read in conjunction with Article 5 EEC (now Article 10 EC), providing for the principle of solidarity, placed obligations upon and granted rights to individuals, thereby strengthening the horizontal direct effect of the equal pay right. Moreover, the *Worringham* case[34] made it clear that the European Court's interpretation of Article 119 EEC had extended its scope in order to go beyond the narrow criterion of equal work. In this case the European Court held that the Equal Pay Directive was essentially a definition of Article 119 EEC and thus by being part of the Treaty it not only imposed an obligation on Member States to ensure that national law complied with it but was also binding on private employers. The most salient aspect of this ruling was the ECJ's conceptualization of the Community's social objectives placing them on an equal footing with its economic central goals. This decision also entailed a shift towards a more human rights perspective. In particular, the European Court in pursuing its integrationist agenda (Streeck 1995: 399) recognized the market-correcting as well as market-making dimension of the social provisions of the Treaty of Rome (Barnard 2006: 53). In its landmark ruling the Court highlighted the twin objectives of Article 119 EEC and said that:[35]

> Article 119 EEC pursues a double aim. First . . . the aim of Article 119 EEC is to avoid a situation in which undertakings established in states which have actually implemented the principle of equal pay suffer a competitive disadvantage in

---

29 Last amended by a 2006 Regulation (Council of the European Union 2006) providing new rules for the period 2007–2013.

30 For a critical analysis of these Directives, see Kenner (2003: 26–42).

31 This Directive was amended in 1998 (Council of the European Union 1998a) and consolidated in 2001 (Council of the European Union 2001b).

32 Amended in 1992 (Council of the European Union 1992) and consolidated in 1998 (Council of the European Union 1998b).

33 See Case 43/75 [1976] ECR 455.

34 See Case 69/80 *Worringham and Humphries v. Lloyds Bank* [1981] ECR 767.

35 See *Defrenne (No. 2)*, paras. 9–10 and 12.

intra-Community competition as compared with undertakings established in states which have not yet eliminated discrimination against women workers as regards pay.

Second, this provision forms part of the social objectives of the Community, which is not merely an economic union, but is at the same time intended, by common action, to ensure social progress and seek the constant improvement of the living and working conditions of their peoples . . . This double aim, which is at once economic and social, shows that the principle of equal pay forms part of the foundation of the Community.

According to Kenner (2003: 47), in this ruling 'the Court revealed an understanding of the evolutionary development of Community social policy, moving on from purely negative integration and recognizing that the social policy provisions were as important as the economic ones . . . The Court's equalities jurisprudence has been at the forefront of this evolutionary process.'[36] In this context, it may be argued that the *Defrenne* ruling was contrary to the text of the Treaty and, ultimately, by extending the scope of the proviso contained in Article 119 EEC, it went against the will of the Member States. However Kahn-Freund (1960: 329) observes that Article 119 EEC did not confer any rights or impose any obligations on any individual based on the principle of equality and that it created only an obligation binding the Member States according to the rules of inter-national law.

Furthermore, it became clear subsequently that the principle of equality as a funda-mental right went beyond this provision. Hence Article 119 EEC should be seen as part of the implementation of this principle and not the source (Docksey 1991). In *Defrenne (No. 3)*[37] the European Court held that the right not to be discriminated against on grounds of sex was a fundamental right embodying as such one of the general principles of Community law.

These legislative measures and the favourable approach of the ECJ towards social intervention on a European level signified a shift in emphasis towards social action but they were still confined to labour market policies and were far from embracing a broader notion of social policy. Moreover, the early 1970s enthusiasm for social action at Community level was short-lived because of major economic challenges with which Member States were confronted (Hervey 1998: 18–19). Pressures to compete with the less regulated labour markets of the United States and Japan and to adapt to new technologies led to an increased focus on "flexibility" debates, with the parallel abandonment of social policies other than those that were centred on labour market measures. Hence, by the end of the 1970s, European social action had reached a situation of stagnation which was aggravated by the unanimity voting procedure in the Council required for the adoption of social measures under the general Treaty legal bases, Articles 100 and 235 EEC (now Articles 94 and 308 EC), ensuring that Member States retained complete control over EC social regulation.

2.4 A period of stagnation in social action, 1980–1986

The deregulatory policies and measures adopted in the social field in the early 1980s constituted a response to increased pressures of structural changes in global economy in the late 1970s and early 1980s. As a consequence the 1980s were years of re-embedded liberalism and thus stagnation or crisis for social action. The neo-liberal approach to the

---

36 By drawing on the *Defrenne (No. 2)* decision the Court held in *Jenkins* that the principle of equal pay applied to both direct and indirect discrimination, see Case 96/80 *Jenkins v. Kingsgate (Clothing Productions)* [1981] ECR 911; see also Case 170/84 *Bilka-Kaufhaus v. Weber von Hartz* [1986] ECR 1607.

37 See Case 149/77 *Defrenne v. Sabena (No. 3)* [1978] ECR 1365.

social sphere is illustrated by the preference for soft law instruments in the restructuring of the labour market (Nielsen and Szyszczak 1997: 28).[38] As a result, few legislative measures were adopted in this period. Two Directives promoted the equal treatment programme, one on occupational social security (Council of the European Union 1979) and one on equal treatment for the self-employed and their spouses (Council of the European Union 1986a). These were supplemented by soft law measures such as Action Programmes which set out goals to be achieved within a given period as well as providing a framework for developing Community policy. Soft law instruments were also employed in the area of vocational training (Council of the European Union 1976a) and disability (Council of the European Union 1981).

However, most of the Commission's legislative proposals for adopting Directives, for example on parental leave, reversal of the burden of proof in sex discrimination cases and atypical work were not passed by the Council and were to be adopted only in subsequent years during the more politically and economically favourable 1990s. The area where most legislative measures were enacted was health and safety at work and it was during this period that the first Framework Directive on the protection of workers from risks related to exposure to chemical, physical and biological agents at work was adopted (Council of the European Union 1980a).[39] This Framework Directive paved the way to other Directives in areas such as lead (Council of the European Union 1982),[40] asbestos (Council of the European Union 1983) and noise (Council of the European Union 1986b).

The early years of the 1980s were disappointing not only for the paucity of legislative measures in the social sphere. Soft law instruments were employed to avoid any further developments in the legislative arena and any binding commitment to social action. Soft law therefore became a means for ensuring social inaction rather than action and measures remained within the realm of rhetoric and exhortation. Conversely, as we shall see in the course of the book, post-Maastricht, and particularly with the Treaty of Amsterdam, the use of soft law becomes a way of expanding Community intervention in the social sphere in sensitive policy areas such as social exclusion and social protection and a means for introducing change. In particular, post-Maastricht, soft law is transformed into a new mode of policy making, becoming a valuable means for breathing new life into social regulation within the broader processes of the Community's decision-making system.

Despite the few legislative measures and the use of soft law to prevent further commitment to social intervention at Community level, the ECJ gave a series of bold rulings in social law cases which signified a shift towards a more favourable approach to the development of the Community's social dimension. In particular, through some of these cases the European Court developed important principles of EC law to ensure that the procedural and remedial laws of the Member States governing the enforcement of causes of action derived from Community law are effective, thereby strengthening the substantive protection afforded to individuals by EC social legislation.[41] In so doing, the European Court recognized that national courts have the task of determining procedural issues in accordance with their national legal system,[42] provided domestic rules are not less favourable than

---

38 E.g. Recommendation on a forty-hour working week and four weeks' annual paid holiday (Council of the European Union 1975b).

39 This Directive was replaced by another Directive in 1998 (Council of the European Union 1998c).

40 The Directive on lead has been replaced by another Directive in 1998 (Council of the European Union 1998c).

41 For a critique of the Court's approach to effective judicial protection and its principles, see Kilpatrick (2001).

42 See Case 33/76, *Rewe v. Landwirtschaftskammer Saarland* [1976] ECR 1989, para. 5; Case 45/76 *Comet v. Produktschap voor Siergewassen* [1976] ECR 2043, paras. 13 and 16.

those governing similar domestic actions (the principle of equivalence)[43] and that they do not render excessively difficult the exercise of rights conferred by Community law (the principle of effectiveness).[44] Ultimately, therefore, 'the effectiveness of the protection afforded to the individual under Community law depends to a large degree on the robustness of national legal and administrative procedures' (Kenner 2003: 51). Moreover, in *Johnston*[45] the Court held that the requirement of judicial control provided for in Article 6 of the Equal Treatment Directive (Council of the European Union 1976) embodied a general principle of law. In the *Marshall* case,[46] even though the Court rejected the horizontal direct effect to Directives,[47] it gave a broad notion of public body in order to broaden the purview of effective judicial protection afforded to individuals. The Court further strengthened the protection of EC social rights in the *Von Colson* case,[48] where it not only held that Article 6 of the Equal Treatment Directive required that the sanction chosen by the Member State against a discriminatory act must guarantee real judicial protection[49] but also took the opportunity to develop the principle of indirect effect according to which Member States – namely, national courts – are obliged, pursuant to Article 5 EEC, to take account of provisions of Community law in interpreting provisions of national law, both those which implement EC provisions, and others.[50] As we have seen in Chapter 2, the duty of consistent interpretation has particular significance for the effect of soft law measures on national legal orders. In effect with *Von Colson* the European Court developed a Community method of construction which in practice could override national constitutional norms as well as established judicial principles such as the doctrine of precedent (Docksey and Fitzpatrick 1991: 117–118).

The objective of ensuring that Community law was effective in the national legal systems led to the European Court's seminal decision on state liability in the *Francovich (No. 1)* case.[51] The European Court ruled that in order to ensure the full effectiveness of Community law, and in accordance with Article 5 EEC (now Article 10 EC), Member States should take all appropriate measures to fulfil their Community law obligations, the state was liable for 'loss and damage caused to individuals as a result of breaches of Community law'.[52] However, while this principle is certainly of great importance for ensuring effective judicial protection, it is not devoid of problems. As stated by Advocate General Van Gerven in his Opinion in *Marshall (No. 2)*:[53]

---

43 An extension of the principle of non-discrimination provided for in Article 12 EC.

44 See Case 33/76, *Rewe v. Landwirtschaftskammer Saarland* [1976] ECR 1989; Case C-246/96 *Magorrian and Cunningham* [1997] ECR I-7153, para. 37; Case C-352/96, *Levez v. T. H. Jennings (Harlow Pools)* [1998] ECR I-7835, para. 18.

45 See Case 222/84 *Johnston v. Chief Constable of the RUC* [1986] ECR 1651.

46 See Case 152/84 *Marshall v. Southampton and South West Hampshire Area Health Authority (Teaching)*, [1986] ECR 723.

47 As Kenner explains (2003: 53) while the Equal Treatment Directive (Council of the European Union 1976) was of general application as part of the principle of equality, it was not founded upon Article 119 EEC and was therefore derived from the broad social policy objectives in Article 117 EEC and adopted by virtue of Article 235 EEC (now Article 308 EC). This is why the direct effect of the Directive was considered as being only vertical.

48 See Case 14/83 *Von Colson and Kaumann v. Land Nordrhein Westfälen* [1984] ECR 1891.

49 However, there is no directly effective right to a remedy arising from Article 6, *ibid.*, para. 35.

50 See Case C-106/89, *Marleasing v. La Comercial Alimentation* [1990] ECR I-4135.

51 See Joined Cases C-6 and 9/90, *Francovich (No. 1) and Bonifaci v. Italian Republic* [1991] ECR I-5357.

52 See *Francovich (No. 1)*, para. 35.

53 See Opinion of Advocate General Van Gerven in Case C-271/91 *Marshall v. Southampton and South West Hampshire Area Health Authority (Teaching) (No. 2)* [1993] ECR I-4367, para. 12.

[State liability] does not remedy the fact that individuals who are operating in a Member State which implemented the Directive correctly and are therefore bound by the obligations . . . are disadvantaged in comparison with individuals (perhaps their competitors) who are operating in a Member State which has not yet correctly implemented the Directive.

Further, from an employee's perspective it is far more desirable to have an employer respecting the substantive right provided for by Community law enforceable through a direct contractual claim rather than via a non-contractual procedural action against the state given that, *inter alia*, a domestic judicial system may not guarantee a successful state liability claim (Ryan 2000: 155). The effectiveness of national judicial remedies has been central in the procedural protection conferred by the Equality Directives. Originally, Article 6 of the Equal Pay Directive (Council of the European Union 1975) required Member States to ensure that the principle of equal pay was applied and that adequate means would be made available to ensure the respect of this principle. Article 2 of the same Directive required Member States to ensure those who consider themselves wronged by the failure to apply the principle of equal pay to pursue their claims by judicial process. This Directive has now been replaced by the Recast Directive (Council of the European Union 2006a), Article 17 of which requires Member States to ensure that, after every possible recourse to other competent authorities, judicial and/or administrative procedures for the enforcement of the Directive are available for cases concerning the failure to apply the principle of equal treatment. In addition, Article 18 of this Directive also requires Member States to introduce adequate measures ensuring real and effective compensation or reparation in a way which is dissuasive and proportionate to the damage suffered.

2.5 The Delors Commission, the Single European Act and the 1989 Community Social Charter: some first attempts at social action renewal

The legislative impasse in the social sphere characterizing the early 1980s terminated with the appointment of Jacques Delors as President of the Commission. Delors was a strong supporter of the creation of the Internal Market, which he considered to be a means through which to pursue European political integration. He also envisaged social regulation and, in particular, the creation of an *espace sociale européenne* as being a *sine qua non* for the completion of the Single Market programme by the end of 1992.[54] In his speech to the European Parliament he maintained that (EC Bulletin 1986: 9):

> The creation of a vast economic area, based on market and business co-operation, is inconceivable – I would say unattainable – without some harmonization of social legislation. Our ultimate aim must be the creation of a European social area.

---

54 In 1985 the European Commission submitted to the European Council its White Paper on the completion of the Internal Market, which set out a timetable for the measures required for the completion of the Internal Market by the end of 1992, at the very latest; see European Commission (1985).

In Delors's view,[55] developing a social dimension to the Internal Market was necessary to ensure its smooth functioning and also to prevent the practice of "social dumping", which gives a competitive advantage to companies and businesses through lower standards of social protection or low wage costs rather than through fair competition based on productivity levels.[56] Delors believed that, without some degree of social harmonization, employers in Member States with high levels of social protection and high wage costs would be in a situation of competitive disadvantage in comparison with the employers of Member States with lower wage costs and lower levels of social protection. This in turn would lead to industrial relocation and to lower wage costs and social protection generally to reduce competitive disadvantage as well as, in the longer term, unemployment (Hervey 1998: 10). To this end the Commission issued a report, *The Social Dimension of the Internal Market* (European Commission 1988), which analyzed the negative impact of the Internal Market on Member States' social systems, including the problem of "social dumping". The report identified two possible but alternative approaches to social regulation: a centralized approach centred on harmonization and a decentralized one based on flexibility (Kenner 2003: 77–78). The first approach favoured the use of binding legal instruments to achieve harmonization. The report found that although this method could be effective in some instances it was lacking in flexibility, did not promote innovation, limited the autonomy of the social partners and did not give due consideration to the diversity of Member States' industrial relations and labour market systems. With regard to the second approach, the report maintained that by favouring social minimization – with the exception of such areas as health and safety where harmonization was considered the desirable form of regulation – it respected Member States' diversity, it promoted innovation and greater autonomy of the social partners while ensuring a certain degree of social intervention. At the same time, the report found that this approach also had its limitations because of certain areas of social law and policy requiring more than the mere definition of minimum Community rules or standards to prevent discrimination, mistreatment and abuse. The report, therefore, suggested a "middle ground" approach that would benefit from the strengths of both approaches and give equal consideration to both the economic and social objectives of the Community. According to the Commission this could be achieved by way of creating a "European industrial relations area" which would provide a platform for dialogue between management and labour. This provided the template for the subsequent European Social Dialogue established with the SPA annexed to the EC Treaty. The Commission also suggested a range of methods such as harmonization where necessary, convergence of social standards in areas such as social protection, vocational training and public health and the adoption of a body of basic social provisions at Community level. In broader terms, a tension between two extreme positions (which to date has remained unresolved) underscored this report:

> one which suggests that it is disparities between national rules which create impediments to the establishment and functioning of the market (such disparities may, depending on the context, be seen as either barriers to free movement or distortions

55 Delors's view of social intervention may be associated with the social democratic tradition of French socialism, according to which social policy is necessary to "humanize" the market in order to ensure fairness and distributive justice. Hence the focus of the Community should no longer be exclusively on economic efficiency but on creating a European social market economy.

56 For analysis and comment on social dumping, see Barnard (1999: 503) and Barnard (2009).

of competition), and a second which is tolerant of the existence of national regulatory diversity.

(Syrpis 2007: 49)

Despite the aforementioned shift in emphasis, subsequent developments in the European integration process did not signify a major change in social action. In particular, the 1986 SEA was still based on economic neo-liberalist premises according to which the effective functioning of the market would ensure both economic and social prosperity. The Cecchini Report (1988) emphasized the importance of the Single Market programme in terms of the benefits it could bring to employment levels. Hence few social provisions were inserted in the Treaty of Rome. Article 7(2) EEC (now Article 12(2) EC) was amended in order to change the voting procedures of the Council to qualified majority voting (QMV) and to increase the involvement of the European Parliament with the introduction of the co-operation procedure (Article 189c EEC, now Article 252 EC). A new Article 8a EEC (Article 14 EC) was added which referred to the free movement of persons as one of the fundamental principles of the Internal Market. New Articles 130a–130e EEC (Articles 158–162 EC) were inserted to strengthen economic and social cohesion and thus in 1988 the Community's Structural Funds were reformed (Council of the European Union 1988a). The aim of these reforms was to ensure the adoption of structural measures on the basis of five objectives: (1) promoting development and structural adjustment of the regions whose development is lagging behind; (2) converting the regions, frontier regions or parts of regions (including employment areas and urban communities) seriously affected by industrial decline; (3) combating long-term unemployment; (4) facilitating occupational integration of young people; (5) speeding up adjustment of agricultural structures and promoting the development of rural areas; they also led to the creation of the European Agricultural Guidance and Guarantee Fund (EAGGF). However, the most important provisions introduced by the SEA were Articles 118a (now Article 137 EC) and 118b EEC (now Article 139 EC). Article 118a EEC extended QMV and the co-operation procedure to measures concerning the health and safety of workers, although matters 'relating to the rights and interests of employed persons'[57] still required unanimity in the Council. Article 118a(1) EEC provided for the general use of Directives and required that Directives adopted in the area of health and safety should contain 'minimum requirements for gradual implementation, having regard to the conditions and technical rules obtaining in each of the Member States'. The same article also contained a "safeguard" for ensuring that Member States would still retain the power to maintain or introduce more stringent measures for the protection of working conditions compatible with the Treaty (Article 118a(3) EEC). Article 118a EEC was the legal basis of several important Directives in the area of labour law such as the second framework Directive on the Safety and Health of Workers at Work (Council of the European Union 1989).[58] As Kenner (2003: 100) aptly says, one important feature of this Directive is that 'it represents a flexible guideline method of Community legislation, laying down general objectives and obligations on employers and workers, while leaving as much scope as possible for the application of detailed rules at the appropriate level'. Hence the object of the Directive was to facilitate the adoption of further "daughter Directives" based on Article 118a EEC. In the *Working Time Directive*

---

57 See Article 100a(2) EEC (now Article 95 EC).
58 It was amended first by a Regulation in 2003 (European Parliament and Council of the European Union 2003) and by a Directive in 2007 (European Parliament and Council of the European Union 2007).

case,[59] the United Kingdom sought the annulment of the Working Time Directive (Council of the European Union 1993a),[60] arguing *inter alia* that Article 118a of the Treaty was not the appropriate legal basis as the Directive dealt with the functioning of the Internal Market, the proper legal basis being, therefore, either Article 100 EC (now Article 94 EC) or Article 235 EC (now Article 308 EC). The ECJ held that the concepts of working environment, safety and health in Article 118a EEC should not be interpreted in a restrictive manner and they included all aspects and factors, physical or otherwise, which would be capable of affecting the health and safety of the worker. It followed that since the main objective of the measure in question was the protection of the health and safety of the worker Article 118a EEC was the appropriate legal basis.

Article 118b EEC aimed at developing a 'dialogue between management and labour at European level', known as the European Social Dialogue. The idea of creating a forum at European level for management and labour to discuss social issues was strongly supported by Delors. He considered it to be an important facet of the completion of the Internal Market, as it would enable Member States to adapt to structural change. Two working parties made up of European inter-sectoral social partners, that is, representatives of employers' organizations – the Union of Industrial and Employers' Confederations of Europe (UNICE) and the European Centre of Employers and Enterprises providing Public services (CEEP) – and representatives of workers' organizations – the European Trade Union Confederation (ETUC) – were set up: one working party was entrusted with the task of looking at the implications of new technology and work while the other working group was entrusted with the task of examining effective employment and macroeconomic measures. These working parties were known as the Val Duchesse talks, from the name of the place where the meetings took place. While these talks provided a valuable forum for discussion, few concrete initiatives were taken because of strong disagreement in relation to the use and status of collective agreements at European level. Hence in the period between 1986 and 1992 nine opinions, mainly declaratory in nature, were issued in relation to vocational training, new technology and adaptability of workers to industrial change.[61]

One of the reasons which may explain the foregoing limitations is that the provision contained in Article 118a EEC was not very clear in relation to a series of important matters: the definition of the process in the context of which the social partners deliberated and adopted decisions on social issues; the extent to which the parties to the collective agreements envisaged in Article 118a EEC were to be considered representative of management and labour nationally (both inter-sectoral and sectoral levels) and the nature of the decisions taken by these parties. Another reason is the imbalance in power position between management and labour at European level: European employers' organizations have no particular interest in European regulation on social issues whereas labour, on the other hand, does not have the bargaining power to get management to the negotiating table on issues it considers important (Smismans 2008: 165).

The paucity of social provision introduced by the SEA in the Treaty of Rome was compensated by the signing of the Community Charter of Fundamental Social Rights of Workers (hereafter, the Social Charter) by all the Member States (with the exception of the United Kingdom) during the 1989 Strasbourg European Council meeting. The Social Charter at the time significantly strengthened the social dimension of the Community.

---

59 See Case C-84/94 *United Kingdom v. Council* (*Working Time Directive*) [1996] ECR I-1705.
60 Amended by a Directive of the European Parliament and of the Council of the European Union (2000).
61 For a list of these opinions, see European Commission (1993: Annex IV, 100).

Under this Charter the Community is obliged to provide for the protection of the fundamental social rights of workers under the following headings:

- Freedom of movement (Articles 1–3).
- Freedom to choose and engage in an occupation and to be fairly remunerated (Articles 4–6).
- Improvement of living and working conditions (Articles 7–9).
- Social protection (Article 10).
- Freedom of association and collective bargaining (Articles 11–14).
- Vocational training (Article 15).
- Equal treatment for men and women (Article 16).
- Information, consultation and participation for workers (Articles 17–18).
- Protection of health and safety at the workplace (Article 19).
- Protection of children and young persons (Articles 20–23).
- Protection of the elderly (Articles 24–25).
- Protection of the disabled (Article 26).
- Member States' action (implementation) (Articles 27–30).

The Charter has no legally binding effect, as, in the words of the Preamble, it was a 'solemn proclamation of fundamental social rights'. However, the ECJ has used it as an interpretative guide in litigation concerned with social and labour rights.[62] The main limitation of the Social Charter is that the fundamental social rights that it aims to protect are still conceived in the framework of the Internal Market programme and they are associated with the free movement of persons/workers provision rather than being considered as embodying a concept of "social citizenship".[63] The Social Charter, therefore, protects workers *in primis* and does not grant rights to those citizens who are not workers. Moreover, the Social Charter is firmly based around issues of employment rather than a broader notion of social policy (Freedland 1996: 278–279).[64]

At the Strasbourg European Council meeting it was also agreed that the protection of the fundamental social rights listed in the Charter would be ensured through the adoption of the Social Charter Action Programme and that measures adopted pursuant to this Action programme would be based on Treaty provisions (European Commission 1989). The implementation of the Action Programme, however, was not as successful as had been expected. Out of the forty-seven proposals made by the Commission there were only seventeen Directives, of which there were only six main labour law Directives outside the area of health and safety. These were:

- Directive on an employer's obligation to inform employees of the conditions applicable to the contract or employment relationship (Council of the European Union 1991).
- Directive on the approximation of the laws of the Member States relating to collective redundancies (Council of the European Union 1975b).[65]

---

62 See e.g. Joined Cases C-397/01 to C-403/01 *Pfeiffer v. Deutches Rotes Kreuz* [2004] ECR I-0000, para. 91.
63 Marshall (1975) defined social citizenship as 'the whole range from the right to a modicum of economic welfare and security to the right to share to the full in the social heritage and to live the life of a civilised being according to the standards prevailing in society'.
64 For comment and critique, see Bercusson (1990) and Silvia (1991).
65 Amended by a Directive in 1992 (Council of the European Union 1992) and subsequently consolidated in 1998 (Council of the European Union 1998b).

- Directive relating to measures to encourage improvements in the safety and health of pregnant workers and women workers who have recently given birth and women who are breastfeeding (Council of the European Union 1992a).
- Directive on certain aspects of the organization of working time (Council of the European Union (1993a).[66]
- Directive on the protection of young people at work (Council of the European Union 1994).
- Directive on the posting of workers in the framework of the provision of services (European Parliament and the Council of the European Union 1996).

The main reason explaining the weak implementation of the Action Programme is that the few social provisions contained in the Treaty could not provide a sound legal basis for a social programme at Community level. Moreover, the lack of political will of the Member States prevailing at the time made it difficult to adopt social measures at European level.

The period in between the mid-1980s and the beginning of the 1990s pre-Maastricht has been considered by labour lawyers as being either a period of dynamism during which the "social" gradually started to gather momentum or, on the contrary, and in a more pessimistic vein, as being a period of minor significant changes in European social regulation. These conflicting views are based on different interpretations of the measures adopted in that period and on the predilection for a typology of legal instruments which fell in the broad category of soft law. In his analysis of the legal instruments used in this period, Kenner (2003: 127) shows how soft law became a 'tool for furthering and deepening European integration by building upon and around the legal *acquis* without directly creating strict legal obligations'.[67] Moreover, in order to evaluate the impact of the Community Social Charter, the Action Programme and other non-binding measures, Kenner (2003: 128) categorizes the use of soft law in the field of social policy into four groups:

- Joint institutional resolutions or declarations that have the aim of fostering social activism.
- Recommendations that have the aim of maintaining the momentum of existing programmes or of reactivating unfulfilled programmes.
- Recommendations, resolutions and memoranda designed to supplement hard law measures or to bring specific policy areas on the Community agenda.
- Broad statements of political principle regarding policy areas where there are no legislative proposals in the near future.

The Social Charter and the Action Programme may be said to fall within the first category whereas the soft law measures that followed may be said to fall within the other three broad groups. Despite the declaratory nature and intent of the Social Charter and the few legislative measures that were adopted, it may be argued that the Social Charter nevertheless served as a catalyst for action and it represented an important instrument in furthering the protection of fundamental social rights. The emphasis on fundamental rights was an important step forward in the promotion of rights within the Community and thus a continuum may be traced between the 1989 Social Charter, running through the Treaty

---

66 Amended by a Directive in 2000 (European Parliament and of the Council 2000).
67 For an analysis of the Community Social Charter as a soft law instrument and its contribution to the social dimension of the Community, see Kenner (2003: 126–131 and 200–212).

of Amsterdam (with the reference to fundamental social rights in Article 136 EC) and the Charter of Fundamental Rights of the European Union (*ibid.*: 131).[68]

Another important feature of this period is the strong activist role of the Commission in ushering in social action by way of employing soft law instruments, chiefly in situations of legislative deadlock due to the lack of political will on the part of the Member States. The proactive role of the Commission was also important in providing the grounds for establishing the European Social Dialogue through the Val Duchesse talks.

Hence the years prior to the ratification of the Treaty of Maastricht were important in providing the basis for the significant changes that were to come in the years that followed. In particular, during this period the Community was no longer considered solely as an international organization driven purely by the pursuit of economic objectives but also as a quasi-state polity, with the European Parliament becoming a stronger player in the legislative arena through the co-operation procedure. In this context, soft law became a key tool for fostering and deepening European integration and Community intervention in new policy areas with the participation of new actors such as the social partners. All of these features will acquire visibly more importance in the period starting with the Treaty of Maastricht.

3 The Maastricht Treaty on European Union and the shift in Community social policy making

In the early 1990s, the need for a certain level of social policy regulation at European level became an important Community objective (Trubek and Mosher 2003: 30–31). By then the Community was grappling with major economic challenges affecting most of the Member States (Barnard 2006: 15–16). These were caused by the structural transformation of the economy involving the internationalization of corporations and the concentration of the labour force away from agriculture and traditional industries towards services. These structural economic changes caused problems of industrial adjustment (such as for example a mismatch between supply and demand for skills) and revealed how obsolete West European welfare states had become. In turn, post-industrial economic development led to a series of economic crises and major recessions in the early 1980s and again in the early 1990s, with high levels of unemployment. These economic changes were accompanied by a general move to the right in national government policy making, reflected by a shift in the economic balance of power away from employees and trade unions and towards employers and managers.

The Treaty on European Union with its major amendments to the EC Treaty was the Community's response to these trends. At the end of the 1980s, and following the Hanover European Council meeting in June 1988, a Committee for the Study of Economic and Monetary Union was set up, chaired by the President of the Commission, Jacques Delors (1989). The Committee recommended a three-stage process for attaining EMU: (1) closer co-ordination of national economic and monetary policies; (2) the creation of a European Central Bank; and (3) a European single currency to replace national currencies. To this end new provisions should be inserted in the Treaty focusing on major institutional reform at European level.

The creation of EMU had a major impact on welfare and labour market policies, as

---

68　On the EU Charter of Fundamental Rights, see further in Chapter 5.

it required a tightening of Member States' public expenditure and fundamental structural reforms at domestic level. The economic emphasis of the European integration project was causing growing dissatisfaction across most of the Member States. Delors, therefore, suggested the adoption of policies in the social field to counterbalance the impact of EMU on Member States' socio-economic systems. In particular, Delors envisaged the introduction of a Social Chapter in the Treaty and the establishment of a macroeconomic European strategy to co-ordinate national policies to combat unemployment and social exclusion.

When the Treaty on European Union was signed in 1992 the Heads of State first agreed to reform the Community in order to establish a political union, improving the functioning of its Institutions and regulating new areas such as justice and home affairs and a common foreign and security policy which signalled a move towards expanding the external dimension of the Community. This led to the creation of a new legal entity with the establishment of the European Union in the form of a three pillar-base structure: the first "pillar" would correspond to the European Community – the supranational pillar of the Union – whereas the other two pillars would concern home and foreign affairs and would be left to intergovernmental co-operation. The Maastricht Treaty was also important because it introduced provisions on EMU in the Treaty of Rome (Articles 102a–109m EC, now Articles 98–124 EC) with the transfer of monetary and exchange rate policy to the European Community,[69] and, at the same time, it started a process of gradual expansion of EC social competence to be completed with the Treaty of Amsterdam. Besides these important changes, the Treaty of Maastricht was also significant for the new method of governance it put in place, particularly in the context of economic policies. Under the new provisions an iterative and co-ordination process was established, with Member States required to conduct their economic policies in accordance with the objectives set out in the "soft" BEPGs laid down by the European Council and within a system of multilateral surveillance, combining intergovernmental and supranational elements of policy making. As we shall see, this mode of governance provided the blueprint for the European Employment Strategy set up with the Treaty of Amsterdam.

The further enlargement of the Community and the favourable political scenario for expanding EC competence in the social sphere[70] led to a gradual departure from the neo-liberal approach which had prevailed until then and the EEC Treaty was officially renamed the European Community (EC) Treaty. However, because of the strong opposition of the United Kingdom to the insertion of a new Social Chapter in the Treaty, a Social Policy Agreement (SPA) and a Social Policy Protocol (SPP) were annexed to the EC Treaty (which taken together formed the European Union's Social Chapter).[71] Considered by many legal scholars as being one of the first examples of a two-speed Europe (Shaw 1994; Barnard 2006: 17), the United Kingdom reserved itself an opt-out from the Social Chapter as well as from the provisions on EMU. The United Kingdom's opposition to increasing the scope of Community intervention in the area of social policy also explains why no direct reference was made in the Treaty on the European Union to the European Social Charter or to the international standards laid down by the ILO.

A significant amendment to the Treaty of Rome made by the Treaty of Maastricht was

---

69 For a detailed analysis, see Chapter 3.
70 In particular Sweden, Finland and Austria, which officially became Member States on 1 of January 1995, were in favour of increasing the EU role in the field of social policy.
71 On the legal status of the Protocol and Agreement, see Watson (1993), Weiss (1992) and Bercusson (1994); Kenner (2003) 223–226.

the insertion of a new Part Two introducing the concept of Citizenship of the Union (Articles 8–8e EC, now Articles 17–22 EC). Any person holding the nationality of one of the Member States would also be a Union citizen. This legal concept was defined according to a set of positive (and chiefly political) rights: the right to free movement (Article 8a EC); the right to stand and to vote in municipal elections and elections to the European Parliament (Article 8b EC) and the right to diplomatic or consular protection by any of the Member States in a Third State; the right to petition the European Parliament and the right to apply to the European Ombudsman (Article 8d EC). The concept of EU citizenship, as defined in the Treaty, has been criticized for not including a human rights dimension, for not embracing a concept of "EU social citizenship" and participatory forms of citizenship. The rights to which Union citizens were entitled under the new title were mainly a consolidation of existing rights attached to the freedom of movement along with some limited political rights (Everson 1995; Weiler 1996).

3.1 Subsidiarity, the Social Chapter and the generalization of the rules and procedures of the European Social Dialogue

3.1.1 Subsidiarity

Subsidiarity is both a political and a legal principle that was introduced in the Treaty of Rome to address matters relating to Community competence and the exercise of power between the Member States and the European Institutions, and it should be seen as part of the Maastricht Treaty's institutional reform package.[72] As the Community was growing bigger in size and in power (and significantly through the ECJ's judicial activism) the inclusion in the EC Treaty of a set of principles to help identify the appropriate level of decision making had become a necessary requirement for the Community's effective functioning and, from a political point of view, for its very own existence. As de Búrca (1999) posits, subsidiarity should also be 'understood as part of a language which attempts to articulate and to mediate ... some of the fundamental questions of political authority, government and governance which arise in an increasingly interlocking and interdependent world'. It should also be understood against the backcloth of decreasing centrality of the nation-state, the increase of legal sites and legal pluralism and the blurring of the public–private divide which were examined in detail in Chapter 2.

A new Article 3b EC (now Article 5 EC), therefore, was inserted in the Treaty of Rome defining the concept of subsidiarity (para. 2) to be applied to fields of Community law characterized by shared or supporting competence.[73] The rationale was simple: public powers should normally be located at the lowest tier of government where they can be exercised effectively. This principle applied and applies to most issues of social policy and thus the insertion of Article 3b EC constituted a significant change for EU social intervention, for both the Member States and the Community Institutions. In 1992 the Commission issued a Communication to the Council and the European Parliament explaining the application of subsidiarity (European Commission 1992). The Communication bluntly stated that the powers of the Member States represented the rule whereas the powers of

---

72 There is an extensive literature on the principle of subsidiarity. See, among others, Estella (2002), Wyatt (2003) and Ippolito (2007).

73 Two other key principles were included in the same article: conferred competence and proportionality; paragraphs 1 and 3 respectively of Article 3b EC.

the European Institutions were the exception and the functions transferred to the Community were only those that the Member States at various levels of decision making could not perform satisfactorily. The "legitimate need" requirement was stressed also in the Presidency Conclusions of the European Council in Edinburgh in December 1992 (European Council 1992: Part II, para. i). In particular, the Edinburgh European Council issued another Communication on the definition and application of the principle of subsidiarity and a three-stage test was to be applied to new and existing EC legislation. First, has the Community the competence to act? Second, if so, is it impossible to achieve the desired result at national level? Third, if measures are not attainable at national level, what is the minimum Community intervention necessary?

The Edinburgh European Council also called for the Commission to submit to the European Council and the European Parliament an annual report on the application of Article 3b EC.[74] In 1993, due to the vagueness of its meaning, the Commission issued another report explaining once again the purpose and application of the subsidiarity principle (European Commission 1993d). Kenner (2003: 231) argues that subsidiarity was defined somewhere in between the concept of attribution of powers and proportionality.

It was hotly debated, in the early days following the insertion of Article 3b EC, whether the principle of subsidiarity was justiciable (Toth 1994). These doubts have subsequently been dissipated by the European Court's case law.[75] Initially the principle of subsidiarity was designed to regulate the distribution of competence between the Community and the Member States – so-called "vertical subsidiarity" – subsequently, and with the creation of the "European Social Dialogue", it has been extended to cover also the allocation of competence between actors operating at the same level of policy making – so-called "horizontal subsidiarity". More generally, the term "horizontal" is based on the premise that the European Union has become a multi-layered system where tasks can be assigned to different actors at the same level of policy making. Horizontal subsidiarity has a wider meaning, therefore, than that envisaged by Article 5 EC, which refers exclusively to the relationship between Member States and the European Community (Barnard 1999: 493).

3.1.2 The Social Chapter

The bulk of the new social provisions were placed in a separate protocol and agreement annexed to the EC Treaty. However, important amendments were made to the Treaty itself which together with the Community Social Charter and the 1990s White and Green Papers of the Commission[76] signified a change in the way of conceiving of the social with an emphasis given to high levels of employment and social protection, that is, a gradual shift from a purely labour market perspective to one comprising employment creation.

In the White Paper on *Growth, Competitiveness and Employment* (European Commission 1993a), considered as the watershed document for the Community's approach to unemployment, the Commission provided an array of solutions to tackle unemployment

---

74 These reports have subsequently been entitled "Better Lawmaking".
75 E.g. Case C-84/94 *United Kingdom v. Council of the European Union* [1996] ECR I-5755; Case C-376/98 *Germany v. European Parliament and Council* [2000] ECR I-8419; Case C-377/98 *Kingdom of the Netherlands v. European Parliament and Council* [2001] ECR I-7079. Case C-491/01 *The Queen v. Secretary of State for Health, ex parte British American Tobacco* [2002] ECR I-11453; Joined Cases C-154/04 and C-155/04, *The Queen, on the application of Alliance for Natural Health and Others, v. Secretary of State for Health and National Assembly for Wales* [2005] ECR I-6451.
76 These Green and White Papers aimed at developing consensus building based on shared values to create a "European social model"; this is discussed further below in this chapter.

and strategies to enhance job creation. This White Paper was particularly significant since it not only launched an overall debate on the co-ordination of economic and employment policies at European level, but also brought the issue of employment on to the Community's top agenda. The White Paper was also innovatory in the way that it aimed at reforming labour markets by introducing flexibility and promoting atypical forms of work and drew on the conclusions of the Green Paper *European Social Policy* (European Commission 1993), which called for new responses and measures to address technological and structural change in world economy.

Article 2 of the Treaty of Rome, which defines the tasks of the Community, was amended to include high levels of employment and social protection, the raising of the standard of living and quality of life, economic and social cohesion and solidarity among the Member States. Title III of Part Three of the EC Treaty became Title VIII of Part Three and was renamed "Social Policy, Education, Vocational Training and Youth". Articles 117–127 EC remained the same but Article 123 EC extended the scope of the European Social Fund to facilitate the adaptation of workers to industrial changes, in particular through vocational training and retraining. In addition, Article 125 EC was amended in order to simplify the rules regarding the European Social Fund and to introduce co-operation as the main legislative procedure with the aim of facilitating the free movement of workers and improving their employment opportunities within the Internal Market. In a new chapter entitled "Education, Vocational Training and Youth", Articles 126–127 EC introduced a distinction between education and vocational training, the latter being given particular emphasis in the context of the Internal Market.

These provisions assigned a supplementary role to the European Institutions and Member States retained strong decision-making powers in these fields of social policy. The Treaty on European Union also strengthened economic and social cohesion in Articles 3(j) EC and Article 2 EC and provided a new Chapter XIV (Articles 130a–130e EC; now Articles 158–162 EC). The essential aim of the Community's economic and social cohesion policy remained the same,[77] although the Structural Funds were subject to review (European Commission 1992a, b, c) and a sixth objective was added to the Structural Funds' existing objectives.[78]

Apart from these changes to the Social Policy Title, the bulk of the Chapter on Social Policy was inserted in the Social Policy Protocol and Agreement. The SPP authorized the then eleven Member States 'to have recourse to the Institutions, procedures and mechanisms of the Treaty for the purposes of taking among themselves and applying as far as they are concerned the acts and decisions required for giving effect to the [Social Policy Agreement]'. The Protocol was considered legally binding and in accordance with the general rules of public international law and Article 239 EC (now Article 311 EC) was considered as an integral part of the Treaty of Rome.[79]

The main purpose of the SPA was to implement the Social Charter (Kenner 2003: 236). The SPA also served three other purposes. First it redefined and extended the shared social policy objectives of the Community and the Member States. Second, it provided a set of procedural rules for the adoption of legislation and in so doing it broadened the scope of

---

77 Article 130d EC (now Article 161 EC) was amended and it required the Council of Ministers to establish a Cohesion Fund by 1994, which would contribute to projects in the fields of environment and trans-European networks on transport infrastructure.

78 Objective 6 was added following the accession of Finland and Sweden – the development of the Arctic regions.

79 For comment and analysis, see below, note 87.

Community competence in the social field as well as increasing the areas in which measures could be taken by QMV (as part of the co-operation procedure under the then Article 189c EC). Hence measures concerning working conditions, information and consultation of workers, equal opportunities and equal treatment at work and social inclusion could be adopted by QMV (Article 2(1) and (2), now Article 137 (1) and (2) EC). Third, it provided a better definition of the role of the social partners in the EC social decision-making system (*ibid.*). The key provisions were to be found in Articles 1–4. Article 1 established the shared competence of the Community and the Member States in the area of social policy and emphasis was given to the objectives of promoting employment, improving living and working conditions and social protection, although it continued to subordinate social policy to the economic objectives of the Treaty. Article 2(1) emphasized that the decision-making power of the Member States in the area of social policy should be the rule whereas Community powers should be the exception. Article 2(2) provided that Directives should be adopted on the basis of the co-operation procedure.[80] However, because of the United Kingdom's opt-out the voting procedure within the Council of Eleven was changed so that decisions could be reached with fifty-two out of seventy-six votes instead of sixty-two out of eighty-six.[81] Certain areas of social policy were subject to the unanimity rule, with the consultation of the European Parliament. These fields were:[82]

- Improvement of the working environment to protect workers' health and safety.
- The information and consultation of workers.
- Equality between men and women in labour market matters.
- Integration of persons excluded from the labour market.
- Social security and social protection of workers.
- Redundancy.
- Representation and collective defence of the interests of workers and employers, including co-determination.
- Conditions of employment for third-country nationals (TCNs) legally resident in the Community.
- Financial contributions for the promotion of employment and job creation.

Article 2(4) provided that Member States could entrust the social partners, at their joint request, with the implementation of Directives adopted under paragraphs (2) and (3). Article 2(5) restated the provision laid down in Article 118a(3) EEC according to which Member States would not be prevented from 'maintaining or introducing more stringent protective measures compatible with the Treaty'. Article 2(6) excluded pay, the right of association, the right to strike or the right to impose lock-outs from the content of any measures adopted under paragraphs (1) and (3).

3.1.3 Towards a European Social Dialogue

The central provisions concerning the European Social Dialogue were to be found in Articles 3 and 4 and their purpose was to reinforce Article 118b EC (now Article 139 EC).

---

80 These Directives had to be based on minimum requirements for gradual implementation, having regard to the conditions and technical rules in each Member State. See Article 2(2) of the SPA.
81 See Protocol on Social Policy, point 2, para. 2.
82 See Article 2(3) of the SPA (now Article 137(3) EC).

Article 3 provided that the Commission would give "balanced support" for the consultations of management and labour and that it had an obligation to consult the social partners on the possible direction of Community action before submitting proposals. If, after this consultation, the Commission felt that Community action was advisable it should then consult the social partners on the content of the draft proposal. Subsequently, the social partners would forward an opinion or a recommendation to the Commission. The social partners could also inform the Commission that they wished to invoke the procedure of Article 4 according to which they could reach an agreement on the Commission's initiative. The social partners would then have nine months in which to act, although this period could be extended. Article 4 provided that, should the social partners so desire, the dialogue between them at Community level could lead to contractual relations, including agreements. It also provided that these agreements could be implemented either in accordance with the procedures and practices specific to the social partners and the Member States or, in matters covered by Article 2, at the joint request of the social partners by a Council decision on a proposal by the Commission. The Council would vote either by QMV or unanimity according to the subject matter of the agreement. Furthermore, Article 2(6) provided that the SPA did not apply to pay, the right of association and the right to strike or the right to impose lock-outs. Hence the SPA was particularly significant in that it gave a greater role to the social partners in the Community's decision-making process: not only would they be consulted on the possible direction of Community action and on the content of a proposal, but they could, if they so chose, negotiate collective agreements which could be given *erga omnes* effects by a Council decision.[83]

The generalization of the procedures and rules concerning the implementation of the social dialogue at European level with the establishment of a European collective bargaining system were put into effect in accordance with the principle of *horizontal subsidiarity* (de Búrca 1999: 6). As explained above, this principle applied during the second consultation of the Commission may lead to contractual relations between the social partners, including agreements. This process, authorized by the Commission, suspended the Commission's initiative with regard to a specific Community action for nine months, unless the social partners concerned and the Commission decided jointly to extend it. The principle of horizontal subsidiarity was therefore being applied within the framework of the European Social Dialogue and based on a binary scheme procedure which, starting with a consultation of the social partners, could lead to strict co-operation of management and labour with the Commission and the Council or to the total or partial regulation of a specific issue through the adoption of a collective agreement. These collective agreement were considered as being a source of law supplementing EU legislation.

Hence the application of the principle of *horizontal subsidiarity* had a significant impact on the EU decision-making process and on the entire system of sources of EC labour law, including the relationship between sources of EC law and sources of national law. The social dialogue process could lead either to a simple consultation of management and labour – which was compulsory but not binding – or to the adoption of a collective agreement by the social partners to have direct effect at both EU level and national levels or, finally, to a collective agreement to be implemented by a Council decision on a proposal

---

83   Under Article 4 of the SPA (now Article 139 EC), "decision" is not used in the sense of Article 249 EC (ex-Article 189 EC) but as a legally binding Act, including Directives.

from the Commission.[84] Hence for the first time in the social sphere private agents could be involved in the adoption of public policy decisions.[85] Barnard (2006: 19) argues that the European Social Dialogue also 'highlights the multi-faceted and paradoxical nature of the principle of subsidiarity. Although the social partners are negotiating [a form of "horizontal" subsidiarity], they are doing so at European level at a time when decentralized collective bargaining is the trend in many states.' Five Directives have been adopted *via* the European Social Dialogue.[86] However, the result achieved so far has not been very satisfying in terms of transparency, efficiency and output. Procedural problems remain, for example the negotiations between the social partners on the content of the Directives have been time-consuming, leading to a low number of agreements with binding effect (Vigneau: 1999; Lo Faro 2000: 115–121; Smismans 2008) and the whole process takes place behind relatively closed doors. Moreover, the number of Directives adopted so far has been rather scant. Finally, the content of the Directives may be subject to criticism for the 'dilution of the quality of rights it recognizes' (Barnard 2002),[87] although Smismans (2008: 170) observes that it is difficult to make a proper assessment on the substantial content of the European collective agreements as it 'raises questions about what European social policy is supposed to deliver and how normal legislation would have dealt with it'.

In her detailed analysis of the evolving quasi-public role of the social partners at both European and national levels, Barnard (2002) examines the reasons that led to their participation in the EU law-making process and the weaknesses and paradoxes underscoring their inclusion and the lack of participation of the European Parliament *vis-à-vis* the new governance agenda.[88] In so doing, Barnard identifies the central questions regarding the

84 For an examination of statutory collective agreements and non-statutory collective agreements, see Smismans (2008: 162–164). In the first category he includes Commission-initiated and Council-implemented collective agreements (COCOCAs) and self-initiated but Council-implemented collective agreements (SICOCAs). In the second group he includes Commission-initiated but self-implemented collective agreements (COSICAs) and self-initiated and self-implemented collective agreements (SISICAs).

85 See Smismans (2008), who analyzes the European Social Dialogue from the perspective of principal–agent theory.

86 Three Directives regarded the inter-sectoral level: Directive on Parental Leave (Council of the European Union 1996; (for the United Kingdom) Council of the European Union 1997c), which was based on the Framework Agreement between UNICE, CEEP and ETUC, OJ L 145, of June 1996 (on 18 June 2009 the European social partners signed a new framework agreement on parental leave according to which parental leave will be increased from three to four months and will apply to all employees regardless of the type of contract; this is the first time that a pre-existing framework agreement has been reviewed by the European social partners); Directive on Part Time Work (Council of the European Union 1997e), which was based on the Framework Agreement between UNICE, CEEP and ETUC, OJ L14, of 20 January 1998; Directive on Fixed Term Work (Council of the European Union 1999), which was based on the Framework Agreement between UNICE, CEEP and ETUC of 18 March 1999. Two Directives concerned the sectoral level: Directive on the Organization of the Working Time of Seafarers (Council of the European Union 1999a); Directive on the Organization of the Working Time of Mobile Workers in the Civil Aviation Industry (Council of the European Union 2000). For a detailed analysis of the Framework Agreements and Directives, see Kenner (2003: 266–291); Smismans (2007a); Smismans (2008).

87 See also Lo Faro (2000: chapter 5). Particularly interesting is the distinction he introduces between "tied agreements" and "weak agreements" or "inconsequential agreements". Only the former types of agreement, which are implemented via a Directive of the Council, have legal relevance in the European Union. The latter form of agreement implemented 'in accordance with the procedures and practices specific to management and labour and the Member States' has no legal relevance at Community level. Moreover, the implementation of the agreements by way of Directives – with the agreements annexed separately to them – has raised a series of perplexities regarding the difficulty of maintaining intact the collective autonomy part of the agreement, especially with regard to the fact that a high margin of discretion is left to the Member States in the implementation of Directives.

88 For a critical analysis, see Betten (1998); Armstrong (1999); European Parliament (1994).

creation of the European collective bargaining system and, chiefly, subsidiarity, effectiveness, legitimacy and democracy. As regards subsidiarity, the main contention is that the involvement of the social partners rather than embodying the principle of subsidiarity in the social sphere is an example of centralized law making and specifically a form of "centrally co-ordinated decentralization" (Ferner and Hyman 1998).[89] With respect to effectiveness, the introduction of the social dialogue at European level represented one of the means to confront the "sclerosis" of the traditional legislative process or, more critically, a way of "defusing" the problem of effectiveness of Community law.

An important reason explaining the establishment of the European Social Dialogue is the need to increase the legitimacy without parliamentary democracy of the European Union in the adoption of social policy measures (Bercusson 1996: 72–78).[90] In particular, given the dependence on hierarchy,[91] both in terms of threat of legislation and public intervention to ensure implementation, the European Social Dialogue may be said to have been introduced as a regulatory technique rather than an additional level of bipartite negotiation in an autonomous multi-level collective bargaining system (Lo Faro 2000). The legitimacy of the European Social Dialogue remains a controversial matter and it is associated with the problem of representativity of the European social partners. The quasi-public function assigned to them is at odds with the majority of the Member States' collective bargaining and industrial relations systems, as it has entailed a loss of autonomy of the social partners which historically has always typified their role in private contractual law (Lo Faro 2000: 104–108).[92] In this respect, Bercusson (1996: 34–36) has defined the inclusion of the social dialogue in the European legislative process as 'bargaining in the shadow of the law'.[93] Whereas in the national context the development of collective autonomy in a separate industrial relations system, through autonomous rule-making procedures and judicial bodies, has always preceded heteronomous regulation in the supranational context, supportive legislation has preceded the separate development of collective autonomy (Lo Faro 2000).[94] Bercusson (1999: 164) has criticized the constitutional perspective of the European Social Dialogue which makes it akin to a new level, transnational, of collective bargaining superimposed on national systems and has stressed that the social dialogue provisions should be interpreted in such a way that the autonomy of the social partners is respected. In more recent years the European Social Dialogue has started to depart to a certain extent from this narrower regulatory function and it now focuses also on a more bottom-up process of softer sectoral governance on the basis of OMC-like methods. At the inter-sectoral level two frameworks of action, one on lifelong learning (March 2002) and another on gender equality (March 2005), and three framework agreements on teleworking (July 2002), work-related stress (October 2004) and harassment and violence at work (April 2007) have been adopted. At sectoral level an agreement on musculo-skeletal disorders in the agricultural sector (November 2005) and in a multi-sector agreement (April 2006) to

---

89 See also Weiler (1999a); Lo Faro (2000: Chapters 3–6).
90 For comment and analysis on the constitutional view on the European Social Dialogue and its critique by labour lawyers, see Smismans (2007a).
91 On hierarchy, see Bercusson (1996) further below.
92 See Lo Faro (2002: 104–108). He criticizes the discretion with which the Commission assesses the outcome of the bargaining process, particularly the legality of the agreements, which is intended to examine whether the clauses of the agreements may be contrary to Community law. The author argues that the Commission has arrogated to itself the 'competence to perform a purely jurisdictional role' which pertains to the European Court.
93 More specifically, the "shadow" of the Commission weighs on the whole Social Dialogue process.
94 See also Caruso (1997); Fredman (1998: 386, 408 and 410).

reduce health risks associated with the use of crystalline silica have been adopted.[95] The Commission (2008: Chapter 2) has also stressed the importance of the European Social Dialogue for achieving the goals of the Lisbon Strategy, such as active labour market policies and the flexicurity agenda.

As regards the representativity of the social partners, in the Communication *New Procedures introduced by the Agreement on Social Policy and the Role of Management and Labour* the European Commission (1993c) outlined the representativity criteria which needed to be met by the social partners in the consultation process.[96] Some commentators have argued that the Commission introduced a distinction between the social partners' consultative role and their contractual relations role "with subtle and studied ambiguity" by applying the above criteria only to the former (Bercusson and Van Dijk 1995). At present the ETUC, CEEP and UNICE have a monopoly of the inter-sectoral social dialogue (Barnard 2002: 90). The representativity, internal democracy and accountability of these three major organizations have been called into question in relation to the way they operate and with regard to issues of membership and affiliation (Britz and Schimdt 2000; Keller and Sörries 1999).

The *UEAPME* case is illustrative.[97] As Bercusson and Van Dijk (1995: 12–13) posit, representativity is pivotal to establish the identity of the social partners and, therefore, it was a key criterion for the admissibility test before the CFI.[98] The salient parts of the judgment in which it declared the action lodged by *UEAPME* inadmissible may be summarized as follows (Bercusson 1999; Betten 1998; Schmidt 1999: 162–163). The CFI held that the consultation stage is different from the negotiation stage and there is no general right for those consulted to take part in the negotiations under Articles 3(4) and 4 SPA[99] or an individual right to participate in negotiations of the framework agreement. In so doing, the CFI emphasized the dual nature of EC labour law. Moreover, it stated that in the context of the SPA democratic legitimacy derives from the European Parliament's participation in the conventional legislative procedure provided for by Article 2(2)[100] whereas under the procedure of Article 4(2)[101] the European Parliament was not called to participate. According to the CFI, democracy as a fundamental and foundational principle of the

---

95 On further developments at both cross-sectoral and sectoral levels, see European Commission (2008).

96 The criteria for organizations to be eligible are the following: cross-country or belong to specific sectors or categories of the economy and be organized at European level; they must consist of organizations, which are themselves an integral and recognized part of Member State social partner structures, have the capacity to negotiate agreements and be representative of all Member States as far as possible; and they must have adequate structures to ensure their effective participation in the consultation process. The list was confirmed by in a Communication in 1998 (European Commission 1998).

97 See T-135/96 *UEAPME v. Council* [1998] ECR II-2335. The case concerned a challenge to the legality of the Directive on Parental Leave by UEAPME (European Association of Craft, Small and Medium-sized Enterprises), which claimed to represent the largest number of small and medium-size employers (SMEs) at pan-European level. UEAPME's main contention was that since it had been involved in the first consultation procedure it should have necessarily been involved in the second consultation process given that the interests of SMEs were different from those of UNICE.

98 On the question of representativity, see Milman-Sivan (2009).

99 Now Articles 138(4) and 139 EC.

100 Now Article 137(2) EC.

101 Now Article 139(2) EC.

Union under Article F(1) TEU (now Article 6(1) TEU) required that democracy could be otherwise assured, in this case through the participation of management and labour in the legislative process (Bercusson 1999: 164–165).[102] On this basis, the Commission and the Council, therefore, had a duty to verify the representativity of the signatories to the agreement and to refuse to implement the agreement if they were found to be insufficiently representative. In this case, the CFI found that the Commission and the Council had taken sufficient account of the representativity of the parties to the agreement on parental leave. In so doing the CFI insisted that the "collective representativity" of the parties had to be seen in relation to the content of the agreement. Since the signatories were general inter-sectoral organizations with a general mandate, they were sufficiently representative. The CFI also noted that the interests of SMEs were adequately represented by UNICE. On these grounds, the CFI concluded that UEAPME did not have the required individual concern to bring proceedings under Article 173 EC (now Article 230 EC).

The ruling was subject to criticisms on many points. First, the CFI did not assess the validity of the representativity criteria but only whether they had been applied correctly. It also failed to take into account the representativity issue with regard to those workers who are not members of trade unions. Second, it differentiated between the informal consultation stage and the formal negotiation stage in order to strengthen its statement and in so doing it implicitly endorsed the monopoly of the three major organizations. Third, and linked to the former, the 'CFI favoured a narrow representation-based model of democracy, which is concerned with the procedural rather than a wider participatory model that legitimates on the basis of the outcomes' (Kenner 2003: 92), leading to a narrow approach to the rules on the standing of private associations. Fourth, it did not address the issue of '*who* has legitimacy to negotiate and *how* to balance wider participation with effective negotiation' (*ibid.*)

The *UEAPME* case in broad terms exemplified the legitimacy, democracy and effectiveness problems of the European Union and, more specifically, it illustrated the limitations of using the European Social Dialogue as a regulatory technique at European level (Smismans 2007a) as well as the problems generated by giving a quasi-public role to the social partners in terms of their diminished collective autonomy. In this context the CFI decision left many unanswered questions. It also brought to the surface the complexities of subsidiarity and how challenging its application may be in practice.

3.2 The 1993 White Paper on Growth, Competitiveness and Employment and the Essen Strategy

In the 1993 White Paper *Growth, Competitiveness and Employment* (European Commission 1993a) the Commission provided an array of analyses and strategies in order to identify potentially viable employment policies. This White Paper was particularly significant as it not only launched an overall debate on the co-ordination of economic and employment policies at European level but also, and most important, brought the issue of employment on to the Community's top agenda.[103] The White Paper was also innovatory in the way

---

102 In particular, Bercusson criticizes the fact that the CFI considers the European Social Dialogue as being part of the European legislative process, thereby depriving the former of its autonomy which generally typifies industrial relations systems.

103 For a detailed analysis of the White Paper also in relation to the OECD Jobs Strategy, see Ashiagbor (2005).

that it aimed at reforming labour markets, introducing flexibility and promoting atypical forms of work. To address the European Union's problem of high levels of unemployment it put forward a package of proposals with a mix of deregulation, infrastructure investment and active labour market measures (Barnard 2006: 21).[104] These ideas had already been considered in a Green Paper entitled *European Social Policy* (European Commission 1993) in which the Commission said that in order to adapt to technological and structural changes to the economy adequate responses and measures had to be taken and in the White Paper *European Social Policy* (European Commission 1994), which provided instruments for action to develop a "European social model". The striking feature of these three documents is the emphasis placed on social goals, such as the promotion of high levels of employment and the elimination of social exclusion, and the move away from harmonization of social rights to greater reliance on convergence, technocratic support and soft law (Barnard 2006: 21; Cullen and Campbell 1999: 263). While employment has been a main feature of post-TEU debates on social policy, the issue crystallized as a priority with the conclusions of the European Council meeting at Essen in December 1994 (EU Bulletin 12–1994). On the basis of this White Paper, the European Council drew up five priorities (European Council 1994). The five priorities were:

- Improving job opportunities for the working population by promoting investment in educational training: particularly the acquisition of qualifications by young people (education policy).
- Increasing the intensity of the work content of economic growth (macroeconomic policy).
- Reducing unsalaried labour costs, particularly for non-qualified workers (labour market policy).
- Improving the efficiency of employment policies by avoiding measures that negatively affect the availability for work and by replacing passive policies by active ones (flexibility).
- Improving the measures concerning the assistance to groups that have been most affected by unemployment: young people, long-term unemployed workers, women and older employees (social inclusion).

The Essen Presidency Conclusions may be considered as the "daughters" of the 1993 White Paper for the similarity of the solutions put forward. The most visible change is a shift from harmonization towards a more flexible approach to policy making. The European Council at Essen requested the Commission (together with the Council) to monitor employment trends in the European Union and national policies and to report back to the European Council.[105] It was agreed that the Council would recommend the Member States to invest in vocational training, increase employment intensive growth, reduce non-wage labour costs and increase active labour market policies in order to reduce youth and long-term unemployment. Each Member State would present a multi-annual employment programme to the Commission. Furthermore, a benchmarking process was introduced to increase the use of best practice focusing mainly on long-term and youth unemployment and equal opportunities for men and women at the work place. The Green Paper *European Social Policy Options for the Union* (European Commission 1993) and the *Medium Term Social*

---

104 This policy mix also underpins the EES.
105 E.g. European Commission (1995a); European Commission (1995b).

Action Programme for 1995–1997 (European Commission 1995c) both considered unemployment as being the central priority of social policy and the Commission's role mainly involved studies on and monitoring of national labour markets as set out at Essen.

The Essen Strategy was implemented throughout the 1995 Madrid and Dublin Summits and, subsequently, at the 1996 Cannes and Florence Summits.[106] The Commission encouraged Member States to take account of the Essen objectives in their convergence programmes[107] and made a number of proposals for decisions in the employment field and approved projects relating to the Essen employment strategy (European Commission 1995c). The fact that initiatives were mainly taken by the European Council and the Commission highlights the political rather than the legal orientation to employment policy. In some ways this may be explained by the growing social unrest, by increased feelings against the European Union which were perceived as concentrating excessively on the EMU project and by concerns over preserving Member States' sovereignty. Public support was particularly important in the run-up to the entry into force of the Treaty on European Union and thus for the further development of the EMU. It became clear that the EMU project was going to be accepted by nationals of the Member States only in so far as the social dimension would be given equal consideration at European level.

The Essen Conclusions brought to the fore two main diverging views about how to tackle the then high levels of unemployment. On the one hand, there was the view that some form of European social intervention was a *conditio sine qua non* for the completion of the Internal Market, the EMU and, more broadly, the very existence of the Community. This view was sustained by the Delors Commission. On the other hand, there were those who were strongly opposed to any further expansion of Community competence in the social sphere (*in primis* the United Kingdom). The compromise was the adoption of a "minimalist solution". Nevertheless, it may be argued that the Essen process, while not transferring competence to the European Union in the employment policy area in any extensive way, certainly contributed to widening the debate on the employment crisis at EU level, and, most important, the Community had finally achieved a role in the area.

The Essen Strategy, however, failed to have a real impact on the employment situation across the European Union, with unemployment levels remaining substantial in most of the Member States. The closure of Renault's Vilvoorde plant in Belgium in February 1997 caused general discontent in Europe due to the number of lay-offs announced. The Vilvoorde case highlighted the lack of effective protection of workers at European level (EIRR 1998: 22–25).[108] Meulders and Plasman (1997: 31–33) have identified some significant contradictions inherent in the Essen Strategy. First, and more generally, the convergence criteria of the EMU project together with the Essen priorities imposed heavy constraints on national fiscal policies to the detriment of social protection and social security. Second, there were significant contradictions between three of the five Essen priorities. "Priority two" aimed at introducing more flexibility in the labour market regulations, potentially undermining the concept of the working environment which is well established in the Nordic–Scandinavian system (Nielsen and Szyszczak 1997: 330–331). Moreover, the introduction of flexibility entailed more instability and uncertainty with regard to the durability of employment contracts and reduced the level of salaries. Social protection systems in many Member States were still based on traditional ideas of full-time

---

106 For a detailed account, see Régent (2002: 3–6).
107 For a definition of convergence programmes, see Chapter 3.
108 For detailed information on the Renault case, see the EIRO (1997).

and lifetime employment and had to adapt to changing working patterns, characterized by greater worker mobility, new forms of work organization and new types of employment contract. "Priority three", by aiming at reducing unsalaried costs in an attempt to enhance job creation on a broader scale, ended up favouring firms. The measures adopted under this heading combined with "Priority four" led to cuts in social expenditure, with detrimental effects on low-qualified workers. Furthermore, multilateral employment monitoring introduced by the Essen Strategy lacked sufficient institutional co-ordination and focused more on convergence of employment policies (Szyszczak 2001: 177). Nevertheless, it may be argued that the Essen Strategy provided a blueprint for the formalized procedure set out subsequently in the Amsterdam employment title and brought into effect by the Luxembourg process (Kenner 1999: 48).

A Reflection Group chaired by the then Spanish Secretary of State for European Affairs, Carlos Westendorp, presented a report at the Madrid European Council meeting in December 1995 which proposed a revision of Article 103 EC in order to include employment as one of the objectives of the Union (Council of the European Union 1995). In addition, at the Turin European Council meeting in March 1996 the *Memorandum pour un modèle social européen* presented by the French government clearly stated that employment was to be one of the main priorities of the European Union (European Council 1996a). These developments taken together signify an important shift towards the strengthening and formalization of Community intervention in the area of social policy.

3.3 The dynamics of European social policy after the Treaty of Maastricht

The Treaty on European Union marked an important move towards the regulation of social policy at European level. More precisely, it fostered a shift in policy emphasis from labour market policies to employment policies to be later formalized by the Treaty of Amsterdam. This change in the conceptualization of social policy had its best example in the creation at European level of a strategy to promote employment creation – the Essen Strategy – which provided a blueprint for the subsequent European Employment Strategy and also in the SPA provisions on a European collective bargaining system which *de facto* introduced a new mode of decision making alongside the more classical Community Method.

However, the development of an EU social policy was still far from complete and many problems remained, some of which would be considered at the Amsterdam European Council meeting. First, social policy remained subordinate to the overarching economic objectives of the Union and, in particular, to the EMU project. In addition, the scope of EU citizenship was limited in that it was anchored to the free movement provisions and it did not seem to including a notion of social citizenship. As envisaged then, Union citizenship was also criticized for not encompassing a human rights dimension and it was still restricted to the notion of market and political citizenship. Moreover, the Treaty on European Union further entrenched differences in approach to European social policy by their institutionalization in the SPA, from which the UK opt-out (Hervey 1998: 25) acted as a brake in the evolution of social policy. Further, the internal contradictions of the Essen Strategy emphasized the fact that its implementation was still subordinate to the Union's overarching economic objectives. Finally, the *UEAPME* case not only illustrated the problems which could arise within the European Social Dialogue, chiefly in relation to the consultation and negotiation stages but, from a broader perspective, it also showed the nature and scale of legitimacy, democracy and effectiveness problems facing the European

Union. Despite these serious shortcomings, progression towards the generalization of a European social policy in the EC Treaty by then was well under way.

4 The Treaty of Amsterdam and the establishment of a European Strategy for Employment

4.1 Introduction

With the Amsterdam European Council the European Union entered a new distinctive sixth phase which was further developed by the Lisbon Strategy and by subsequent European Councils. This phase is characterized by an even stronger proactive role of the Commission in the social sphere which may be said to have begun in 1985 under the Presidency of Jacques Delors; a tendency for negative forms of integration; an increase in the use and typology of non-binding legal instruments and, in particular, a shift towards decentralized modes of policy making and employment policies rather than labour law; the establishment of a set of goals and their achievement through processes, strategies and action programmes decided at European Council meetings rather than harmonization through the use of Directives. In addition, as explained in the next chapter, the adoption of the EU Charter of Fundamental Rights has fostered a debate on a catalogue of rights to be included in the EC Treaty.

4.2 The Treaty of Amsterdam: a new era for Community social regulation

At the 1997 Amsterdam European Council meeting, employment was not initially on the agenda. However, due to the slow or lack of progress in other policy areas, for example the Common Foreign and Security Policy (CFSP), and in furthering institutional reform, the future of the European integration process seemed to be in great peril. Employment, therefore, being a common concern to the majority of the Member States, became a valuable token for furthering European integration (Goetschy 1999: 124). Moreover, the election of Blair in the United Kingdom and Jospin in France, respectively in May and June 1997, provided the political momentum for a new centre-left and for pursuing a stronger Social Europe, which by then had the support of most Member States, including the Benelux countries (Goetschy 1998).

At the Amsterdam European Council meeting the Scandinavian countries were pushing for a "full employment objective" and for establishing specific EU employment criteria similar to the EMU convergence criteria and the SGP criteria (*ibid.*). At the time both proposals were rejected, as were the proposals for direct EU intervention and job-creating spending. As we have seen, the SPA annexed to the EC Treaty provided the basis for a certain level of regulation at European level but many important areas of employment policy remained within the remit of Member States' decision making. Furthermore, by the time of the entry into force of the Maastricht Treaty the traditional regulatory approach showed signs of decay and there was the need for adopting a more flexible approach which would rely on an increased use of soft law instruments and procedures. This explains why the adoption of Directives that went beyond setting minimum standards proved to be problematic and why the general political climate of the late 1980s and early 1990s had made it difficult to ensure the effective implementation even of those Directives that had been adopted. The solution to this political impasse was achieved through compromise and, in particular, agreement on a "new" regulatory approach that would provide a middle ground between harmonization and deregulation. Heads of State, therefore, agreed to use a mode of governance similar to the Essen Strategy that was based on a multilateral system of co-operation and surveillance of Member States' employment policies as well as formalizing the European collective bargaining system provided for in the SPA.

Hence, at the behest of France and the Scandinavian countries, a new title on "Employment" was inserted in the EC Treaty, Title VIII (Articles 125–130 EC) and amendments were made to old Title VIII, on "Social Policy, Education, Vocational Training and Youth", which became new Title XI (Articles 136–150 EC). This title, as revised, finalized the establishment of the European Social Dialogue. The Maastricht Social Protocol was thus repealed and in its place an amended version of the SPA was incorporated in the EC Treaty. A significant change introduced by Amsterdam with regard to the Employment Title was that the promotion of employment was raised to a 'matter of common concern' (Article 127 EC) and the direct reference to the joint contribution of the Community and the Member States to achieving high levels of employment (Article 126(2) EC).

The EES was formally created with the objective of 'promoting a skilled, trained and adaptable work force and labour markets responsive to economic change with a view to achieving the objectives defined in Article 2 EC' (Article 125 EC), namely high levels of employment and social protection. The EES was immediately fast-tracked by the so-called "Luxembourg Process" (European Council 1997a: 4–5) before the ratification of the Treaty of Amsterdam. The strategy was structured as an iterative and annual process, based on the co-ordination of national employment policies with a supervisory role for the European Institutions and on ideas of benchmarking and mutual learning. The bone structure of the EES as envisaged by Title VIII differed in some aspects from the current *modus operandi*.[109] It entrusted the Council with the task of drawing up employment guidelines, on the basis of European Council Conclusions and after consulting the European Parliament, the Economic and Social Committee (ECOSOC), the Committee of the Regions and the Employment Committee,[110] which Member States had to follow when adopting and implementing their national employment policies. In particular, each year Member States had to submit NAPs to the Commission (Article 128(4) EC). The amended EC Treaty also provided that after having examined Member States' performance, the Council could make recommendations to individual countries in relation to their domestic employment policies (Article 128(4) EC) and adopt incentive measures in support of Member States' policies and to encourage co-operation between them (Article 129 EC). After examining Member States' national reports, the Council and the Commission would submit a joint annual report to the European Council on the employment situation in the Community and on the implementation of the EPGs (Article 128(5) EC).

The creation in 1997 of a new strategy at European level for fighting high levels of unemployment, the EES, was considered to represent a sea change with regard to the law-making process in the European Union at both national and European levels. The extent to which Title VIII may be said to have introduced a new form of governance in the EU system remains open to debate among scholars.[111] Undoubtedly at European level it has

---

109 This is explained in more detail in Chapters 5–7.

110 The Employment Committee had an advisory role; it had been established to monitor the employment situation in the European Union and the implementation of the EPGs and to assist the Council. See Article 128(2) EC and Article 130 EC.

111 See Chapter 2.

entailed a shift from social law and legislative initiatives towards soft law, or rather policies aimed at employment creation which for the most part eschew legislation (Ashiagbor 2001: 317). It also highlighted a shift in emphasis in the Union, from measures protecting those in employment to addressing high levels of unemployment in Europe. This was a direct response to the growing socio-economic crisis faced by the majority of the Member States and of what Rhodes (2005: 281) has defined as "welfare without work": expensive social welfare programmes which were not generating high levels of employment and were putting "euro zone" countries in a position of being in breach of the budgetary commitments laid down by EMU (Barnard 2006: 25). Moreover, as we saw in Chapter 3, because of the constraints imposed by the SGP, national monetary and fiscal policies could no longer be used to fight high levels of unemployment. The EES, therefore, was based on the adoption of supply-side policies focusing on increasing productivity levels, stimulating business while, at the same time, improving the quality of the workforce. Freedland (1996) and Barnard (1999: 487) maintain that this shift in social policy took place with the publication of the White Paper *Growth, Competitiveness and Employment*. Given that employment represented a highly sensitive policy area, it was felt that a new method of policy making had to be developed which would enhance job creation without, however, undermining national sovereignty. As explained in more detail in the next chapter, the EES was modelled on the economic co-ordination process of the EMU. Again, as a compromise for having some form of regulation at European level the strategy was developed to enable co-ordination of national employment policies and not to grant rights to employees.

In addition, soon after the entry into force of the Treaty of Amsterdam the *European Employment Pact* (EEP) was launched at the 1999 Cologne European Council meeting, highlighting once again Member States' commitment to boosting employment and improving employability with the key involvement of the social partners (European Council 1999a).[112] Concerted employment initiatives or pacts had been adopted since the 1980s in several Member States, playing an important role in labour market reforms. The EEP may be considered as part of these national social pacts with the added value of being conceived as a long-term initiative.

With regard to Title XI, Article 136 EC charged the Community with giving due consideration to fundamental social rights and, in particular, those protected in the 1961 European Social Charter and the 1989 Community Charter of the Fundamental Social Rights of Workers. However, the centrality of such rights was mitigated by the need to maintain the competitiveness of the Community's economy. Article 137 EC was basically a refashioned replica of Article 2 of the SPA and Directives adopted under this proviso were subject either to QMV or unanimity in the Council, depending on the area of social policy being regulated. Moreover, the proposals in the areas listed in paragraph 1 were subject to the co-decision procedure under Article 251 EC, which meant that the Council and the European Parliament would be acting as co-legislators. Paragraph 4 empowered national social partners to implement Directives, while paragraph 5 retained the provision enabling Member States to define the fundamental principles of their social security systems and to maintain and introduce more stringent protective measures compatible with the Treaty. Paragraph 6 replaced Article 2(6) of the SPA by way of excluding pay and collective rights from legislation provided for by the Article. Articles 138 EC and 139 EC are an exact replication of Articles 3 and 4 of the SPA examined earlier.

The third significant change brought about by the Treaty of Amsterdam concerned the

---

112 See also Special Issue (1999).

importance of equality between men and women. The centrality of this principle was reinforced by its inclusion in Article 2 EC as one of the tasks of the Community and as one of the activities of the Community in Article 3 EC. This provision also contained a reference to gender mainstreaming by stating that 'in all the activities referred to in this Article, the Community shall aim to eliminate inequalities, and to promote equality, between men and women'. Article 141 EC replaced old Article 119 EEC and Article 6 of the SPA. The new provision strengthened Community powers in the area of sex equality. First, it added an important specification to the right to equal pay for equal work, that of 'work of equal value'. Article 141(2) EC replicated the same proviso of Article 119 EEC with regard to the notion of pay whereas Article 141(3) EC provided a new legal basis for the adoption of measures ensuring the protection of sex equality and the use of QMV and co-decision. Article 141(4) EC made reference to substantive equality – 'full equality in practice' – and provided for the use of positive action measures.

Another significant change introduced by the Treaty of Amsterdam in the field of social policy was the insertion of new Article 13 EC, which provided the legal basis for Community competence in anti-discrimination legislation (Meenan 2007). This article has been the legal base of two non-gender Directives, namely Directive 2000/43/EC implementing the principle of equal treatment between persons irrespective of racial or ethnic origin (the "Race Equality Directive") (Council of the European Union 2000a) and Directive 2000/78/EC establishing a general framework for equal treatment in employment and occupation (the "Framework Employment Directive") (Council of the European Union 2000b) and one gender-related Directive, Directive on the principle of equal treatment between men and women in access to and the supply of goods and services (Council of the European Union 2004)[113] as well as the Decision on establishing a Community action programme to combat discrimination for 2001–2006 (Council of the European Union 2000c).

The amendments introduced by the Treaty of Amsterdam reinforced the legislative power of all the actors involved in social policy making, shedding new light on the role of the European social partners: at EC level, a new legal source – contractual agreements – was introduced in parallel with the more conventional forms of decision making; at national level, social partners were to play an important role in the implementation of the EES. However, the role of the social partners had not been clearly defined. Moreover, no reference to the their role could be found in new Title VIII, contrary not only to the provisions of Title XI but also to EC documents and to practice (High Level Group on Industrial Relations and Change in the European Union 2002). In addition, there were still the "left-overs" of the *UEAPME* decision, namely the representativity of the European social partners, the question of social partners' traditional private autonomy and the effectiveness and justiciability of collective agreements in the light of the strong diversity of national welfare and industrial relations systems.

5 A comparison of the EES and the OECD Jobs Strategy[114]

The OECD Jobs Strategy was first set up in 1992 following the persistence of high levels of unemployment in most European countries. It represents another example of a European

---

113 For comment and analysis, see Caracciolo di Torella (2007).
114 For a detailed study of the two strategies, see Noaksson and Jacobsson (2003); Ashiagbor (2005: 72–100).

system of multilateral co-operation and surveillance in the field of employment policy (Marcussen 2002) and like the EES it focuses essentially on the adoption of supply-side measures. The overall objective of the OECD Jobs Strategy is similar to the EES, namely 'to frame a common value system and shared definition of policy problems and solutions' (Visser 2002: 3) which involves a similar cyclical process based on guidelines, exchange of information, best practice and formal and informal meetings between officials of the OECD and member countries (OECD 1994). However, the aim of the OECD Jobs Strategy is more humble in comparison with that of the EES in that basically it constitutes an information mechanism, albeit important, that facilitates the understanding of social and labour market trends in Europe since it focuses not only on individual member countries but also on specific regions of Europe.

The OECD Directorate for Education, Employment, Labour and Social Affairs is the institution assigned with the task of examining employment and labour market patterns. The annual "Employment Outlook" offers an analysis of key labour market trends and policies and the Economic and Development Review Committee (EDRC) examines economic trends and policies in each member country of the OECD every twelve to eighteen months.[115] The document normally contains an assessment of economic developments and macroeconomic policies, a chapter reviewing progress in structural reform and a chapter on a specific structural problem.

Since 1999 attention has been primarily on three areas – ageing, tax reform and environmentally sustainable growth – with a view to drawing some lessons from cross-country experience in these areas. To this end synthesis reports have been produced in 2000 and 2001. The EDRC, therefore, plays a pivotal part in the process of the OECD multilateral surveillance of economic policies. After each examination the committee's country survey and policy conclusions are published.

There are mainly two differences between these strategies. First, whereas the OECD Jobs Strategy is based on a centralized academic and technocratic approach which mainly sees the involvement of European countries at ministerial level, the EES by contrast is based on a multi-tiered and iterative mode of governance involving the participation of an array of state and non-state actors. The EES also leaves more manoeuvre to Member States in the type of employment-related policy measures they need to adopt in following the recommendations made to them by the Council or the Commission. In addition, the OECD Jobs Strategy has always had a more explicit neo-liberal programme focusing on labour market flexibility. Even though under the Barroso Commission there has been a shift in focus towards the orthodoxy of a more deregulatory labour market agenda, with EU Institutions accepting more readily the need to combine labour market flexibility with employment security, the EES contrasts significantly with the OECD Jobs Strategy at discourse level in that it builds on two opposing rationales. As explained earlier, the EES is centred on social solidarity and social justice rationales together with open market economy efficiency. Moreover, and linked to this, the EES differs profoundly from the OECD Jobs Strategy because with its focus on co-ordination rather than co-operation it attempts to change the logic of policy making by fostering "bottom-to-top" governance even though, as explained in the next chapter, it has not fully succeeded in achieving this.

---

115 More information is available on the OECD Web site, <htttp://www.oecd.org/document/23/ 0,3343,en_21571361_37949547_37970135_1_1_1_1,00.html>.

6 Conclusion

This chapter looked at the development of EU social law and policy and explained how Community social regulation has developed into two distinct branches: on the one hand, European labour law, which is linked to the Internal Market and is part of both the integrationist and economic rationales of the Community, and, on the other, social and employment policies which abandon the idea of legal harmonization by focusing on the achievement of goals and eschew the use of traditional legal instruments. However, this distinction is not always so clear-cut. As posited by Syrpis (2007: 10–11, 52) policy rationales have a core and a periphery. The peripheries may at times overlap so that it becomes difficult to determine whether, for example, an intervention aimed at reducing unemployment should be classified as economic or social. Likewise, it may be difficult or impossible to distinguish between integrationist and economic policies because measures aimed at ensuring a free and competitive market economy may also ensure the effective operation of the Single Market.

The chapter also showed how the evolution of EU social policy is a story of tense cohabitation between convergence/isonomy and divergence, autonomy and heteronomy, positive and negative integration, continuity and discontinuity and stability and instability forces in an evolving European Union. Since the foundational period and the minimalist and non-interventionist approach of the Community in the social field which heavily relied on the Ohlin and Spaak reports, EU social policy has undergone different paths of evolution and involution which highlight its fragmented structure. In particular, prior to the SPA annexed to the EC Treaty there was no firm legal basis for EU social policy. Regulations were initially adopted in the field of social security and social protection providing minimum standards to guarantee the completion of the Internal Market and Directives focused primarily on employment law or health and safety conditions in the workplace.

Moreover, since the Treaty of Maastricht EU social policy is no longer limited to ensuring the free movement of workers on the basis of the principle of non-discrimination on grounds of nationality (Article 39 EC). It has gone further, reinforcing and strengthening substantive labour law, creating the basis for the establishment of a body of fundamental social and labour rights (Rusciano 1996; Sciarra 1995).[116] In this context, the ECJ has played a crucial role in developing and shaping concepts and principles of social policy at European level through what Weiler (1991) has effectively described as a "process of mutation", although the Court's judicial activism and legitimacy have been called into question because of several poorly reasoned judgments and lack of consistency. The institutional role of the social partners in accordance with this change in the conceptualization of EC labour law has been given support and enhanced at various levels and sectors of the economy. The increased role of the social partners, however, has been overshadowed by the existence of significant problems, as discussed earlier.

Over an arch of time that starts from the 1993 White Paper *Growth, Competitiveness, Employment* (European Commission 1993), through the Essen (June 1994), Amsterdam (June 1997), Luxembourg (November 1997) and Lisbon (March 2000) European Council meetings, and continuing through the Barcelona (March 2002) and the Brussels European Council (2005) and beyond, it is possible to trace a progressive commitment to issues regarding employment, social cohesion, competitiveness and new technology with the

---

116 In this context, Sciarra (1995: 60) refers more broadly to 'social values and multiple sources of EC Social Law' rather than to social rights.

introduction of non-binding legal tools which enhances forms of horizontal as well as vertical subsidiarity.

In addition, from a governance perspective, there has also been an increase in the use of measures based on soft law instruments, and, in particular, with the EES soft law becomes the main instrument at European level for creating and developing a process within the broader EU system and not merely an *ad hoc* instrument to fill in the gaps in situations of legislative deadlock within the Council (Kenner 1995: 307). Back in 1992 the Edinburgh Council considered soft law measures preferable to hard law, especially in relation to the implementation of Article 3b EC (EC Bulletin 12/1992: 25–26).

The chapter also brought to the fore the main problems besetting EU social intervention which explain its paroxysmal development throughout the fifty years of existence of the European Community/Union. The social rationale for EU intervention is underdeveloped. Articles 2 EC and 2 TEU define the social objectives of the European Union in general terms, and give no indication of the way in which the balance between the Union's economic and social objectives is to be struck. Article 136 EC is also not sufficiently clear (Syrpis 2007: 67). This lack of specificity is damaging for the development of EU social law and policy because it affects the capacity and willingness of the European Institutions to act on the basis of the social rationale (*ibid.*). It is equally damaging for the integrationist rationale because the European integration project has at its core a series of objectives, among them the pursuit of social progress, social justice and social cohesion. Hence, if those objectives are unclear, the criteria with which political choices in the European Union's market-building process are made will equally be unclear (*ibid.*: 68). D'Antona (1994: 704) defines this situation as being the "genetic anomaly" of Community social law and policy in comparison with the constitutional traditions of national welfare states (at least those of Continental and Mediterranean countries). This anomaly is caused by the absence of a 'principle of the welfare state or at least of labour protection' that counterbalances the unconditional principle of an open economy and free and competitive market (*ibid.*: 697; see also Giubboni 2006: 26–27). Likewise, Lo Faro (2000) talks about the impossibility of regarding European labour law as a self-contained and homogeneous system of norms endowed with an autonomous rationality of its own. The existing tension between opposing views of social law and policy, coupled with the lack of a clear legal basis for EC social policy explains the tendency for EC social policy measures to focus on process rather than substance (Hervey 1998: 23), two key examples being the European Social Dialogue and the EES.

5   The European Employment Strategy and its implementation through the Open Method of Co-ordination

1 Introduction

This chapter examines the origins and further development of the EES unfolding the reasons for its creation and exploring its significance in the context of the sixth phase of EU social policy. In this context the chapter also provides a thorough examination of its main mode of operation, namely, the OMC.

The purpose of this chapter is twofold. First, it aims at analyzing the elements of continuity and break with previous regulatory instruments in the field of social policy and, in particular, it seeks to explain why and how employment policy has taken on an independent identity from the beginning of the 1990s and, more precisely, the reasons for the displacement of employment and economic discourses over social policy and social law. As seen in the preceding chapters there is a series of composite factors – political, economic and social – which explain the creation and further development of the EES. From the perspective of decisional supranationalism,[1] the strategy and its mode of governance, the OMC, present elements of continuity with existing EU modes of regulation in the sense that they represent one of the means of intense dialectical exchanges between centre (the European Union) and periphery (the Member States). Moreover, co-ordination and net-working are not new in the EU system. Hence, from this point of view, the EES is not entirely new and may be said to constitute what Sabel and Zeitlin (2003) have termed "pragmatic constitutionalism". In this context, the chapter seeks to unravel in what way the EES may be said to constitute an experimental form of EU governance and the extent to which as a soft co-ordination process it may be said to differ from previous or extant soft modes of governance. On the level of normative constitutionalism,[2] however, there are significant differences between the classical Community Method based on hard law, legal sanctions, enforceable EU rights and the involvement of mainly public bodies and the EES, which is structured around the participation of an array of stakeholders (both public and private actors), is built on the blurred definition of targets (apart from the more well-defined structural indicators) and relies on the use of soft sanctions.

The second aim of the chapter is to provide a preliminary evaluation of the functioning of the EES. As explained in Chapter 4, there is an existing tension between opposing views of social law and policy which together with the lack of a clear legal basis for EC social policy explains the tendency for EC social policy measures to focus on process rather than

---

1 As defined by Weiler (1981: 267).
2 *Ibid.*

substance. The EES is a case in point. Given that legally binding measures in the social and employment fields may be adopted at national level pursuant to the strategy, what effects may the EES have on the exercise and protection of EC social rights?

The study focuses on the multi-tiered and iterative nature of the strategy made up of a series of levels of decision and policy making – European, national, regional and local – and it seeks to unfold the soft and hard layers of the strategy. In so doing, it analyzes the quality of its democratic and participatory elements and whether the EES provides a valid platform for policy learning to take place. In particular, the chapter seeks to examine whether it provides a common cognitive framework for understanding and describing problems in national labour markets and for identifying workable solutions that are adaptable to the different socio-economic context of different welfare systems. The analysis carried out in the subsequent sections covers chiefly the period in between 1997 and 2005 and focuses chiefly on three key phases of the EES:

- *First period* (1997–2002). Creation and development of the EES (including its major revision in 2002–2003).
- *Second period* (2003–2004). Consolidation of the EES (including the first and second Kok reports).
- *Third period* (2005 to the present). Integration in the Lisbon Strategy (including the 2004–2005 mid-term review of the overall Lisbon Strategy).

In this context, the analysis of the EES also takes into consideration further social policy developments and its role in relation to the strengthening of the "European social model".

The chapter concludes by providing a preliminary evaluation of the strategy's strengths and weaknesses. A more exhaustive assessment of the EES is given in Chapter 7 on the basis of both the theoretical governance model developed in Chapter 2 and the comparative case study undertaken in Chapter 6.

2 Genesis and first years of implementation of the European Employment Strategy [3]

2.1 Unemployment as a "European" policy concern

The EES emerged from a crisis in social policy which became a matter of common concern to all the Member States in the mid-1990s (Goetschy 1999: 118–119; Kenner 1999; Esping-Andersen 1996). Unemployment had reached levels comparable only to the years preceding the Second World War. Although there was recognition that action needed to be taken with no further delay, the European Institutions and the Member States were faced with two challenges. On the one hand, reformers were confronted with the number and magnitude of the measures required: it became clear that extant social policy measures were inadequate to fight unemployment and significant changes were needed. On the other hand, they were confronted with the complexity of the unemployment problem and the limitations of existing regulatory methods. Hence, while there was awareness of the fact that unemployment was a matter of common concern requiring a Europe-wide

---

3 See Appendix 1 for key phases in the development of the EES; see also de la Porte (2008: 71–103), who identifies five stages in the emergence of the EES.

response, there was no strategy available at European level to deal with these problems and given the diversity of Member States' welfare state and industrial relations systems there was also a certain degree of resistance and/or scepticism in relation to the idea of Europeanizing labour market and employment policies. Further waves of enlargements in the 1980s and 1990s had also increased the aforementioned heterogeneity (Ferrera *et al.* 2001).

By the mid-1990s, therefore, Europe had to deal with high levels of unemployment[4] and, at the same time, rethink the way employment policies were defined and how to restructure welfare systems in the light of major economic and structural changes at Member State level. Measures to fight joblessness that had worked in the past such as encouraging early retirement proved to be unsustainable and new measures were urgently required. It was thus necessary to go beyond short-term job creation schemes and adapt industrial relations and welfare state systems to a changing labour market and labour force in order to adjust to external shocks caused by globalization, the Single Market and the EMU.

Traditional European industrial relations systems were organized and directed principally towards a male labour force employed in most cases in one firm on a full-time basis and for a lifetime. However, economic and social patterns had been subject to a deep process of change and by the mid-1990s working patterns reflected these changes, with women entering the labour market in large numbers. In addition, these structural changes required more skilled workers and vocational training. The volatility characterizing the European economy brought about mainly by globalization and the creation of the Single Market further increased the need to ensure the free movement of workers and basic social rights. In this context, employment contracts were also reviewed with the creation of atypical forms of work and the increased demand for and supply of part-time work. In turn, these major changes required a reform of social security and social protection systems to deal also with an ageing population and the negative impact that social benefits had on employment. Moreover, the fight against unemployment had to be tackled in a period of recession and slow economic growth and, from a political perspective, in the realm of neo-liberal ideological resurgence.

Further, most Member States were confronted with severe budget constraints to meet the convergence criteria for joining EMU.[5] For some policy makers and politicians, the solution was a strong centralized system at European level reproducing the structures of domestic social systems. According to this view, the Community was to be endorsed with regulatory and spending capacities similar to those of the Member States (Rhodes 1995). However, there was strong opposition to increasing the decision-making power of EU Institutions in the social policy field (Streeck 1995; Teague 2001) because issues regarding the welfare state and social policy *sensu lato* are at the heart of Member States' sovereignty. In addition, furthering the Europeanization process was considered by many to be anachronistic and in most Member States it increased anti-European feelings with the added risk of further alienating an already disillusioned populace, thus undermining the TEU ratification process. The Community needed to give itself a new image, a more "human face", and the renaissance of actions favouring social policy that were undertaken in the following years must be considered in this political climate. Moreover, the Community's

---

4 The European average exceeded 10 per cent and several Member States had even higher levels (European Commission 1999: 7–12).
5 For a detailed analysis of the effects and impact of the EMU on Member States' economic policies, see Chapter 3.

self-imposed budget constraint made it almost impossible to fund employment policies apart from those policies that were implemented via regulations (Majone 1993). Thus the Community's competence was limited *ab initio*.

The Employment Strategy launched in 1997 must be analyzed in the context of this scenario, which helps us to better understand why the choice fell on this particular mode of policy making.[6] The EES represents an experimental approach to governance combining the use of soft law instruments such as guidelines and recommendations with traditional modes of regulation to create a partnership approach or, more broadly, a common response to fighting unemployment. The first years of the existence of the EES and its further implementation via the OMC are the focus of the ensuing analysis.

2.2 The development of a European employment policy

In the early 1990s the need for a certain level of social policy regulation at European level became an important Community objective. In addition, the further enlargement of the European Union and the favourable political scenario for expanding the EU Institutions' role in the area of social policy[7] changed the general perception of how the latter should be implemented.

As we have seen,[8] the Commission played a crucial role in the formation of the EES in relation to both its policy objectives and its institutional model mainly through discourse framing.[9] In the 1993 White Paper *Growth, Competitiveness and Employment* (European Commission 1993a) the Commission provided various perspectives and strategies to identify viable employment policies. The novelty in the policy discourse developed by this White Paper was to shift attention away from unemployment rates towards employment rates and active labour market policies in order to increase the overall number of people in employment. It was also important in that it not only launched an overall debate on the co-ordination of economic and employment policies at European level but it also brought employment on to the Community's top agenda for the first time.[10] While employment has been a main feature of post-TEU debates on social policy the issue crystallized as a priority with the conclusions of the European Council at Essen in 1994. On the basis of the White Paper, the European Council agreed to adopt a European employment strategy, namely the Essen Strategy, based on co-operation, a benchmarking process and a multilateral employment monitoring system under the aegis of the Commission. The Essen Strategy had failed to meet its objectives.[11] Multilateral employment monitoring introduced by the Essen

---

6 For a detailed analysis of the reasons leading to the launch of the EES, see Arnold (2001).
7 In particular Sweden, Finland and Austria, which officially became Member States on 1 of January 1995, were in favour of increasing the EU role in the field of social policy. This was also possible for the change in position of the big EU countries such as the United Kingdom, France and Germany.
8 See Chapter 4.
9 Some scholars (e.g. Johansson 1999; Kulachi 2004) contest the role of the European Commission in the early stages of the EES and argue that the EES has its origins in the European political party organizations. According to Johansson (1999) the "European Employment Initiative" (EEI) working group under the auspices of the Party of European Socialists defined a strategy for combating unemployment, *Put Europe to Work* (the so-called Larsson Report, after the name of the chair of EEI) around the same time as the studies and analyses conducted by the European Commission in the early 1990s. Both Johansson (1999) and Kulachi (2004) maintain that the EES originated in this report.
10 For a detailed analysis of the White Paper also in relation to the OECD Jobs Strategy, see Ashiagbor (2005).
11 See Chapter 4.

Strategy lacked sufficient institutional co-ordination and focused more on convergence of employment policies (Szyszczak 2001; Goetschy 1999). Moreover, the Social Policy Agreement annexed to the EC Treaty created the basis for a certain degree of regulation at European level but many important areas of employment policy were left to the Member States. It also became clear by then that new regulatory approaches had to be defined and replace traditional forms of regulation based on harmonization. This explains why the adoption of Directives that went beyond setting minimum standards proved to be challenging and, similarly, why the effective implementation of those Directives that had already been adopted was equally difficult.

Moreover, following the failure of the Essen Strategy there was still the need to identify an effective Community employment policy. As Régent (2003: 194) aptly maintains, soft law in this period focused mainly on convergence and it was still far from becoming the main policy instrument to manage social policy pluralism. Nevertheless, post-Essen the Community maintained the commitment to strengthening employment policy. In particular, at the Cannes European Council the fight against unemployment was reaffirmed as an important target and Member States were to adopt more measures pursuant to the Essen Strategy priorities (European Council 1995). The Madrid European Council identified further objectives and specific spheres of action, particularly long-term unemployment and youth and female unemployment, and also emphasized the need to adopt common indicators for assessing national employment policies (European Council 1995a). At the Dublin European Council it was agreed to identify better instruments for effective monitoring and evaluation of Member States' labour market and employment policies such as employment indicators and benchmarking (1996b).

The soft law discourse that emerged in the mid-1990s developed into a fully fledged process with the 1997 Amsterdam and subsequent European Councils. At Amsterdam it was agreed that a revitalized Employment Strategy would be based on a regulatory approach that had already been employed in the context of the EMU, in particular in the area of economic co-ordination, by way of adapting the multilateral surveillance process developed for EMU to employment policy (Hodson and Maher 2001). By adapting a similar approach to the field of employment it was possible to achieve a compromise between those who supported an increased role for the Community and those who instead were against any further extension of the powers of the European Union. In this context, the EES and the co-ordination model of the OMC have been explained in neo-functionalist terms and, in particular, as processes of functional and political spill-over from the EMU, since the co-ordination model of the EES (and then the OMC) was inspired by EMU guidelines, benchmarks, national reporting, peer review and multilateral surveillance (de la Porte 2008).

Hence a new Title on Employment was inserted in the Treaty, Title VIII (Articles 125–130 EC) and amendments to the old Title VIII, on Social Policy, Education, Vocational Training and Youth, were made which became new Title XI (Articles 136–150 EC). The latter finalized the establishment of the European Social Dialogue. Title VIII is to be read together with Title VII on Economic and Monetary Policy: the combined effect of these two titles is a strategy to promote employment based on the co-ordination of Member States' macroeconomic policies and structural reforms. Article 126 EC obliges Member States to pursue their employment policies in a way that is consistent with the broad guidelines of the economic policies of the Member States and of the Community.

The strategy was immediately fast-tracked by the "Luxembourg process" (European Council 1997a), *inter alia*, with the immediate implementation of two initiatives, one concerning an action plan by the European Investment Bank (EIB)[12] and a second one regarding the creation of a new budget heading defined "European Employment initiative".[13] Moreover, as part of the EES, the European Union has used Structural Funds to create "flanking policies". Central to the operation of the Structural Funds is partnership which is based on a sharing of responsibility across different levels of government and between a variety of actors both public and private. The Commission has long aimed at establishing what Hartwig (2007) defines as a functional relationship between the EES and the ESF. Article 146 EC provides that the ESF has 'to render the employment of workers easier and increase their geographical and occupational mobility within the Community, and to facilitate their adaptation to industrial changes and to changes in production systems'. Since the launch of the EES the European Commission has considered it necessary to ensure co-ordination between the EES and the ESF priorities and that there should be 'consistency of assistance from the structural funds with employment policy' (European Commission 2002a: 5). The synergy between the two governance methods was stressed by the Commission in a Communication on the Structural Funds (European Commission 1999) where it stated that 'the plans, drawn up on the basis of common employment guidelines adopted by the Council, will serve as the overall framework for measures to support employment policies under the Structural Funds'. In 1999 the structural funds were charged with promoting a high level of employment (Council of the European Union 1999b) and a new integrationist approach was introduced for all structural funds in order to ensure economic and social cohesion. The ESF was reformed in the light of the EES and Article 2 of Regulation 1262/99 listed five priority areas which the ESF can support in line with the then four "pillars" on which the Employment Strategy was based (European Parliament and Council of the European Union 1999a). The ERDF was also revamped and Article 1 of Regulation 1261/99 stated that the Fund should contribute to promoting sustainable development and the creation of sustainable jobs (European Parliament and Council of the European Union 1999b). In addition, the criteria for determining the regions eligible for funding were the level of total unemployment and long-term unemployment. The amount of Structural Funds devoted to boosting employment is quite significant: in the period 2000–2006 it amounted to 35 per cent of the entire Structural Funds budget and the ESF represented up to half of the total spending on employment policy in some Member States.

While Title XI may be said to consolidate horizontally accepted judicial and political practice,[14] Title VIII on the other hand may be said to consolidate political and proactive thinking in the social field elaborated by the Commission through the use of *ad hoc* soft law instruments (Szyszczak 2000: 197–198). These changes have greatly contributed to the further development of a European social and employment policy, departing from the

---

12 This initiative was designed to 'find up to an extra ECU 10 billion for small and medium-sized enterprises, new technology, new sectors and trans-European networks, which sum will be able to generate a total volume of investment of ECU 30 billion' (European Council 1997a: 2).

13 This initiative, based on an agreement between the EU Parliament and the Council, was designed to the 'redeployment of appropriations', creating a new budget heading, 'intended in particular to help small and medium-sized enterprises and to create sustainable jobs. It was planned to allocate ECU 450 million to this heading over the next three years' (European Council 1997a: 2).

14 See Arrigo (1998: 175–188). The author elaborates the concept of "double subsidiarity" in referring to the provisions of Title XI in order to emphasize the coexistence of vertical subsidiarity, i.e. the institutional dialogue between the Community and the Member States, and horizontal subsidiarity, i.e. the European Social Dialogue, in which management and labour co-operate with one another in stipulating collective agreements, which may then be transposed into EU law.

narrow guise of labour law and labour market regulation, with major repercussions on Member States' competence in this area. Since then, EC employment policy has gradually taken on an independent identity and has helped to revive and reconceptualize the "European social model". The events preceding Amsterdam and the various European Councils before 1997 clearly indicate that the initiative of including an Employment chapter in the EC Treaty originated and was driven by the Member States. During this stage the Commission's influence was low because of its weak legislative powers in employment policy, which largely remains a domain of the Member States. More broadly, it may be argued that during stages of emergence of a new policy area the Commission does not have an unconditional greater influence than the Member States rather it can define the EU policy objectives in a given area where the European Union has weak legislative powers only in so far as the Member States are receptive to its proposals (de la Porte 2008: 96).

When it was set up and in its first years of implementation, the EES was greeted with great enthusiasm by those who advocated a stronger "Social Europe". The EES was considered to represent a sea change in the EU law-making process at both national and European levels, owing to its reliance on iterative processes, "bottom-to-top" policy making and deliberative forms of democracy (e.g. Goetschy 1999, 2001; Régent 2002). Further, it was touted as entailing a shift from 'social law and legislative initiatives, towards soft law, or rather policies aimed at employment creation, which for the most part eschew legislation' (Ashiagbor 2005: 317). However, most of these initial evaluations of the EES were limited in scope, since they focused chiefly on the procedures employed in the EES and policy formulation rather than on its real impact in terms of the content of national policies and policy outcomes. In the years that followed, both theoretical analyses and empirical studies have revisited and assessed more critically the "newness" of the EES and its regulatory tool, the OMC, and their much claimed participatory nature, and have highlighted their failure to meet initial expectations, particularly in terms of policy results (e.g. Chalmers and Lodge 2003; Hatzopoulos 2007; Jacobsson and Vifell 2007; Beveridge and Velluti 2008). The examination of the EES and its implementation through the OMC which follows in the next sections benefits from this copious literature and builds upon some of these more recent empirical accounts of the functioning and efficiency of the EES and the OMC.

3　Structure and mode of operation of the European Employment Strategy

The EES is an iterative and multi-level governance process and it attempts to establish a nexus between different EU policy areas by widening its scope of action, which goes beyond the field of social policy *stricto sensu*. More precisely, the EES aims at developing a social dimension to the activities of the European Union (European Council 1997).[15] This iterative process involves the adoption of several key documents:

- A Joint Employment Report (JER) by the Council and the Commission (from 2006 part of the Annual Progress Report, APR).
- Conclusions by the European Council on the employment situation within the Member States.

15　The major policy areas called into play were taxation, research and innovation, trans-European transport networks, structural funds and the information society.

- Guidelines by the Council (now part of the Integrated Guidelines) and the concomitant adoption of National Action Plans by the Member States (now National Reform Programmes).
- Recommendations by the Council to the Member States upon a proposal of the Commission.
- Incentives measures by the Council designed to encourage co-operation between Member States and to support their action in the field of employment through initiatives aimed at developing exchanges of information and best practices
- Opinions by the Employment Committee (EMCO) which has the task of monitoring the employment situation and policies in the Member States and formulating opinions on the labour market performance.

As explained further below, the EES does not entail any systemic or institutional change at European level. The EMCO is the only new European Institution that has been created specifically for the implementation of the EES (Council of the European Union 2000d). The EMCO consists of two nominees from each Member State and two from the Commission (Article 130 EC), selected from among senior officials or experts possessing outstanding competence in the field of employment and labour market policy in the Member States. It has an advisory status to promote co-ordination between Member States on employment and labour market policies and its tasks are to monitor employment policies both within the Member States and the Commission and to formulate opinions at the request of the Commission or the Council or on its own initiative. It must also contribute to the preparation of the EPGs. In carrying out its tasks the EMCO must consult the social partners who are represented on the tripartite Standing Committee on Employment (Council of the European Union 1999c).[16] The EMCO was created with the idea of representing a bridge between the Commission and the Member States and, in particular, as a deliberative body (Barnard 2006: 112). Instead it remains essentially an intergovernmental institution and continues to be driven by interest-based bargaining rather than being results oriented (*ibid.*).

Trubek and Mosher (2003) have identified several steps in the implementation of the EES as provided in Articles 128 to 130 EC and prior to the streamlining process of the employment and economic policy co-ordination processes:[17]

- *Theory development.* The Commission develops a theory of what is hindering employment growth. It develops these ideas after consulting the European Parliament, ECOSOC, Committee of the Regions and the EMCO.
- *Identification of best practice.* The Commission then identifies best-performing Member States and best practices. It identifies successful Member States' performance in order to incorporate their best practices into the Strategy.
- *Employment Policy Guidelines proposal.* The Commission then presents a proposal for the adoption of EPGs. Specific guidelines are drawn up indicating measures that Member States should implement to modify their national employment policies. An

16 The social partners represented on this committee are only European-level social partners. These are UNICE, CEEP, UEAPME, COPA (Committee of Agricultural Organizations in the EC) and EUROCOMMERCE on the employers' side and ETUC, EUROCADRES (Council of European Professional and Managerial Staff) and CEC (Confédération Européenne des Cadres) on the employees' side.
17 See also Appendices 1 and 2 for a description of the key phases of the EES and the changes made following its inclusion in the Lisbon Strategy.

attempt is made to produce a multi-area strategy cutting across a range of different areas that affect the trend of employment, such as taxation policies, unemployment policies, education policies and equal opportunities policies.

- *Approval of Employment Policy Guidelines.* The first EPGs were presented for approval to the European Council at the special Luxembourg Summit on Employment in 1997. In the years that followed, the EPGs and the Joint Employment Report (JER) have been considered at the December European Council meeting, where an overall general assessment of the employment situation is made. The EPGs are then passed by QMV at the joint ECOFIN and Social Affairs Council meeting that takes place after the December European Council (following the streamlining process this now takes place after the June European Council). On that occasion, Member States may review the Commission's proposals.[18]

- *Adoption of National Action Plans for Employment.* Once the Council adopts EPGs each Member State prepares NAPs (now NRPs) in accordance with the EPGs, followed by Implementation Reports, both of which are submitted to the Council and the Commission.

- *Monitoring procedure, recommendations and incentive measures.* The Commission each year examines the implementation of the EPGs by the Member States. It uses the NAPs, implementation reports, its own inquiries with the aid of the EMCO to assess the national reports.[19] In particular, the evaluation is a two-day meeting held in Brussels at which each Member State briefly presents its NAP. Other countries can use this opportunity both to learn about what is being done and to ask questions. This peer reviewing session is also known as the "Cambridge process". Subsequently, the Commission organizes a series of "bilateral" meetings with the Member States where a draft of its JER is may also be discussed.

The Council may decide by QMV on a recommendation from the Commission to issue recommendations to the Member States. The recommendation is without sanction and it is part of the "naming and shaming" process. In practice, Member States have been involved in drafting the recommendations to be issued against them through their representatives in EMCO. The result has been that the Commission's draft recommendations have been significantly watered down and simplified so as not to represent a considerable burden on the Member States concerned (Barnard 2006: 113). The Council, after consulting the ECOSOC and the Committee of the Regions, may also adopt incentive measures designed to encourage co-operation between Member States and support their action in the field of employment through initiatives aimed at developing exchanges of information and best practices, providing comparative analysis and advice as well as promoting innovative approaches and evaluating experiences, in particular by recourse to pilot projects (Article 129 EC). These measures shall not include harmonization of the laws and regulations of the Member States. Two declarations issued at the time of the adoption of the Amsterdam Treaty

---

18 As explained later in the chapter, further to the streamlining process of the employment and economic co-ordination processes, the two key European Council meetings at present are the Spring and June European Councils. The first summit reviews implementation and, on that basis, provides general guidelines for main priorities. The second summit approves the guidelines package presented by the Commission. See also Appendix 4 for an overview of the streamlining process.

19 As explained later in this chapter, following the streamlining process the assessment of the national reports is made by the Commission in its implementation package after the month of October and in its spring report within a three-year period.

limit the scope of Article 129 EC. The first sets limits to the validity, duration and funding of measures under this Article and the second says that incentive measures may not rely on the financing of the European Structural Funds. These limitations show how the Member States resisted any significant expansion of Community powers in relation to expenditure aimed at boosting job creation.

- *Adoption of a Joint Employment Report.* At the end of the annual cycle, the Commission and the Council write a JER (now part of the APR) on the employment situation in the Union and on the implementation of the EPGs by the Member States.
- *New process.* While the JER is being written, EPGs for the following year are being prepared and drafted.[20] It is at this stage that the Commission revises its conclusions on the situation of employment in the European Union and modifies, if necessary, its overall strategy for the EES.

From a governance perspective, the EES aims at introducing innovation while maintaining intact the main institutional design of the European Union, as a result of the political compromise for having a certain level of EU competence in the field of employment. Moreover, even though the policy cycle begins with policy objective setting by the Commission by drafting guidelines proposals, the Member States represented collectively by the Council must approve the Commission proposal through QMV (after consulting the European Parliament, the ECOSOC, the Committee of the Regions and the EMCO). In practice this amounts to a clear veto role which prevents the Commission from developing too much power in the definition of policy objectives (de la Porte 2008: 88). Further, the guidelines draw on the Presidency Conclusions of the European Council, 'which means that political priorities of the Member States (collectively) are institutionalized in steering the process' (*ibid.*). The EES does not cover all policies that are related to employment. Important areas such as monetary, fiscal and wage policy that concern economic and employment growth in the European Union are not included in the EES. Until the streamlining of the EES with the economic co-ordination processes within the Community Lisbon Programme (examined below), these policies have been addressed at European level by the economic co-ordination process through the adoption of BEPGs and, more broadly, in the context of the "Macroeconomic Dialogue".[21] As explained in more detail below, the EES was initially based on a four-pillar structure, with employment guidelines centred on these pillars:

- Improving employability.
- Creating a new culture of entrepreneurship.
- Promoting and encouraging the adaptability of firms and their workers.
- Strengthening equal opportunities policies.

The main objectives were: higher employment participation, increasing active unemployment systems, the number of highly skilled workers and employment intensive growth indicators, helping maintain the lower-skilled workers in employment, striking a balance between flexibility and security, supporting and promoting the start-up of smaller companies and entrepreneurship and promoting gender equality.

---

20 As explained later in this chapter, the annual cycle has been replaced by a three-year cycle, although the Employment Guidelines may be subject to interim reviews.
21 For detailed analysis see Chapter 3.

Although the pillars and guidelines have a clear Treaty basis in Title VIII, they pertain to the sphere of soft law, since they are not produced in the form of legally binding instruments such as Directives or regulations. Despite their "soft" nature, these guidelines have important implications for policy and law making within the Member States. In addition, the EC Treaty provides that legislation and regulation is still a matter for Member States. Articles 127 EC and 129 EC make it clear that Member States' competence in the field of employment must be respected and that measures taken by the Council to promote employment shall not include harmonization of the laws and regulations of the Member States. Moreover, there are no legal sanctions to be imposed on any Member State that fails to comply with the employment guidelines. Article 129 EC, however, has led to the launch of the peer review procedure.[22] Under this procedure Member States hosted reviews of their own programmes and visited programmes presented by other Member States. Some assessments of the first years of implementation of the Employment Strategy show that little learning was achieved and there was no evidence of significant policy transfer (Casey and Gold 2005: 23).

Apart from the equal opportunities guidelines, which are linked to the gender equality objectives of the EC Treaty, all the other guidelines are part of a supply-side strategy that focuses on the structural problems of unemployment, in line with a neo-liberal conception of economic integration (Scharpf 2002: 654–655). Theoretically, they are a combination of neo-liberal policy objectives stressing deregulation and individual responsibility for training and labour market mobility and neo-corporatist strategies which envisage collective solutions to the reconciliation of flexibility and security. However, their "accent" remains strongly neo-liberal (Velluti 2009: 146). The EES is essentially a soft co-ordination process which 'apes the business-oriented model of "management by objectives" aimed at delivering targets within a given timeframe' (Barnard 2006: 114). As explained later in this chapter the predilection for better regulation and good governance with a focus on output efficiency over social rights and social justice discourses is problematic, and rather than representing a means of strengthening the "European social model" the EES risks undermining its very existence.

The EES is conceived in a way that does not challenge the *acquis* of the Internal Market and EMU, as they remain the paramount objectives of the Community. Even when responding to the guidelines, therefore, Member States continue to operate under exactly the same legal and economic constraints of economic integration which limit their policy choices when they are acting individually (Scharpf 2002: 655). For example, if unemployment rises to high levels within the "euro zone", the EPGs cannot recommend the ECB to lower interest rates; likewise if unemployment is high in a given Member State, the EPGs cannot recommend the Council to relax the strict rules of the SGP, nor the Commission to relax competition or state aid rules; similarly EPGs cannot suggest increases in taxation on capital incomes, or controls on capital exchange to reduce cuts in social expenditure imposed by fiscal constraints (*ibid.*). The EES, however, covers a much larger number of social policy areas than have been addressed through traditional EU level social policy regulation, and the EPGs concern a wider range of important policy issues. The EES trades off the legal force of traditional regulations in order for the European Union to deal with some key areas of social policy that have been until 1997 solely reserved to the Member States (Trubek and Mosher 2003: 37).

---

22 In 2005 peer review was incorporated into the Mutual Learning Programme. See, e.g., <http://www.mutual-learning-employment.net/>.

Following an impact evaluation report in 2002 and key communications in which the Commission outlined a redesign of the EES (European Commission 2002b, 2003), the strategy was simplified, with the employment guidelines reduced to "ten commandments", streamlined with the economic co-ordination process and transformed into a three-year policy cycle, the focus being on full employment, quality and productivity of work and cohesion and inclusion. The EES was subject to another significant revision in 2005 following the relaunch of the Lisbon Strategy pursuant to the recommendations of the Kok Report (2004). This new process sees the adoption of Integrated Guidelines for Growth and Jobs (2005–2008). Reduced from ten to eight, the employment guidelines are now part of the package of twenty-four guidelines of the Lisbon Strategy. The guidelines are presented in conjunction with the macroeconomic and microeconomic guidelines (previously named "Broad Economic Policy Guidelines") for a period of three years. Despite these changes, the employment guidelines have maintained the same principles on which they were initially based.[23] Hence the underlying neo-liberal rationale remains untouched if not strengthened by the reform process and, as shown later in this chapter, it may be argued that with the significant reduction of the employment guidelines there has been a loss of visibility of other guidelines centred on more social democratic and social justice discourses, the equality guidelines being a case in point.

4 The first years of the Employment Strategy: the adoption and implementation of the Guidelines for Employment for 1998 and 1999

The EES, as we have seen, was implemented before the entry into force of the Treaty of Amsterdam. The French government had insisted that an Extraordinary Summit on Employment should be scheduled in the autumn of 1997. The Luxembourg Summit, which took place in November 1997, fast-tracked the EES and on 15 December 1997 the first EPGs were issued[24] on the basis of detailed working papers and documents presented by Member States, social partners, the Commission and the EU Parliament.[25] The Commission's proposals, however, were watered down. Quantitative targets and a timetable for the increase of employment were not agreed notwithstanding the Commission's proposal of a target of 65 per cent of those of working age to be employed within five years. Similarly, the Commission's proposal to reducing the EU unemployment rate to 7 per cent of the working population was not included (Kenner 1999: 52; Goetschy 1999: 128).

A common structure for the NAPs was agreed at the end of January 1998 and the Member States agreed to submit their reports by mid-April to the British Presidency and the Commission. These first NAPs represented the basis for preliminary discussions at the Cardiff Summit of 15 June 1998. In December 1998 the Vienna European Council examined the implementation of the NAPs and new guidelines were adopted for the following year. The EPGs were based on four pillars (Council of the European Union 1999d):

---

23 See Appendix 3 for a comparison of the main characteristics of the co-ordination processes in fiscal, economic and employment policy.

24 Nineteen EPGs were issued.

25 These guidelines were broadly based on the Commission proposals (European Commission 1997b).

- *Employability*. Member States had five years to adopt measures and schemes that would guarantee the young unemployed (between fifteen and twenty-four years of age) vocational training and work experience within the first six months of unemployment; for adults, within the first year. Spain pushed for an extension of these periods for those states with particularly high levels of unemployment. The proportion of unemployed receiving training should be increased to 20 per cent, which corresponded to the three best-performing Member States.[26] A guideline also provided for a reduction of the levels of young persons not completing the years of study but no specific target was agreed notwithstanding the Commission's proposal.
- *Entrepreneurship*. Member States were to support start-ups and businesses with specific measures and incentives. A new action plan of ECU 10 billion was approved for the EIB funding of new businesses. A new budget of ECU 450 million to provide loans for small and medium-sized enterprises (SMEs) was also agreed. In this context, Member States were required to foster self-employment and the creation of new jobs. This would be achieved, *inter alia*, through reductions in taxes, indirect labour costs (including labour productivity costs) and VAT on labour-intensive services, which could be seen as inhibiting the demand of new labour force.
- *Adaptability*. This is the area where the social partners were called to play an important role through the adoption of agreements at sectoral and company levels. The objective was the modernization of work organization, increasing the competitiveness of firms and attempting to strike a balance between flexibility and security of the workers. The United Kingdom declared that national differences in working time should be respected.
- *Equal opportunities*. The objective was to reduce discrimination against women at the work place. The Commission had initially proposed that the target regarding the reduction of the gap between men's and women's unemployment rate should be of 50 per cent within five years. The Commission had also included the provision of child care services in order to achieve the same standard of the (average of) three best-performing Member States in the rest of the European Union. Again no specific targets were agreed at the Summit.

The EPGs aim at achieving the following objectives (Trubek and Mosher 2003: 37–38):[27]

- *Higher employment participation*. Because of the ageing of the population and the threat this poses to social security systems, the European Union needs a higher proportion of its working-age population working. This also explains why early retirement schemes are considered as being detrimental to this objective and why female employment and part-time work have been given greater emphasis at European level.
- *More active unemployment systems*. Passive unemployment systems with generous social and employment benefits are a disincentive to actively seek work and to improving working skills necessary for workers to find work.
- *More skilled workers*. Increased economic and technological change requires workers to be better skilled at the outset as well as the ability to develop new skills throughout life.

---

26 The Luxembourg Presidency was pushing for 25 per cent but Germany was against it.
27 By and large the objectives of the Employment Guidelines have remained unchanged in subsequent years even after the streamlining and simplification processes.

- *More employment intensive growth indicators.* The European Union lags behind in the provision of services which are said to provide employment intensive growth. This is true in particular in the "social economy", including services provided by non-profit groups and private companies. Europe must encourage the social economy and decrease direct taxes on labour-intensive services.
- *Fewer obstacles to low-skill workers.* The European Union must also ensure the employment of low-skilled workers. Tax systems, especially high flat-rate social charges, discourage low-skilled workers from working and impede more appointments of low-skill workers. Tax systems, therefore, should be adjusted in order to ensure employment for low-skilled workers.
- *Strike a balance between flexibility and security.* Economic and technological change requires more flexibility in the way work is organized and workers organize their lives. The model of a male worker working full-time on a normal work week for one firm his entire life must be replaced by a model that allows firms more flexibility in terms of working time, envisions greater heterogeneity in the types of workers (men, women, full-time, part-time), and at the same time supports and protects workers, who will be changing jobs much more often. In practice, this requires the definition of new mechanisms ensuring a balance between flexibility and the security of the workers.
- *Support and promote the start-up of smaller companies and entrepreneurship.* In the majority of the Member States SMEs represent the most dynamic areas of the economy. A way of supporting and fostering self-employment and the setting up of more SMEs is reforming and simplifying national tax systems.
- *Promote gender equality.* The various forms of disadvantage faced by women in the labour market need to be addressed at European level in order to increase employment participation of women and ensure equal opportunity. These may include pay discrimination, higher levels of unemployment, and obstacles to combining work and family life.

The stress on working flexibility and the role of entrepreneurship in creating jobs embodies the "Third Way" emphasis (Kenner 1999) on overcoming dependence and shows acceptance of the need to promote risk taking and adapt social protection to the need by business for flexibility (*ibid.*: 52). Nonetheless, the EES foresees an important role for the state and for the social partners: it presume that the core of the welfare state will remain in force and does not envisage major changes in the organization of industrial relations. The role of the social partners is not mentioned in a formal institutional sense in the Employment Title (Szyszczak 2001a: 1148). On this point, Smismans (2004: 7) says that it is striking that Article 128(3) EC, which asks the Member States to submit national reports, does not make any reference to the role of the social partners and to the sub-national public authorities in drafting the national reports, particularly since the EES is defined as being a decentralized form of governance. The Treaty does recognize explicitly the autonomy and role of the social partners in employment policy at national level (Article 126(2) EC). However, the phrasing that Member States in co-ordinating their action to promote employment should have regard to 'national practices related to the responsibilities of management and labour' can hardly be said to be a proactive approach to encourage decentralized participation (Smismans 2004: 10). Moreover, the reference to "national practices" does not include a recognition of the role in the EES of the European social partners. This silence in the Employment Title 'does not rightly reflect the framework in which an EES should develop' (*ibid.*). However, while the social partners do not have the same powers that they have been given under Title XI, their consultation is envisaged at several stages in the articulation and implementation of employment policy. Moreover, national social partners are considered as playing an important role in the preparation and drafting of the national reports. Throughout the Employment Guidelines there is recognition that the social partners have a key role in employment creation. Under what used to be the Adaptability and Employability pillars the social partners were considered as being the main actors to ensure the adaptability of workers and the modernization of work organization as well as the employability of workers through partnerships and lifelong learning strategies. The Lisbon European Council confirmed the importance of the social partners in the drawing up, implementation and follow up of the guidelines and post-Lisbon Horizontal Objective C called social partners to be actively involved in supporting the EES by developing their own process of implementation of the guidelines for which they have responsibility and to report on progress. In so doing, it fostered a strong relationship between national and European social partners. Similarly, the Integrated Guidelines for 2005–2008 envisage an important role for the social partners, regional and local governments and for civil society in the implementation of the guidelines.

Moreover, the EES is a strategy which looks at reform and recalibration in the short run, with a gradual shift towards major restructuring in the long run. The documents submitted to the Vienna European Council included the JER for 1998, the *Employment in Europe 1998* report, the EPGs for 1999 and six specific studies on benchmarking, statistics, employment rates, job creation in the IT sector, modernization of work organization, public services and public investment. What emerged was a stronger commitment to establishing a link between the EPGs and the BEPGs and between structural policies and employment policy. The Commission was asked to prepare various communications for 1999 on such matters as tax systems, international financial markets, investment in infrastructure and human capital, economic policy co-ordination, mainstreaming EU policies and the establishment of an EEP. "Consolidation" and "continuity" were considered pivotal aspects of the strategy and only minor amendments were made compared to the previous EPGs. The NAPs submitted were documents which summarized measures that had been adopted previously, or actions and schemes which had been decided by the Member States without really taking into account the EPGs. The nature of these national reports highlighted the difficulty Member States had in changing their employment policies in such a short period of time (Biagi 1998: 331).

At the Vienna European Council it was agreed that the structure of the 1999 EPGs should be based on the four pillars established for the 1998 EPGs. The employment guidelines were centred on the methodology rather than the content of the NAPs, with particular focus on benchmarking of best practice, statistical data, quantified targets and indicators. Furthermore, the NAPs had to be presented in a standard and simple format and one per Member State.

Member States were also required to present an Implementation Report together with the NAPs. This report constituted 'an annual report on the principal measures taken to implement its employment policy in the light of the guidelines for employment' which Member States had to submit to the Council and the Commission (Article 128(3) EC). On 15 June 1998 the Commission provided Member States with a questionnaire to facilitate the drafting of the Implementation Report. The questionnaire was divided into two parts. The first part laid out a series of general questions addressed to all the Member States.[28] In

---

28 The questions concerned issues regarding the social partners, the distribution of resources, the extent of funding provided by the European Social Fund, monitoring procedures and the nature of the methodologies employed.

the second part, the questions were addressed to individual Member States with a request for specific explanatory studies. For example, Italy was asked to explain the role of the regions in relation to preventative measures for the fight against long-term unemployment (G 1 and G 2) since its NAP reported of institutional devolution from the central government to the regional authorities in the field of public services (Italy 1998). Through a careful formulation of these questions the Commission was able to implicitly exert pressure on the Member States and to direct them towards achieving specific targets.

In its Communication *From Guidelines to Action: The National Action Plans for Employment* (European Commission 1998b) and in the 1998 JER the Commission and the Council evaluated the NAPs, which can be succinctly summarized in six main points (European Commission 1998c):

- Measures focused on the "employability" and "entrepreneurship" pillars and only marginally on the "adaptability" and "equal opportunities" pillars. More precisely the implementation of the strategy under the four pillars was uneven.
- Most of the initiatives listed were general programmes reproducing measures adopted in the national employment pacts and not specific responses to the guidelines.
- There was an insufficient distribution of resources for the measures to be implemented and no attention on the effects of the measures on the employment situation.
- Insufficient attention was given to long-term unemployment preventative measures.
- The funds of the ESF were not addressed satisfactorily.
- Most NAPs failed to define precise quantitative targets, an implementation timetable and to provide statistical data.

Moreover, the NAPs reported that the social partners were actively involved in the preparation of the NAPs in Austria, Belgium, Germany, the Netherlands and the United Kingdom,[29] although the final drafts were prepared by the central governments and on the whole only a few measures may be said to have been adopted on the basis of the social partners' initiatives. Once again, the Commission was able to direct Member States to the pursuit of specific targets and thus exert pressure on them by avoiding any direct reference of those Member States that had failed to implement the guidelines. It mentioned only those NAPs that in accordance with the EPGs had provided the most effective measures to fight unemployment. The governments of the defaulting Member States saw the lack of reference of their report as a form of criticism, although the Commission had not made any explicit criticism (Biagi 1998a; Rampini 1998).

With regard to the content of the NAPs, the Commission stated that the national reports were in most cases declaratory in nature rather than operative instruments. It observed that only four Member States – France, Spain, Luxembourg and the United Kingdom – had adopted a preventative approach in relation to G 1, G 2 and G 3. Once again the lack of reference to certain Member States indicated that they were still not in line with the EPGs, especially G 3. This form of political sanction used by the Commission as opposed to the more traditional legal sanction was intended to exercise peer pressure on the Member States, focusing on the psychological effect that it entailed (Smith 1998). This form of sanction was "self-binding" and "self-imposing" in that the national government concerned would end up feeling compelled to take the necessary measures to meet the targets

---

29 In Germany, the Netherlands and the United Kingdom the joint contributions of the social partners were included in the NAPs.

required. Consequently, the implicit comparison with the more "successful" Member States and implicit criticism of their mode of operation exerted a strong pressure on national governments since this soft sanction could have a significant impact on them in the domestic arena and be used against them either by the public media or the opposing party.

In 1999, following the second evaluation of the NAPs, specific recommendations to the Member States for the year 2000 were issued for the first time. The Commission stated that the measures implemented at national level were insufficient in eight areas, namely:

- The fight against youth unemployment (Belgium, Greece, Spain, Italy).
- Preventative measures against long-term unemployment (Belgium, Germany, Spain, Italy).
- Tax and unemployment benefit reforms (Germany, Greece, Italy, the Netherlands, Austria).
- Job creation in the service sector (Belgium, Germany, Greece, Spain, France, Ireland, Italy, Portugal).
- More employment-friendly tax systems (Belgium, Germany, France, Italy, Austria, Finland, Sweden).
- Modernization of work organization (Greece, France, Portugal, United Kingdom).
- The fight against gender inequalities (Germany, Spain, Greece, Ireland, Italy, Luxembourg, Austria, United Kingdom).
- Improving indicators and statistical tools (Germany, Greece, Spain, Italy, the Netherlands, United Kingdom).

The best-performing Member States were the Scandinavian countries and those where unemployment was fairly low such as Luxembourg, the Netherlands, Portugal and Austria. While employment growth generally increased in the European Union in 1999,[30] the positive trend varied between the Member States. In most Member States this increase was a result of economic growth and labour market reforms. In other Member States employment growth was also linked to lower labour productivity rates, as in the case of Denmark, Germany, Italy and the United Kingdom. Other countries, such as Spain (15.9 per cent), Italy (11.3 per cent), France (11.3 per cent), Finland (10.2 per cent) and Greece (11.6 per cent), were still faced with higher levels of unemployment.

The 2000 JER emphasized the existence of four major issues related to unemployment: youth unemployment and long-term unemployment still persisted and the percentage of early retirement of older workers from the labour market remained high.[31] Differences in unemployment rates between Member States varied significantly: whereas Austria, Belgium, France and Italy had the highest rates, Sweden, Denmark and Portugal instead had the highest rates. Another employment-related problem was linked to the nature of the labour markets, including those countries with high levels of employment: most of them showed signs of tightness, bottlenecks and skill shortages. The JER for the year 2000, therefore, called for the implementation of activation policies and measures aimed at promoting labour mobility (European Commission 2000a).

---

30 Unemployment fell again in 1999 to 9.2 per cent and in 2000 it went down to 8.7 per cent. Despite moderate growth in 1998/1999 strong employment gains were achieved, with 4 million new jobs created. The overall EU employment rate rose to 62.2 per cent, of which, however, only 56.5 per cent corresponded to full-time). The employment rate went back to the same levels as the early 1990s before Member States were subject to economic recession.

31 In 1999 the employment rate of those aged fifty-five to sixty-four was below 37 per cent.

Prior to their accession to the European Union in 2004, the new Member States had been defining labour market and employment policies in line with European standards and progressively adjusting institutions and policies to the EES in order to allow the full implementation of the Employment Title as from accession. To this end, in 1999 the Commission initiated a co-operation process on employment with these countries, which also aimed at ensuring that both the present EU financial support for accession and the preparation for ESF implementation would focus on supporting the identified employment policy priorities (European Commission 2003a). Moreover, at the European Council in Stockholm in 2001 it was decided that the future Member States should be actively involved in the goals and procedures of the Lisbon Strategy. The National Plan for the Adoption of the *acquis* required candidate countries to take responsibility for drawing up long-term market strategies as a basis for the detailed annual action plan, which had to be drawn up each year under the EES (European Commission 2002c). Several of the candidate countries drew up employment action plans containing programmes that were structured on the basis of the EES. Moreover, candidate countries and the Commission analyzed the key challenges for employment policies in Joint Assessment Papers (JAPs) on the basis of studies funded by the Commission in co-operation with the European Training Foundation. At the beginning of 2002 seven CEECs had been evaluated.[32] Candidate countries and the European Commission subsequently agreed to monitor the implementation of the JAP commitments. Shortly after the signature of the JAPs the main targets were discussed in technical seminars between the European Commission and representatives of different Ministries, regional authorities, the public employment services (PES) and the social partners to encourage policy action (European Commission 2003a). In late spring 2002 the JAPs were reviewed in a second round. This reviewing process helped to identify strategic challenges, some of which were shared with the current Member States (European Commission 2003b). Studies (Khol and Platzer 2003; Celin 2003; Editorial 2003) conducted on these countries showed that:

- Sectoral characteristics of employment in the candidate countries were quite different from those in the current EU Member States. In CEECs agriculture and industry had a much higher share of total employment. The restructuring process had severely damaged the industrial sector, leading to high levels of unemployment. The service sector now represents the main source of new jobs.
- Labour relations in CEECs were developing along nationally characteristic lines and were showing considerable variations. A comparison of structural developments in labour relations in the eight CEECs candidate countries at company, sectoral and national levels showed that change was difficult to achieve. Significant common features, except for Slovenia, were weak and fragmented structured companies with widespread absence of a sectoral level of action and organization and a pronounced emphasis on the state.
- Educational and training levels were generally lower than those of current EU Member States.
- Labour productivity levels varied widely, due to the specificities of each candidate country.

32 The first JAPs were signed with the Czech Republic, Slovenia, Poland and Estonia in 2000 and early 2001, followed by Malta, Hungary, Slovakia, Cyprus and Lithuania in late 2001/early 2002 and by Romania, Bulgaria in autumn 2002. The JAP with Latvia was signed in early 2003.

- High levels of long-term unemployment as a consequence of structural and economic reform, which affected marginalized groups, such as minorities, the disabled, the low-skilled, older workers and people living in remote regions. The restructuring process also entailed an increase of informal employment.
- Education and vocational training levels were generally lower than those in most current EU countries.
- High levels of regional and social disparities.
- Inefficiency of PES to adapt to the new economic and social scenario and their incapacity to create new jobs. This emerged during the transition period.
- Lack of national financial resources for implementing effective labour market and employment policies.

Furthermore, in most cases the drafting of the JAPs has been a purely administrative exercise, with a lack of political commitment from most governments of the candidate countries. In its report on progress on the implementation of the JAPs the Commission maintained that, despite significant differences, candidate countries had made progress in transforming their labour markets and in adjusting policies to EU standards. The report identified the following strategic priorities for the labour markets of candidate countries:

- Increase labour supply, employment rates, particularly in the service sector, together with productivity rates and skill levels.
- Restructure the CEECs' economic system and the labour markets by way of taking into consideration the specificities and levels of adaptability of CEECs to change.
- Linked to the former, reduce the reliance on agriculture and traditional industrial sectors.

The first years of the EES were pivotal in further addressing the unemployment problem across the European Union representing, therefore, a collective response to what had become a matter of common concern to the majority of the Member States. Furthermore, the various documents and texts produced in the context of the Employment Strategy brought to the fore existing problems within individual Member States and the different socio-economic rationales underpinning European labour markets. In this context, it confirmed the existence of clearly identifiable groups of Member States with similar welfare state systems, labour market and socio-economic structures and trends, which were confronted with similar problems in relation to unemployment. The review of Member States' policies also revealed significant differences between northern European and southern Mediterranean countries not only in the way labour markets were structured, the composition of the labour force and the nature of employment-related problems but also in the typology of measures used and, more broadly, in the regulatory approaches to tackling the unemployment problem. Overall, it also showed the difficulty most Member States had in falling into line with the EPGs and, at the same time, the limitations of extant regulatory measures. From a policy perspective, the main innovative feature of the EES was the policy mix that it promoted, namely, the combined use of measures in different policy areas such as structural policy, economic policy and social policy, albeit in a limited way.

From a governance perspective, what is significant of these first years is the central proactive role of the Commission in the policy objective setting of the strategy. While not always succeeding in having its EPGs proposals passed by the Council it was still able to exert a strong pressure on the Member States in ensuring better compliance with the EPGs.

Hence, in the first years of implementation while the EES may be said to have been predominantly intergovernmental the Commission has been nevertheless a significant player in ensuring the further development of the strategy and, chiefly, in avoiding the "errors" of the Essen Strategy. However, the analysis conducted above also seems to suggest that a close connection between key political actors in the Member States and the Commission was an important factor in the emergence and first years of implementation of the EES. The policy agenda proposed by the Commission would not have been adopted had it not coincided with the policy aims of the majority of the Member States (de la Porte 2008: 96). With regard to its purported promotion of "bottom-to-top" policy making and democratic participatory element, some NAPs reported that social partners had been involved in the preparation of the first NAPs but only in relation to the first drafts while the final drafts were prepared by the central governments and thus it is difficult to evaluate the extent to which they have been actively involved in the definition of new measures.

5 The European Employment Strategy after the Lisbon Summit and the "ratification" of the OMC

In the years that followed, EC employment policy still gathered momentum. In the year 2000 employment improved considerably while growth increased significantly in most European countries. It was this positive socio-economic scenario that provided the political drive for launching the Lisbon Strategy. Degryse and Pochet (2001: 11) maintain that the OMC was in a sense ratified at the Lisbon Summit, in that it was extended to other aspects of social policy. More broadly, Member States agreed 'a new strategic goal for the Union [for the next decade] in order to strengthen employment, economic reform and social cohesion as part of a knowledge-based economy' (European Council 2000: 1–2)[33] The underlying aim was to put the European Union on an equal footing with the United States and Japan. The major objectives were:

- *Education and training for living and working in a knowledge-based society.* Among the various measures and aims there was Internet access in schools; an EU framework of basic skills – IT skills, languages, technological culture, entrepreneurship and social skills; increasing mobility of students and teachers. Furthermore, a quantified target was agreed of halving by 2010 the number of eighteen to twenty-four-year-olds leaving lower secondary education who were not in further education or training.[34]
- *More and better jobs for Europe: developing an active employment policy.* The quantitative target of achieving the 70 per cent on average by 2010 and for women the 60 per cent by 2010 was combined with the qualitative aspect of the target by recognizing Member States' different situations and by allowing them to establish national employment targets for improving the employment rate.[35] Four key areas were to be addressed by the Council and the Commission: improving employability and reducing skill gaps; giving higher priority to lifelong learning; increasing employment services; furthering all aspects of equal opportunities.

33 See also European Council (2000a); European Council (2000b: paras. 24–28).
34 This target was later introduced in the EPGs for 2001.
35 The Stockholm Summit, in March 2001, defined interim targets for employment rates: 67 per cent overall and 57 per cent for women for January 2005; and set an EU target for increasing the average EU employment rate among older women and men (fifty-five to sixty-four) to 50 per cent by 2010; European Council (2001).

- *Modernizing social protection.* The European Council invited the Council to strengthen co-operation between Member States through the exchange of best practice and agreed that the High Level Working Party on Social Protection would have to support this co-operation with the main priority of achieving the sustainability of pension systems by 2020 and beyond.
- *Promoting social inclusion.* Policies for combating social exclusion should be passed on the basis of the OMC combining national action plans with the Commission's initiatives. In particular, the Commission and the Council should promote social inclusion through: (1) exchange of best practice and information on the basis of commonly agreed indicators; (2) mainstreaming the promotion of inclusion in Member States' employment, education, training policies, health and housing policies, with the funding of the Structural Funds.

The key achievement of the Lisbon Summit was to provide a clear and positive link between social, employment and economic issues and to place the renewal of the "European social model" at the heart of an integrated economic and employment strategy (Ashiagbor 2005: 190). In particular, Lisbon emphasizes a fundamental transformation of the "European social model" from merely activating the unemployed to the "adult worker model" goal of promoting employment for all adults (Annesley 2007: 195). This entails increasing economic activity rates overall, getting all adults – including those conventionally excluded from the labour market – into employment and ensuring adequate levels of social protection (European Commission 2005: 28). One of such measures agreed at Lisbon was to shift the target from 'high levels of employment' (Article 2 EC) to 'full employment' (European Council 2000).

The Presidency Conclusions of the European Council listed sixty actions to be taken in ten different fields. The detailed list of new actions, initiatives and measures emphasized a more decisive and less rhetorical approach to social policy issues with the further implementation of the EES and with the use of a new regulatory tool, the OMC, which refers to the alternative "softer" method of policy making that is used either in areas in which there has traditionally been a very narrow margin of opportunity for action at European level or in areas which have never been in the remit of Community decision making. In particular, it was decided that the priority areas in the framework of the OMC were to be employment, social protection, social security and education. Hence the rigid traditional procedures were replaced by the "soft" approach in which the Luxembourg (employment), Cardiff (economic reform) and Cologne (macroeconomic reform) processes have become increasingly co-ordinated.

The Conclusions of the Lisbon Summit were very similar to those already proposed by the White Paper *Growth, Competitiveness and Employment* (Degryse and Pochet 2001: 14). The White Paper analyzed ways of improving the European Union's competitiveness in comparison with the United States and it aimed at tackling unemployment with the creation of new technology jobs. To that end, various measures were agreed with the definition of EU funding to invest in European infrastructure networks in the fields of telecommunications (ECU 150 billion), energy and transport (ECU 250 billion) and environmental projects (ECU 174 billion). In the White Paper the Commission identified three types of unemployment: cyclical, structural and technological (European Commission 1993a: 3–4). It also proposed to reduce labour costs with compensatory fiscal measures.[36]

---

36 The Member States adopted the White Paper, without the most ambitious targets, i.e. 15 million jobs to be created by 2000, the funding of the trans-European networks and plans for European energy taxes.

Although the Lisbon Presidency Conclusions were similar to the White Paper in terms of objectives, policy mix and the typology of measures to be used, the approach was very different. Whereas the latter prescribed numerical objectives for reducing unemployment, the former provided numerical targets for increasing the employment rate. Moreover, in the Lisbon Strategy the competitiveness targets are to be met by means of further liberalization (e.g. telecommunications, gas, electricity, postal services and public transport) with the concomitant reduction in state intervention and state aid. Goetschy (2001: 6) posits that EU economic integration was not an end in itself but a means to support employment and social cohesion. At the same time, social cohesion and high employment levels had to underpin conditions for economic growth. More precisely, the Lisbon Summit aimed at 'modernizing the "European social model" by investing in people and building an active welfare state' (European Council 2000: 7 ff.). An earlier official definition of the "European social model" reflected this "utilitarian" approach to social policy with respect to the economic objectives of the Community: in addition to the recognition of social justice as a policy target and the importance of a high-level bargaining between the social partners, emphasis is placed on 'the acceptance of the productive role of social policy and its contribution to economic efficiency' (European Council 1997b).

The OMC, launched at the Lisbon Summit, has its origins in the "hard" fiscal provisions and "soft" economic provisions of the EMU (de la Porte 2002: 40–41; de la Porte and Pochet 2002: 32–34). With regard to the former, Articles 98–104 EC (ex Articles 102a to 104c EC) and Article 121 EC (ex-Article 109j EC) together with the Protocol on the Excessive Deficit Procedure, the Protocol on the Convergence Criteria and the SGP introduce basic rules for budgetary soundness and establish procedures for the surveillance of national fiscal policies.[37] Member States have agreed to meet certain convergence criteria in the form of benchmarks, namely, a sound government budgetary position with budget deficits that should not exceed 3 per cent of GDP and a public debt ratio of no more than 60 per cent of GDP. In the event of non-compliance with the SGP, the Council is empowered to issue a recommendation and a formal sanction in case of infringement of the SGP. In the context of economic policy co-ordination, a multilateral surveillance system has been set up to guarantee that national economic policies do not hinder EU economic policy objectives and, for those Member States that had joined the EMU, also compliance with the objectives of monetary policy. In this case, the BEPGs set up a framework for the "soft" co-ordination of economic policies laying out the main objectives and substituting the strict requirements of the "hard" monetary policy provisions with peer pressure (Article 99 EC). Hence the OMC is based on the "hard" procedures regarding national fiscal policies and the "soft" co-ordination process regarding national economic policies.

The same definition of this novel regulatory tool as an "open method"[38] signifies the decision to include different policy areas of EU law in this co-ordination process as well as illustrating the fact that targets are for the most part not quantified. On this point Smismans (2004: 2) criticizes the OMC's openness as being circumscribed to meaning open ended in its outcomes rather than in terms of increased participation of stakeholders and public scrutiny. There is no single OMC method. Belgian Minister Vandenbroucke (2001) – who played a key part in launching the social inclusion and pension OMCs during his country's 2001 EU Presidency – suggestively defined the OMC as 'a kind of cookbook

37 See Chapter 3.
38 For an analysis of the meaning of "open" in the OMC, see Telò (2001).

that contains various recipes, lighter and heavier ones'.[39] The 'OMC is thus given the freedom to evolve and continues to supply a safety net for the creation of policy objectives and their normative development' (Szyszczak 2006: 490). Post-Lisbon the OMC has been applied to and variously implemented across other policy areas of the first pillar (Laffan and Shaw 2005).

This experimental mode of EU governance can be described as constituting an enmeshment of open participation in the implementation of policies, consensus building, exchange of best practice and information, use of benchmarking and more broadly co-operation and co-ordination within a multi-tiered framework of governance (Velluti 2003: 360). As Borrás and Jacobsson (2004: 187) have effectively put it, the OMC 'perches on the fence between the Community method and the international method, it coaxes Member States into co-ordinating their national public actions within a collectively decided framework, it spreads widely into different policy areas, and it cuts across the national–EU borders using persuasion but not coercion'.

This new process defined in general terms by the European Council, structured in more detail by the Commission and the Council and implemented under the supervision of the executive body of the European Union and in most cases *ad hoc* EU committees, relies upon peer pressure. The constraint on Member States is not a legal one, since the OMC lacks any system of sanctions and enforcement procedures; it may be defined as a moral constraint, or better said, as a form of political pressure. Because of these characteristics this governance method is defined as being "soft" in nature as opposed to the traditional "hard" law instruments (Abbott and Snidal 2000: 421). The OMC is thus the 'means of spreading best practice and achieving greater convergence towards the main EU goals' (European Council 2000).

According to the Presidency Conclusions of the Lisbon Summit this method involves:

- Fixing guidelines for the Union combined with specific timetables for achieving the goals which they set in the short, medium and long term.
- Establishing, where appropriate, quantitative and qualitative indicators and benchmarks against the best in the world and tailored to the needs of different Member States and sectors as a means of comparing best practice.
- Translating these European guidelines into national and regional policies by setting specific targets and adopting measures, taking into account national and regional differences.
- Periodic monitoring, evaluation and peer review organized as a mutual learning process.

It was also agreed that a fully decentralized approach would be applied in line with the principle of subsidiarity in which the European Union, the Member States, the regional and local levels as well as the social partners and civil society (ECOSOC 1999) would be actively involved, using variable forms of partnership (European Council 2000). As explained in Chapter 2, it is open to debate whether we may refer to subsidiarity being applied in the context of the OMC. Smismans (2008a: 172) for instance maintains that the OMC may represent a threat to subsidiarity in that it allows the European Union to intervene in new policy areas without apparently having to justify itself in subsidiarity terms. In his view the application of the OMC entails rather a fusion of competences,

---

39 See also European Convention (2003: para. 39).

with target setting and definition of policy priorities which may equally take place at European and national levels (*ibid.*).

Moreover, according to a traditional understanding of subsidiarity, Article 5(2) EC applies to the field of shared legislative competence and thus co-ordination processes are outside its scope of application. If we departed from a traditional conceptualization of subsidiarity there would still be other problems in relation to its possible application to the OMC, given that subsidiarity is an *ex post* judicial mechanism of accountability. In particular, because of the aforementioned fusion of competences it would be difficult to establish exactly who should be held accountable to whom and for what (*ibid.*: 173). The Commission does not have the same institutional role as under the Community Method where it has the nearly exclusive right of legislative initiative, representing the common European interest, and thus the European Institution that would need to provide justification. The OMC is a cyclical process, with a central role assigned to the European Council and the Council of Ministers (as explained further below) and it has been designed as a decentralized co-ordination process. Hence would the Commission be required to provide justification for co-ordination at European level in its role as drafter of guidelines or rather the European Council or the Council of Ministers as agenda setters? This second scenario would lead to the paradoxical situation whereby the Member States would have to provide justification to themselves (*ibid.*: 174).

In this context, Smismans (*ibid.*: 174–175) welcomes the Protocol on subsidiarity and proportionality of the Lisbon Treaty as it provides for an *ex ante* mechanism through which national parliaments can require the Commission to reconsider its proposal on the ground that it would not respect subsidiarity. However, the new Protocol on subsidiarity of the Lisbon Treaty only applies to legislation.[40] Thus, while the Protocol could provide some political teeth to the principle of subsidiarity regarding legislative initiatives, it cannot do so for the OMC. Nevertheless, it could be possible in accordance with the governance model elaborated in Chapter 2 to envision a similar "flagging down" power for national parliaments in relation to the OMC. While any such warning mechanism would have significant procedural problems such as the short time available for national parliaments to react and co-ordinate their action it would at least provide the platform for encouraging national parliaments to become more actively involved with the OMC.

Shortly after the Lisbon European Council, the Commission maintained that the OMC is used on a case-by-case basis (European Commission 2001a: 21), that the use of guidelines

---

40 The Lisbon Treaty replaced Article 5 EC with new Article 5 TEU, where it adds an explicit reference to the regional and local dimension of the principle of subsidiarity. Furthermore, the Lisbon Treaty replaces the 1997 protocol on the application of the principles of subsidiarity and proportionality by a new protocol with the same name, the main difference being the new role of the national parliaments in ensuring respect for the principle of subsidiarity. The Lisbon Treaty introduces an early-warning mechanism whereby national parliaments have eight weeks in which to submit opinions to the Commission on draft legislative Acts, which it must send to them at the same time as to the European Parliament and the Council. If one-third of national parliaments contest the conformity of a draft legislative Act with the principle of subsidiarity, in a reasoned opinion, then the Commission must re-examine the draft and explain why it is maintaining it (the "yellow card" procedure). This threshold must be one-quarter of national parliaments for draft legislation relating to the area of freedom, security and justice. In addition, if a simple majority of national parliaments challenge the conformity of a draft legislative Act with the principle of subsidiarity (the "orange card" procedure) and the Commission maintains its proposal, the matter is referred to the Council and European Parliament, which issue a decision at first reading. If they believe that the legislative proposal is incompatible with the principle of subsidiarity they may reject it, subject to a 55 per cent Council majority or a majority vote in the European Parliament. This notification right is granted to all national houses of parliament.

for Member States may sometimes be backed up by NAPs as in the case of employment and social exclusion, that in some areas, such as employment and social policy or immigration policy, it complements the programme-based and legislative approach (European Commission 2001b) while in others it adds value at European level, where there is little scope for legislative solutions. This is the case, for example, of education policy. Moreover, the Commission said that the use of the method must not upset the institutional balance nor dilute the achievement of common objectives in the Treaty. In particular, it should not exclude the European Parliament from a European policy process and that the OMC should be a complement rather than a replacement for Community action.

Following the Lisbon Summit, various institutional reforms particularly relevant to social policy *sensu lato* were made regarding the Committee of the Regions, the Economic and Social Committee (ECOSOC) and the Social Protection Committee. The Committee of the Regions was given a more proactive role in examining policy through the preparation of exploratory reports in advance of Commission proposals, in organizing the exchange of best practice at local and regional levels and in reviewing the local and regional impact of certain Directives (Article 2 ToN; European Commission 2001a: 14). The ECOSOC was assigned an important role in developing a new relationship between Institutions and civil society. Like the Committee of the Regions, the ECOSOC was to be more active in developing opinions and exploratory reports in order to help shape policies at a much earlier stage (Article 2 ToN; European Commission 2001a: 15). Finally, the Social Protection Committee's advisory status was strengthened in order to monitor and promote co-operation and the exchange of best practice in the field of social protection (Article 2 ToN).

At the Lisbon Summit, it was also agreed to hold an annual European Council meeting every spring, aimed at monitoring the implementation of the overall strategy agreed in Lisbon. More precisely, these special meetings were to be devoted to the examination of economic and social matters on the basis of the synthesis report prepared by the Commission and relevant reports from the Council. The first meeting was held on 23 and 24 March 2001 in Stockholm (European Council 2001). Furthermore, at the Laeken Summit, the Council welcomed the decision to create and institutionalize a European Social Affairs Summit, to be held before each Spring European Council Summit (European Council 2001b: 7). The first one was held in Brussels at the eve of the Laeken Summit, where representatives of management and labour, members of the Presidency of the European Union, the European Commission, and, more generally, the European Council met in order to discuss issues regarding social and economic policies in the European Union.

In this context, the Sustainable Development Strategy established at the Göteborg Summit should be seen as a follow-up to the Lisbon strategy with the further inclusion of a third environmental dimension to it (European Council 2001a). The European Council in Göteborg emphasized that this strategy lies within the framework of the OMC.[41] It, therefore, invited Member States to draw up their own national sustainable development strategies and to this end it invited them to establish appropriate national consultative processes. Moreover, the European Council set up a monitoring and review system with the supervision of the Commission which would present an annual synthesis report based on a

---

41   This can be seen also by the terminology used. See European Council (2001a: para. 24, second indent), where there is reference to a *horizontal preparation* of the Sustainable Development Strategy, to be co-ordinated by the General Affairs Council; see also European Council (2001a: para. 23, second indent), where consultation with all the *relevant stakeholders* is underscored. Emphasis added.

number of headline indicators together with a report assessing how environment technology could promote growth and employment. In addition, as seen earlier, prior to the Feira Summit in June 2000 a High Level Forum was held in Brussels in June 2000 in order to evaluate the co-ordinated implementation of the Luxembourg, Cardiff and Cologne Processes.

Hence a "pre-eminent and co-ordinating role" was given to the European Council 'to ensure overall coherence and effective monitoring of progress towards the new strategic goal' (European Council 2000). In this context, Cafaro (2003) referred to the European Council as being the *chef d'orchestre* of the OMC. The European Commission (2001a: 22), however, emphasized its active co-ordinating role in the OMC and specified that the main function of the European Council should be that of 'shaping the strategic direction of the Union in partnership with the Commission. It should not deal with the day-to-day detail of EU policies, since the requirement for consensus in the European Council often holds policy making hostage to national interests' (*ibid.*: 29). It was clear that the Commission wanted to reduce the intergovernmental element of the OMC and preserve its important proactive role created and promoted under President Delors and, in particular, maintain its role in shaping and defining the development and implementation of the strategy by structuring the behaviour of the various actors involved, channelling conflicts and fostering consensus building.

This new way of implementing policies at European level with the inclusion of all the relevant stakeholders,[42] including civil society (European Commission (2001a: 14–15; ECOSOC 1999), in the decision-making process had important effects on the Community's division of powers although it certainly did not entail a systemic change like the Single Market and the EMU. At the time this form of policy making was greeted as being a new form of governance based on a transverse form of policy making. This new process was said to be based on a transnational basis of self-regulation, voluntary networking links and, more specifically, on the interaction of actors distributed across various levels of policy making. Hence co-ordination processes and co-regulation[43] of EU policies were given formal recognition within the multi-tiered system of the European Union to either substitute in some cases, or complement in others, classical forms of regulation of the Community Method.

The Lisbon Summit was particularly important for EC social policy in that it formalized the mode of governance through which the EES was being implemented, the OMC. The open method rapidly became the main mode of policy making for expanding Community competence in sensitive social policy areas.[44] In addition, the Lisbon Summit strengthened the powers of the advisory bodies of the Community and institutionalized regular meetings on social policy thus improving the overall regulatory framework of EC social policy.

---

42 The importance of including more actors in the decision-making process had already been highlighted at the 1998 Vienna European Council, where it was agreed that 'for the future success of the Luxembourg process a broad and intensive dialogue between all the actors involved, i.e. the Council, the Commission, the European Parliament, the social partners, the European Central Bank and the European Investment Bank, is of prime importance, contributing to the overall strategy for employment, growth and stability' (European Council 1998b); see also European Commission (2001a: 9 and 13), where the Commission refers to "concerted action" and to "systemic dialogue".

43 For a definition of co-regulation, see European Commission (2001a: 21).

44 For a list of areas where the OMC has been applied to, see Laffan and Shaw (2005) and Szyszczak 2006.

6 Amendments to the 2001 guidelines for employment following the Lisbon Summit

In September 2000 the Commission proposed its EPGs as part of the Employment Package which also included the JER and the Recommendations on the Implementation of Member States' employment policies. Some relevant changes were brought to the EPGs 2001 which may be explained by various factors: the new paradigm promoted by the Lisbon Summit, the mid-term review of the three years of experiences with the EES and the assessment of the process made in the JER. Prior to the Feira Summit in June 2000, a High Level Forum was held in Brussels on 15 June 2000 which brought together the social partners, the EU's Institutions, the ECB and the EIB to assess the co-ordinated implementation of the Luxembourg, Cardiff and Cologne Processes. 'It confirmed that there was a high degree of consensus on the Lisbon Strategy, identified the possible contributions of the various actors, each within its own sphere of action, and demonstrated the importance of broad political debate, social concertation and social dialogue' (European Council 2000b) In particular, the social partners presented a Joint Declaration on their position regarding important issues such as temporary work, telework, lifelong learning and provisions for joint monitoring of industrial change.

The Mid-term Review of the EPGs introduced some significant changes such as the adoption of clear indicators for the evaluation of the NAPs, the insertion of so-called "horizontal objectives" in the EPGs and an increased role for the social partners, particularly under the Adaptability pillar (European Commission 2000b). The Mid-term Review carried out by the EMCO stated that the OMC and the four-pillar structure of the guidelines demonstrated their value and should not be changed at least until the end of 2002 when an overall evaluation of the strategy would be made at the end of a five-year cycle. In particular, the changes introduced in the 2001 guidelines concerned the following:

- *Social partners.* The social partners were expected to be responsible for developing and reporting on actions within their own sphere. In particular, they had exclusive responsibility in the implementation of two guidelines in the Adaptability pillar: G 13 concerning the modernization of work organization and G 15 on the contribution of education and lifelong learning to adaptability; on both issues they were invited to negotiate agreements. With regard to modernization of work organization, they had to issue an annual report on the negotiations achieved and on the status of their implementation and impact on employment and labour market functioning. The same type of report was expected for education and lifelong learning. Finally, the social partners were invited, together with the Member States, to strengthen their contribution to active policies to combating emerging bottlenecks (G 6), undeclared work (G 9), to take part in local action for employment (G 11), to tackle gender gaps (G 17) and to reconcile work and family life (G 18);
- *Horizontal objectives.*[45] The main innovation of the EPGs for 2001 was the introduction of five horizontal objectives which were meant to shape the already existing objectives of the four-pillar structure in relation to the Lisbon Strategy goals: (1) raise the average EU employment rate to 70 per cent by 2010 (60 per cent for women); (2) increase the involvement of the social partners, particularly in relation to the Adaptability pillar; (3) enhance lifelong education and training, particularly in relation

---

45 For a detail analysis see Degryse and Pochet (2001: 16–19).

to the Employability and Adaptability pillars; (4) ensure a better balance between the four pillars of the EES; (5) improve the definition and use of structural indicators necessary for the evaluation of the NAPs.

The content of the 2001 EPGs remained for the most part similar to those of the year 2000.[46] The new objectives of the 2001 EPGs concerned mostly education and lifelong learning, discriminatory aspects of the labour market, social exclusion, emerging bottle-necks, undeclared work, active labour market policies, the promotion of good jobs, higher employment rates among older workers through policies in support of active ageing. The Joint Commission/Employment Committee evaluation report (European Commission (2000a)), contained various general considerations, among which:

- New structures and institutions for decision making and the evaluation of employ-ment policies combined with the OMC had put employment policies on the Community and national agendas.
- While the cyclical and multi-layered structure of the EES was fostering the involve-ment of various actors, more participation by representatives of civil society should be promoted at grass-roots level in the Member States.
- A stronger commitment of the governments and other actors to the implementation of the EES was required; in particular, the social partners were said to have been insufficiently involved in the Employment Strategy.
- More transparency in the definition of targets, exchange of best practice and peer review was necessary.

A first general assessment may be made of the implementation of the EES carried out so far on the basis of the first three JERs. First, most NAPs focused on employability and not enough importance was given to the other pillars. In addition, these national reports were mainly programmatic. With regard to the Employability pillar, there was visible progress in relation to preventative and active measures because of the definition of quan-tified targets at European level. As regards to the Entrepreneurship pillar, the reduction of the tax burden on labour was not implemented as required by the guidelines. In addition, there was little progress in relation to the modernization of work organization under the Adaptability pillar. With regard to the Equal Opportunities pillar, Member States improved the level of gender mainstreaming across the four pillars although the measures to reconcile work and family life varied greatly between Member States. The JERs also stated that in relation to the European Structural Funds most NAPs recognized the import-ance of the ESF for funding employment-related projects but not enough attention was

---

46 The EPGs for the year 2001 numbered nineteen: *Pillar 1, improving employability:* tackling youth unemployment and preventing long-term unemployment (G 1), a more employment-friendly approach: benefits, taxes and training systems (G 2), developing a policy for active ageing (G 3), developing skills for the new labour market in the context of lifelong learning (Gs 4, 5, 6), active policies to develop job matching and to prevent and combat emerging bottlenecks (G 7), combating discrimination and promoting social inclusion by access to employment (G 8); *Pillar 2, developing entrepreneurship:* making it easier to start up and run a business (Gs 9 and 10), new opportunities for employment in the knowledge-based society and services (G 11), local action for employment (G 12), tax reforms for employment and training (G 13); *Pillar 3, encouraging adaptability:* modernizing work organization (Gs 14 and 15), supporting adaptability in enterprises as a component of lifelong learning (G 16); *Pillar 4, strengthening equal opportunities policies for women and men:* gender mainstreaming approach (G 17), tackling gender gaps (G 18), reconciling work and family life (G 19). The EPGs were adopted jointly by the Council of Social Affairs and the ECOFIN Council.

paid to the other existing structural funds. Moreover, social partners remained insufficiently involved in the drafting, preparation and implementation of the NAPs. In particular, the consultation of the social partners did not lead to the adoption of new initiatives or strategies to fight unemployment (Foden 1999).

The recommendations for 2001 took into account the diversity among different EU countries. The recommendations for 2001 were mostly a repetition of previous recommendations and focused on the following subject areas:

- The fight against youth and long-term unemployment (Belgium, France, Germany, Greece, Italy, Spain and the United Kingdom).
- Tax reforms and unemployment benefits reforms (Belgium, Finland, Greece, Spain, Sweden).
- Job creation in the service sector.
- Making the tax system more employment-friendly (Austria, Belgium, Denmark, Germany, Finland, France and Sweden).
- The EU tax rate on labour remains 15 per cent higher than that of the United States, with an average of approximately 40 per cent of GDP within the European Union.
- Modernizing the organization of work (Greece, Spain, Luxembourg, the Netherlands, Portugal and the United Kingdom).
- The fight against gender inequality (Austria, Denmark, Finland, Germany, Ireland, Luxembourg and Spain).
- Encouraging ageing workers to remain longer in employment (Austria, Denmark, Germany, Finland and Italy).
- Improving job creation in the service sector (Greece and Portugal).

Added to these recommendations, another set of new recommendations were included regarding two broad issues:

- The NAPs were to adopt a more overall and strategic approach with regard to their employment policies, taking into consideration all four pillars of the EES (United Kingdom, France, Greece, Ireland and Italy).
- The NAPs needed to focus more on education and lifelong learning, where policy action by Member States remained too modest (Belgium, France, Germany, Greece, Spain, Ireland, Italy, Luxembourg, Portugal, United Kingdom).

At the 2001 Stockholm Summit, the Commission presented its Communication *Realizing our potential: Consolidating and extending the Lisbon Strategy* (European Commission 2001c), evaluating progress made since the Lisbon Summit. In this Communication the Commission highlighted the major achievements in economic and social policy and suggested the way forward for the future. In particular, the Commission proposed the following priority fields where action should be taken:

- Intrinsic quality of jobs.
- Labour market reforms.
- Integrating financial markets.
- Identifying ways of achieving a better regulatory environment.
- Accelerating the process of introducing information and knowledge-based technology, the *e*Europe 2002 project.
- Tackling the IT skill gaps.

- Strengthening Europe's capacity for research and innovation.
- Developing and investing in new technologies, e.g. biotechnology.
- Enhancing social inclusion and modernizing social protection systems.

With regard to social and employment issues, the Commission also introduced some intermediate targets, 67 per cent on average and 57 per cent for women by 2005. Important issues concerning the notions of quality of jobs and the new European labour market needed to be analyzed in more detail. The Commission also stressed the need to set up comparative structural indicators for the fight against social exclusion through the OMC and to reduce public debts in order to allow interest savings to support pensions and healthcare. In addition, more importance should be given to the employment of the elderly, restricting early retirement, increasing tax incentives, training and re-skilling of older workers; pension systems needed to be reformed, in particular private pensions should be benefiting from the Internal Market.

A list of twenty-eight indicators that covered all of the four pillars and seven more general economic background indicators,[47] drafted on the basis of an earlier Communication by the Commission were annexed to the report (European Commission 2000c). Structural indicators may be defined as monitoring, benchmarking and peer pressure instruments for assessing Member States' employment and economic trends. These were the following:

- Employment indicators (seven).
- Innovation and research indicators (seven).
- Economic reform indicators (seven).
- Social cohesion indicators (seven).

These structural indicators provided important tools for gathering information and for assessing the development of the EES and, more broadly, for assessing to what extent the European Union had achieved its target established at the Lisbon Summit.

The changes made to the 2001 EPGs and the adoption of these structural indicators emphasized the fact that a soft law discourse had clearly emerged in the area of social and employment policy that was ratified at the Lisbon Summit. In this context, Szyszczak (2000: 218) defines these changes as entailing a shift from "court watching" to "agenda watching". More broadly, from a governance perspective these changes showed that an experimental regulatory technique based on soft law, benchmarking, promoting policy learning, policy co-ordination, policy interaction and a partnership approach had been systematized within the broader decision-making system of the European Union. Scholars, however, have criticized or questioned the purported effectiveness of the Employment Strategy. For example, de la Porte, Pochet and Room (2001) argue that the benchmarking process developed

---

47 The *employment indicators* were: the employment rate; the female employment rate; the employment growth rate; the employment rate of older workers; the unemployment rate; the tax rate on low-wage earners; lifelong learning, i.e. adult participation in education and training. The *social cohesion indicators* were: the distribution rate; the poverty rate before and after social transfers; a persistence of poverty rate; jobless households; regional cohesion; early school leavers not in further education and training; long-term unemployment. These indicators had to be flexible enough to keep up with economic, employment and social cohesion developments further to the implementation of the EES. The Commission listed, therefore, a series of complementary indicators regarding the employment field: long-term unemployment flows; quality of work; vacancies; marginal effective tax rate. In the social field these complementary indicators were to be defined by the High Level Group on Social Protection.

within the EES has not been very effective as it has been difficult to reach agreement on common objectives and guidelines and even once benchmarks are agreed, the way to pursue it may not be. Moreover, as pointed out by Barnard (2006: 115), the achievement of objectives and targets may also be a "hostage to fortune" and it will often depend on external factors such as economic trends over which Member States have no control.[48]

7 Social policy developments post-Nice

At the Nice Summit in December 2000, Member States agreed to adopt a new Social Policy Agenda for 2000–2005 (European Commission 2000d)[49] which created the basis for the creation of a new "European social model" (European Council 2000c). The objectives of the Social Policy Agenda were:

- The creation of more and better jobs.
- The adaptation to the new working environment striking a balance between flexibility and security.
- The promotion of mobility.
- The promotion of social inclusion.
- The strengthening of gender equality.
- The reinforcement of fundamental rights.
- The fight against discrimination.
- The reduction of poverty.
- The modernization of social protection systems.
- The promotion of social dialogue.
- The preparation for enlargement and for international co-operation.

Member States also agreed to adopt a European Charter of Fundamental Rights, which came into force on 26 February 2001.[50] Although declaratory in nature and non-binding,[51] the Charter fosters a 'closer union' among 'the people of Europe' based on common values[52] and includes a set of fundamental social rights, some of which may be said to be distinctly "European".[53] Kenner (2001: 11, 12–15) argues that the Charter should be considered as a

---

48 See also Szyszczak (2001a: 1146), who questions the legitimacy of the benchmarking process, which ends up creating "league tables" not envisaged by the Member States when Title VIII was inserted in the EC Treaty.

49 This new social policy agenda was part of the Commission's strategic objectives for 2000–2005 (European Commission 2000e: 9–10).

50 The Charter was issued with a joint Act by the European Parliament, the Council of the European Union and the European Commission on 7 December 2000. The Charter enumerates fifty specific rights apart from the general provisions contained in Articles 51–54. These rights are subdivided into six chapters: Chapter I, 'Dignity', Articles 1–5; Chapter II, 'Freedoms', Articles 6–19; Chapter III, 'Equality', Articles 20–26; Chapter IV, 'Solidarity', Articles 27–38; Chapter V, 'Citizens' rights', Articles 39–46; and Chapter VI, 'Justice', Articles 47–50.

51 Moreover, Article 51(2) outlines very clearly the limited scope of the Charter by stating, 'This Charter does not establish any new power or task for the Community or the Union, or modify powers and tasks defined by the Treaties.'

52 See First Recital of the Preamble of the Charter.

53 The rights of most relevance for EC social law are to be found in Chapter I, 'Dignity', in particular the right to human dignity, Article 1, which is drawn from the Preamble of the 1948 Universal Declaration of Fundamental Rights, the right to integrity of the person, Article 3, which includes a general right of respect for everyone's 'physical and medical integrity' and specific protections with regard to medicine and biology provided in the Convention on Human Rights and Biomedicine of the Council of Europe (ETS 164 and additional protocol ETS 168), and the prohibition of slavery and forced labour, Article 5, which corresponds to Article 4(1) and 4(2) ECHR and has therefore the same meaning and scope as the ECHR by virtue of Article 52(3) of the Charter; Chapter II, 'Freedoms', Chapter III, 'Equality', Chapter IV, 'Solidarity', Chapter V, 'Citizens' rights', Chapter VI, 'Justice'.

dynamic soft law instrument; more precisely as 'a declaratory form of aspirational soft law that, like the Social Charter, is capable of furthering and deepening European integration by building upon and around the *acquis* without directly creating strict legal obligations' (*ibid.*: 12–13). The Charter has formulated a new architecture of fundamental rights and social rights and recognized their indivisibility and their universal character.[54] As seen in Chapter 2, even though it has no binding effects it still bears a significant impact (and not merely a political one) for the protection of social rights.[55] The Charter also establishes certain basic social values which are necessary for the consolidation and further development of the "European social model". Since 2006 the European Court has used the Charter as a consolidating document and, in particular, one of a range of sources it may use to identify general principles of law without creating new rights.[56] Moreover, in line with the wording of the Preamble of the Charter and its horizontal provisions, the European Court has used it to reaffirm rights as they result from various other international sources.

The Nice Treaty also amended three EC Treaty Articles regarding social policy:

- Article 13 EC, where a new paragraph[57] was added so as to allow the European Union to adopt incentive measures in the field of discrimination.
- Article 137 EC, where the scope of action in the field of social policy was broadened to include new areas.[58]
- Article 144 EC, which formalized the creation of the Social Protection Committee.[59]

These amendments are particularly important to the development of EC social policy. Szyszczak (2002) argues that the reform of Article 137 EC has broken the division between industrial relations and social protection and, more generally, she argues that the Nice Summit created a trilateral link between welfare policy, macroeconomic policy and employment policy. The reform did not include, however, QMV for taxation and social protection matters, which still require unanimity, whereas measures regarding the Internal Market and the liberalization/deregulation of public services or public monopolies can be adopted with QMV.

7.1 The importance of mainstreaming quality in employment policies

In the Social Policy Agenda for 2000–2005 (European Commission 2000d) quality is considered central to the modernization of the "European social model" and to the

---

54 For a less optimistic reading of the value of the Charter for the strengthening of social rights in the Lisbon and post-Lisbon context, see Ashiagbor (2005: 174–178).

55 See Opinion of Advocate General Tizzano in Case C-173/99, *Broadcasting, Entertainment, Cinematographic and Theatre Union (BECTU) v. Secretary of State for Trade and Industry* [2001] ECR I-4881, paras. 22–28. See also C-122/99P *D. and Sweden v. Council* [2001] ECR I-4319. For further analysis, see Chapter 2.

56 See Case C-540/03 *Parliament v. Council* [2006] ECR I-5769; Case C-432/05 *Unibet* [2007] ECR I-2271; Case C-303/05, *Advocaten voor der wereld* [2007] ECR I-3633; Case C-438/05 *International Transport Workers' Federation, Finnish Seamen's Union v. Viking Line ABP, OÜ Viking Line Eesti* [2007] ECR I-10779; Case C-341/05 *Laval & Partneri v. Svenska Byggnadsarbetareförbundet, Svenska Byggnadsarbetareförbundets avd. 1, Byggettan, Svenska Elektrikerförbundet* [2007] ECR I-11767.

57 Article 13(2) EC.

58 The amended provision excludes the adoption of harmonizing measures as regards combating social exclusion and the modernization of social protection for individuals other than workers.

59 The Social Protection Committee was already established by a Council Decision (Council of the European Union 2000e).

implementation of the Lisbon goals. The new Social Policy Agenda differs from previous action programmes in that it attempts to provide a redefinition of the "social" and to that end it articulates a new working method (Degryse and Pochet 2001: 32). A key message of the Social Policy Agenda is that growth is not an end in itself but essentially a means to achieving a better standard of living for all the focus being on employment relations, social policy and industrial relations. With regard to work, the Social Policy Agenda provides that, while it pursues full employment and thus more jobs, at the same time it also aimed at ensuring quality of jobs, namely, creating better jobs and a better balance between work and personal life. Quality in employment policy making is meant to ensure higher living standards by addressing both unemployment and underemployment, which includes 'manifestations such as delayed labour market entry by young persons, the reduction in activity rates among the over-fifties, non-voluntary part-time work and the labour market phenomenon represented by the significant numbers of "discouraged" persons who have given up the idea of participation' (Goetschy 2001a). According to the new Social Policy Agenda, the injection of a quality approach in social policy ensures higher levels of social protection, good social services, equal opportunities for all and the guarantee of fundamental and social rights. In addition, quality in industrial relations fosters consensus building and helps to adapt to industrial change and corporate restructuring.

The main initiatives and measures to be adopted pursuant to the Social Policy Agenda included, *inter alia*, strengthening the lifelong learning and the adaptability themes, promoting benchmarking processes, developing qualitative as well as quantitative indicators,[60] supporting the local and regional dimensions of the EES, supporting initiatives related to corporate social responsibility, adapting and improving existing legislation, taking into account Community case law, promoting IT initiatives that foster employability, the formalization of the Social Protection Committee, submitting an annual report on social protection, including the ESF in funding EU social activities, adopting and implementing action programmes to combat discrimination based on gender and race and increasing the involvement of the social partners. In its Communication *Employment and Social Policies: a Framework for Investing in Quality* European Commission (2001d), the Commission identified ten areas contributing to quality in work. These are the following:

- Intrinsic job quality.
- Lifelong learning and skills.
- Gender equality.
- Health and safety at work.
- Flexibility and security.
- Inclusion and access to the labour market.
- Work organization and work–life balance.
- Social dialogue and workers' involvement.
- Diversity and non-discrimination.
- Economic performance and productivity.

These areas have been used by the EMCO to construct a series of indicators. The new indicators for monitoring the EPGs 2002 include quality as a key element in the set of employment indicators (Employment Committee 2002).

---

60 See Biagi (2002: 157–159), who suggests a series of indicators which may contribute to ensuring an effective industrial relations system.

Quality of work may also be associated with the definition of "full employment". As we have seen, Lisbon introduced it as a policy goal although no precise definition of it was given of it in the Portuguese Presidency Conclusions beyond the employment targets set for the Member States. The academic literature is also divided on the meaning of full employment. The Pisani-Ferry Report provides three meanings of full employment (Pisani-Ferry 2000). The first way of assessing full levels of employment is by using the 'Non-accelerating Inflation Rate of Employment' (NAIRU) which refers to the rate of structural unemployment and rate of equilibrium unemployment. The NAIRU indicator is a threshold above which unemployment can be reduced by the spontaneous operation of the market and below which specific structural reforms will be necessary. According to Ashiagbor (2005: 166–167) this economic perspective of full employment refers to a situation whereby 'employment is as high as it can be without labour shortages that lead to rising wages and hence prices'. This type of full employment, however, does not ensure that everyone who wants a job has got one. The second method is the one employed by the EES, based on the average of the three best-performing Member States. There is also the Beveridge (1944) definition according to which full employment is a 'situation where the number of vacancies exceeds the number of candidates for any given position and the positions and job locations are such that unemployment does not extend beyond brief waiting periods'. Ashiagbor (2005: 167) argues that this definition is more compatible with the European Union's goal of social cohesion, and the International Labour Organization (ILO: 1996) draws on the Beveridge perspective by defining full employment as 'the absence of involuntary unemployment or the availability of jobs for all active job seekers'.

A new conceptualization of full employment that includes the notion of quality would include all three definitions in order to take into account real convergence factors and not only nominal convergence. Quality of work became one of the objectives of the 2002 EPGs (Council of the European Union 2002). The Stockholm European Council (2001: 6) agreed that the Council should include quality in work as a general objective in the 2002 EPGs. This was reflected in a new Horizontal Objective B, which spelled out the main aspects of quality of work on the basis of the Commission Communication *Employment and Social Policies: a Framework for Investing in Quality* (European Commission 2001d). Other horizontal objectives also emphasized the importance of quality, for example Horizontal Objective C regarding the development of a comprehensive strategy for lifelong learning and Horizontal Objective D on the development of a partnership involving the social partners. In addition, new references to the quality aspect were integrated in a number of relevant thematic guidelines, namely G 3, G 7, G 10, G 11 and G 13.

In its Communication *The Future of the European Employment Strategy (EES): a Strategy for Full Employment and Better Jobs for All* (European Commission 2003) the Commission described quality at work as being one of the three overarching objectives required for a knowledge-based economy.[61] The Communication therefore proposed both the creation of better jobs but also more effective delivery services, strong involvement of the social partners, mobilization of all the relevant actors and adequate financial support. The importance of quality at work was further buttressed by the Working Group XI on Social Europe of the European Convention, which recommended that the promotion of quality in work should be included among the aims of the European Union in Article 3 of the Constitutional Treaty (European Convention 2003: 2).

---

61 The other two being full employment and social cohesion.

The 2005 Social Policy Agenda while maintaining the goal of full employment recognized that the 2010 deadline for achieving it was unrealistic (European Commission 2005a). In the Lisbon Strategy 'the discourse on "modernizing" welfare states in the context of full employment means a shift from extensive employment protection and social benefits, towards an emphasis on investment in human capital, thus improving "employability" and equipping individuals to be self-sufficient' (Ashiagbor 2005: 168). In this register, it may be argued that the Lisbon Strategy further encapsulates the "Third Way" agenda which the EES has been said to exemplify, namely a middle course in between neo-liberalism and traditional social democracy. It is neo-liberal in relation to markets, which it aims at liberalizing and, at the same time, it embraces social democratic values in its pursuit of social justice and social inclusion.

However, the "Third Way" approach's main limitation is that it focuses excessively on "supply-side citizenship" (Plant 1998) or "supply-side egalitarianism" (Streeck 1999). Hence, although social justice is an objective to be achieved and ensured, it should be attained through reforming the welfare state around a strict work ethos as opposed to a social democratic perspective of citizenship according to which citizenship confers membership and rights independently of the market. In this register, citizenship is seen as an achievement through actively participating in the labour market and reaping the rewards that accrue from that (Plant 1998) and equal opportunities for all are ensured through investment in skills (*idem*).

This is why it may be argued that the Lisbon Strategy may fall short of social democratic ideals of social solidarity and social rights. Moreover, quality in work has remained somewhat in limbo in the last few years, explained in part by new waves of economic downturn and recession worldwide. In the EU context this situation may also be explained further by the functioning of the EES as a procedure. Because of the focus on the Employment Strategy as a process, quality in the Employment guidelines has consequently been conceived of as a means to other ends rather than being intrinsically valuable *per se* in the pursuit of ensuring better living and working conditions for all (Raveaud 2007: 419). According to the Horizontal Objective B, introduced in 2002, the promotion of quality is a way to 'raise employment rates, promote social cohesion and social progress, enhance competitiveness, productivity and the functioning of the labour market'. In particular, job characteristics (such as intrinsic job quality, wages, skills and lifelong learning and career development) and working conditions (such as diversity and non-discrimination, equal opportunities, inclusion, work organization and work–life balance, social dialogue and worker involvement) are referred to only as indicators rather than as objectives to be pursued for ensuring the exercise of certain basic social rights and, more broadly, a better quality of life for European citizens.[62]

The difficulty of promoting quality at work at European level is exemplified by the contradictory approach of the Commission in its 2003 Communication referred to above. On the one hand, the Commission takes the view that temporary jobs are to be promoted because they facilitate entry into the labour market and thus contribute to a high employment rate. On the other, the Commission also seems to be taking the view that fixed-term jobs are associated with a high risk of unemployment and premature exit from the labour market. These conflicting views in relation to the meaning of quality at work can be found also in the EES which essentially ends up favouring market mechanisms as a way to promote employment in the European Union (*ibid.*: 423).

---

62 For further critical analysis, see Raveaud (2007: 420–423) and Ashiagbor (2005: 178–185).

7.2 Further developments in social policy and the strengthening of EC employment policy

The European Council held in Laeken in December 2001 under the outgoing Belgian EU Presidency discussed a number of employment-related topics, including progress towards the targets set by the Lisbon Strategy. In this context, the Council emphasized the importance of the Spring European Council, which is now held annually in Brussels in the month of March. This IGC was intended to provide the political leadership and strategic direction towards the achievement of the objective of becoming the most dynamic knowledge-based economy in the world, with full employment and increased levels of social cohesion, by 2010. It was, therefore, devoted to the examination of economic and social matters as agreed at the Lisbon Summit, on the basis of the annual synthesis report prepared by the Commission on progress in relation to employment, innovation and social cohesion. The report was based on key economic indicators and targets which helped European Council to provide both short and medium-term directions for economic and social policy in the Union.

In addition, *ad hoc* European Social Affairs Summits would be held before each Spring European Council. The first meeting took place on 13 December 2001 and it highlighted the social partners' willingness to develop social dialogue at European level by jointly drawing up a multi-annual work programme before the European Council in spring. The social partners endorsed the creation of this European Social Affairs Summit,[63] as they considered it the place where the European Council would take their resolutions into consideration. Moreover, it introduced more transparency in the EU decision-making system by further reducing what Bercusson (2000: 9–16) defined as the "non-institutionalization" or "institutional marginalization" of the social partners that was contrary not only to the provisions of Title XI but also to EC documents and to practice at domestic and European levels which saw the active involvement of social partners in both private and public debates.

With regard to the "European social model", the Laeken European Council (2001b: 8–9) welcomed a number of developments, including the political agreement in the form of a conciliated text between the Council of Ministers and the EU Parliament on the proposed Directive on the Protection of Workers in the Event of Insolvency of their Employer and on the proposed Directive establishing a general framework for improving information and consultation rights of employees in the European Community.[64] The European Council maintained that it was necessary to adopt measures aimed at preventing and resolving social conflicts, particularly those of a transnational nature, by means of voluntary mediation mechanisms. The European Council also tackled other social policy issues, namely gender equality, social inclusion and pensions. It held that is was necessary to modernize pension systems in order to ensure the sustainability of pensions and improve access to occupational pension schemes.

63 E.g. see Confédération Européenne des Cadres (CEC), 'Preparation du Conseil Européen de Laeken', Information pour la presse, Brussels, 12 December 2001, ref. 0640101.

64 The favourable political climate for a Directive establishing a general framework for improving information and consultation rights of employees in the European Community eventually led to the adoption of such a Directive in 2002 (European Parliament and the Council of the European Union 2002).

8 The 2002 review of the European Employment Strategy and the 2003 guidelines

Following the Barcelona Spring European Council in March 2002, which called for a strengthening of the EES centred on the axis of simplification, implementation and liberalization,[65] the Commission issued a series of Communications. In its Communication *Taking Stock of Five Years of the European Employment Strategy* the Commission reviewed the experience of five years of the EES and broadly outlined a redesign of the EES for the future (European Commission 2002b). Ten topics were the subject of the evaluation:

1   Prevention and policies of activation to employment.
2   Tax reforms and benefits.
3   Lifelong learning.
4   Social inclusion.
5   Administrative simplification and the self-employed.
6   Creation of jobs in services, at local level and in the social economy.
7   Taxation.
8   Modernizing work organization.
9   Equal opportunities.
10 Changes in policy making.

The Communication identified the need to reform the EES in relation to four key aspects:

1   Setting clear objectives in response to policy challenges.
2   Simplifying the policy guidelines without undermining their effectiveness.
3   Improving governance and partnership in the execution of the strategy.
4   Ensuring greater consistency and complementarity with respect to other EU processes.

The above Communication stimulated an active debate. The European Parliament (2002) issued a resolution in which it suggested the adoption of various measures to strengthen the EES, and the EMCO and the Economic Policy Committee (2002) reached a joint position on the future direction of the EES that was submitted to the Council. The Commission further developed the objectives outlined in the above Communication in a subsequent Communication on the future of the EES (European Commission 2003), where it provided examples of concrete objectives and considerations and suggestions for possible new targets. The Commission also issued a Communication on streamlining EPGs and BEPGs (European Commission 2002) with a shift towards a more medium and longer-term approach in order to ensure progress towards full employment, sustainable development and, more broadly, the strengthening of the "European social model".

From a governance perspective, the aim of the new process was to improve coherence and complementarity between the various processes and instruments, foster the participation and involvement of both European and national parliaments, a better consultation of

---

65 On the philosophy underpinning the Barcelona European Council and subsequent European Council in 2003 and 2004, see Ashiagbor (2005: 185–190), who notes how the repeated "mantra" in those years was delivery and effective implementation.

social partners and civil society, and increase the transparency of policy co-ordination.[66] In April 2003, in line with the new streamlined approach, and as part of the overall Lisbon agenda follow-up, the Commission presented a Guidelines Package which included formal proposals of BEPGs and EPGs and the annual recommendations to the Member States covering a three-year policy cycle up to 2006. Guidelines were to be issued annually only in the case of major new developments. Likewise, and consistently with the Cardiff process, and pursuant to the Lisbon Strategy, the Internal Market Strategy included in the Guidelines Package covered a three-year policy cycle up to 2006. According to these new procedures, after the June European Council considers the economic and social situation, the Council adopts the BEPGs, the EPGs, the Employment Recommendations to Member States, and/or adopts action plans in their areas of competence. The first full application of the proposed new arrangements for reviewing implementation took place in the autumn of 2003. As a transitional measure the draft Joint Employment Report was adopted in the autumn of 2002 (European Commission 2002d).

Hence, as a result, the timetable of the EES was brought into line with the BEPGs and the structure of the 2003 Employment Guidelines was reviewed in quite a significant way. The four pillars were dismantled in favour of three 'overarching and interrelated objectives' of 'full employment, quality and productivity at work, and social cohesion and inclusion', thus reflecting the Lisbon agenda's goals (European Commission 2003). These objectives were embedded in ten guidelines, the so-called "ten commandments". However, the 2003 guidelines still reflected the content of the original four pillars and accompanying guidelines, the only exception being G 9 on shifting gainful employment into regular employment and G 10 on overcoming regional disparities in employment, their insertion being a response to the ten new Member States which joined in 2004, particularly CEECs, where undeclared work and regional differences remain a serious problem (Celin 2003: 99). For example, there was emphasis on the need to encourage people into training and to update their skills, on the need to reduce burdens on business and to modernize work organization, although no reference to underemployability. There was also further emphasis on regional disparities as well as the need to foster economic migration of TCNs due to the ageing population and the need of high-skill workers. The 2003 guidelines also included a number of specific targets such as 25 per cent of the long-term unemployed actively participating by 2010 in training, work practice or other employability measure, with the aim of achieving the average of the three most advanced Member States; the provision of child care by 2010 for at least 90 per cent of children between three years old and the mandatory school age and at least 33 per cent of children under three years of age; at least 85 per cent of twenty-two-year-olds in the European Union should have completed upper secondary education by 2010.[67] The 2003 guidelines also reduced the number of indicators to sixty-four (thirty-nine key indicators and twenty-five context indicators) and placed greater emphasis on marginalized groups in the labour market such as the long-term unemployed, undeclared workers and also immigrants. However, while policies aimed at women were still on the agenda, the focus became less about the different issues of

---

66 The revision process of the EES was initially a joint Danish–British initiative within EMCO calling for more simplification of the overall process and a change in the conceptualization of the guidelines so as to have only a few output-oriented guidelines.

67 Mailand (2006: 40) notes that while the number of guidelines decreased the number of quantitative targets increased.

family and professional conciliation and more about a quantitative increase in female employment rate targets (de la Porte 2008: 113).

From a governance perspective these guidelines placed significant emphasis on partnership and good governance, with a multiplicity of actors to be involved (including parliamentary bodies and the social partners) at all levels of decision making. Reference was also made to the potential of the European Structural Funds, especially the ESF, to support the delivery of policies and to strengthen the institutional capacity in the field of employment.

Studies on the EES revision process see it as yet another expression of a weakened Commission and stronger Member States in influencing the development of the EES (Mailand 2006: 41–42). In particular, EU presidencies have been quite active in preparing documents to be subsequently considered by the Commission and EMCO. For example, the 2002 Danish EU Presidency was very active in preparing the simplification of the guidelines, whereas the 2003 Greek EU Presidency was particularly active in adding new guidelines (*ibid.*: 42). The European social partners were all in favour of a revision of the EES, although they each had different views about the changes made to the EES. Moreover, they did not have any direct input into the changes made to the strategy. UNICE welcomed the simplification and synchronization with the BEPGs but was disappointed by the fact that the final version of the Entrepreneurship guideline had been 'really watered down' (*ibid.*: 44). The ETUC instead, while being in favour of a revision of the EES, did not support the streamlining process because it entailed the subordination of the EES to the objectives of the BEPGs.

From a governance perspective, this revision process confirmed the predominance of elitist and diplomatic elements of the Employment Strategy. The review took place entirely at civil servant and ministerial levels and was far from exemplifying a model of deliberative supranationalism that it purported itself to be. Most decisions were made through informal channels on the basis of coalitions between different national governments' representatives and/or European social partners (de la Porte 2008; Mailand 2006).

8.1 The 2003 European Employment Task Force

Another key event in the evolution of the EES which took place at the same time as the EES revision and simplification was the setting up of the European Employment Task Force chaired by Wim Kok, former Dutch Prime Minister, and its so-called Kok Report. The initiative to set up a more intergovernmental employment initiative aside the EES was made by Blair, Schröder and Chirac prior to the Spring European Council in Brussels in March 2003. The mandate of this task force was to identify ways in which the implementation of the EES could be improved. The European Council 'invited the Commission to establish a European Employment Taskforce to help identify practical reforms that could have the most direct and immediate impact on the implementation by Member States of the revised Employment Strategy' (European Council 2003). The final report, entitled *Jobs, Jobs, Jobs* (European Employment Task Force 2003) listed four key objectives to ensure more effective implementation of the EES:

- Increase the adaptability of workers and enterprises.
- Attract more people into the labour market.
- Invest more and more effectively in human capital.
- Ensure effective implementation of the reforms through better governance.

The Commission framed the EES employment recommendations according to the four commandments of the Kok Report, which was said to be a balanced document which focused on economic as well as social concerns of the EES. Moreover, Member States have been criticized for giving insufficient recognition in their national reports to the contribution of the ESF in underpinning their labour market policies. The new ESF regulation for the period 2007–2013 continues the use of the ESF for developing and implementing the EES and for meeting the employment objectives and targets of the Lisbon Strategy. In particular, pursuant to the 2003 Kok Report, it stresses the importance of the ESF for investing in human capital. However, the link between the ESF and the EES continues to be weak, which is explained in part by the inconsistent approach of the Council towards linking the ESF with the EES. In the first five years of implementation of the EES the Council changed its stance towards the functional relationship fostered by the Commission almost annually (Hartwig 2007: 126). In 2003 the Council embraced the same approach as the Commission in promoting a more functional relationship between the EES and the ESF and called for a more coherent approach in implementing both. Member States' reaction has been mixed. However, national reports show that despite taking into consideration the objectives of the EES in ESF allocations, most Member States seem to have implemented this functional relationship in a formal manner rather than in a strategic way. In particular, although Member States made sure that the ESF programmes were consistent with the national reports and the EES objectives, they did not fundamentally modify their ESF priorities because of the EES or their national report (*ibid.*: 129). The guiding principle in allocating the ESF remains mostly a national priority and only to a smaller extent an EES objective, and the EES and the national reports are built into the programming documents only after they have been drafted (*ibid.*: 130). Moreover, the strategic orientations of the ESF and the EES differ, and the former leaves some manoeuvre for Member States to decide to which specific orientation or objective they want to allocate their ESF share (*ibid.*).

The European Parliament has criticized the Member States for not sufficiently linking the ESF to the EES in their national reports (European Parliament 2002). However, the European Parliament criticized the Commission because the guidelines for the programming period 2000–2006 linked the ESF to the EES very loosely. The European Parliament has also suggested establishing a conditional link between the allocation of structural funds and the performance of the Member States in relation to the recommendations of the EES (European Parliament 2003). In other words, Member States that follow the recommendations should receive more structural funds than those that do not. However, this proposal would be difficult to implement (what does it mean to be in line with the recommendations?) and it would run the risk of introducing inequality of treatment between the Member States, chiefly between the southern Mediterranean/Continental block, the new Member States and the northern European countries (in the case of the former group there are often structural problems which impede compliance, so would programmatic measures be sufficient to ensure compliance?) as well as being politically incorrect.

Nevertheless, even though the EES may not have triggered changes to the ESF strategy in the different Member States, it may still have influenced the allocation of funds to different priorities. Hartwig (2007: 138) argues that, at strategic level, the Commission supports a spill-over from the EES to the ESF because the EES serves as a source of legitimation to influence Member States' structural funds strategies while, at administrative level, the Commission favours the spill-over from the ESF to the EES because it has a much more powerful role in the control of the Structural Funds implementation than in the operation of the OMC within the EES.

9 The relaunch of the Lisbon Strategy

9.1 The Kok High Level Group and the 2004–2005 mid-term review of the Lisbon Strategy

The 2004 *Employment in Europe* report showed that the European Union was still far short of the Lisbon objectives and targets (European Commission 2004). At 63 per cent, the 2003 employment rate overall was 7 per cent below the Lisbon target while the employment rate for women and older workers fell short by 5 per cent and 10 per cent respectively. Concerns over the achievement of the Lisbon objectives were also raised at the 2004 Brussels European Council, which mandated the Commission to set up a High Level Group 'to contribute to the mid-term review of the Lisbon process' (European Council 2004). Wim Kok was once again appointed as chairman of this High Level Group. In the final report, entitled *Facing the Challenge: The Lisbon Strategy for Growth and Employment*, key actions were defined under five main headings (Kok 2004):

- Knowledge society.
- Internal Market.
- Business climate.
- Labour markets.
- Environmental sustainability.

The key focus of the report was on growth and employment, sidelining social cohesion and sustainable development. It called Member States and social partners to give urgent attention to four structural challenges (adaptability of workers and enterprises to changing economic conditions and labour market demands, attracting more people into and remaining in the labour market and making work a real option for all, improving the quality of employment, and investing in human capital). The 2004 Kok report emphasized the need to improve governance of the EES in order to encourage "ownership" of the Lisbon Strategy both within national governments but among civil society.

The Commission's Communication to the 2005 Spring European Council, *Working Together for Growth and Jobs: A New Start for the Lisbon Strategy* (European Commission 2005b) restated the new priority of the Lisbon Strategy from the second Kok Report: growth and jobs. According to the Commission the failure of the Lisbon Strategy to deliver was caused by poor implementation and it did not question the overall goals of the strategy. Rather it pointed out to the quantity of objectives and a lack of focus. The Lisbon Strategy contained twenty-eight main objectives, 120 sub-objectives, 117 different indicators and a reporting system which required Member States to produce up to 300 annual reports. The communication did not include the actual guidelines but listed a series of actions giving a good indication of what was to be expected. The actions were grouped under three headings: (1) a more attractive place to invest and work; (2) knowledge and innovation for growth; (3) creating more and better jobs. With regard to the EES, the key change was the creation of a so-called "European Youth Pact" (European Commission 2005c). Other important changes concerned governance aspects and, in particular, the proposal to integrate the BEPGs and the EPGs, not only by cross-referencing, as in 2003, but by including them in a single set of Integrated Guidelines; second, NRPs would replace the NAPs. In addition, to increase national ownership, Member States' governments should appoint a "Mr or Mrs Lisbon" to co-ordinate the different elements of the Lisbon Strategy.

The most significant institutional change regarding the mid-term review of the Lisbon

Strategy was the increase in the power of the DG Enterprise of the Commission, the reason being the stronger emphasis on aspects such as innovation and entrepreneurship.

9.2 Changes to the governance of the Lisbon process and the three-year cycle[68]

At the 2005 Brussels European Council it was agreed that the revised governance structure of the Lisbon Strategy would start with the Commission presenting a strategic report concerning the economic policy and employment guidelines with a thorough review every three years. The strategic report would be examined by the various Council configurations and then discussed at the spring European Council. The European Council would then establish political guidelines for the economic, social and environmental strands of the strategy. In accordance with the procedures laid down in Articles 99 and 128 EC, and on the basis of the European Council conclusions, the Council (ECOFIN and EPSCO, respectively) would then adopt a package of Integrated Guidelines consisting of both the BEPGs and the EPGs based on a Commission proposal. These Integrated Guidelines would consist of macroeconomic, microeconomic and employment policy guidelines. Member States would draw up NRPs replacing NAPs in consultation with all relevant actors at regional and national level, including parliamentary bodies. Moreover, Member States would also prepare a single annual report to the Commission on how they would give effect to the Lisbon Strategy and set out also all measures taken in the preceding year to implement the national programmes. The Commission instead would be preparing a Community Lisbon Programme which would include all measures to be taken at Community level in relation to growth and employment. In addition, the Commission would also be reporting on the implementation of the strategy in an EU Annual Progress Report in which it would also, if necessary, make proposals for amending the BEPGs, the EPGs and the Union Lisbon Programme. In turn, the European Council would be reviewing progress every spring on the basis of the Commission's evaluation and decide on any necessary changes to the Integrated Guidelines.

The new cycle started in April 2005 with the Commission's proposal of Integrated Guidelines for Growth and Jobs for the period 2005–2008 which were approved by the Brussels European Council in June 2005. Guidelines 1–6 concern macroeconomic matters, Guidelines 7–16 relate to microeconomic matters and Guidelines 17–24 concern employment issues. These guidelines were subdivided into Council recommendations for macroeconomic and microeconomic policies and a Council Decision for Employment Guidelines (European Commission 2005). The 2005 EPGs were based on three "overarching and interrelated objectives" of "full employment, quality and productivity at work, and social cohesion and inclusion", reflecting the Lisbon agenda's goals, already included in the 2003 EPGs, the only change being the explicit reference to territorial inclusion. Integrated Guideline 17 contains the overarching objectives of the EES mentioned above. Worthy of mention is the explicit reference to promoting flexibility combined with employment security (Integrated Guideline 20) and the fact that there are no targets or benchmarks attached apart from those included in the 2003 guidelines, which have been consolidated and placed in a separate annex Council of the European Union 2005c). Two Integrated Guidelines are clearly a response to problems affecting more significantly the new Member States that

68 See Appendix 4.

joined in 2004, namely, Integrated Guideline 18 on ensuring inclusive labour markets for job seekers and disadvantaged people and Integrated Guideline 19 on improving matching of labour market needs, which includes, *inter alia*, the modernization and strengthening of labour market institutions, notably employment services. Many of the new Member States, particularly of Central Eastern Europe, are confronted with problems of marginalization and social exclusion of large parts of the population due to the significant proportion of long-term unemployed among those without a job and also with improving the institutional capability of PES, which in countries such as the Czech Republic plays a key role in the governance and modernization of labour market policies. Moreover, the synergy between the two main components of the Integrated Guidelines has been strengthened. For example, Integrated Guideline 4, which calls on Member States to ensure that the development of salaries contributes to macroeconomic stability and growth, explicitly refers to Integrated Guideline 22, which refers to ensuring employment friendly labour costs developments and wage-setting mechanisms. However, as explained in part in Chapter 3 and as will be examined further in Chapter 7, the EU overarching economic objectives continue to take precedence over the social policy objectives. In this case, nominal wages increase and labour costs have to remain inferior or equal to productivity gains. This policy of wage moderation is considered as being employment-friendly at Community level. However, as seen in Chapter 3, rather than stimulating growth the primacy afforded to price stability increases unemployment levels because 'it locks Europe in a vicious circle of low consumption, low demand, low investment and stagnation of productivity' (Raveaud 2007: 429). Hence, as argued by many scholars, the BEPGs end up taking precedence over the objectives of the EPGs.

Based on these guidelines the Member States prepared their first NRPs[69] and the Commission also drew up a Community Lisbon Programme drawing on the three priority areas for action identified by the Spring European Council in 2005 (European Commission 2005d). Moreover, the European Commission (2006) assessed Member States' national reports and adopted its Annual Progress Report in January 2006 entitled *Time to Move up a Gear*. This report is made up of three main parts. First, it contains an assessment of the Member States' national reports; second, it highlights the strengths in the NRPs with a view to fostering exchange of best practice; third, it identifies where there have been shortcomings and proposes a set of concrete action at EU and national levels. An important section of the Annual Progress Report is the Annex, which contains important documents and, in particular, a more detailed analysis of the macroeconomic, microeconomic and employment elements of the Integrated Guidelines. The Commission proposed that the guidelines should remain unchanged, and in July 2006 the Council adopted the same guidelines (Council of the European Union 2006c).

9.3 An assessment of the relaunch of the Lisbon programme

The Lisbon Strategy is probably one of the most important initiatives of the European Union of the twenty-first century, notwithstanding its limitations and weaknesses, as explained further below. The reason for this is twofold. First, from a substantive perspective the Lisbon agenda has broadened in a significant way the scope of the European Union's action for economic growth. With its focus on competitiveness and economic growth, the

---

69 These reports are available at <http://ec.europa.eu/growthandjobs/national-dimension/member-states-2005–2008-reports/index_en.htm>.

strategy seeks to expand the Single Market and to strengthen the economic dimension of the EMU while, at the same time, going beyond them by emphasizing economic-related institutional reforms at all levels of policy and decision making. Second, from a procedural view point, it has widened the forms and procedures of EU public action. More precisely, it has combined the achievement of its ambitious substantive agenda with the use of an array of instruments and thus not only conventional EU regulatory and economic instruments but also a series of experimental governance techniques.

Assessing whether or not the Lisbon Strategy has been effective is not an easy enterprise. In terms of goals and objectives there is now evidence that the European Union has been unable to meet its targets, and observers and politicians at both Community and national levels agree that the Lisbon Strategy has failed to deliver. The failure of the Lisbon Strategy cannot be attributed *sic et simpliciter* either to its goals or to its principles. The Lisbon goals continue to reflect the major challenges that European economies are confronted with in the context of globalization.[70] The goals in the Lisbon Strategy are important regardless of the fact that the strategy has been inadequately implemented in the Member States. The failure of the Lisbon Strategy, therefore, is explained by a combination of other factors such as the lack of clarity of the objectives (apart from the ones setting clear quantitative targets) and policies to achieve them, excessive complexity and inadequate process. Moreover, specifically in relation to the Employment Strategy, there is the feeling among some officials of the DG Employment that there has been limited "success" so far because the Commission itself has limited powers and is unable, therefore, to exert real pressure on the Member States to actually do something.[71] In addition, the lack of political commitment on the part of the Member States represents a major shortcoming.

However, in relation to Member States' performance it may not be all that simple to assess to what extent a government may be held responsible for meeting or missing these goals, especially in the case of dynamic growth or sustainable public finances. Two sets of problems may be envisaged here. First, overarching and worldwide economic problems which countries and international organizations cannot fully master or solve would make such assessment meaningless save for the purpose of obtaining politically destabilizing effects within that country. Second, governments that come into power may inherit inevitably a legacy of previous administrations' debt management and accumulated social entitlements that cannot be easily undone within one or two terms of office (Schelkle 2007/2008: 1).

Be that as it may, the Lisbon Programme remains essentially a cyclopean and overly ambitious project, notwithstanding the changes introduced further to its mid-term review and its relaunch as "Lisbon II", aimed at simplifying the overall process and improving its delivery. The Lisbon process seems to have been suffocated by the overwhelming detail of indicators and benchmarks and the distribution – or, better, the fusion – of competence remains opaque and has spread to include a rather unclear array of actors. Hatzopoulos

---

70 This point was raised by Mr Robert Strauss (Head of Unit D/2, Employment Strategy, CSR and Local Development, DG Employment), Interview of 5 November 2008 and 19 November 2008, European Commission, DG Employment, Brussels. See also the OPTEM qualitative study on the EES in which respondents in twenty-eight countries were asked to assess the strengths and shortcomings of the EES, European Commission (2007a).

71 Interview with Mr Radek Malý (Head of Unit D/1 Economic Analysis), 19 November 2008, European Commission, DG Employment, Brussels. He also maintains, however, that in the new Member States the Lisbon Strategy constitutes a strong incentive to reorganize their labour market policies.

(2007: 317) adds that the limitations of the Lisbon agenda are not only linked to its objectives which he finds contradictory but also to the fact that it is idealistic to set specific time frames and try to keep them with OMCs as the main means for the implementation of the relevant policies (that is, with non-binding instruments where the costs of non-compliance are too low; *ibid*.: 313). This explains why the 2010 target, included in the initial formulation of the Lisbon Strategy as a plausible time frame for the realization of its objectives, has been dropped after the mid-term evaluation and the project has become more open ended (*ibid*.: 317). According to Barnard (2006: 168):

> the Lisbon Strategy in its various forms is like nailing blancmange to a wall. There is no obvious way of grasping what is actually required, just a sense that (lots of big) "things have got to be done". It would be unfair to say that the Lisbon relaunch has the feeling of deckchairs being reorganized on the *Titanic*, but achieving the Lisbon goals does require the turning round of a large and unwieldy steamship.

Others have criticized the review of the Lisbon Strategy because other original goals such as gender equality, the fight against discrimination and poverty and environmental objectives have been set aside in favour of growth and employment. Moreover, the streamlining of the Lisbon Strategy has elevated the role of the ECOFIN Council. Similarly, within the Commission the DG ECfin has acquired a stronger role in comparison with the DG Social Affairs. The streamlining of the economic and employment co-ordination processes was meant to provide more political salience to the employment dimension but the result has been a significant loss of visibility of the social goals of the Lisbon Strategy. Gender equality is a case in point (as the next chapter will go on to show). In this context, Raveaud (2007: 429) argues that the Lisbon Strategy under the Barroso Commission has been reduced to an employment strategy itself limited to making labour markets more flexible and increasing labour supply in line with a neo-liberal conception of social policy. The limitations of the Lisbon Strategy, however, should be linked to the framework of the Union's economic governance. As Schelkle (2007/2008: 4) suggestively puts it:

> the governance framework of EMU before the reforms was based on a "Dr Jekyll and Mr Hyde" view of government. While government is Mr Hyde and must be restrained when it comes to macroeconomic policy making, it should turn itself into Dr Jekyll when it comes to microeconomic reforms to improve incentives for growth and innovation . . . The original SGP was based on a Mr Hyde view of government that cannot easily reconcile with the demands on Dr Jekyll requested by the Lisbon Agenda.

My argument is that this situation has remained unchanged even after the relaunch of the Lisbon Strategy. Nevertheless the relaunch, while not bringing about major substantive policy revision, provided an opportunity to refocus priorities and re-evaluate the governance structure of the OMC, drawing on the Kok reports and the "New Start" report issued by the European Commission (2005b). The revamped strategy emphasized the need to generate support for the implementation of the Lisbon Strategy by bringing it closer to EU citizens. It called for greater "ownership" of the strategy by national institutions, particularly national parliaments and greater participation of civil society and the social partners at national and sub-national levels.

The 2009 Swedish Presidency of the European Union worked on reviewing the Lisbon

Strategy to make it more focused and more efficient. The stated employment and social affairs priorities of the Swedish Presidency were: full employment and more inclusive labour markets; promoting good health for an ageing workforce (primarily through negotiating the patient mobility Directive and *e*Health co-operation and progress on the pharmaceuticals package); emphasizing the importance of gender equality for economic growth and employment (Sweden 2009).

The Commission envisions a new narrative for the Lisbon Strategy, although no radical changes in substance are expected, with competitiveness, research, innovation and the environment as its main pillars. While the strategy has been disappointing in terms of what it has actually delivered, at the same time it remains an important legitimacy token for the Commission and, more broadly, for Community action, particularly as it is becoming harder to obtain Member States' consent to adopt legislation.[72] In particular, the Commission will be launching a wide Internet-based consultation of European and national stakeholders on the post-2010 Lisbon Strategy in view of proposals for new Integrated Guidelines, country-specific recommendations and the Community Lisbon Programme.

The Commission has also called upon the European Parliament to become more involved in the process by providing input on the Commission's strategic annual report to be taken into account by the Council. In addition the Kok report proposed that the European Parliament should acquire an active role in scrutinizing the role of the Commission in the context of the Lisbon Strategy (Kok 2004: 41–42). The Bruegel Policy Brief (Pisani-Ferry and Sapir 2006) provided comparative data on the involvement of national parliaments in the design and adoption of the National Reform Programmes and showed that there is still very little involvement. The report suggests establishing minimum standards for national parliament involvement in the National Reform Programmes to address the uneven engagement of national parliaments.

The European Parliament, however, seems to have been taking on a more active role in the Lisbon process and in so doing it has also helped to increase the involvement of national parliaments. In 2004 the Conference of Presidents of the European Parliament established a group of thirty-three members of the European Parliament drawn from all the European Parliament's standing committees dealing with issues relevant to the Lisbon Agenda (the so-called G-33 group). The main task of the G-33 group is to establish the position of the European Parliament in relation to the operation, objectives and results of the Lisbon Strategy, submit recommendations to the Conference of Presidents of the European Parliament Political Groups and organize fora with, among others, the national parliaments. On the basis of these recommendations a resolution is drawn up annually. The resolution is debated and approved by the European Parliament in plenary session and then sent as input for the deliberations of the Spring Council (European Parliament 2007). Before the resolution is sent to the Spring Council the European Parliament holds an annual meeting with representatives of the national parliaments on the main priorities to be discussed in the Spring Council, with working groups co-chaired and made up of members of national parliaments and of the European Parliament to discuss and report on each priority area.[73] Importantly, the Presidents of the Commission and the Council, representatives of other EU institutions, civil society and the social partners also attend these meetings. Through the G-33 group and the annual joint meeting European

---

72 Interview with Mr Robert Strauss (Head of Unit D/2, Employment Strategy, CSR and Local Development, DG Employment), 5 and 19 November 2008, European Commission DG Employment, Brussels.
73 Three such meetings were held, in 2005, 2006 and 2007.

political parties and party coalitions are able to develop examples of good practice facilitating cross-country mutual learning. In addition, such new configurations could trigger political confrontation and realignments through public deliberation and justified on the basis of either constitutional or policy reasons in the context of a more comprehensive framework.

Concluding on a more optimistic note, it may be argued that 'to the extent that the Lisbon Process is based on a firm (though incremental) social "acquis" built by the European Courts and legislative institutions the fears linked to the ambiguity of its objectives and the inefficiency of its methods may be partially appeased' (Hatzopolous 2007: 1634).

10 A critical analysis of the European Employment Strategy and its key objectives

This section provides a first evaluation of the Employment Strategy and its aims in terms of both policy learning and policy formulation as well as democratic participation and deliberative supranationalism. In so doing it identifies the main achievements and short-comings of the EES. This preliminary assessment is going to be further developed in Chapter 7 on the basis of the theoretical bone structure and governance model provided in Chapter 2 and the empirical findings of Chapter 6.

What follows is a critical examination of the key objectives of the EES. The Employment Strategy aims at achieving six major objectives at both European and national levels:[74]

- Legitimacy of Community action.
- Promotion of transnational forms of governance while maintaining a certain degree of convergence.
- Efficiency of policy making.
- Increase policy co-ordination among all levels of government.
- Promotion of greater interaction between different policy areas.
- Promotion of policy learning.

The first objective, legitimacy, has always been pursued by the EC Institutions in the difficult achievement of promoting further integration in policy areas which have traditionally been considered as pertaining to the national domain.[75] From this perspective, the EES may be defined as constituting a *tertium genus*, that is, a middle way representing elements of continuity with previous methods of policy making in the field of social law and, at the same time, representing an innovative and qualitative break from the past, chiefly in the *way* in which these objectives are pursued.

The difficult aim of promoting further convergence while respecting the diversity of national labour markets and industrial relations systems was already an objective of the SPA, annexed to the EC Treaty. Its aim was to introduce a multi-tiered system of decision making at Community level combining the use of different regulatory tools such as Directives with non-binding legal instruments as well as co-ordinating these new methods of

---

74 This section draws on the works of Trubek and Mosher (2003) and Goetschy (2003).
75 See Chapters 2–4.

regulation with national measures.[76] As seen in Chapter 4, the result was the power assigned to the social partners to negotiate European framework agreements which could become European law, the formal consultation of the social partners in the drafting of social policy Directives and finally the possibility of implementing Directives by way of national collective agreements rather than legislation. The Treaty of Amsterdam added further impetus to differentiation and subsidiarity by institutionalizing the European Social Dialogue and, more broadly, by making the subsidiarity principle a more pervasive part of the Community's legal and political culture through the inclusion of such guidelines in forms and instruments of increasing legal significance which culminated in their constitutionalization in the protocol added to the EC Treaty on the application of the principles of subsidiarity and proportionality (de Búrca 1999). This protocol also made it clear, *inter alia*, that subsidiarity is a dynamic concept and, therefore, Community action can be equally expanded or restricted or discontinued where it is no longer justified. It also gave preference to the wider use of Directives and Framework Directives as opposed to regulations and detailed measures.

Within the EES, the objective is to integrate Member States' policies with the EPGs in a medium and long-term perspective with results that are to increase at the end of every cycle transcending short-term policies (Goetschy 2003). Goetschy (1999: 132) posits that 'the EES is a way to "depoliticize" the unemployment problem from its immediate national contingencies and to address it in a longer-term perspective'. Moreover, the very existence of the EES with its EPGs and its NAPs shows that efforts are being made to integrate the various levels of governance at both European and national levels, strengthening the co-ordination of national and European social policies and ultimately increasing the efficiency of social regulation. In this respect, the EES has several cardinal features:

- Most policies must be carried out at national or local level. There is relatively little direct action by the EC Institutions and bodies, the only exception being the use of the European structural funds to support the implementation of the EES.
- The primary role of the EU Institutions is to provide the general framework of the strategy, to develop specific guidelines, establish a monitoring system and finally to make annual recommendations to the Member States, where necessary.
- The institutional and legislative reforms are established and implemented at national or local level.

The question is how effective the co-ordination of national and European social policies is in integrating the various levels of governance and in increasing the efficiency of social regulation. Some Member States have failed to respond to the EPGs to change national policies and there is concern that the regional authorities and the social partners have not been adequately involved in the strategy. The guidelines stress explicitly the role of both social partners and regional and local authorities. Yet the role attributed to them differs according to the different areas covered by the guidelines. However, there is also a difference in the intensity with which the guidelines refer to vertical and horizontal decentralism in that the role of the social partners is much more stressed than that of the regional and local authorities (Smismans 2004: 12). The EES was expected to increase the legitimacy of Community social intervention by giving voice to representatives of civil society and by

---

76 In most Member States, such as France, Spain, Germany and Italy, social issues were also or mostly dealt with through non-legislative regulatory tools such as collective agreements.

increasing the participation of Member States in the modernization of the "European social model" (European Commission 2000d). The EES, however, has scored poorly on both accounts. The involvement of sub-national actors in the EES has been considered to be largely insufficient.[77] The invisibility of the sub-national authorities in the EES and, more broadly, in the Lisbon Strategy has been confirmed in the Integrated Guidelines for 2005–2008 and 2008–2010.[78]

However, some changes have already occurred, suggesting that the strategy has gradually introduced different regulatory approaches to social policy. Among the most salient features used in the EES there are what Jacobsson (2004) has defined as "discursive regulatory mechanisms" which although not unique to this method are herein employed systematically. In particular, the EES provides a common cognitive framework for understanding and describing problems in national labour markets and for identifying workable solutions that are adaptable to the different socio-economic context of different welfare systems. Thus, concepts and categories developed in the context of the iterative process of the EES are increasingly used in national labour market policy discourse and have had at least a symbolic impact nationally. Moreover, peer review and critique are now seen by the Member States as a legitimate exercise and have been institutionalized as a governance procedure to take place on a regular basis.[79] Similarly, Ashiagbor (2005: 233) talks about the emergence of a common discourse among elite actors. She argues that we can identify a transfer effect generated by the EES via the OMC which, although less coercive than the one resulting from traditional hard law measures, may change policy discourse within Member States, altering the boundaries of what is considered an acceptable range of policy choices for Member States.[80]

Particularly with the Lisbon Strategy, a policy paradigm emphasizing prevention, activation and lifelong learning has clearly been established. It follows that the legal significance of national reports lies in the *way* in which Member States interpret and use the concepts developed in the EES, as well as how the Commission and Council use the information and knowledge gathered in transforming them into standards and structural indicators that Members States then use to develop their labour and employment policies.

The creation of the EES was also meant to introduce change in the objectives of the EU agenda. Previous EU social policy and legislation was oriented to labour market policies linked to the completion of the Internal Market and to the creation of EMU without taking into account core issues of national social policies. On the contrary, the EES aims at addressing issues that directly affect national employment policies and industrial relations systems. This is explained by the fact that 'the more nationally sensitive a subject and the more difficult to resolve at national level, the more likely are Member States to become involved in an EU co-ordination procedure' (Goetschy 1999: 133). Syrpis (2002) maintains that 'in performance legitimacy terms, the focus has shifted away from the completion of the Internal Market, towards the redistributive implications of European integration'. However, since its inception the EES has been devoid of its more social democratic

---

77 As Smismans (2004: 13) notes, it is remarkable that there is no reference to sub-national authorities under what used to be the Employability pillar, given that regions may have a key role in relation to training and employment services and may be also responsible for tax and benefit systems.

78 See <http://ec.europa.eu/growthandjobs/european-dimension/index_en.htm>.

79 See e.g. <http://www.mutual-learning-employment.net/>.

80 See OPTEM qualitative study on the EES (European Commission 2007: 55 ff.), in which respondents consider the effectiveness of the Employment Strategy at national level.

objectives and with the emphasis placed on growth and jobs the Employment Strategy seems to have been re-embedded in the Internal Market agenda.[81]

Another feature of the EES is that it attempts to integrate separate policy domains. This objective was reflected initially with the selection of the four areas constituting the four pillars on which the employment guidelines were adopted. Previously, measures aimed at fostering entrepreneurship, vocational training and gender equality were not only dealt with by different authorities, institutions and bodies, but were also treated as completely separate policy domains and thus regulated separately. The employment guidelines and the national reports both illustrate how the EES and subsequently the Integrated Guidelines and other documents/texts produced in the context of the Lisbon Strategy have identified a series of key areas in which the independent operation of the various actors involved and policy boundaries are to be substituted by strict co-operation, co-ordination and with the implementation of horizontal, preventative and active measures and initiatives at all levels. Effective cross-cutting among the various policy domains has been insufficient. Already in the 2000 JER the Commission had expressed concern over the fact that the Employment Strategy was being considered as an agenda driven solely by the Ministries of Labour rather than an integrated strategy committing different levels of policy making (European Commission 2000a: 89).

With regard to the participation and functional representation of the social partners, there is evidence that there has been little participation of the social partners in the shaping of the employment guidelines and national reports (de la Porte and Nanz 2004: 280–281) and the 'varying quality of social partners' participation shows that their level of involvement is vulnerable to political changes' (*ibid.*: 280). Moreover, the interest of the social partners to participate in the draft of the national reports seems to be weak because these reports are often perceived as being a bureaucratic exercise documenting for the most part governmental measures, responding to objectives that were decided without their consultation. While some trade unions reported favourably on their participation in the process of drafting the NAPs/NRPs, other social partners complained of not having been able to contribute in a significant way (ETUC 2001). Several national union confederations reported having less than two weeks to provide input into plans or reported that no real effort had been made by the governments to ensure their participation in the process (ETUC *et al.* 2000: 3). In this context, Lafoucrière (2000: 22–24, 29–31) argues that the effective implementation of what used to be the Adaptability pillar could have been guaranteed only by the wider use of what she defines as "positive social dialogue", namely by introducing more specific guidelines and by clearly assigning an active role to the social partners within the iterative process of the EES. It may be argued, therefore, that the EES still remains heavily driven by bureaucratic top representatives both at European and national levels of policy making. Instead of broad participation the EES – and within it the OMC – seems to have fostered institutional change at national centralized level and a transnational, highly professionalized elite of experts, leading to a new form of epistemic community. In this register, Casey and Gold (2005: 37) have described peer review as 'a learning process for a limited community of labour market technicians and experts'.

With regard to convergence, the EPGs leave Member States with a great deal of discretion in relation to the typology of measures to be adopted. The EES, therefore, aims at achieving mostly convergence of results. In addition, the strategy covers only some aspects of employment policy and many areas remain exclusively within the domain of the

---

81 For an economic analysis of the EES and the Lisbon Strategy, see Schmid (2008).

Member States. In this context, the EES may be said to present the same intrinsic logic as a Directive. Although Directives are part of EC secondary law they are binding only 'as to the result to be achieved, upon each Member State to which it is addressed, leaving to the national authorities the choice of form and methods' (Article 249(3) EC). According to Goetschy (1999: 132) the difference between the two regulatory methods lies in the fact that whereas the EES is a deliberative form of governance, Directives, on the contrary, are based on a diplomatic approach because of the composition of the Council, which is made up of Ministers of national governments. The second main difference is that the EES, as a soft law instrument, does not provide any kind of legal sanctions in the event of Member States' non-compliance with the EPGs, whereas in the case of a Member State failing to implement a Directive the Commission may initiate enforcement action against the Member State concerned in accordance with Articles 226–228 EC.

Independently of its soft nature, establishing whether or not Member States have complied with the EES is challenging *per se* because of the fairly small number of quantified targets contained in the guidelines. It would be difficult, therefore, to establish whether a Member State, given its socio-economic structure, has achieved the objectives established by the EPGs. Even in cases where the target to be achieved has to correspond to the average of the three best-performing Member States[82] it would appear politically incorrect for the Commission and the Council to impose legal sanctions on those Member States which have failed to achieve quantified targets, precisely because of strong differences between the industrial relations systems and labour markets of each country. This explains why the use of recommendations and the adoption of incentive measures by the Council designed to encourage exchange of information and best practice between Member States and to support their action in the field of employment may be a more effective way of promoting policy learning in the Member States.[83]

The question of whether the EES promotes policy learning represents a core aspect of the overall assessment of the strategy. According to Casey and Gold (2005), while there is evidence at European level of policy convergence through the adoption of certain labour market targets, there is little evidence either of systematic learning or of significant efforts at emulation at Member State level. Their research findings identify three types of constraints: institutional, attitudinal and administrative/financial (*ibid.*: 30–35). With regard to policy convergence at European level, the most significant change to the content of the Employment Guidelines was made in 2001 with the insertion of the so-called "horizontal objectives" and new guidelines specifying these objectives (Council of the European Union 2001).[84] While some were an attempt to refine the previous EPGs, other guidelines introduced new objectives and targets. Examples of these changes are the addition of an obligation to modernize Member States' public employment services and apprenticeships systems (G 1 and G 10 and G 4), with an effort to change the measures from passive to more preventative and active ones. Other changes concerned the new obligations to eliminate the levels of poverty by reforming tax and social benefit systems (G 1, G 2 and G 11); improving skills qualifications (G 4), providing training for future entrepreneurs (G 9), introducing policies to keep older workers in the workforce (G 3) and finally

---

82 This is the case for example of G 2, regarding the Employability pillar.
83 For a detailed analysis of the causal mechanisms of policy learning reforms both from the perspective of the Member States (policy learning *stricto sensu*) and the European Union (mimicking), see Hemerijck and Visser (2001); see also Radaelli (2000), who examines policy transfer and isomorphism in the context of the single currency, tax policy and media ownership policy.
84 See also European Commission (2001e).

adopting new labour market policies to create a European knowledge-based society (G 5). That said, the changes made to the employment guidelines while exemplifying exchange of information and ideas at *European* level are not evidence that mutual learning is occurring at *national* level. In other words, there is still the question of what amounts to compliance in the context of the EES and, more generally, the OMC and the extent to which Member States are constrained in what they can do with their employment policy.

During its first years of implementation, scholars argued that the promotion of policy learning represented one of the key features of the EES (Ferrera *et al.* 2001; Teague 2001). The iterative and cyclical process of the Employment Strategy was considered to exemplify the way the "reregulation" or "renationalization process" (Sciarra 2000: 270–271; Lafoucrière 2000: 7) may operate in practice, furthering the Europeanization of social policy and, at the same time, strengthening national social pacts (Goetschy 2000: 55). Easterby-Smith, Crossan and Nicolini (2000) have listed various regulatory mechanisms which enhance policy learning such as mechanisms that reconfigure policy networks, foster co-operation between different policy areas, promote multi-tiered forms of policy making and decentralization, produce information on innovation, foster the exchange and benchmarking of best practice or promote deliberative modes of governance for problem solving.

Prima facie the EES may be said to have (or at least to promote the development of) most of these features. First, the overall iterative and cyclical process of the EES which entails the adoption of employment guidelines, national reports and recommendations to the Member States may be said to reconfigure policy networks and foster co-operation between different policy areas, particularly since its inclusion in the Lisbon Strategy. The EES also aims at introducing change in the way of implementing national policies and in the way of conceiving the function and objectives of domestic welfare state systems. Moreover, the Employment Strategy also attempts to promote partnerships between different stakeholders at different levels of authority. There are also several benchmarking mechanisms, and the Commission has issued various documents on structural indicators (European Commission 2000c; European Commission 2005e).[85] Such comparative indicators are important in order to be able to identify target groups for each measure, to measure policy effort (in terms of financial resources, staff and technical support) and to compare policy outcomes (Ashiagbor 2005: 200). In particular, benchmarking in the EES consists of evaluating Member States' performance against the average of the three best-performing Member States for that given indicator. Be that as it may, in practice what does benchmarking entail and achieve?[86]

Benchmarking was first introduced in the private sector as a means of enhancing efficiency by measuring the performance of one organization against a standard (Tronti 1998). In essence, this means improving performance by looking at and analyzing the achievements of others. Benchmarking has suggestively been defined as 'the practice of being humble enough to admit that someone else is better at something and being wise enough to learn how to match and even surpass them at it' (Rolstadås 1995: 212). In the context of the EES and, more broadly, the OMC, benchmarking cannot be equated with a simple transfer of best practice, due to different national structures, institutional environments and societal preferences. Policy benchmarking, therefore, should always take into account national contexts and national diversity. Returning to the question of what

---

85   For the full database of structural indicators, <http://epp.eurostat.ec.europa.eu/portal/page/portal/structural_indicators/introduction>.

86   For detailed comment and analysis on benchmarking and peer review, see Ashiagbor (2005: 199–208).

benchmarking entails, it is necessary to consider the fact that it has been introduced in the EES as a key tool for comparing Member States' performance precisely because 'it appeared to offer a means to solve two sets of conflict which intersect: the conflict between state action/intergovernmentalism and Community competence/supranationalism; and the conflict between regulation and deregulation. Benchmarking by avoiding more social regulations would seem to neutralize the fears of those concerned about centralization and over-regulation' (Ashiagbor 2005: 201). Hence a word of caution seems in order at this juncture: as the intergovernmental element is quite strong in the EES, the exchange of best practices, benchmarking, peer review and the mutual learning programme, which are key elements of its implementation, may result in a mere window-dressing exercise although there is some evidence of policy change, as illustrated by the definition of new EPGs. This has been particularly the case of the early years of the EES. Since 2003 and following the simplification and streamlining processes the employment guidelines have remained virtually unchanged (Mailand 2006: 31). In addition, as noted by Arrowsmith, Sisson and Marginson (2004: 312) 'political consensus is still required to identify and implement benchmarking projects, and that peer group pressure may be insufficient to this end. A second more technical problem is that the promise of benchmarking as a powerful tool of learning can be undermined by the elevation of quantitative criteria over more complicated issues to do with context and processes'. The Lisbon Strategy is a case in point and the mid-term review as well as subsequent evaluations of the Lisbon Strategy's "partial success" is associated with the vast amount of national reports to be submitted by Member States and the significant number of performance indicators and quantitative targets which have led to a situation of "checking and verifying rather than doing" to the detriment of quality of outcomes (*idem*).

With regard to policy learning there is also the issue of whether in the case of the EES we may talk of voluntary policy learning or coercive policy transfer. The Dolowitz and Marsh (2000) model develops a framework to analyze the process of policy transfer.[87] According to this model a continuum may be traced that runs from voluntary policy learning to coercive policy transfer without this process resulting necessarily in institutional change. Throughout this chapter we have seen that the intergovernmental element of the EES is very strong. This would suggest that Member States voluntarily "mimic" what they consider as being best practice and successful policies become transferred deliberately and willingly. While the Commission plays a significant role as "norm entrepreneur" it is the Member States that ultimately either through the European Council or the Council of Ministers decide what they want to be "bound" to with the EPGs. Bulmer and Padgett (2005: 123) argue that 'transfer outcomes under governance by facilitated unilateralism are significantly weaker than under hierarchical modes of governance. Informal rules and "soft" compliance mechanisms . . . entail, at best, only the very weakest forms of transfer effect'. However, this perspective presupposes that soft co-ordination processes such as the EES are essentially supranational, aiming at achieving Europeanization and thus some degree of convergence of national policies/measures pursuant to what are seen as being chiefly "European" objectives. As argued by Ashiagbor (2005: 233), it may be possible to identify a transfer effect generated by the Employment Strategy via the OMC. Hence, using the language of "policy convergence", it may be possible to argue that the EES is

---

87 The model is built around six questions: (1) Why do actors engage in policy transfer? (2) Who are the key actors involved in the policy transfer process? (3) What is transferred? (4) From where are lessons drawn? (5) What are the different degrees of transfer? (6) What restricts or facilitates the policy transfer process?

achieving such convergence by changing the direction of Member States' policies and, most important, through the 'emergence of a common discourse among elite actors (EU Institutions, national Ministries, the social partners)' (*ibid*.: 232).

In the light of the above analysis, the argument put forward here is that voluntary lesson drawing remains pivotal in the EES: either the Member States agree to it and are happy to go ahead with the process of policy learning, or policy transfer will not occur. Second, because of the soft nature of the Employment Strategy and lack of legal sanctions there is no guarantee that voluntary policy learning will occur at national level and that within the Member States it will take place through decentralization, involving regional and/or local levels and civil society. Linked to this, there is also a methodological difficulty in measuring "compliance".

A series of case studies which assessed the implementation of the EES at national level bring to light the existence of significant limitations to the EES (de la Porte and Pochet 2002; Zeitlin and Pochet 2005; Bredgaard and Larsen 2005; Beveridge and Velluti 2008). As regards the causal link between the EES and the national employment and labour market policies, the case studies showed that the EPGs and national social policies either aimed at achieving similar objectives or, on the contrary, had different targets (de la Porte and Pochet 2002: 18–19). In the former case, empirical studies had to assess whether there was any influence of the strategy on the adoption of national policy objectives and second, if any influence was found to have taken place, the extent of reciprocal influence of both levels of governance, namely whether the input was supranational or national and, more precisely, whether it was the supranational or the intergovernmental element to prevail in the strategy. In the event of different policy objectives, the research aimed at analysing national labour markets in order to explain why there was a divergence of policy objectives.

The second step was to assess the effective implementation of the strategy at national level. In the case of non-convergence of policy objectives, the research studies were conducted in order to provide some valuable proposals of reform in line with the EPGs. The case studies showed that the level of "policy distance" between a given national context and the European objectives determines the level of European influence on the national level (Anderson 2002: 256). The studies also revealed an interesting scenario. In the first place, even where the EPGs appear to be mostly influential, as in the case of Sweden and Denmark, research showed that there was little direct correlation between domestic labour market and employment-related measures and the Employment Strategy and that the apparent "success" of the EES was mainly due to a commonality of policy objectives and targets. Moreover, the whole process was mostly administered at ministerial level, chiefly, Ministries of Economy and Finance and Social Affairs. Jacobsson and Schmid (2002: 70) argue that EES is 'a rather insular process of interaction' between administrative top-level professionals and civil servants in the Directorate General of Employment and Social Affairs and national Ministries. Even though the participation of social partners in these two countries was higher compared to other countries, the case studies revealed that their involvement was still more formalistic and passive – 'more a matter of information than real consultation or negotiation with the government' – than at domestic level of policy making (*ibid*.: 86–87).

In France, research showed that the NAPs process is still in the phase of formal adaptation and there is no "real" reformulation of national policy objectives. Particularly relevant in this case was the fact that, at European level, France retained a sizeable amount of manoeuvre and directly influenced the drafting of the EPGs. Under the French Presidency of the European Union, there has been increased emphasis on the concept of quality of work. As a result, new horizontal objectives were introduced in the 2001 EPGs which also included quality of work. In Spain, the Employment Strategy promoted a rethinking of policy making by fostering the co-ordination between different administrations and the rationalization of employment and labour market policies, one important aspect being the increase in expenditure for employment-related policies. However, the case studies show that the impact of the EES was not particularly significant, due to specific political patterns and to the existence of persisting structural problems. With regard to CEECs' gender equality policies, Fuszara (2008) and Koldinská (2008) argue that there has been mostly formal adaptation and that the OMC is having only very limited effect in orienting domestic policies towards the issue of gender equality. Their research indicates that some of the perceived benefits of the OMC – its flexibility, its discursive nature and its promotion of mutual learning – cannot be relied on to deliver improvements in gender equality in the particular circumstances of these countries. Their research points to the importance of domestic political commitment, on the one hand, and indigenous capability in relation to gender equality, on the other, as twin prerequisites for successful implementation of equality policy through OMC processes.

The foregoing studies confirm that the intergovernmental element in the strategy is quite strong, with the implementation of the EES being carried out at civil servant and ministerial levels. This is confirmed by the weak involvement of the social partners in the adoption and implementation of the NAPs. Social partners have not been properly consulted and have not been included in an official process of negotiation with the government. This situation contrasts with the proviso of the employment guidelines, particularly those concerning adaptability, which gave the social partners a key role in the modernization of work organization and in lifelong learning measures.[88] Moreover, national reports indicate that it was mostly national confederations that were involved in the process and little information was provided on the extent of the social partners' participation at sectoral level (Keller and Bansbach 1999/2000: 84).[89] Even so, several national union confederations reported having less than two weeks to provide input into plans or reports and that no real effort had been made to ensure their participation in the NAP process (ETUC *et al.* 2000). Moreover, there is not enough information about the interaction between national and European social partners in the development of the strategy and the ETUC has said to have been insufficiently involved (ETUC 2001).

The EES, therefore, has various weaknesses that are inherent in its soft law nature. First, the very nature of the EES as a non-binding legal instrument does not allow an accurate assessment of the results achieved, given that national measures might also not refer explicitly to the EPGs and that many of the EES objectives are already part of national policy programmes. Second, the subordination of the strategy's implementation to the economic and political situation within the various Member States combined with its soft law nature does not guarantee its further development in moments of economic recession or political instability. Moreover, the paucity of specific procedural rules and detailed guidelines, the insufficient information on the operationalization of the benchmarking exercise (particularly on how parameters and structural indicators are selected and applied), the absence of a clear definition of the distribution of competence (Szyszczak

---

88 E.g. G 13, G 14 and G 15. See also G 6 (combating emerging bottlenecks); G 17 (equal opportunities) G 18 (reconciling work and family life) and horizontal objectives B (quality of work); C (lifelong learning strategy) D (partnership) and F (common structural indicators).

89 It is not clear at European level how the joint declarations adopted in each sector are then channelled in the wider context of the European Social Dialogue.

2001: 1138) and, finally, the lack of a system of legal or formal sanctions in the event of non-alignment of a given Member State with the EPGs seriously undermine the legitimacy and the effectiveness of the strategy, considering that the guidelines are normative in character (Biagi 2000: 160). The whole process seems to be taking place "between elites for elites" (Barnard and Deakin 2001). In addition, despite the increased role of both the European Parliament and the Committee of the Regions, these institutions still have a minor consultative role in the implementation of the Employment Strategy (Szyszczak 2001a: 1141) and the ECJ is absent from the process.

This overall picture of the EES underlines the opacity and complexity of its institutional framework (Hodson and Mayer 2001: 730–732). In addition, these regulatory deficiencies confirm the fact that the EES cannot be used as an alternative to the traditional Community Method but rather as a complement and that New Governance, law and constitutionalism should be seen as forming part of the same *corpus unicum*, each performing a specific role in ensuring the effective functioning of the Union by compensating for each other's weaknesses. In particular, the analysis conducted in this chapter reinforces the fact that there is the need to reconsider accepted and fixed understandings of law and constitutionalism and to develop and strengthen a strong hybridized system of co-regulation. Specifically, the aim is to develop and employ a governance model[90] which draws on the combination of direct, representative, participatory and deliberative forms of democracy in which both European and national parliaments could have a key role in setting a meta-governance frame defining objectives and procedures, monitoring progress towards agreed goals and revising the processes in light of the results achieved. In their renewed role national parliaments could pass framework legislation containing commitments to a broad set of goals such as OMC objectives, establishing administrative infrastructures to stimulate decentralized experimentation, monitor the efforts of local units to improve their performance against them, pool resulting information and set provisional standards in light of what they have learned, reviewing the results and revising framework objectives and administrative procedures accordingly (Zeitlin 2005: 224–225). As seen in Chapter 2, this renewed role may give national legislators access to insights and tools for producing better legislation and provide them with grounds for criticizing governmental legislative and administrative measures. In this context, courts would retain an important monitoring function of deliberative problem-solving units and, in particular, they have a process-perfecting function by ensuring that decision makers themselves make policy with explicit reference to constitutional reasons and to policy reasons. This governance model would ensure more transparency and accountability as well as participatory and reflexive forms of democracy whilst ensuring, at the same time, efficiency and output delivery without reverting to a command-and-control rationale typifying classical forms of regulation.

11 Conclusion

The chapter analyzed the genesis, development and further implementation of the EES through the OMC. In so doing, it showed that the EES presents at the same time elements of continuity with and break from pre-existing and more conventional regulatory instruments employed in the Community Method and received a relatively high level of consensus among the Member States. During its first years of implementation it was considered to be a successful mode of governance compared to the more traditional hard

90 See Chapter 2.

law methods in allowing Member States to introduce radical changes in the social policy sphere at their own pace and discretion. Moreover, the sovereignty of the Member States remains intact in an area which is deeply embedded in the history and economic and social culture of the Member States. In this respect, Mailand (2006: 77) maintains that 'whereas a plurality of actors were decisive for the setting up of the EES in the mid-1990s, in its further development the Member States have been the dominant actors, even though the Commission (DG Employment and to some extent DG ECOFIN and DG Enterprise) has also continued to exercise a strong influence. The social partners and the European Parliament – who have been pointed out as part of the coalition establishing the strategy – have been less influential.' Similarly, the processes around the two Kok reports demonstrate more clearly an intergovernmental process. Especially the first Kok report – a process where the Member States (Germany and especially the United Kingdom) set the agenda, and where the Commission acts reactively – could be seen as a government-driven process (*ibid.*: 78). However, while the political–institutional structure of social solidarity in Europe has remained national, its substance has changed. In this context, the EES within the Lisbon Strategy plays an important role in changing the policy rationales and discourses on which labour and employment measures adopted at domestic level are premised.

The EES is consistent with its attempts to create an active welfare state in the context of "competitive solidarity" (Streeck 2000: 245), replacing protectionist social protection systems with a focus on measures that improve employment and earning capacity and remove the disincentives for activity, either within or outside the formal labour market. Embedded in a policy environment which has removed their control over traditional instruments of macroeconomic policy, the EES is an attempt to reduce the willingness of national governments and politicians to condone high unemployment and inactivity, and strengthen their resolve to engage in reform (Visser 2002). According to Visser, by focusing on the employability of workers in combination with adaptability policies, the supply-side egalitarianism on which the EES is premised would make *ex post* political redistribution less pressing (*idem*). However, as shown throughout this chapter, the EES has fallen short of reaching these initial expectations.[91]

The chapter also explained how the iterative process, upon which the EES is based, operates and how it aims at strengthening the role of new actors at different levels of governance. In this context the analysis has shown a rather different picture from the one that has been portrayed of the EES. Empirical studies confirm that regional authorities and the social partners have not been adequately involved in the Employment Strategy. Instead of broad participation the EES – and within it the OMC – seems to have fostered institutional change at national centralized/ministerial level with the participation of professionalized experts transnationally. Hence the EES stands far from the standard democratic narrative of representative democracy as well as from the democratic ideal of directly deliberative polyarchy (Cohen and Sabel 1997; Gerstenberg 1997). In particular, it does not provide the coherent institutional framework that can encourage decentralized self-regulation in an accountable and democratic way.

With regard to the Employment Strategy's key objectives, we have seen that the creation of the EES has been developed also as a governance response to solving the Community's democratic and legitimacy problems, which became particularly obvious during the ratification process of the Treaty of Maastricht and have bedevilled the European Union at every (attempt at) Treaty amendment and wave of enlargement. Smismans (2004: 10)

---

91   By contrast, see the Commission's recent evaluation report of the EES (European Commission 2007).

effectively summarizes the limitation of the EES and its mode of operation as a form of decentralized deliberative democracy and as promoting democratic participation, which deserves to be quoted at length:

> The Employment Title does not provide a comprehensive framework for what might be a European employment policy in a multi-level context. The Treaty provisions read as an EES built on the Member States, and not as a European employment policy built on a multitude of actors in a multi-level polity, including regional and local authorities and civil society organizations organized at European, regional and local level (in addition to "traditional" national, sectoral and firm-level social partners' associations). If one can read in the Employment Title the intentions of the Member States when creating a European employment policy, there are few signs to believe that the OMC was intended to be a prime example of a decentralized approach, a radicalization of subsidiarity or the realization of the democratic experimentalist dream.

The chapter showed that the EES's main strength lies probably in providing a common cognitive framework for understanding and describing problems in national labour markets and for identifying workable solutions that are adaptable to the different socio-economic context of different welfare systems. Thus concepts and categories developed in the context of the iterative process of the EES are increasingly used in national labour market policy discourse and have had at least a symbolic impact nationally. In this context, we have seen that through its cyclical process and production of texts and information produced it promotes new employment and labour market paradigms in the Member States. However, it is difficult to assess (especially from a methodological perspective) whether the EES results in policy transfer and, most important, in voluntary lesson drawing. It is not possible to establish whether the changes in national legislation are a direct result of the implementation of the EES. In this context, questions remain regarding its soft law nature and, in particular, the effectiveness of the Employment Strategy, given that it lacks any legal sanctions and enforcement system.

The simplification of the EES, its inclusion in the Lisbon Strategy and its streamlining with the economic co-ordination process have left the above problems unsolved or, in some instances, it has exacerbated them, such as the loss in visibility of the more exclusively "social" objectives, the unbalanced relationship between quality and quantity as well as between democratic participation and efficiency. Moreover, as seen above, the Lisbon Strategy has not been able to meet most of its ambitious goals and the European Union is already thinking ahead to develop a "new narrative" for the Lisbon agenda. As Hatzopoulos (2007: 1628) puts it:

> the attainment of the Lisbon objectives may be seen, from a neo-functional point of view, as the next big "bet" of the European Union, nourishing and streamlining its integration process: after the completion of objectives such as the Internal Market (1992), EMU (1999), enlargement (2003–2005) and in view of the unhappy fate of the Constitutional Treaty . . . the Lisbon Strategy [with all its inbuilt limitations][92] seems to be offering the necessary impetus for keeping the European Union steaming ahead.

92 My addition.

However, a key question remains unanswered, namely: are democratic experimentalism or directly deliberative polyarchy or reflexive harmonization *descriptively* appropriate names for OMC processes (Ashiagbor 2005: 227–230), given that empirical studies indicate that far from being truly open and participatory they seem to be largely "top-down" driven? And if the answer is no, what then should be the adequate measures or instruments to ensure that OMCs, and in broader terms New Governance processes and practices, may embody (and not merely be capable of embodying) the principles of one or more of the afore-mentioned theories of governance? This question will be addressed in full in Chapter 7 on the basis of the theoretical governance model developed in Chapter 2 and the empirical case study which is the focus of the next chapter.

6 Gender equality and mainstreaming in the rearticulation of labour market policies: Italy, Denmark and the Czech Republic

1 Introduction

This chapter examines whether the European Employment Strategy may effectively promote gender equality in the context of the reorganization of European labour markets. By adopting a gender audit approach it identifies synergies and conflicts between measures aimed at encouraging the adaptability of businesses and their employees to structural, economic and industrial change and measures aimed at promoting gender equality in the labour market. In particular, the chapter examines the implementation of the EES as a New Governance tool and uses a comparative analysis approach to evaluate how effective it is to implement and enforce social policy measures. The countries selected are Italy, Denmark and the Czech Republic representing ideal-type southern Mediterranean, Scandinavian and Central Eastern European social policy systems.

The chapter seeks to answer the following two questions. Given that gender mainstreaming[1] is considered one of the most important objectives of the EES, how have gender equality and equal opportunities issues been mainstreamed in the modernization of European labour markets at national level? And, following the simplification and inclusion of the EES in the Lisbon Strategy and the disappearance of the Equal Opportunities pillar, have gender equality and gender mainstreaming lost momentum? The findings of the study underpin a general analysis of the operation of the EES and its impact on social policies at national level. The study also illuminates the impact of the OMC on the constitutional and institutional structures of the Member States and, more generally, on EU social governance. In particular, the significance of this chapter lies chiefly in subjecting the theoretical assumptions of how the EES operates (for example, the distribution of competence between the European Union and the Member States and within the state

---

1 Gender mainstreaming entails a paradigm shift both in theory and in action from previous measures designed to achieve equality between women and men such as equal treatment, equal opportunities and positive action. Gender mainstreaming addresses the problem of gender inequality at a more structural level in comparison with previous generations of equal treatment and equal opportunities measures which mainly provide for a set of equality rights and create the conditions for exercising them but still hold individuals primarily responsible for exercising them. In addition, preferential treatment consists of specific measures aimed at facilitating equality for specific targeted groups of women whereas gender mainstreaming is based on a more systematic approach and it identifies gender biases in current policies, assessing the impact of gender biases in the reproduction of gender inequality (Verloo 2005).

between the central government and the regional and local policy makers) to further critical analysis in order to evaluate the effectiveness of the EES in the wider context of EU social governance.

The aim of the chapter is not so much to identify and comparatively assess individual Member States' performance to evaluate whether policy transfer does occur in the context of the EES and, if so, to establish the level of policy transfer in each of the different typologies of welfare states, but rather to examine how policy change, if it does take place, may impact on the exercise of social rights within each of the welfare state clusters taken into consideration. In this context, it seeks to examine the nature and scale of the effects of the EES on national social systems. As explained in previous chapters of the book, the Employment Strategy is built upon two conflicting rationales, namely a social policy discourse and a neo-liberal agenda. From the perspective of social rights this means that the EES promotes two conflicting visions of social rights. On the one hand, it fosters a "workfare" or employability approach whereby individuals have a duty to work and job seekers have a responsibility to look for work and social rights are residual or curtailed rights. In this context, the 'role of state intervention is not to secure equality of outcomes, but equality of opportunity, to invest in skills so as to improve and equalize the *marketability* of individuals, rather than protecting them from the market' (Ashiagbor 2005: 292). On the other hand, it fosters a social inclusion or capabilities approach premised on the effective freedom a person – be it natural or legal – has when embarking on achieving a set objective (independently of its nature) and based on social solidarity and employment protection, whereby the duty to work is balanced with the right to work and social rights are conceived of as individual and collective procedural rights (ensuring participation) and substantive rights (Salais 2001: 272–273, 277). While both may be said to build on the Hayekian perspective that contractual and property law enables individuals to enter the market and take part in mutually beneficial exchange relations, the difference lies in the fact that the capabilities approach ensures that 'a range of basic social rights is required if meaningful participation in the market is to be possible. From this perspective, certain social rights, such as the right to non-discrimination and the right to fair treatment at work, can be thought of as "institutionalized capabilities" ' (Barnard *et al.* 2001: 466). In this context, the freedom to enter the labour market, therefore, becomes a substantive freedom because a series of other substantive rights will be ensured through employment. Hence, in consideration of these conflicting rationales underpinning the EES, the comparative analysis undertaken in this section seeks to examine its effectiveness in different welfare state systems.

The chapter also shows that, while the 2003 and 2005 simplification and streamlining of the EES with the BEPGs has reduced the visibility of the gender equality dimension to the EES, the problems regarding the implementation of gender equality go beyond the governance debate and are linked to the complexities of conceptualizing a clear vision of gender equality. Any study of this policy area, therefore, must take into account that the legal construct of equality and the social construct of gender are based on different premises: while equality is based on likeness or similarity, gender is based on difference (Barbera 1991).

The chapter is structured as follows. The next section provides an overview of the reform of the EES, with a focus on the changes that have affected adaptability and equal opportunities measures. In this context, the chapter also looks at the role of the social partners and "flexicurity" debates. The EES assigns an important role to the social partners in ensuring good governance of employment policies and in the implementation of the strategy, particularly in promoting "flexicurity" measures in the context of adaptability. Prior to the reform of the EES and the Lisbon Strategy, the Employment Guidelines assigned a prominent role to the social partners across all the then four pillars of the EES, including the Equal Opportunities pillar (Council of the European Union, 2002). The simplification of the Employment Guidelines and their inclusion in the Integrated Guidelines have entailed a decrease in importance of the social partners in the Strategy, with Member States regaining centre stage in the implementation of the EES (Council of the European Union 2005). In so doing, the chapter explains the importance of injecting a gender perspective into adaptability measures in the light of global socio-economic changing patterns and the feminization of the labour market. Following on from the analysis conducted in the previous section, the chapter then proceeds to explaining the need for change in the way of conceptualizing gender equality measures. The third section analyzes welfare state cluster classifications and examines whether it is possible to identify a welfare state regime unique to CEECs or whether their welfare state regime(s) can be incorporated into one of the existing clusters which typify the "old" Member States. The fourth section focuses on the joint study of adaptability and equal opportunities in order to assess to what extent measures aimed at modernizing European labour markets take into account the promotion of equal opportunities for women and men at work. In this context, it provides a comparative study of Italy, Denmark and the Czech Republic. This analysis allows us to evaluate the effectiveness of the EES and, in particular, to assess how the EES operates in three Member States with different economic and social structures which nevertheless share similar problems. In considering the factors which shape domestic policies as well as the interaction between policy dynamics and political structures in the European Union and the interplay of different levels of governance – in accordance with Europeanization theories (Héritier and Knill 2000; Radaelli 2000, 2004) which explain change and, more broadly, examine the variables affecting the performance of public policy – this section focuses on policy measures, the legal and institutional framework (the rules, the actors and their relationships), and resources (funding, the level of competence and influence). In this context, implementation is intended as a process that does not necessarily lead to the mere implementation of a given policy, but rather to the redefinition of its goals and reinterpretation of outcomes (Majone and Wildavsky 1979). More precisely, the aim is to look at how EU soft co-ordination processes may "frame" or, better, "re-frame" domestic policy by providing legitimate policy ideas to domestic actors (Knill and Lehmkuhl 1999). From this perspective, the EES may be seen as a form of framing integration policy in that it does not necessarily lead to institutional change, but rather promotes certain values and principles which underpin legislative and policy measures at domestic level, thereby altering the beliefs and expectations of national actors. In addition, the comparative case study looks at the distribution of agency within the implementation process of the Employment Strategy. In this context, the chapter seeks to illustrate how the transfer process may have a more voluntary character when the involvement of domestic (governmental) actors is predominant and conversely policy transfer may be more coercive when EU intervention is decisive for implementation as illustrated by the pre-accession process of candidate countries. Furthermore, the level of adaptation of national policies to EU law and – for the purposes of this book – to the policy objectives of the EES also depends crucially on domestic institutional structures and efficiency of national decision-making systems. The final section brings together the main arguments put forward throughout the chapter and makes some suggestions for strengthening the synergy between adaptability and equal opportunities in domestic social policy systems within the broader context of the EES.

2 The importance of linking the modernization of work organization to equal opportunities policies

2.1 The ups and downs of gender equality and gender mainstreaming in the European Employment Strategy

In the first year of implementation of the EES in 1998, the employment co-ordination process centred around four key areas named "pillars": employability, entrepreneurship, adaptability and equal opportunities. The Equal Opportunities pillar included policies aimed at fostering gender equality, reducing gender gaps and promoting gender main-streaming. Four guidelines were formulated referring to tackling gender gaps, reconciling work and family life, facilitating the return to work and promoting the integration of people with disabilities into working life (Rubery *et al.* 2003). In 1999, at the end of this first cycle, a mainstreaming approach to equal opportunities was adopted for the fourth pillar, with the aim of strengthening the integration of equal opportunities issues into the employment framework and reducing gender pay gaps. Subsequently, the employment guidelines under the fourth Equal Opportunities pillar were developed on the basis of four principles (EGGSIE 2007). The first referred to the need to adopt a gender-mainstreaming approach. The guidelines included promotion of equal access to active labour market policies (ALMPs)[2] among women and men in unemployment, assessment of the gender impact of tax and benefit systems and application of the principle of equal pay for work of equal value. The second principle required Member States to tackle gender gaps. Guidelines included the reduction of the unemployment gap through supporting female employment growth (possibly in line with a national target), action to reduce sex segregation, initiatives to diminish the gender differential in income and measures to further women's advance-ment in employment. The third principle required Member States to encourage the recon-ciliation of work and family life. The fourth principle referred to facilitating reintegration into the labour market.[3] At the Lisbon Summit, the European Council re-emphasized the importance of the gender dimension to employment (European Council 2000). Member States should strengthen their efforts to include and make visible a gender perspective across all the pillars and quantitative targets for higher employment rates were agreed: 70 per cent for all in employment and 60 per cent for women, to be reached by the year 2010. In 2001 the Stockholm European Council added other quantitative targets: inter-mediate targets of 67 per cent (total) in employment and 57 per cent (for women) by the year 2005 and an additional employment target of 50 per cent for older men and women (fifty-five to sixty-five years old) by 2010 (European Council 2001). Following the 2002 Barcelona spring European Council, which called for a strengthening of the EES (European Council 2002), the Commission issued a series of Communications. As seen in Chapter 5, in its Communication *Taking Stock of Five Years of the European Employment Strategy* (European Commission 2002b) the Commission reviewed the experience of five years of the EES and broadly outlined a redesign of the EES for the future. The most significant change introduced was a streamlining of the Employment Strategy with other key policy co-ordination processes, including the BEPGs and the Internal Market Strategy (European Commission 2002) and the adoption of three overarching and interrelated objectives: full

---

2 For detailed analysis and comment on ALMPs, see Barbier (2004), Serrano Pascual (2007), Eichhorst, Kaufmann and Konle-Seidl (2008).

3 From 2001 this principle was no longer included under the pillar of Equal Opportunities.

employment, quality and productivity at work and social cohesion and inclusion and the disappearance of the four pillars. Moreover, the guidelines were simplified and reduced to ten (Council of the European Union 2003). Employment Guideline 6 referred to gender equality and emphasized, again, the integrated approach of combining gender mainstreaming and specific policy actions. This approach should focus on the reduction of gender gaps (chiefly the gender pay gap) and reconciling work and family life. Moreover, it included the goals that by 2010 Member States should provide child care for at least 90 per cent of children between three years old and the mandatory school age and at least 33 per cent of children under three years of age. This review was followed by another major revision of the EES and in 2005 the Brussels Spring European Council adopted Integrated Guidelines for Growth and Jobs for the period of 2005–2008. Reduced from ten to eight, the Employment Guidelines are now part of a package of twenty-four guidelines of the Lisbon Strategy (corresponding to Integrated Guidelines 17–24). The Guidelines are presented in conjunction with the macroeconomic and microeconomic guidelines (previously BEPGs) for a period of three years and the NAPs are replaced with the NRPs.

Gender equality is no longer included as a specific guideline, although gender mainstreaming and the promotion of gender equality are included as a general principle. For example, Integrated Guideline 17 refers to the employment target of 60 per cent for women and Integrated Guideline 18 addresses the reduction of gender gaps and the introduction of reconciliation policies as a means to promote a life-cycle approach to work (EGGSIE 2007). However, due to the disappearance of a specific gender equality guideline, the visibility of gender and the attention paid to both gender equality policies and gender mainstreaming in the national reports has declined (Fagan *et al.* 2006). The loss of focus and the increasing invisibility of gender are also mentioned in the Joint Employment Report for 2006–2007: 'through the European pact for gender equality Member States were asked to include a perspective of gender equality when reporting on implementation. In spite of this, the promotion of female employment and systematic gender mainstreaming of policies are rarely emphasized' (Council of the European Union 2007a: 4). The disappearance of the equality guideline in the EES explains why the NRPs give less importance to the gender equality dimension of employment policies, particularly gender mainstreaming. In 2008, however, the European Commission (2008) recognized the importance of policies aimed at ensuring a balance between professional, private and family life, stating that they are at the core of Europe's strategy for growth and jobs.[4] It has presented, therefore, a work–life balance package which includes, *inter alia*, two legislative proposals to revise existing Directives and a report on progress made by Member States towards the Barcelona targets for child care provision. The legislative proposals (on amending the Directive on the protection of pregnant workers (Council of the European Union 1992a)[5] and the Directive on the protection of self-employed women during pregnancy and motherhood (Council of the European Union 1986a) aim to strengthen women's legal entitlement to family-related leave, namely maternity leave, and ensure equal treatment of the self-employed and their assisting spouses. The main points of the new maternity leave proposal are an extension of the duration of maternity leave from fourteen to eighteen weeks;[6]

4 Interview with Mr Laurent Aujean, Unit G/1, Equality between Men and Women, DG Employment, 4 December 2008, European Commission, Brussels.
5 This is under revision at the time of writing this book, see European Commission (2008).
6 The extension of the duration of maternity leave to eighteen weeks has been recommended by the ILO since the year 2000, see ILO (2000).

the principle of full pay during the eighteen weeks, with a possibility, however, for Member States to introduce a ceiling that must not be below sickness pay; the right for women coming back from maternity leave to ask for flexible work arrangements. The employer must examine such a demand but has no obligation to accept it; the proposal also increases the flexibility for women to decide when to take their maternity leave, before or after giving birth. The other legislative proposal aims at ensuring a better balance between the need to improve the protection of self-employed women and the recognition of the specificities of self-employment. It also provides that Member States must ensure that assisting spouses can, at their request, benefit from at least an equal level of protection to that of self-employed workers. The Commission consulted European employers' and trade union representatives on possible work–life balance measures in two stages during 2006 and 2007, covering all forms of leave, such as maternity, paternity and parental leave. This consultation eventually led to a new agreement between the European social partners. In June 2009 European social partners signed a new framework agreement on parental leave according to which parental leave will be increased from three to four months and will apply to all employees regardless of the type of contract. This is the first time that an existing framework agreement (on which the Directive on Parental Leave, Council of the European Union 1996, is based) has been reviewed by the European social partners.

2.2 Understanding adaptability in a "flexicurity" context in the European Employment Strategy

2.2.1 The notion of adaptability in the European Employment Strategy

Prior to the reform of the EES, the Adaptability pillar, as the title expressly stated, encouraged adaptability of businesses and their employees to structural, economic and industrial change. Measures adopted under this pillar were developed and implemented at workplace level. The three main interdependent elements of the pillar were: partnership, creation of a new working environment at enterprise level and adoption of policies which promoted the development of workers' capacities. In particular, the Adaptability pillar aimed at promoting policies that pursued the modernization of work organization, including flexible working arrangements and also measures that contributed to the strengthening of lifelong learning strategies, high skills of workers and quality at the workplace. More precisely, the Adaptability pillar covered two sets of policies: on the one hand, policies that contributed to making firms productive and competitive in the context of new technology and, on the other, measures that improved the quality of jobs, ensuring a proper balance between flexibility and security.

2.2.2 The role of the social partners

The objective of establishing a balance between flexibility and security has been included in the EES since its inception in 1998. Flexibility and security were included in the third pillar, 'encouraging adaptability of business and their employees', from 1998 to 2002, and emphasis on their importance has been confirmed in subsequent years. The social partners were invited to take an active role in establishing this goal. They were asked to negotiate (and, as of 2000, also to implement) agreements to modernize the organization of work, including flexible working arrangements, with the aim of making undertakings productive and competitive (as of 2002, also adaptable to industrial change) and achieving the required balance between flexibility and security.

In 2001 the task of the social partners was broadened, as they were asked to report annually which elements of work organization were covered by negotiations, what the level of implementation was, and what the influence on employment and labour market functioning was (Council of the European Union 2001). Moreover, from 2001, the part of the modernization of work organization for which the Member States are held responsible was reformulated so that the notion of security for workers in atypical contracts should not only meet business needs but also the aspirations of workers. Member States would have to examine their legislation in co-operation with the social partners or based upon the negotiated agreements between the social partners. The social partners have also been given a prominent role in supporting the adaptability of enterprises, with a specific focus on making agreements about lifelong learning. Since the reform of the EES and its inclusion in the Lisbon Strategy the role of the social partners in the context of adaptability and flexibility of the labour markets has lost prominence. In particular, no reference to their role is made in Integrated Guideline 20 concerning the adoption of measures for the promotion of flexicurity and the reduction of labour market segmentation (or in Integrated Guideline 4 concerning the adoption of measures for the promotion of greater coherence between macroeconomic and structural policies). Moreover, Integrated Guideline 21 on measures ensuring the development of adequate frameworks for wage bargaining systems at national level refers to the role of social partners only incidentally by referring to the respect of their role in setting up such systems. This seems to be in contrast with the emphasis placed on the role of the social partners in the Kok Report (2003) and the Green Paper *Modernizing Labour Law* (European Commission 2006a) where they are urged together with the Member States to examine the degree of security for non standard workers who work under alternative forms of contracts to standard open-ended contracts.

With regard to CEECs, the Soviet-style trade union movement completely disappeared after 1989, while free trade unions are still in the process of finding their new niche. They could serve a useful purpose in monitoring equal opportunities legislation by giving opinions on draft laws, representing workers in meetings with employers, disseminating information in the workplace, and bringing cases of discriminatory behaviour before the relevant authorities. Unfortunately, trade unions across CEECs are generally not dedicated to improving gender equality in the labour market and are thus unable to exert significant pressure on employers. Furthermore, many workers remain apathetic about their own labour market interests. During the pre-accession stage, the Joint Assessment Papers (JAPs, see further below) reported minimal involvement of the social partners in CEECs. While the role of social partners varies across Central Eastern Europe it is possible to identify common developments. In particular, since 2004 not only are trade unions politically weak and employers' organizations slow to develop but often governments have adopted a centralized approach to regulation, thus limiting the involvement of organized civil society *lato sensu*.

2.2.3 *From adaptability to flexicurity*

In 2003 the Adaptability pillar underwent drastic changes, also affecting the formulation of flexibility and security. The distinction in the pillar between guidelines concerning the modernization of work organization and guidelines concerning the adaptability of enterprises disappeared, and, more important, the need for a balance between flexibility and security was replaced by the less restrictive and less balanced formulation of 'the need for both flexibility and security':

Member States will facilitate the adaptability of workers and firms to change, taking account of the need for both flexibility and security and emphasizing the key role of the social partners in this respect.

(Council of the European Union 2003: 18)

Member States were encouraged to examine overly restrictive elements in their employment legislation which affected labour market dynamics and the employment of target groups. In addition, the pillar suggested that Member States should address labour shortages and bottlenecks, for example by promoting occupational and geographic mobility and simplifying mobility, by improving the recognition and transparency of qualifications and competences, and simplifying the transferability of social security and pensions rights. The 2004 guidelines remained the same, whereas in 2005 another major change was introduced in order to anticipate, trigger and absorb economic and social change. In this respect, emphasis was given to employment-friendly labour costs, modern forms of work organization and well functioning labour markets that allow more flexibility combined with employment security to meet the needs of both companies and workers. Although this implicitly refers to the need for a balance between flexibility and security, the actual formulation of Integrated Guideline 21 merely mentions the promotion of flexibility combined with employment security. It also reduces the broad term of security to the more specific term of employment security. Moreover, as mentioned above, the former *key role* of the social partners is now seen only as a *role* (Integrated Guideline 21).

In 2006 "flexicurity" was placed high on the European political agenda and balancing flexibility and security became a priority in the context of the Lisbon Strategy. Following the evaluation of Member States' practice early in 2006, the Commission stressed the importance of establishing further conditions of flexicurity. In the conclusions of the Austrian Presidency later that year the European Council endorsed the joint initiative by the Commission, the Member States and the social partners to identify a set of 'common principles' on flexicurity (European Council 2006) and the following year the Commission issued a Communication on flexicurity (European Commission 2007b).

There is no single flexicurity model, and very different models and strategies can be subsumed under the term "flexicurity". The concept of flexicurity exemplifies deep changes in the labour market, in the workforce and in labour law.[7] Fredman (1997) suggestively talks about labour law being in flux, although, as Kenner (2009: 288) aptly cautions, its inherent purpose, that of acting as a countervailing force against the inherent inequality of bargaining power between the contracting parties of an employment relationship (Davies and Freedland 1983: 18), remains untouched. Flexicurity was first introduced and used in the Netherlands in the mid-1990s as well as in Denmark and it may be said to entail a twofold departure from the European labour market debate of the 1990s (Keune 2008: 6). First, it promotes a holistic approach to labour market analysis because it presents a view of the labour market as representing the interplay of a number of different types of flexibility and security and, therefore, dismisses the one-directional analytical approach of promoting deregulatory measures. The flexicurity approach argues that it is the combined effect of these different types of flexibility and security that determines the functioning and performance of the labour market. Closely related to this, the flexicurity approach aims to

---

7 In this context, the binary distinction between employees and the self-employed is considered by some to be obsolete in that it is no longer an adequate depiction of the socio-economic reality of work, see e.g. Freedland (2003); for a detailed and stimulating analysis, see Kenner (2009).

overcome the traditional dichotomy of labour market flexibility and security (*ibid.:* 7) and argues that they can be mutually reinforcing.

Flexicurity as developed and employed by the Commission draws on the ILO's (1999) concept of "decent work" and it is developed through procedural methods in the form of "common principles" and "pathways" to be taken forward and put into practice at national level (Kenner 2009: 283). The first time the Commission referred to striking a balance between flexibility and security was in the 2002 JER. The notion of a balance between flexibility and security was considered central to the Adaptability pillar (European Council 2002). Flexibility was broadly defined as the capacity of firms to adjust to market demand. In addition, the Commission identified an external and internal dimension to flexibility. External flexibility was defined as the flexibility of companies to "hire and fire", whereas internal flexibility implied the reorganization of the existing workforce, for instance in terms of working time, working methods, training and mobility. In her analysis of how the EU Institutions have conceptualized and used the concept of flexibility, Ashiagbor (2005: 154–166) identifies five areas of the labour market where – according to the Commission – more flexibility is required. First, the Commission identifies a link between flexibility and employability. In this context, flexibility is intended as ensuring that labour market policies, and specifically, employment measures, impose low burdens on business. This explains why the focus of the Lisbon Strategy seems to be on how to reduce unemployment rather than how to maintain overall employment levels high. The second area of labour market flexibility referred to by the Commission is in relation to the reorganization of the labour market and working patterns, which is the focus of this chapter and is explored further below. The third type of labour market flexibility used by the Commission is in relation to wages and salaries. In this context, the Commission emphasizes the importance of ensuring that wage developments are in line with productivity levels. The fourth area of labour market flexibility identified by the Commission is ensuring higher levels of labour mobility across Member States. The fifth area of labour market flexibility, which is also the focus of this chapter, is associated with what Ashiagbor (*ibid.:* 157) defines as sectoral or occupational mobility. This type of flexibility is central to the flexicurity debate and raises the important and complex question of how to combine the concerns of firms and employers pre-occupied of overarching economic changes brought about by globalization processes and the concerns of the workers, namely job security. Security can be seen from a static and a dynamic perspective, the former referring to the idea of a stable employment relationship and the availability of a safety net in case of unemployment; the latter on non-discrimination between different forms of working contracts and arrangements and the acquisition and preservation of employability.

The Commission explicitly referred to the term "flexicurity" in 2006. Flexicurity has rapidly become one of the key concepts in the debate on reforming European labour markets. According to the Commission the core of adaptability lies in finding the right combination of flexibility and security and the reduction of labour market segmentation and calls for creating efficient conditions of flexicurity, which are:

> Sufficiently flexible work contracts, coupled with effective active labour market policies to support labour market transitions, a reliable and responsive lifelong learning system, and modern social security systems combining the provision of adequate income support with the need to facilitate labour market mobility.
>
> (European Commission 2006a: 6)

In its 2007 Communication the European Commission (2007b) called for increased flexibility through limited dismissal protection, as well as the normalization of non-standard contracts, while security is largely limited to employment security, to be fostered through lifelong learning and active labour market policies. The 2007 Communication on flexicurity ends with the statement that flexibility and security can be mutually reinforcing and serve the interests of both the employer and the employee. This implies that an integral approach to flexibility and security is deemed possible. However, the Commission's Communication makes no reference to striking a balance and does not put forward any design for combined flexibility and security policies. Moreover, Keune (2008: 11) observes that: 'where modern social security systems are concerned, the Commission remains vague and ambiguous, arguing that good unemployment benefit systems are necessary to offset negative income consequences during job transfers, but also that unemployment benefits may have a negative effect on the intensity of job search activities and may reduce financial incentives to accept work'. In his analysis of the European Commission's (2007c) recommendations to the Member States on economic and employment policies, Keune (2008) shows how the Commission advises a number of countries to review employment protection legislation with a view to reducing labour market segmentation (that is, to reduce employment protection) and increasing the use of flexible contracts. But in no country does it recommend an increase in employment protection, suggesting that even in the countries where it is lowest its level remains adequate. Similarly, in relation to unemployment benefits the Commission in its country-specific recommendations does not request an improvement of such benefits. From the above we can see that the level of integration of flexibility and security has changed over time and that policy suggestions included in the guidelines and recommendations to the Member States mostly address flexibility and security as separate issues. The guidelines and proposed measures concerning adaptability are extensive, covering many different terrains and involving various actors (Bekker 2007). This does not contribute to the clarity of the notion of balancing flexibility and security and thus it might hinder a coherent implementation by the Member States. In the Adaptability pillar the flexibility measures mostly concerned internal and external numerical flexibility and functional flexibility. This contrasts with scholars who consider flexicurity as a deliberate policy strategy to deal simultaneously with flexibility and security in a co-ordinated manner (Wilthagen, Tros and van Lieshout 2004) and the need for an integrative approach (Madsen 2006).

In its opinion on the Commission's Communication the European Parliament stated that the Commission is one-sided and too focused on flexibility and has, therefore, taken a different approach towards flexicurity, emphasizing the importance of the traditional open-ended employment contract (European Parliament 2007a). The European Parliament argues that employment protection and longer-term employment relations act as incentives for firms to invest in human resources, which in turn is good for productivity and innovation (*idem*). Flexibility, therefore, should not be achieved by introducing flexible employment contracts but rather by ensuring quality in education, improving training and apprenticeship programmes, promoting measures against discrimination, removing obstacles to mobility (*idem*).

The flexicurity model promoted by the Commission has also been criticized for not taking into sufficient account the situation of part-time and agency workers, mostly female workers who are often in the most precarious position at the edge of the legislative framework provided by labour law (Fredman 2004).

2.2.4 Injecting a gender perspective in adaptability measures

Studies have often analyzed adaptability as a gender-neutral issue and likewise the promotion of equal opportunities has been mostly conceived as an extra-work organization issue. European labour markets, however, have become increasingly feminized, particularly in the "third sector" jobs and thus the traditional "gender contract" on which the organization of work is based is no longer adequate for the adaptability of undertakings and the labour force to the new economic, structural and industrial changes. The traditional "gender contract" consists of a set of implicit and explicit cultural and quasi-legal rules governing gender relations which allocate different values, responsibilities and obligations to women and men not only at the workplace but also with regard to education and family welfare issues. Furthermore, the European Union is confronted not only with external challenges posed by new technology but also with internal ones, chiefly, changing demographic patterns caused by low fertility and birth rates and an ageing population. In addition, most Member States have become immigration countries and participation rates in the labour market are still relatively low compared with the United States (Stalford, Currie and Velluti 2009).[8] This explains why increasing employment rates for women, bringing the representation of women and men in certain economic sectors and occupations into balance and increasing career opportunities for women have also become important for improving the competitiveness of European labour markets.

The above analysis highlights the importance of linking the modernization of work organization to equal opportunities policies. The new changing patterns and the implications for economic and social policies described above have compelled the EU institutions to adopt and implement new strategies and action programmes in order to promote structural reforms at national level. The role of the social partners is particularly important in this context because collective bargaining may be a useful tool for challenging organizational cultures, breaking down occupational segregation and reducing gender pay gaps by encouraging a more equal distribution of paid and unpaid work. Indeed, collective agreements cover a wide range of equal opportunities policies (Bercusson and Dickens 1996).

3 Changes in the conceptualization of gender-equality policies: the impact of globalization

"Flexibilization" processes of European labour markets and more specifically of working patterns such as the new forms of employment contracts and working time arrangements involving part-time, casual, fixed-term, teleworking, self-employed, independent or home workers, to name but a few, fostered the adoption of policies which promote equality. At the same time, the increased variety of legal instruments and atypical working contracts has entailed a greater need for protection against discrimination. There is an important gender dimension to the debate on the effects of globalization on employment patterns and chiefly on atypical work, as men are disproportionately represented in standard employment relationships and increasing numbers of women in the labour force work under "atypical" conditions. The persistent gender pay gap is one of the main consequences of the differences and inequalities which women face on the labour market owing to the increased difficulty of reconciling their professional and private lives and the unequal division of domestic and family responsibilities, which remain very marked. Women earn an average

8 See also European Commission (2001g).

of 15 per cent less than men for every hour worked and thus women's earnings remain, on average, significantly below those of men across the Union (European Commission 2007b). It was at the 1994 Essen Summit that equal opportunities between women and men were defined as being a "paramount task" of the European Union and its Member States and a requirement for the further development of the Internal Market (European Council 1994). The promotion of equal opportunities has since then been considered pivotal in EU economic planning and policy. To this end, the regulations on the Structural Funds for 2000–2006 increased the funding for gender mainstreaming initiatives and programmes and the *Framework Strategy for 2001–2005* (European Commission 2000f) provided further funding for promoting gender equality. The year 2006 saw the adoption of a new regulation for the Structural Funds (Council of the European Union 2006a) and of the Community strategic guidelines on cohesion for the period 2007–2013 which provide specific measures and the integration of a gender perspective in all actions (Council of the European Union 2006a: Article 16). Their implementation will primarily be the task of the Member States, in the form of national strategic reference frameworks and operational programmes. The remit of the ERDF also includes the principle of equality between men and women (Council of the European Union 2005d: Article 8) in rural development support policy. In addition, the Community's Progress programme (Council of the European Union 2006b) contains a section dedicated to gender equality which will support the implementation of Community policy on equality between women and men in the areas of employment and social solidarity.

The EES may be considered to be a product of globalization and in this context a new form of EU social governance seeking to promote gender mainstreaming within adaptability policies and rejecting a gender neutral approach to the modernization of work organization. Globalization has fostered the promotion of different living standards and lifestyles. Economic constraints have led to a situation whereby men are no longer the only breadwinner of the family and there are many dual-earner households. Moreover, women's participation in the labour market has become very important due to an ageing population. A report on low fertility, families and public policies (Bagavos and Martin 2000) posits that low levels of fertility across all Member States are not so much a consequence of women entering the labour market as the result of an asymmetrical division of family responsibilities. If policy makers enabled women to better reconcile work and family life and men took on a greater share of the household tasks couples wanting to have children would realize their plans more readily (Eurostat 2002). The report added that the process of modernization does not necessarily engender low fertility figures. The example of Scandinavian countries illustrates that people will choose to become parents if the efforts undertaken to raise employment go hand in hand with policies incorporating a gender equality perspective. It also shows that the exercise of a pro-natalist choice and the creation of a better environment for children will be possible only through modernized family policies and alternative child care policies (Bagavos and Martin 2000). Finally, the report added that fertility and female unemployment have a reverted proportional relationship: higher levels of female unemployment are most likely to cause low levels of fertility and vice versa, high female occupational levels will increase fertility levels. Scandinavian countries have been able to modernize gender relationships and the concept of the family without undermining the importance of the latter. Another issue which has risen up the policy agenda in recent times as a consequence of the socio-economic changes brought about by globalization, such as for instance the feminization of the labour market, is the need to increase women's representation in the decision-making process, where there is still an under-representation of women. Gender balance in decision making is one of the five core priorities identified by the *Framework Strategy for 2001–2005* (European Commission 2000f) and its importance has been confirmed in the Commission's *Roadmap for Equality* (European Commission 2006b). A *de facto* gender-balanced working environment can be achieved only if changes to society's cultural and political perspectives on gender roles are made. Adopting and implementing awareness strategies and initiatives represent a first step in this direction (Council of the European Union 2000c). To this end, the action programmes adopted by the Commission in the framework of gender mainstreaming are to be welcomed. Moreover, since the year 2000 the BEPGs (Council of the European Union 2002a) have addressed the impact of globalization, with the inclusion of various recommendations concerning not only labour market policies but also social cohesion and employment policies, including the EES and, in particular, the promotion of appropriate wage developments, the modernization of labour markets and the promotion of a stronger knowledge-driven economy. In addition, the BEPGs emphasized the importance of linking adaptability measures to equal opportunities and assigned an important role to the social partners in the framework of growth and stability-oriented macroeconomic policies. In particular, social partners are called upon to promote appropriate wage developments taking into account productivity differences, such as, for example, skills, qualification or geographic areas, when determining wage levels and finally to pursue policies aimed at reducing gender pay differences due to *de facto* discrimination.

Furthermore, the BEPGs pointed out that modernization of welfare systems must ensure that structural change does not compound the existing social problems, such as unemployment, social exclusion and poverty. Hence the BEPGs stressed that more efforts had to be made on equal opportunities policies by improving incentives in tax and benefits systems and by promoting policies to reconcile work and family life. While priority is still largely given to guaranteeing the macroeconomic objectives of the Lisbon Strategy there has also been an emphasis on the adoption of policies which strengthen the "European social model". Particular emphasis has been given to gender pay gaps and to reconciling work with family life. In 2006, the Commission launched a formal consultation among the social partners on the possible thrust of Community action regarding the reconciliation of professional, private and family life, including the promotion of flexible working arrangements, the development of crèche and care services and the possible revision of existing provisions regarding maternity leave and parental leave (European Commission 2006c). As seen earlier, this consultation process has led to the adoption of a work–life balance package which includes, *inter alia*, two legislative proposals for amending existing Directives and to the review of the framework agreement on parental leave. However, a close examination of the integration of the EES with the BEPGs in the NRP highlights the link between the EES to the overall growth and macroeconomic policy and indicates the limits placed on the commitment to gender equality. The general macroeconomic rationale for promoting female employment is to raise the fiscal base and reduce the share of the population dependent upon state welfare payments (Fagan *et al.* 2006).

While some positive results for gender equality can be expected in the form of child care provision, there is also a risk of negative impacts, for example, those pension reforms that make it even more difficult for women to obtain full pension entitlement or the promotion of flexible employment that fails to offer job security or career opportunities (Fagan *et al.* 2006). Furthermore, the macroeconomic emphasis on reducing public expenditure has negative implications both for the development of services to support families and for women's employment opportunities given that they are disproportionately employed in the public sector (Fagan *et al.* 2006).

Hence globalization processes have exacerbated certain gender equality problems in employment and working patterns and while emphasis has been placed on the adoption of measures to tackle them, the overall growth and macroeconomic rationale indicates how the commitment to gender equality remains limited by the prevailing economic objectives of the Lisbon Strategy.

4 Classifying welfare states in an EU-27: beyond the Esping-Andersen typology

This section will proceed to the analysis of welfare state cluster classifications and examine whether it is possible to identify a welfare state regime unique to CEECs or whether their welfare state regime(s) can be incorporated into one of the existing clusters which typify the "old" Member States. The starting point of this analysis is Esping-Andersen's seminal work. Esping-Andersen's (1990) central argument is that welfare states fall within three distinct welfare regimes. He defines the concept of welfare state regime as referring to:

> the institutional arrangements, rules and understandings that guide and shape con-current social policy decisions, expenditure developments, problem definitions, and even the respond-and-demand structure of citizens and welfare consumers. The existence of policy regimes reflects the circumstance that short-term policies, reforms, debates, and decision-making take place within frameworks of historical institutional-ization that differ qualitatively between countries.

Esping-Andersen distinguishes the three regimes by the degree of "decommodification" which 'occurs when a service is rendered as a matter of right, and when a person can maintain a livelihood without reliance on the market' (Esping-Andersen 1990: 21–22) and the kind of "stratification" they produce in society. Stratification refers to the intensity of redistribution and the level of universality of solidarity that is imposed by the welfare state. In particular, Esping-Andersen's classification is based upon three ideal-type welfare states. He distinguishes between a "liberal", a "conservative corporatist" and a "social democratic" welfare state.[9] The first typology, which may be equated to the "Anglo-Saxon" welfare state cluster is characterized by means-tested assistance; modest universal transfers or modest social insurance plans;[10] underdeveloped public social services beyond health and education; poor family services; low levels of employment protection and no legacy of active labour market policies; uncoordinated industrial relations, with moderately strong unions, decentralized wage bargaining and low levels of collective bargaining coverage. The second cluster, which may be equated to the "Continental European" welfare state model is influenced by a mix of statist, corporatist and familialist traditions and it is characterized by a moderate level of decommodification. The direct influence of the state is restricted to the provision of income maintenance benefits related to occupational status. Labour market participation by women (especially with children) is generally discouraged and the state will interfere only when the family can no longer provide for its members. Hence very modest levels of public social services beyond health and education; consider-able reliance on the "third sector" and private delivery; passive family policies still largely

---

9 Some scholars radically reject the idea and usefulness of a general welfare typology, e.g. Kasza (2002).

10 Social benefits are mainly for the low-income, usually working-class, state dependants, with little income redistribution.

premised on the conventional male breadwinner family; strict levels of employment protection; in some countries such as Germany, Austria and the Netherlands there are also comprehensive systems of vocational education and training; strong social partnerships; co-ordinated industrial relations, with a predominance of sectoral wage bargaining; high levels of bargaining coverage and moderately strong trade unions. In the "social democratic" type which is represented by the "Scandinavian" welfare state model, the level of decommodification is high. This cluster is characterized by citizenship-based universal entitlements; generous replacement rates in transfer programmes; general revenue financing; a broad supply of social services beyond health and education, active family policy encouraging gender egalitarianism and women's integration in the labour market; low (Denmark) to high (Sweden) levels of employment protection, with strong emphasis on active policies and training programmes linked to general education; and corporatist industrial relations, with peak-level bargaining, strong trade unions and high levels of collective bargaining coverage. Some scholars have suggested the addition of a fourth welfare typology, that of a "southern" or "Mediterranean" welfare state regime (Bonoli 1997; Ferrera 1996).

More broadly, there is a wide variety of different typologies of welfare states, each based upon different factors and indicators. For instance, Leibfried (1992) identifies four social policy or poverty regimes, on the basis of different policy models: modern, institutional, residual and rudimentary. He distinguishes between the "Scandinavian" welfare states, the "Bismarck" countries, the "Anglo-Saxon" countries and the "Latin rim" countries (Spain, Portugal, Italy, Greece and France) although with the exclusion of the latter, the classification of the other types is the same as Esping-Andersen's typology. Ferrera (1996) develops a very similar classification, including a fourth, "southern European" model on the basis of four dimensions of social security systems – the rules of access, the conditions under which benefits are granted, the regulations to finance social protection and the organization and management of social security administration. Bonoli (1997) instead bases his classification on the extensiveness of the welfare state (indicated by social expenditures as a proportion of GDP) and the way the welfare state is financed (indicated by the percentage of social expenditures financed through contributions). In particular, he classifies the resulting types the British, Continental European, Nordic and southern countries. The first three clusters are close to Esping-Andersen's typology, the differences between this typology and Esping-Andersen's original classification stemming from the addition of the southern type.

Some authors argue that Esping-Andersen does not sufficiently take into account the gender inequality dimension in his attempts to classify welfare states. For instance, Siaroff (1994) proposes a more gender-sensitive typology that is based on the work and welfare choices of men and women across countries. He distinguishes between a "Protestant social democratic", a "Protestant liberal", an "advanced Christian democratic" and a "late female mobilization" type of welfare regime. While the first three types show a strong overlap with the original typology, the last category resembles the group of countries that other authors have labelled the "southern" or "Mediterranean" type.

Having looked at the main welfare state regimes, we may now examine whether CEECs present certain common characteristics which may be said to constitute a unique welfare state regime or whether each or some of these countries may be incorporated into one of the foregoing groups. According to Fenger (2007: 13), although these countries all share the characteristic of being post-communist countries there are quite significant differences in terms of institutional characteristics and paths of development. Central Eastern Europe includes a wide variety of countries that range from the prosperous region of Slovenia to the impoverished military state of Belarus, and from the new EU Member States whose development and institutional framework have been greatly influenced by the pre-accession process to countries like Moldova and Ukraine that until recently stood under the influence of the Russian Federation. Any attempt to classify the welfare states of Central and Eastern Europe should thus take this variety into account.

On the basis of the hierarchical cluster analysis developed by Esping-Andersen (1990)[11] it may be argued that the Eastern European welfare states can be clearly distinguished from the traditional European welfare states (*ibid.*: 22). According to Fenger (2007: 24–26) the group of post-communist countries may be subdivided into three sub-groups. The first sub-group is the "former Soviet Union" type (Belarus, Estonia, Latvia, Lithuania, Russia and Ukraine), which resemble the conservative–corporatist type. However, there are differences in the social situation and level of trust in public authorities. The second sub-group, which Fenger defines as the "post-communist European type" (Bulgaria, Croatia, Czech Republic, Hungary, Poland and Slovakia), to some extent resembles the previous cluster. The major difference lies in better and more stable economic development over the last few years. This is reflected in the levels of economic growth and inflation. Moreover, the level of social well-being is higher than in the former Soviet countries. Finally, this group of countries is based on a more egalitarian system than the previous group. The third sub-group is the "developing welfare state type" (Georgia, Romania and Moldova). This cluster represents countries that are still in the process of developing into well defined welfare states and still lag behind the countries of the other sub-groups, particularly in relation to their social situation, which is characterized by high levels of infant mortality and generally low life expectancy.

Overall, the level of trust in public authorities, the level of public expenditure on social programmes and the social situation in the post-communist countries are considerably lower in comparison with other European countries. The sub-group of Central and Eastern European post-communist countries is the one that most closely resembles the Western European countries because of the pre-accession phase, which enabled these countries not only to prepare themselves for EU membership but also to undergo a radical process of transformation as regards to the socio-economic underpinnings of their economic system, which is still *in fieri*.

Fenger's study (2007: 26) shows that there are methodological problems in assessing whether Eastern European countries are converging towards Western European types of welfare. If convergence is occurring, the transitional stage is taking much longer than anticipated. The differences between the Western countries and the post-communist countries stem primarily from differences in the social situation, not so much from differences in the governmental programmes. Whereas the three Western subtypes clearly represent different perspectives on the welfare state and governments' role in it, the post-communist subtypes mix elements of the conservative-corporatist and, to a lesser extent the social-democratic type. (*Idem*)

---

11 This technique may be defined as follows: 'Hierarchical cluster analysis allows grouping countries that have similar characteristics across a set of variables, thus leading to homogeneous empirical types. It is called hierarchical because it divides a set of cases (the countries) into ever more numerous and specific subsets, according to the distance measured among all pairs of cases, taking into account their position across the whole set of variables under analysis' (Saint-Arnaud and Bernard 2003).

The empirical analysis of post-communist and Western welfare states conducted by Fenger (2007) shows large differences between these welfare states. The differences between the group of post-communist countries and the traditional Western welfare states are bigger than the differences between the countries within any of those groups. At present, post-communist welfare states cannot be incorporated in any of Esping-Andersen's or any other well known types of welfare state. However, the empirical analysis does not show a distinct, specific type of post-communist welfare state, and the only clearly identifiable common traits shared by post-communist countries are low levels of governmental social intervention and the nature of the social problems. Cerami (2008) argues that CEECs are moving towards a new world of welfare capitalism which combines old with new social policy characteristics. Systematic research and especially clustering countries is difficult due to lack of stability of the policy outcomes and their temporary character (Szelewa and Polakowski 2008: 117). Esping-Andersen (1996: 267) himself rejected the idea of applying his regime typology to a comparative analysis of CEECs. In order to overcome this methodological problem in a study conducted on child care policies in CEECs, Szelewa and Polakowski (2008) have developed an analytical approach which takes into account both synchronic and diachronic perspectives. In particular, they present a comparison between countries but also between different policies and indicators in the course of time. In this way it is possible to identify specific welfare clusters within CEECs – specifically, "explicit familialism", "implicit familialism", "female mobilizing" and "comprehensive support types"[12] – and, at the same time, to consider the dynamics of change, policy trends and diversity among these countries. The advantage of this approach is that it enables us to include a country in one of these clusters within a specific period and to move the same country to another cluster if the policies adopted or dependent variables indicate a change in the socio-economic rationale underpinning those policies. They do so by relying on the fuzzy set theory (Ragin 2000), which is a type of comparative approach that has also been employed to study complexity, diversity and changes in social policy (Kvist 1999; 2006). 'The fundamental assumption of the fuzzy set approach is that empirical phenomena have a complex character. This configurational character stems from the presumption that theoretical constructs can rarely be described by one aspect, and only multidimensional treatment of cases can provide their sufficient reflection in the process of research' (Szelewa and Polakowski 2008: 119). For example, one of the components for assessing child care policies is parental leave provision. They argue that two key features concerning parental leave are universality and generosity. Together they give rise to four combinations: low universality and high generosity, low universality and low generosity, high universality

---

12 In the "explicit familialism" model, the state pursues more active policies to support the traditional family model. The periods of paid parental leave therefore are longer (usually two to four years) as well as parental leave payments. Women are mainly perceived in their traditional role as primary carers, which explains long periods of paid maternity and parental leave. At the same time, the state does not subsidize child care centres because of the promotion of private child care. In the "implicit familialism" model, child care policies are residual and formally neutral. These policies neither suggest the locus of responsibility for care, nor do they explicitly mobilize women to join the workforce. However, due to gender inequalities in the labour market, the lack of affordable and available child care leaves the sphere of care to families. In the "female-mobilizing" model, the rate of children in child care services is high, although the quality of services provided is not always very good. There are shorter periods of paid parental leave. Hence, even though parents may have a universal entitlement to parental leave, they may not be incentivized to taking it, especially women. The "comprehensive support" model supports the dual-earner type of family. Hence families and women are both paid and relieved in their care responsibilities because of the availability of more diversified and high-quality child care services as well as long periods of paid parental leave.

and high generosity, high universality and low generosity. The configurations of the extreme values of sets (0 and 1) are treated as Weberian ideal types. Hence different configurations of sets and their values yield different parental leave types. If we apply this model to the Czech Republic, we can see that in the period between 1989 and 1995 that country presented the characteristics of the "female mobilizing" cluster, whereas in the period 1997–2004 it presented the characteristics of "explicit familialism" (*ibid.*: 127).

5   The implementation of "adaptability" and "equal opportunities" policies in Italy, Denmark and the Czech Republic

5.1 The economic and employment context of Italy, Denmark and the Czech Republic

Since the launch of the EES, Italy and Denmark have had relatively stable economies and for different reasons suffered from a tightening of the labour market, that is, a shortage in labour supply, and from an ageing population which emphasized the need to avoid an increase in wages and prices (European Commission 2006c). The Czech Republic instead has had to deal with an excess of labour supply further to the transition process to an open market economy which has also led to excessively low wages. Hence, while Italy and Denmark are confronted with the long-term challenge of increasing the active labour force, the Czech Republic is confronted with significant problems of mismatch between labour demand and supply. At the same time, as the analysis below illustrates, the Czech Republic and Italy share common problems in relation to female employment, namely discrimination at the workplace associated also with difficulties in establishing a work–life balance, labour market segmentation, job precariousness as well as increase in unemployment levels. (For the Czech Republic this is a direct consequence of the transition process.)

Moreover, large differences exist between these countries, particularly in terms of labour market performance, industrial relations system and the employment situation. In Italy, both labour and productivity growth have increased less than the EU average (European Commission 2007c). Even though the overall and female employment rates have increased significantly as a consequence of new flexible work arrangements (63 per cent) the female employment rate continues to be well below the EU average (45–46 per cent against 63.8 per cent) with a highly segregated labour market. In addition the gender gap and gender pay gap remain substantial (European Commission 2006d). Furthermore, Italy is confronted with highly asymmetrical regional economic and employment trends, due to the situation in the Mezzogiorno. Differences in activity rates are very high: 58 per cent in the north, 55.1 per cent in the centre and 36.3 per cent in the south of Italy. There are also strong differences in unemployment rates: 6.5 per cent in the centre/north and 19.2 per cent in the south (ISTAT 2005). Finally, the critical state of public finances in Italy explains the low levels of expenditure on the implementation of the EES. The labour market reforms enacted in recent years (Italy 1997, 2003) have led to an increase in employment,[13] although employment data may have been somewhat boosted by flows of previously

---

13 According to Mr Paolo Sestito (Director of the Research Unit of the Bank of Italy and formerly Chief Economic Adviser to the Ministry of Labour and Social Affairs of Italy) when the Employment Strategy was launched the Italian government had significant difficulties in implementing the Employment Guidelines and, more specifically, in understanding exactly what had to be done at ministerial level; interview of 1 October 2008.

under-recorded informal labour, especially newly regularized immigrant labour. Moreover, the pension reforms (Italy 2004) should help raise participation rates among older workers in future years. The labour market reforms have made it easier and cheaper to adjust enterprise labour forces via temporary contracts, and tax incentives have facilitated their conversion to permanent contracts. Thus employers have been more willing to take on low-skilled or inexperienced workers on flexible contracts which have allowed employees to gain work experience and build up skills. However, despite recognition that women account for most of the recent growth in employment, and that a further large increase in the female labour supply will be required to improve the overall employment rate, there is no specific strategy towards women's labour supply and their specific needs (Villa 2005). In general, there is an assumption that the measures will produce some positive impact on female employment without any strategic emphasis on a gendered understanding of the labour market or on a gender perspective on policy. In particular, this process of reform has not been accompanied by parallel changes in the social security system and it has been gender-blind as scant consideration has been given to care work and to the distribution of care not only between women and men but also between individual and collectively provided care work. Also, little attention has been given to gender equality in respect of unpaid work at household level. Women, therefore, whose employment situation in comparison with that of men is relatively more precarious, have not benefited greatly from the labour market reform of recent years.

With regard to industrial relations, collective bargaining in Italy primarily takes place at two levels: at industry level – the most important – and at company or, sometimes, district level. In addition, national-level agreements between employers and union have been used to implement EU-level initiatives, such as the agreement on teleworking, and there are also national level discussions between unions, employers and the government, which sometimes lead to tripartite agreements (concertation via social pacts). According to Article 39(4) of the Italian Constitution, collective agreements have *erga omnes* validity, although this constitutional provision has never been implemented. In practice, there is no system that extends the validity of such agreements, and in practice this means that it is necessary to have the agreements confirmed by legislation. The main social partners in Italy are the Confederazione Italiana Generale del Lavoro (CIGL, General Italian Employment Confederation), the Confederazione Italiana dei Sindacati Lavoratori (CISL, Italian Confederation of Workers' Unions), the Unione Italiana del Lavoro (UIL, Italian Employment Union) and, on the employers' side, Confindustria (Confederation of Industry) and Federmeccanica, the Italian Federation of Metalworking Industries. The lack of a uniform labour law system is considered as being one of the reasons for the traditionally conflictual nature of the Italian industrial relations system, which may be also associated with the country's strong ideological and political polarization. The most important collective agreements are national industry-wide agreements which cannot be derogated by individual contracts. Industry-wide collective agreements provide general rules and clauses applicable to the standard agreement which can be supplemented at company level. They provide a minimum set of standards and may override company-level or territorial agreements if these violate any of the general rules or clauses included in the former. The central legislative Act concerning trade union activity at company level is the Workers Statute, Act No. 300/70. The main trade union confederations have established an infrastructure to promote equality, and collective bargaining covers a wide range of gender equality issues in workplace relations. In particular, industry agreements have been seeking to promote equal opportunities for more than a decade. However, the inclusion of specific equal opportunities matters in collective agreements does not form part of a broader co-ordinated equality strategy which aims at addressing the structural problems of gender inequality in the workplace (Velluti 2008). Apart from gender awareness programmes there is no clear articulation of long-term goals. Moreover, there is little evidence to suggest that the approach to equality is preventative or proactive, that is to say, that efforts to promote equality include mobilizing all general policies and measures specifically for the purpose of achieving equality by actively and openly taking into account at the planning stage their possible effects on the situations of both women and men. In addition, both legislation and collective bargaining seem to be focusing on equal opportunities and positive action measures (*idem*). Moreover, few employers' organizations have shown interest in developing a gender equality strategy in their internal policies and have structures to foster and support equality bargaining.

Labour market policies in Denmark have been extremely successful since the mid-1990s, with unemployment decreasing dramatically, leading many scholars and experts to talk about a "Danish job miracle". The overall employment rate continues to be the highest in the European Union, with 75 per cent and just over 70 per cent for women (Denmark NRP 2005). It is, therefore, well above the Lisbon targets for 2010 also with regard to women. The Danish labour market model combines traits of the liberal labour market model with strong elements of the Scandinavian welfare state model and is often referred to as the "flexicurity triangle" (Larsen 2005; Madsen 2006). It supports a flexible labour market while at the same time maintaining a social safety net in the event of unemployment, combined with active labour market initiatives aimed at getting the unemployed back to work. The Danish version of "flexicurity" would seem to be more coherent with regard to equal opportunities, as it apparently affects both men and women equally. However, increasing maternity leave to twelve months, without extending and making paternity leave compulsory for men, initially has had an adverse effect on those women who aim to have a professional career, as the cost incurred by the employer during the maternity leave period appears to have had a negative effect on the employment possibilities of women (Jepsen 2005). However, in response this has led the social partners to agree on the establishment of a common fund to compensate employers for the financial loss incurred during their employees' maternity leave. The contribution to the fund is irrespective of the number of women working in the firm or sector and is a solidarity measure across the various sectors of the Danish economy. Moreover, this woman-friendly approach has not corresponded with tackling the distribution of work in the family sphere, which contributes to the persistence of lower wages for women, as women voluntarily opt for part-time work. This in turn explains why in Denmark there is still a certain level of gender pay gap, 14 per cent for the private sector and 13 per cent for the public sector (Emerek 2006).

With regard to industrial relations, the Danish model is based on bilateral relations between the government and representatives of management and labour: the Danish Federation of Trade Unions (LO) and the Danish Employers' Confederation (DA). The Danish industrial relations system may be defined as a voluntary system in which the mechanism for concluding collective agreements on wages and working conditions is underpinned by basic agreements concluded between the parties in the individual sectors (Stokke 1999; Knudsen and Lind 1999). The Danish Parliament has passed very little formal legislation, giving the social partners the main tasks to regulate the labour market. The use of collective agreements to settle virtually all issues pertaining to working conditions has been defined as the "Danish tradition". Working conditions are covered by legislation only in a few exceptional cases (it applies only to those who are not covered by collective agreements) and there is no statutory definition of a collective agreement. A legal notion of these agreements is to be found in the case law and legal literature. Moreover, various reciprocal recognition agreements between trade unions and employers' representatives have enabled the parties to resolve cases of conflicting interests by concluding collective agreements. Separate procedural rules have been drawn up for concluding these agreements and for defining the scope and use of collective industrial action such as strikes and lockouts. Further rules impose a "peace obligation" which prevents the parties from resorting to hostile action during the period of validity of the collective agreements. These agreements also have mandatory normative effect (although generally they are binding only on those who are parties to them). It is not possible to derogate by contract from rules set out in collective agreements to the disadvantage of the worker. Nielsen *et al.* (2002: 463) maintain that Denmark differs not only from most Continental countries but also from the other Scandinavian countries where collective agreements are defined by legislation as formal, written agreements which do not qualify as collective agreements unless certain requirements are met. In Denmark, EC Directives are mostly implemented by way of collective agreements and subsidiary legislation which ensure the maintenance of the important and traditional role assigned to social partners.

Danish social partners also play a prominent role in relation to gender equality measures, as working conditions are generally covered by collective agreements. Moreover, Denmark's national policy on gender equality and gender mainstreaming is developed via concertation between the government, parliament, the social partners and domestic NGOs. As explained in the next section, the social partners have also been involved in the preparation of the NAPs and are involved in the implementation of the employment guidelines, especially gender equality.

The analysis of the Czech Republic requires a brief overview of the country's labour market structure and economic situation during the 1990s because of its transition from a socialist country centred on a command economy to a neo-liberal country based on an open market economy. With the introduction of economic and social reforms in 1990, earlier strong job stability and employment security were undermined by large-scale structural changes and consequent flows of labour between jobs (an exodus of labour from the public to the private sphere and from heavy industry and agriculture to light industry and services) and from employment to unemployment or inactivity. Some found new jobs immediately, but most were faced with shorter or longer (often repeated) unemployment spells and the necessity to change their occupation, undergo reskilling, or accept commuting for work (rather than a change of residence) before being re-employed (Oxenstierna 1990). In the fight against unemployment growth, newly established labour market institutions have focused on passive labour market measures and, in particular, have increasingly provided job mediation, employment promotion and income support to those who are unemployed. Nevertheless, unemployment has become a widespread phenomenon. To solve the excess of labour supply over demand, policy measures often encourage workers to stay in unemployment, or to withdraw from the labour market (through early retirement, disability benefits, pensions and social assistance). This approach has trapped many (especially the low skilled) in joblessness or inactivity and has heavily burdened national social security systems. It has also led to emerging labour supply shortages in connection with population ageing and, at the same time, fed resistance to flexible adjustment of labour through changes in labour demand. In such circumstances the policy issue is not 'to prevent the rise in unemployment, but to cushion its social costs and to avoid the spread of long-term unemployment' (Boeri 1997: 367).

In the Czech Republic, however, there initially appeared to be more emphasis on keeping unemployment (artificially) low, instead of moderating the consequences of relatively high transitional unemployment, a phenomenon known as the 'Czech unemployment miracle'. There are various reasons both of a political and economic nature (OECD 1995: 132 ff.). Post-1989 governments made social policy an essential part of their transformation project. According to Orenstein (1995: 179) 'despite a continuing feud between neo-liberal and social democratic approaches, the Czech Republic has created a basic framework for a reborn welfare state'. From an economic perspective, Flek and Večerník (2005: 6) explain the Czech employment miracle of the first half of the 1990s with the specific character of the Czech privatization process and the semi-state-owned banks providing generous credit to large enterprises which ensured that levels of labour were further increased. This is not to say that unemployment did not increase. But, because of the above-mentioned specificity of financing of (formerly) state-owned enterprises, these pressures were clearly much lower than they would otherwise have been (*idem*). Moreover, most of those who eventually left the large industrial giants did not enter the pool of unemployed people anyway. Instead, they moved directly to another job or exited the labour market altogether. The country thus enjoyed a remarkably low unemployment rate until the mid-1990s (general unemployment rate was around 4 per cent until 1995; CSU 2009).

However, towards the end of the 1990s the restructuring of private firms as well as bankruptcy enforcements led to a significant increase of redundancies. All this has made the aggregate unemployment figures grow more or less steadily regardless of business cycle fluctuations and/or government policies, and the unemployment rate has risen continuously since 2001 (9.8 per cent in 2002 and 8.9 per cent in 2004; in March 2009 the registered unemployment rate was 7.4 per cent; CSU 2009). The 2000 JAP (Czech Republic 2000) and subsequently the NAPs for 2004–2006 and the NRPs for 2005–2008 and 2008–2010 have reported that one of the main problems of the Czech labour market is the significant lack of flexibility and variability in employment patterns. The Czech Republic has been focusing, therefore, on active labour market policies.[14]

With regard to organized civil society, Saxonberg and Sirovátka 2009 maintain that in the Czech Republic there is a general mistrust of public institutions and low levels of civic and democratic engagement as a consequence of communist rule. This explains why organized civil society is weak and why it is unable to put pressure on post-communist governments to carry out more solidaristic policies (*idem*). Moreover, Herod (1998) and Ost (2000) have pointed out that during the transition phase trade unions have been unsure of their role. This explains why they have found it difficult to organize themselves and be strong representatives of workers' rights. One of the "big" questions during the early years of transition was whether trade unions should be fighting for job security, workers' information rights and co-determination and better working conditions or whether instead they should be supporting rapid privatization processes and open-market measures. Moreover, the establishment of social partnership had a preventive function rather than one of real industrial action. In this sense, the situation in the Czech Republic differed substantially from that in Poland, where "opposition" trade unions already existed under the communist regime and powerfully acted against it (Večerník 2001: 38). Be that as it may, social dialogue in the Czech Republic has developed quite smoothly. The Czech–Moravian Chamber of Trade Unions (CMKOS) is the major union confederation in the Czech Republic, although there are other confederations. The largest union of employers is the

---

14 In this context, Mr Martin Karlik, EU and International Relations Unit, Minister of Labour and Social Affairs of the Czech Republic, maintains that the European Employment Strategy has been pivotal for introducing a new policy discourse in relation to the adoption of labour market policies in the Czech Republic; interview of 21 October 2008.

Confederation of Employers' and Entrepreneurs' Associations. Some employers consider trade unions and collective bargaining as undesirable relics of communism and often try to avoid any dialogue with them.

The most important level of collective bargaining is at company level, although in many companies no bargaining takes place. Moreover, the percentage of employees covered by collective agreements has been falling in recent years. Industry-wide collective bargaining is the other form of bargaining used in the Czech Republic, although this is not as common as the former. In addition, representatives of the social partners and the government may sit on the Council of Economic and Social Agreement. This body does not conclude binding agreements but in the early 1990s it has played a major role through a series of "general agreements" which provided a framework for collective bargaining.[15]

From the above analysis we may argue that, on the one hand, there are some important differences between the "old" and the "new" Member States in terms of institutional capabilities and organized civil society, with the CEECs still being in need of assistance in relation to capacity building, know-how, skills and experience. On the other hand, the social problems of the CEECs and, in particular, the Czech Republic while more intensified are not essentially different from those of the "old" Member States, especially southern Mediterranean countries. For example, persistent unemployment in an unfavourable macroeconomic environment, pension systems overburdened by an ageing population, undeclared work and social inequality.

5.2 Family structure and welfare in Italy, Denmark and the Czech Republic

With regard to gender roles in family welfare and, in particular, in employment law there are great differences between Italy, Denmark and the Czech Republic. Italy was and is still based on a family breadwinner model or, more precisely, a family values-oriented model. The family is seen as the main provider of welfare to its members. Bettio and Villa (1996) have identified a Mediterranean path to the emancipation of women which differs markedly from that of northern countries. The combination of low female participation rates, high unemployment rates and low fertility rates is underpinned by the role of the family, which determines the wealth and welfare of all its members. Moreover, the cultural dimension of family making is a key factor for developing work or career plans, which explains the highly gender-segregated Italian labour market (both vertically and horizontally).

Denmark is based on a social democratic welfare regime characterized by egalitarianism, solidarity, universalism, generous benefit levels and comprehensive social citizenship. In contrast to Italy, Denmark's welfare regime is more woman-friendly and it is not centred on the family but is rather a defamilialized and service-oriented one, taking direct responsibility for the care of children, combined with generous income support for working women (Kjeldstad 2001).

In the Czech Republic the family is considered an institution of fundamental importance in both private and public spheres and the state adopts policies and provides generous social benefits to support the traditional family model. The Czech Republic, therefore, is based on the same type of family structure as Italy, namely a family values-oriented model whereby the family is seen as the main provider of welfare to its members. Women are

---

15 No general agreement has been signed since 1994, although the Council continues to meet and may influence measures adopted by the government.

mainly perceived in their traditional role as primary carers, which explains the long periods of paid maternity and parental leave, and it is mostly mothers who engage in parental leave and full-time child care. The traditional gender roles in family welfare make women's position in the labour market more difficult, and exposes them to discrimination. Another consequence is the segmentation of the labour market.

The different approach to gender issues is clearly reflected in the development of equal opportunities policies and in gender equality law, discussed below. However, if we consider the NAPs and the NRPs in the two periods of 1998–2002 and 2003–2008 there is a difference in the visibility and commitment to gender equality. The removal of the Equal Opportunities pillar and the subsequent removal of the gender equality guideline have meant that the majority of Member States, including Italy, Denmark and the Czech Republic, have paid less attention to gender equality issues. In the following section these two periods will accordingly be considered separately.

6 Gender equality and gender mainstreaming in the period 1998–2002

6.1 Italy

In the context of Italian gender equality legislation the Equal Treatment Directive (Council of the European Union 1976) was implemented through the setting up of specific institutions and bodies with representatives of the social partners (Italy 1977). These included a national committee at the Ministry of Employment responsible for legislative regulation (Italy 1991)[16] and a national commission based in the Office of the President of the Council of Ministers. A department of Equal Opportunities was set up by decree of the President of the Council of Ministers in 1997 (Italy 1997a). At company level, the first bilateral Commissions on Equal Opportunities were set up in 1986 in a number of large Italian companies and the social partners involved agreed to implement measures aimed at promoting positive action measures for women. Moreover, from the end of the 1980s equal opportunities and positive action issues started to be included in national collective agreements for specific employment categories, leading to the creation of an appropriate Joint Commission. Since the end of the 1990s there has been an emphasis on positive action measures and gender mainstreaming even though no definition of the latter can be found in official documentation apart from a repetition of the ones by the Council of Europe (1998) and the European Commission (1996b). Moreover, gender mainstreaming has almost exclusively involved those institutions and bodies which are already responsible for adopting and implementing gender equality measures and certain sections of political parties and trade unions. In turn, the limited development of a gender mainstreaming culture has meant that its practice has been directionless without a clear understanding of what gender mainstreaming is meant to do either procedurally or substantively at national and regional/local levels of policy making. There is also a lack of adequate monitoring procedures and gender impact assessments on policy proposals. In turn these factors explain why gender mainstreaming policies in Italy have been fragmented and not very effective. In the 2001 Italian NAP measures mainly centred on financial and fiscal

---

16 Under Act No. 125/91 the national committee also had the power to monitor the implementation of the law, to draw up behavioural codes, to promote research into male and female unemployment and to assess the funding of positive action plans.

incentives aimed at creating a more favourable environment for job creation. In particular, the Italian 2001 NAP had three main objectives: to foster economic and employment growth in the south of Italy with fiscal incentives and investment in infrastructure; to adopt measures aimed at extending the applicability of flexible labour contracts defined as "co-ordinated and continuing co-operation schemes"; and to promote the modernization of public service and the PES. However, data on quantitative achievements of the pro-grammes were insufficient, particularly in relation to the overall or long-term objectives. In addition, the 2001 assessment report on implementation (ARI) (European Commission 2001e) outlined the delay and/or further postponement of measures announced in recent years: the reorganization of the PES at local level was still very slow, the employment information system (SIL) was not operative; and the announced reform of the benefit system which was urgently needed had not been put into effect. In general, measures remained unspecified and were not implemented in a comprehensive and coherent way. With regard to adaptability, lifelong learning policies were enacted through innovative training schemes at all levels of industry agreed by the social partners, who also managed the newly created inter-professional funds. However, the process of increasing flexibility in the labour market promoted by the government was criticized by some of the social partners, mostly trade unions. As regards equal opportunities, most policies remained mainly programmatic and no detailed information was given on the few measures outlined in the Italian NAP. In the context of Objectives 1 and 3 of the ESF the Department of Equal Opportunities was given a co-ordinating function in matters concerning equal opportunities for men and women, and it monitored the implementation of gender equal-ity measures of central and regional administrations. Female regional and provincial "equality advisers" sat on all the main regional monitoring committees and participated in local social partnership boards in order to promote gender mainstreaming across the Italian territory. However, the NAP did not explain how the co-ordinating role of the Department of Equal Opportunities was to operate in practice. The "Master Plan for the Employment Services" represented a first step towards a more comprehensive approach to gender equality with the inclusion of indicators by gender. However, the NAP failed to explain in detail what these indicators were and how they were to be put into effect. Finally, in accordance with Act No. 125/1991 (Italy 1991), the procedures for financing positive actions in the work place were improved. In particular, the National Equality Committee of the Minister of Labour selected forty-eight projects to enhance positive action measures. A brief analysis of the causes of gender segregation was given but apart from a general description of the budget allotted to these measures no detailed breakdown with explana-tory notes was made available. A National Plan for Female Employment announced in the year 2000 was still in the process of being implemented by the Department of Equal Opportunities. With regard to policies aimed at reconciling work with family life, the government adopted further measures to support families and working mothers by strengthening the enforcement of Act No. 53/2000 (Italy 2000) on parental and training leave schemes and, in particular, by adopting a Unified Code of Regulations in the Matter of Maternity and Leave which simplified and streamlined the existing legal framework. This measure, however, was mainly programmatic, describing in general terms the finan-cial measures enacted. The government's response to the Council recommendation on pursuing active labour market policies and on implementing specific measures to nar-row the wide gender gaps in employment and unemployment (Council of the European Union 2001) was considered disappointing in the ARI and the measures adopted to enhance female employment were considered to be marginal improvements, particularly because of the gender-neutral approach employed in the newly adopted flexible working arrangements. With regard to the document submitted by the subsequent government, the ARI criticized the lack of a gender dimension in the adoption of measures aimed at increasing both female and youth employment rates. The NAP was also criticized for the lack of a gender dimension in the context of positive action measures and for containing insufficient measures regarding part-time work and the issue of undeclared work. The main focus of the 2001 NAP was on the Employability and Adaptability pillars. In particular, the Italian government referred to its White Paper on the Italian Labour Market (Italy 2001), which aimed at, *inter alia*, completing the modernization of the PES, reviewing the benefit unemployment system, continuing the process of improving flexibility in the organization of work and facilitating the introduction of further atypical contracts and measures to combat undeclared work through new fiscal measures. This was the first White Paper to be issued in Italian labour law. It was based on the first pillar of the EES, Employability, and the insider–outsider theory of employment according to which the "insiders" (incumbent employees whose jobs are protected by various labour turnover costs) get market power and affect the "outsiders" (who are either unemployed or work in the informal sector).[17] The White Paper provided the theoretical and economic grounds for the government's major reform plan which aimed at modernizing the labour market and, in particular, at enhancing the competitiveness of Italian firms, to fight against bottlenecks, namely to fight against the 'asymmetry between the flexibility in accessing the labour market and the rigidity in ending an employment relationship' (*ibid.*: 6) and to adapt the standard open-ended employment contract to the new economic environment. This White Paper was subject to fierce criticism, especially in relation to the proposed reform of the rules of unfair dismissal provided in Article 18 of the Workers Statute. Lo Faro (2002) defined it as an '(in)famous refrain of a positive trade-off between flexibility and employment . . . in the government's assertion that less rigid dismissal legislation is not so bad for employees and is extremely good for employment'.[18] The White Paper has also been criticized for its political instrumentalism and, in particular, for its interpretation of the insider–outsider theory, which does not seem to be substantiated by economic analysis (Costabile 2004). In spite of these criticisms, the underpinning philosophy of the White Paper has been used as the basis for the reform of the Italian labour market with Act 30/2003 (the so-called Biagi law).

The report also focused on territorial fragmentation and the need to establish a strong partnership among all different levels of decision and policy making through the development and implementation of TEPs (Gualini 2004),[19] in particular, RAPs and LAPs for employment in line with G 11 and pursuant to the principle of horizontal subsidiarity. As regards equal opportunities policies, the NAP was criticized for the absence of concrete measures for gender mainstreaming, which confirmed that the conceptual framework for developing a gender dimension to the field of employment remained weak. Moreover, the NAP failed to provide more information on equal opportunities policies. The only reference was to the Employment Framework Directive (Council of the European Union 2000b) and how it was going to be implemented at national level. The situation in 2002 remained the same and the NAP was still mainly programmatic. The only significant initiative was the involvement of various Ministries such as the Ministries of the Economy, Education

---

17 On the insider–outsider theory of employment and unemployment, see Lindbeck and Snower (1988).
18 See also Mariucci (2002); interview with Dr A. Megale, President of the Istituto di Ricerche Economiche e Sociali (IRES), the Italian research institute linked to the CGIL, who says that the proposed reform of the labour market was presented to the social partners as a *fait accompli*.
19 In Italy the first TEPs were adopted and implemented before the development of the EES.

and Research, Equal Opportunities, Innovation and Technology and Public Affairs in the drafting of the NAP.

6.2 Denmark

The Danish 2001 NAP listed a number of new measures in the gender equality field. In particular, with the adoption of the Equal Opportunities Act in June 2000 (Denmark 2000), the application of the mainstreaming approach to gender equality was established by statute.[20] Since then 'all new relevant legislation is subject to equality screening'. Moreover, the government launched a major equal pay campaign in 2001. A large number of firms were invited to participate in the establishment of a network of firms with a view to monitoring equal pay measures and using job evaluation to ensure better assessment of employees' qualifications. In this new context the social partners in the municipal and county labour markets initiated a project with the purpose of providing guidance and awareness, in order to fight against gender biased stereotypes. Moreover, the Ministry of Labour launched a project aimed at combating occupational segregation in both the public and the private sectors, and to this end it set up a working group to study gender-segregated labour markets.[21] Finally, a new Equal Opportunities Knowledge Centre ensured a network of information services for women in the workplace. The Danish 2001 NAP also gave a detailed description of the results achieved by the government. In particular, even though there was still a segregated labour market, the number of female managers continued to increase and one-third of young managers were women. Moreover, the degree of coverage for children under ten years in day care facilities and school clubs increased by 1 per cent and in the year 2000 it amounted to 81 per cent. In this context, the Ministry of Social Affairs in co-operation with the National Association of Municipal Authorities and the National Union of Childcare and Youth Workers initiated a joint project with a view to ensuring pedagogic quality in the day care institutions. The only disappointing figures were those relating to men's and women's use of parental leave, which remained the same as the previous NAP. The 2002 NAP was less detailed and also less programmatic than the previous one and it confirmed the further implementation of all the measures enacted since the adoption of the 2000 Equal Opportunities Act. However, the implementation of the measures, especially those regarding gender gaps and gender mainstreaming, was still at an embryonic phase. Hence it was not possible to fully evaluate the effectiveness of these measures. Moreover, gender pay gap issues apart, the information on the social partners' role in the field of equal opportunities and, in particular, in reconciling work with family life (G 18), was insufficient and it did not allow an effective assessment. In addition, the Adaptability and the Equal Opportunities pillars were not treated in a comprehensive and coherent way. However, in comparison with the Italian NAP, where equal opportunities policies received little attention, and where adaptability was still entirely considered as a gender-neutral matter, the Danish NAP represented a great step forward in

---

20 Under this Equal Opportunities Act, Ministries, State institutions and enterprises are required to submit a report every second year about their equality work. These reports are considered to be a central element in the implementation of gender mainstreaming in public planning and administration. The first report was submitted by the Minister of Equal Opportunities in September 2001 and formed part of the annual reports to the Danish Parliament.

21 See also the Danish EQUAL programme approved by the Commission in March 2001. The project looked at gender distribution in occupations with growing employment; within the job hierarchy; and/or in selected female occupation.

the strengthening of gender-equality policies. Finally, adaptability measures were all implemented on the basis of a partnership approach, with the inclusion of the county and municipal sector as well as the social partners pursuant to Horizontal Objective D of the Employment Guidelines.

Denmark has a long tradition of gender mainstreaming in the public employment service and there are equality advisers in all public offices. A new framework for a more efficient and transparent labour market has been set up following the employment service's structural reform which merged employment services and municipalities, creating new job centres. ALMPs apply to all unemployed persons, irrespective of whether they are receiving unemployment benefits, social assistance or sickness benefits, and focus on individualized measures. As such, women should benefit from the policies on a more or less equal footing to that of men. As the ninety-one new local job centres will all have an anchor person for equality and a connection to the new Centre of Equality Consultants, this may result in more efficient gender mainstreaming.

6.3 The Czech Republic

In Chapter 5 we have seen that before becoming members of the European Union CEECs also prepared for the implementation of the EES. As part of the EU accession process, many CEECs had been shadowing the then four-pillar framework of the Employment Strategy (Keune 2003). In particular, as part of the general pre-accession strategy, the European Commission set up the Employment Policy Review on the basis of which it evaluated the labour markets of the accession states with respect to their fitting into existing EU structures and policies. Bilateral JAPs based on a first evaluation set out the challenges to be met and the appropriate policies to be implemented. Through the Employment Policy Review the Commission was able to influence the employment policies of candidate countries in the pre-accession period. The JAP exercise, therefore, helped candidate countries to adopt the *acquis* and the recommendations provided the necessary steps to enable them to participate in the EES once they became members of the European Union.

Before the JAP exercise, in the Czech Republic the Ministry of Labour and Social Affairs launched a new approach to employment policy with the adoption of National Employment Plans (NEP) containing a medium-term strategy on employment policies. The first one was issued in 1999. An institutional development not mentioned in the NEP that was particularly important for gender equality was the establishment in 1998 of a Department for Equality of Women and Men within the Ministry of Labour and Social Affairs which works under the Unit for European Integration and International Relations of the same Ministry. In addition, gender-equality officers were created within each Ministry with the task among others of producing an annual document entitled "Priorities and Progresses in Promoting Equality of Men and Women" which is then incorporated in the government's annual report of the same name. In 1998 the Governmental Council for Human Rights was set up. It acts as an advisory body to the Czech government on issues concerning the protection of human rights and fundamental freedoms. It is responsible for overseeing the government's commitments under the Convention on the Elimination of All Forms of Discrimination against Women (CEDAW) and it has set up the Committee for the Elimination of All Forms of Discrimination against Women.

The Czech Republic was the first accession country to sign the JAP (in 2000). The employment guidelines were understood as focusing on employment creation/activation and prevention of social exclusion. The NEPs adopted these EU objectives and oriented its measures towards the EES priorities. One of its basic objectives was activation, representing a shift of responsibility away from the state towards the unemployed and the worker, the social partners, NGOs and other social actors. However, employment policy was seen as being part of a broader package of measures aimed at achieving an open market economy rather than being conceived as social policy measures. Moreover, the participatory element of the EES was difficult to develop because of the weak role of the social partners and regional and local bodies in the policy-making system of the Czech Republic. However, the PHARE twinning programmes through which candidate countries could receive technical assistance from EU country experts helped the Czech Republic to develop, *inter alia*, social dialogue, equal opportunities and social inclusion measures and occupational safety and health policy. The pre-accession phase, therefore, was pivotal for enabling the Czech Republic to learn how to develop EU concepts and paradigms in the area of employment policy. However, as mentioned earlier, rather than being part of a design to develop social policies in accordance with EU social objectives the aim of the Czech Republic was strategic convergence, in order to enable it to join the European Union.

The transition to an open market economy has been particularly detrimental to women. Before 1989 the socialist state expected women to participate fully in the post-war process of "building socialism": it not only ensured women's economic independence but also enacted protective maternity and child care laws and provided adequate infrastructure such as nurseries, school meals, comprehensive health care provision, cheap and efficient transport (Sloat, 2004: 6). However, the rhetoric of equal rights and gender ideology towards the family and motherhood maintained intact a traditional notion of the gender contract and, consequently, various forms of discrimination against women both in the legal system and in society have persisted. When many state companies were privatized and restructured it was women, therefore, rather than men who were made redundant first and their employment rate, therefore, started decreasing significantly. Another negative consequence of the transition to a market economy was the closure of many child care facilities for lack of funding as they were no longer provided exclusively by the state. Since then female unemployment has been growing sharply (from below or around 3 per cent to 8–10 per cent; CSU 2009) and women at the workplace have been subject to various forms of discrimination (this is particularly the case of the Roma women and, more broadly, women within the age group of twenty-four to thirty-five years of age who generally have young children) and the gender pay gap is persistent. Along with these trends the labour market is being reorganized in a way that supports a sharp division of labour between men and women, with women taking inferior roles. In the Czech Republic a high proportion of women work but the quality of women's jobs is perceivably lower than that of men's. The wage gap is high in the Czech Republic (above 20 per cent; EGGE 2009), and women's managerial chances are lower than in, for example, Hungary. Hence, while Czech women have experienced less resistance to their entry to the labour market than in other countries, once there they face significant disadvantages compared to men. The socialist legacy has also instilled an aversion to the placing of quotas or other positive measures to achieve gender equality in politics (Choluj and Neusuess 2004: 5). Moreover, an overly narrow definition of the "political" has blocked initiatives for a greater level of political participation on the part of women in post-socialist systems (Jalušič and Antić 2000) and demands for the introduction of mechanisms that would ensure the equal participation of women have often been perceived as being illegitimate. Hence, during the years of economic transformation, structural discrimination still persisted due to the assumption that general anti-discriminatory laws and the mechanisms of legal and constitutional complaint would ensure the realization of equality.

Certainly, under Accession negotiation Chapter 13 (social policy and employment),[22] social conditionality required the implementation of both the hard *acquis*, namely EU health and safety rules, a range of EU social laws such as those on working time, parental leave, equal opportunities, mechanisms for social dialogue, and the soft *acquis*. The Czech Labour Code, Act No. 65/1965 (Czech Republic 1965), was amended accordingly in 2001. However, the accession process failed to systematically include elements of the "European social model" (Vaughan-Whitehead 2003). A detailed analysis of the Europe Agreements[23] and Accession Reports shows that they had little social policy orientation (Ferge 2001; Micklewright and Stewart 2000). In addition, the construction of the PHARE programme[24] has been criticized on the grounds that it did not sufficiently focus on the impact, sustainability and relevance for the overall social policy reform of the CEECs (de la Porte and Deacon 2002: 26). According to the 2000 Social Policy Agenda (European Commission 2000d) European agencies were expected to monitor the implementation of the social and employment *acquis* by the candidate countries, give support to the strengthening of social dialogue (European Commission 1998), contribute to the development of non-governmental organizations, prepare a joint analysis in the field of social protection, mainstream gender equality in the pre-accession strategy and ensure the participation of the candidate countries in the Community action programmes in the social area. However, the focus was on the formal implementation of the EU *acquis*.

The above analysis helps to understand why the main concern of the Czech Republic in relation to employment was not so much about how to resolve specific problems affecting the Czech labour market but rather about identifying together with the Commission 'an agreed set of employment and labour market objectives necessary to advance the country's labour market transformation, *to make progress in adapting the employment system so as to be able to implement the Employment Strategy and to prepare it for accession to the European Union*' (Czech Republic 2000).[25] The stated overall objective was developing policy responses that would lead to increased employment and flexibility in the labour market and the adaptability of the workforce, the central aim being to achieve a high and stable level of employment. Hence, besides mentioning that the service sector would increase female employment and help introduce flexible patterns of work that would help women reconcile work and family life, and referring to the then fourth pillar on Equal Opportunities with a generic commitment to combating discrimination also through positive action measures the JAP was to a great extent gender-blind. The main focus of the report was on employability and adaptability measures. In this context, the report made reference to the Employment Act, Act No. 1/1991 (Czech Republic 1991) and Act No. 9/1991 of the Czech National Council concerning employment and competence of the state administration authorities of the Czech Republic (Czech Republic 1991a),[26] which provided the basic legislative framework for adopting employment policy measures.

Nevertheless, during the period under consideration some important institutional

---

22 The other four negotiation chapters concerning labour market and social policies were Chapter 2 (freedom of movement of persons), Chapter 3 (freedom to provide services), Chapter 18 (education and training) and Chapter 21 (regional policy and co-ordination of structural instruments).

23 Detailed information on Europe Agreements is available online, <http://europa.eu.int/comm/enlargement/pas/phare/intro.htm>.

24 Detailed information on PHARE programmes is available online, <http://europa.eu.int/comm/enlargement/pas/europe_agr.htm>.

25 Emphasis added.

26 Both Acts have been amended by Act 220/2002.

changes were made by the Czech government to further promote gender equality. In 2001 the Government Council for Equal Opportunities of Women and Men was established. The Council prepares proposals promoting equal opportunities for women and men. The main activities and tasks of this Council are negotiating and advising the government on measures for the promotion of equal opportunities for women and men, determining the sphere of priorities for the projects of departments aimed at supporting the implementation of equal opportunities and assessing to what extent the principle of equal opportunities for women and men is implemented in practice. The Council may establish committees and *ad hoc* working groups if necessary. Although the Council is under the aegis of the Ministry of Labour and Social Affairs it plays an important role in developing a "bottom-to-top" form of policy making, as among its members there are representatives of NGOs working on gender equality as well as a representatives of labour and management. The involvement of NGOs and social partners ensures a less centralized form of governance and also increases awareness of the multiple forms of discrimination faced by women in the labour market. In addition, their involvement may also promote a more cross-cutting and gender mainstreaming approach. In 2002 the newly elected lower House of Parliament established the Permanent Family and Equal Opportunities Commission. The Commission has ten members representing all parliamentary political parties. The Commission mainly deals with the following issues: gender equality; women's rights; discrimination; home violence; children's rights; and complaints received from citizens. The Commission discusses draft legislation and it has the power to organize hearings and to summon government officials, who have a duty to attend and to provide the information and explanations demanded unless they are prevented from doing so by legislation. The Commission may adopt resolutions, which mainly have an advisory nature. The Commission shares information and co-operates with the Government Council for Human Rights, the Government Council for Equal Opportunities of Men and Women and the Ministry of Labour and Social Affairs. Moreover, as of January 2002 Gender Focal Points have been established in each Ministry which may ensure more gender awareness at ministerial level.

With regard to the social partners, CMKOS set up a specialized Committee for Equality which is a permanent advisory body of the Council of CMKOS. Its primary role is to develop activities and actions promoting equal opportunities. The Committee has faced a series of obstacles such as very limited voluntary membership and lack of funding. Moreover, its first provisions aimed at enforcing gender-equality regulations were adopted only in 2002.

6.4 Comparative evaluation of Italy, Denmark and the Czech Republic in the period 1998–2002

The Evaluation Reports of Denmark and Italy provide important information on the impact of the EES at different levels of policy making. With regard to Italy, the analysis showed how this country is particularly affected by high levels of unemployment due mainly to the peculiarities of the Italian labour market such as, for example, inefficient transition between school and jobs for young people and lack of participation of women in the labour market. In addition, there is also a very high level of early retirement of older people from the market, widespread undeclared labour and serious geographical imbalance and internal segmentation. According to the 2002 draft Italian Impact Evaluation Report of the EES (Italy 2002) and to interviews conducted with representatives of the Italian government and the social partners in Brussels and Italy the Strategy, while representing a major incentive for the adoption of active and preventative measures and the creation of *ad hoc* committees has not contributed greatly to solving the major structural problems in the Italian labour market (Ferrera and Gualmini 2002). This is due in part to delays in the implementation or to the non-implementation of some of the Employment Guidelines and the still mainly centralized system of regulation but also partly to the fact that the EES does not consider Italy's structural problems which cannot be solved exclusively with supply-side measures but also require demand-side policies that take into account the adoption of macroeconomic policies.[27]

The Danish Evaluation Report (Denmark 2002) indicated that employment policies have been implemented in accordance with the principles and objectives of the EES.[28] This explains why the overall objectives of the Strategy have already been met. As in the Italian case, the Strategy has definitely been a source of inspiration for policy developments but it has not entailed a major institutional rationalization. Representatives of the Danish government argue that it is 'hard to detect an explicit change of policy' since the launch of the Luxembourg process.[29] Danish social partners have been to a great extent satisfied with the Strategy particularly because it assigned them important functions in the implementation of the EES and because the Strategy maintained intact their traditional role in the Danish labour market. In particular, the Confederation of Danish Trade Unions (Landsorganisationen i Danmark, LO) maintained that the EES did not introduce any new strategies in Denmark. However, it welcomed the Strategy for bringing employment and labour market issues within the European context.[30] Finally, the Danish government suggested strengthening the quality side of the Strategy and defining a more detailed and selected list of indicators to support the evaluation of the NAPs which would also take into account differences between the various Member States.[31]

With regard to the Czech Republic, the adoption of EU gender-equality law into the national legal system required for accession certainly legitimized women's claim to genuine equality but during the period under consideration it only made a marginal change in practice as the incorporation of EU employment and gender-equality law was part of a broader strategic convergence plan to secure accession to the Union. The setting up of new governmental and parliamentary bodies is evidence of the fact that the Czech Republic was attempting to inject a gender approach into policy making. However, the unfavourable macroeconomic environment of the transition phase severely increased women's unemployment and those women who were able to enter the labour market held less favourable positions in most areas, with significant earning differentials in comparison with men.

7   Gender equality and gender mainstreaming in the period 2003–2010

Following the disappearance of the Equal Opportunities pillar and the subsequent removal of the gender-equality guideline both Denmark's and Italy's 2003 and 2004 NAP and

---

27 Interview with Dr Paolo Sestito, economic adviser to the Italian Ministry of Labour and member of the Italian committee for the drafting of the National Action Plan for Employment, 3 January 2003. See also Sestito (2002).

28 Interview with Mr F. Pedersen and Ms L. Henriksen, consultants of the Danish Ministry of employment, online questionnaire, 12 July 2002.

29 *Idem.*

30 Interview with Mr P. Karlsson, LO representative, Brussels, 17 July 2002, who was directly involved in the drafting of the 2001 NAPS.

31 *Idem.*

2005/2006 NRP reports as well as the Czech Republic NAP for 2004–2006 and NRP for 2005–2008 seemed to have given less importance to gender equality and focused on gender equality issues only incidentally, that is, only in the context of the macroeconomic objectives of the Lisbon Strategy, even though during this period gender equality measures have been adopted in all three countries. In particular, equality policy is concentrated on breaking down the gender-segregated labour market and the reconciliation of working with family life in order to reduce the wage gap between men and women, with little gender awareness in the implementation of adaptability measures. In the Italian NRP for 2008–2010 the focus has been on work-life balance and, more broadly, policies aimed at supporting women's participation in the labour market also through financial incentives (Italy 2008). The primary focus of the Danish NRP for 2008–2010 is on the increase of the labour force because of the high levels of employment (Denmark 2008). As explained below some of the measures proposed may have detrimental effects on the Danish flexicurity model and on gender equality.

In the Czech NRP for 2008–2010 there is reference to the importance of reconciling work and family life following the Commission's 2008 work–life balance package and to a lesser extent as part of the flexicurity objectives of the Union's renewed Growth and Jobs Strategy (Czech Republic 2008). To this end various programmatic measures have been included for the long-term period of 2008–2013. These are analyzed further below. In general, however, the stated central objective of the national report is the strengthening of labour market flexibility with a focus on innovation infrastructure, research and development and increasing company competiveness, social inclusion and education.

7.1 Italy

The measures adopted in Italy between 2003–2008 are very few and do not introduce a notion of gender mainstreaming tailored to the Italian situation or any particularly significant change in the direction of Italian gender equality policies. In recent years a series of programmes have been issued by the Ministry of Labour and the Ministry of Equal Opportunities aimed at promoting the presence of women at different levels and positions within organizations, strengthening female self-employment and developing *ad hoc* positive action projects. However, these programmes are a mere repetition of existing legislation and are purely programmatic in nature, without outlining any clear objective and action for the future.

Among the few measures adopted in the field of equal opportunities worthy of mention there is Law-decree 198/2006 (Italy 2006), which provides for a 'Code for Equal Opportunities between Women and Men' (1) establishing a Committee on Women's Self-employment with the role of promoting female self-employment, for example by establishing a network between the government at ministerial level and the associations of small and medium enterprises and craftsmanship and by fostering research and raising awareness on female self-employment, (2) promoting the adoption of a comprehensive programme of positive action measures including those for promoting female self-employment with the involvement of different actors such as equal opportunities committees and councillors at national, regional and local levels, equality advisers, social partners and private and public employers. This is implemented through a partnership approach ensured by the Equal Opportunities Network which operates at decentralized level. However, the rationale of this law is to reform Italy's public services and simplify legislation in the field of equal opportunities rather than aiming at introducing new gender-equality measures. Moreover, the recent pension reform (see 6.1 above) does not have any gender perspective or awareness and addresses only technical issues of retirement age and post-employment benefit in a strictly macroeconomic and gender-neutral context (Italy 2003a: 23–24).

With regard to the period 2006–2010, the focus of the government has been on strengthening the participation of women in the labour market by adopting various measures on work–life balance. In particular, policies supporting women's participation in the labour market through the provision of childcare services and policies aim at increasing the employment rate through financial incentives. However, the flexicurity approach is still weak. While much has been done to identify flexible contracts to increase female employment rate, there is little emphasis on the security element of flexicurity. In particular, there is no evidence of a complementary strategy for counterbalancing negative effects of this flexibility through adequate unemployment insurance schemes. The weakness of the system of security (of both income and employment) particularly affects female workers, who are overrepresented in all types of precarious contracts (EGGE 2009: 65). Moreover, there is hardly any evidence of a gender-mainstreaming approach in the flexicurity policy objectives pursued by the government. Specifically, in the NRP for 2008–2010 only a section is dedicated to gender-equality issues with exclusive reference to women rather than policies for improving work–life balance for families with children, thus reinforcing gender stereotypes (Italy 2008). In 2007 the Minister of Family Affairs (under the Prodi government) developed a three-year Nursery Plan with the objective of reaching a coverage rate of 13 per cent by the end of 2009. The plan devolved more financial resources to the southern regions in order to tackle regional disparities. This Nursery Plan has been implemented even under the subsequent government and it is discussed in detail in the NRP for 2008–2010. However, the approach adopted to address female employment and gender equality is inadequate. The implicit idea is that it will be enough to encourage employers to use part-timers (by making part-time regulation more flexible) and all other forms of atypical contracts (as they have expanded again) in order to increase female employment. According to the report, as women enter employment more child care services for children up to three years of age will be made available (EGGE 2009: 85). An additional initiative, the so-called "Spring Sessions", has been announced. This is an experimental project aimed at offering care services for children aged between two and three. The government intends to support a complementary offer of care services of a private nature with the disbursement of vouchers or fiscal benefits. This measure should increase the coverage rate of child care services up to 15 per cent by 2013 (well below the Barcelona target of 33 per cent). However, the report does not specify the financial funds available for 2009 to implement this scheme (*ibid.*: 121).

The absence of gender mainstreaming is particularly critical with respect to the reduction in school hours (in all types of schools: maternal, primary and secondary) (*ibid.*: 197). The reform of the education system (the Gelmini Law, Act 137/2008: Italy 2008b) represents the core of the employment chapter of the 2008 NRP. The background analysis reports that Italy has not reached the target of the Lisbon "Education and training 2010" in terms of drop-out rate, key competences level, percentage of people with at least a high school diploma, number of people with a university degree, lifelong learning participation rate. However, it is unclear how the reform with its focus on rationalization of the use of resources can contribute to solving the aforementioned problems of the education system. Moreover, the rationalization of public spending on education does not consider the negative impact it may have on families. In particular, while it is stated that it will be necessary to increase the number of students per classroom and reduce quite significantly the number of school hours in all types of schools (maternal, primary, secondary) it does not take into account how this will increase the already low female unemployment rate, as many teachers are women. In addition, the reduction in school hours will require extra child care provision or alternatively that mothers will be forced to stay at home to look after their children. It is implicitly assumed that the primary responsibility of mothers is to take care of their children. This is in contradiction with the announced efforts to increase the availability of child care services in order to encourage female employment.

With regard to labour market policies, the Berlusconi government has explicitly stated in the 2008 NRP that it intends to break with the previous policy approach of the Prodi government by supporting strong deregulation in the labour market. The approach developed is based on the Green Paper on the future of welfare (Italy 2008a), where the government has developed a new approach to welfare state policies, signalling a shift from a "passive" to a more "active" welfare state based on a "workfare" approach. In order to pursue these objectives, the government announced the intention to implement the Welfare Agreement on Income Support to Workers made Redundant (*ammortizzatori sociali*), PES, apprenticeship and incentives. However, far too much emphasis is placed on flexibility: the simplification and the reintroduction of flexible forms of contract go in this direction (EGGE 2009: 145). The previous government had started to reduce the number of atypical contracts abolishing some of them and also provided atypical workers with more job security, for example in relation to maternity leave. The Berlusconi government reintroduced them without any new measures in relation to job security. Moreover, in the 2008 NRP it is announced that the regulation of part-time work will be modified, and made more flexible particularly in relation to working hours. It is also assumed that this increased flexibility will meet both the needs of employers (facing cyclical fluctuations in production) and employees (especially women with family responsibilities). The employment chapter of the national report has a brief section on female work confirming this approach. The government's view is that atypical forms of contract may help increase female employment and also make it easier for women employed with these atypical contracts to reconcile work and family life with no consideration of the quality of the job, job insecurity and low pay associated with atypical contracts as well as the negative impact on career advancement and training (*idem*).

7.2 Denmark

With regard to Denmark, the most significant measure adopted by the government during the period under consideration is the launch of a new gender-equality strategy (Denmark 2002) following the adoption of the 2000 Equality Act, which included gender mainstreaming among the existing gender-equality measures and made it compulsory to adopt a gender-mainstreaming approach in the adoption of all legislative measures. This new strategy is based on an interministerial gender-mainstreaming project involving both ministerial departments and various agencies and institutions. The main objectives are to ensure that gender-equality perspectives become a natural and integrated part of key ministerial tasks and that Ministries consider society's gender-equality challenges in the context of their own policy areas. An interministerial steering committee has been vested with the overall responsibility for the implementation of the strategy. Each Ministry adopts ad hoc initiatives and is responsible for its own policy areas. The Department of Gender Equality has set up an interministerial network for employees involved in the gender-mainstreaming project in the individual Ministries. In particular, the network gives professional support and expertise to those employees working actively to implement the gender-mainstreaming strategy. Its implementation has helped to provide the necessary tools and techniques for analyzing and assessing

Bills on gender-equality impact (on a par with economic and administrative impacts, impact on trade and industry and environmental impact); analyzing and evaluating budgets in relation to gender-equality impacts; assessing and preparing other types of activities and initiatives for injecting a gender-equality perspective, for example health campaigns, guidelines for trade and industry's social responsibility, guidelines for primary and secondary schools, and so on; generating gender-segregated data, material and statistics and making them easily accessible to employees in their daily work; and producing new information in order to analyze and process material and data in terms of gender equality. In addition, this gender-mainstreaming strategy has helped to set up and develop an organizational and management structure in each Ministry for implementing it. The mainstreaming approach used by the government aims at changing the focus of equal opportunities in Denmark from one which considers the underprivileged, namely women, to one which considers both women and men. The adoption of the interministerial gender-mainstreaming action plan for 2007–2011 (Denmark 2007) confirms the commitment to developing and strengthening further the gender-mainstreaming strategy at interministerial level. The main objective for this period is to improve the ability of Ministries to assess from a gender perspective Parliamentary Bills and the allocation of resources through the development of benchmarks and to this end increase the availability of gender-segregated data. In this context the Ministry of Gender equality has issued a document with a list of initiatives considered examples of good practice.

Moreover, in 2003 the LO adopted an internal gender-mainstreaming strategy as part of its equal opportunities policy for 2003–2007 (LO 2003) with the aim of: (1) improving women's representation in the organizations' top ranks; (2) improving the training of women; (3) creating mainstreaming tools and guidelines; (4) mapping the reasons behind gender wage gaps; (5) fighting against a gender-segregated labour market; and (6) working towards defining a "family-friendly workplace". Among other things, LO's mainstreaming project entails that all recommendations for the day-to-day management and the General Council shall contain a separate recommendation on gender. This recommendation shall define more closely whether there is a gender aspect to the main recommendation and if so what gender-specific consequences and implications this is likely to have at organizational and political levels. LO and its affiliated unions aim to ensure that gender becomes an integrated part of all relevant statistics and all other types of analyses prepared by the trade unions. The political responsibility for the co-ordination of equal opportunities measures is vested in the LO's General Council. In addition, the General Council is presented with a set of reports documenting trade union policy and organization in relation to equal opportunities. These reports include an overview of representation by gender in LO and its affiliated unions, the registration of the number of participants in skills development on gender and mainstreaming, mainstreaming projects and other gender-equality projects. These reports are submitted every year during a four-year period and they may be compared to EU Scoreboards in that they are tools to monitor the implementation of policy objectives and measures. The first reports were produced in 2005 (LO 2005). The 2005 reports included a table with information about LO's mainstreaming strategy and, in particular, which affiliated unions, cartels and members of the LO had been implementing it as a political strategy, as an integrated part of everyday activities and had a dedicated budget for carrying out mainstreaming activities. Examples of a mainstreaming approach were the inclusion of mainstreaming activities in a separate budget by two trade unions and by LO, the creation of a module on mainstreaming in a training course for union representatives and the establishment of a regional equal opportunities network by another two trade unions. Moreover, 2005 was the year in which the LO obtained equal representation of both women and men among LO's elected representatives.

In 2006 the Law on Equal Pay for Men and Women (Denmark 1976, 2003a; Emerek 2006) was amended and now includes the obligation to provide company statistics broken down by gender (Denmark 2006a). This is restricted to companies with a minimum of thirty-five employees ensuring that a minimum of ten women and ten men have the same type of job. However, the most important policy document of recent years, the Welfare Agreement (Denmark 2006), does not discuss pay or equal pay as part of Denmark's future welfare policy.

In the NRP for 2008–2010 the Danish government focuses on the labour market reforms necessary to enlarge the labour force (Denmark 2008). In August 2008 the government launched an ambitious new 2015 plan for the increase of Denmark's labour force. Pursuant to the Growth and Jobs Strategy the measures concern activation employment policies as well as initiatives to increase employment among immigrants. However, the intersection between gender and ethnicity, gender and age, age and ethnicity, and gender, age and ethnicity is not sufficiently taken into consideration in the modernization of the labour markets and investing in people.

Moreover, the main problems affecting women in the Danish labour market concern labour market segmentation and gender pay gaps which are closely linked. One of the main reasons for gender segregation is associated with the division of family duties between women and men. These problems have been taken into account and for the first time equal pay statistics have been published in 2008, following changes in the equal pay law in 2006 (Act No. 562/2006).

Denmark is renowned for its "flexicurity" approach to employment policy, which is based on relatively high unemployment benefits and mobility in the labour market. The mobility is higher than in almost all other Member States. However, according to the National Expert on Gender and Employment Issues for Denmark there is hardly any gender-mainstreaming approach in the Danish "flexicurity" model (EGGE 2009: 139). In particular, there is no discussion or awareness of the economic and non-economic costs of "flexicurity" and the economic redistribution between the female-dominated public sector and the male-dominated public sector that it may lead to. Moreover, in 2005 the benefit system was reformed by the agreement *En ny chance til alle* (A new chance for everybody) (Denmark 2005a) to the detriment of the weaker groups on the fringe of the labour market. These measures may increase job insecurity and result in demands for increasing job security with stricter provisions on dismissal. The low compensation is also a problem for single parents – predominantly single mothers – and the tightening up of the benefit system may result in a backlash for unemployed immigrant women who are more exposed to the possibility of losing their individual right to social benefits.

The government has attempted to increase the labour force for part-time workers by amending the rules on supplementary unemployment benefits (EGGE 2009: 61 and 162). These measures enable employees holding a part-time job with a maximum of 29.6 hours a week to have a supplementary unemployment benefit for the remaining hours of a full-time week of thirty-seven hours if they can either leave their work without notice or be dismissed without notice. The supplementary unemployment benefit is limited to thirty weeks within a period of two years. It is possible to regain the right to a new period of supplementary benefit after twenty-six weeks with at least thirty hours' work within fifty-two weeks. These measures have been met with criticism, especially from the trade unions, as the measures maintain the gender-biased distribution of part-time work in the various sectors of the economy and may end up increasing the precariousness of female employment.

7.3 The Czech Republic

The central aim of the NAP for 2004–2006 was to strengthen ALMP (Czech Republic 2004). Apart from referring to the gender pay gap and labour market segregation and programmatic measures contained in the government's document *Priorities and Procedures in Promoting the Equality of Men and Women*, which entrusts government bodies with the fulfilment of specific measures related to employment, horizontal and vertical segregation and the reconciliation of family and working life, the report is virtually gender-blind. Moreover, between 2004 and 2007 this document contained exactly the same chapter with the same content and the same wording. Policies or specific programmes that would tackle the situation of high gender pay gap were not established (EGGE 2009: 95).

In the NRP for 2008–2010 the Czech Republic has been focusing principally on two areas of gender equality: the definition of work–life balance measures in the broader context of "flexicurity" and the adoption of an Anti-discrimination Framework Act (Czech Republic 2008). The country still lacks such legislation and at present equal treatment and non-discrimination provisions exist as clauses under general law. The idea of adopting an umbrella Act goes back to 2002, when the government issued a report on the "Possibilities of Discrimination" in which it assessed the level of legal protection against discrimination and concluded that it was insufficient. It recommended, therefore, the adoption of a unifying Anti-discrimination Act that would contain procedural rules and include a wide range of anti-discriminatory measures in line with the EU equality *acquis*. The law provides for the establishment of a new monitoring body for cases of discrimination and it envisages two possible solutions: either creating an *ad hoc* body or entrusting the Public Defender of Human Rights with the competence to deal with such matters. The creation of a monitoring body would be an important step forward as the number of cases of gender inequality lodged before ordinary courts still remains relatively small. However, the law is still not in force because the President of the Czech Republic vetoed the Act and the country, therefore, has no framework gender-equality legislation to date. However, some of the newer Acts such as the new Labour Code (Act 262/2006) include a reference to this law, thereby creating a gap in the country's legislation. The Act will be presented in Parliament for an up-or-down vote on the President's veto. This represents a serious drawback, leaving the Czech Republic as the only European country which has not yet implemented all of the Community gender-equality law. The European Commission has threatened the Czech Republic several times via infringement proceedings under Articles 226 and 228 EC for its failure to incorporate EU law into national law. However, disputes about the adoption of wide-ranging anti-discrimination legislation in the Czech Republic have been ongoing for several years. Despite initial reservations with regard to the draft law the fear of EU sanctions eventually led the Czech Parliament to pass the Anti-discrimination Act, albeit in reduced form, at the beginning of 2008. This formal approach to transposing European anti-discrimination legislation into national law (the Senate issued a resolution declaring that it did not identify itself with the umbrella act and that the only reason it passed the act was to comply with European law) explains why the President of the Czech Republic vetoed the Act. Another reason put forward by the President is that existing legislation already complies with EU law. For instance, direct and indirect discrimination is prohibited by the Labour Code and the Employment Act (Act No. 435/2004), which contains other anti-discriminatory provisions (Czech Republic 2004a). This act also provides for the adoption of positive action measures and prohibits discriminatory employment practices such as discriminatory advertisements. Moreover, the principle of equal pay for work of equal value has been sanctioned in the Wages Act (Act No. 54/2001; Czech Republic 2001), and s. 133a of the Code of Civil Procedure (Czech Republic 1963) as amended by Act No.151/2002 (Czech Republic 2002a) shifts the burden of proof to the employer in sex discrimination cases. Instead of adopting an umbrella Act the President of the Czech Republic proposed implementing the specific EU legislation required by further amending existing regulations. The consequence of the veto is that the Czech Republic does not fully comply with EU gender-equality Directives.

With regard to reconciling work with family life, in its NRP for 2008–2010 the Czech Republic presented a package of programmatic measures which signal, according to the government, a shift from passive to active employment policies (Czech Republic 2008). The measures include an increase of incentives for nurseries to adapt their opening hours to the needs of working parents, an increase of incentives for employers to establish nurseries and child care centres at the workplace, subsidies for the training of employees on parental leave and an increase of flexible working patterns. The report also states that a significant increase in funding will be available during the budgetary cycle of 2007–2013 to support the creation of a pro-family environment at the workplace. In particular, the so-called Pro-family package contains the following measures:

- Increasing the number of private child care centres while at the same time promoting start-up of female businesses and reducing female unemployment (targeted group: women of fifty years of age).
- Creation of the institution of "mutual parental aid", namely parents of children caring for the children of other parents on the basis of clearly defined rules.
- Setting up of in-house nurseries at the workplace on a non-commercial basis. Child care services would be provided either by the employer or by non-profit organizations, entities or by local and regional authorities.
- Offering tax allowances for employers providing or subcontracting child care for their employees.
- Adopting financial incentives for employers to promote flexible working contracts such as part-time work, for example the reduction of premiums for social security and unemployment contributions paid by the employer.

The above measures clearly represent an attempt to favour a better work–life balance by facilitating access to child care and introducing flexible working contracts. However, concerns about the security side of "flexicurity" policies have not yet entered the political debates, which still focus primarily on flexibility. There is no awareness or recognition of the negative consequences – greater job precariousness and insecurity – of more flexible contracts that are not backed up by social protection, especially for women. Gender equality is still based on a traditional notion of gender contract and it is restricted to the issue of part-time and flexible work to meet the need of women/mothers to combine work and child care.

Since 2004 parents on parental leave have been allowed to engage in paid employment without any salary limitations while receiving at the same time parental allowances. From February 2006 it is also possible for a parent who is in receipt of a parental allowance to use public child care services for up to four hours a day for a child older than three years. This may be helpful for mothers trying to return to the labour market, as in the fourth year of parental leave they lose the right to return to their original employment. However, even though the combination of parental leave and paid work offers a solution for long periods of absence, the status of "leave" as a transitional stage between being "active" and "non-active" in the labour market becomes rather blurred. If parents may combine leave benefits with gainful employment the actual measure resembles a child care allowance rather than a measure granting time off the labour market (EGGSIE 2007: 61). This approach reinforces and reproduces gender stereotypes which are at the basis of women's discrimination as regards access to employment and equal treatment at work. It also works to the disadvantage of men who decide to go on parental leave (EGGE 2009: 138).

Hence, to date no significant changes have taken place although amendments to the existing policies and legislation have been made. The emphasis on the need to reconcile job and family responsibilities as a women's issue and the introduction of part-time and flexible work to accommodate the needs of women may have a positive impact on some women in the short term but in the long term these measures may have a negative impact on women, especially as they do not address structural inequality. There is a very real danger that if the aspect of job security is not included as part of the debate the changes will not have a positive impact on gender equality (*idem*). In referring to flexicurity, the NRP 2008–2010 (Czech Republic 2008: 72) says that the Czech Republic has further increased the contractual freedom in employment law and adopted measures introducing more flexibility in the labour market. This approach clearly indicates that the security aspect of the "flexicurity" concept is absent in the Czech employment policy even thought the policy approach is labelled as "flexicurity". In addition, these policies are gender-blind. The absence of both the security and the gender-equality dimensions may be highly detrimental to gender equality.

Moreover there is no mention of the role of the social partners in developing a "flexicurity" approach in the "labour market", thus confirming what has been said earlier. On the one hand, trade unions suffer from the legacy left behind by their socialist predecessors and do not have any strong influence on the government in relation to the adoption of gender-equality measures. On the other hand, employers' representatives lack any interest in developing a social dialogue as they see it as a "leftover" of the previous regime. In addition, even though official documents identify women among the groups at risk of exclusion from the labour market (especially women with small children, women after parental leave and women over fifty years of age), ALMPs do not identify the unemployed by gender. The employment policy of the Czech Republic does not provide any specific measures on gender equality and lacks a gender-mainstreaming approach, including the use of gender-impact assessment (EGGE 2009: 60). Part of the explanation lies in the fact that there is still little familiarity with certain concepts such as, for example, the burden of proof in sex discrimination cases, part-time work regulations and self-employment as well as gender mainstreaming, which is a difficult concept to put into practice. Linked to this, the bodies entrusted with the enforcement of gender-equality law lack the necessary knowledge and experience and need to be trained. Legislative harmonization in this area has only ensured formal equality but not equality in practice and the OMC process seems to have achieved little to date. This is also confirmed, *inter alia*, by the fact that the number of cases of gender inequality lodged before ordinary courts remains still relatively small.

7.4 *Comparative evaluation of Italy, Denmark and the Czech Republic in the period 2003–2010*

The analysis of the main policies adopted in the three countries in the period under consideration confirms the different approach to gender equality and gender mainstreaming due to different understandings and meanings assigned to gender equality and to different models underlying their welfare systems. At the same time, however, the analysis also showed a similar change in the emphasis placed on gender-equality measures. In particular, all three countries seemed to have given less importance to gender equality and focused on it incidentally in the context of the overarching macroeconomic objectives of the Lisbon Strategy. During the period under consideration some gender-equality measures have been adopted in all three countries. However, attention seems to have been devoted to "flexicurity" measures and ALMPs without always taking into consideration the gender impact of such measures. At the level of principles and policy, the reforms touch the essence of social citizenship: the emphasis is on the "workfare" or employability approach and the balance between rights and obligations is being reconsidered and conditionality of social rights is on the increase. Surprisingly we also find this scenario in Denmark, where gender mainstreaming is applied to all policy proposals and Bills since the year 2000. Another finding common to all three Member States is the existence of gender stereotyping which at times is exemplified by law and policy and other times either by strong labour market segregation or by employers' behaviour. In part, this may be ascribed to the shift in focus at Community level and, in particular, to the loss of visibility of the gender-equality objectives in the Lisbon Strategy. In part, this may be explained by the peculiarities of the Italian, Danish and Czech labour markets.

In Italy few gender-equality measures have been adopted and the country still lacks any gender-mainstreaming approach, which is particularly disconcerting in relation to the major education reforms enacted in 2008, which contradict the government's nursery plan aimed at facilitating access to child care facilities. Female employment remains among the lowest in the European Union and the measures aimed at introducing further atypical contracts without concurring social protection clearly do not improve women's situation in the labour market. Moreover, in the national reports there is no reference to the role of the social partners in relation to equal opportunities measures. Hence no significant change in the direction of Italian gender-equality policies may be said to have taken place.

By contrast, Denmark remains strongly committed to gender equality. Both the government and the trade unions have been developing a gender-mainstreaming strategy, the most significant measure being the obligation to include a gender-mainstreaming approach in the adoption of all legislative measures since the year 2000. However, some of the "flexicurity" measures that have been adopted in recent years have been criticized for lacking a gender-mainstreaming approach and for not taking into account the negative consequences which some of the measures may have on women, such as the government's measures on part-time work in order to increase the labour force.

Employment policies in the Czech Republic lack systematic focus on gender equality, particularly in relation to the gender aspects of the Lisbon and Barcelona targets and on measures to close the gender gap (EGGE 2009: 201). Policies for gender equality are very limited and mainly concern the reconciliation of work and family life. Some policies that have been announced and could have a positive impact on gender equality have not been implemented. The Czech Republic needs to strengthen the existing institutional structure for implementing gender-equality measures and to ensure that gender equality is not considered merely a matter of formal adaptation to EU law. Another problem is the lack of awareness among the public in relation to changing gender stereotypes and there are still not enough women in politics and the media.

8 Conclusion

The globalization phenomenon and the introduction of new technologies have compelled Member States to shift from a system based on management by regulation to a system of management by objectives (Biagi 2000). Economic change also requires the modernization of work organization and a rethinking of gender-equality policies at all levels of decision and policy making, although the meaning of such modernization and rethinking is unclear and open to debate.[32] In this context, the role of the state and the law has changed and new forms of partnership and co-operation between the state, territorial authorities and the social partners have developed. In turn, these changes have paved the way towards new and more flexible forms of employment in order to adapt to this new economic and social scenario. Furthermore, the feminization of European labour markets has also led to the adoption and implementation of structural reforms with a stronger gender perspective.

In turning to our initial research question as to whether the EES has acted as a framing strategy and introduced change at domestic level, the study showed that the EES has acted as a catalyst for change at discourse level in Italy and the Czech Republic and to a lesser extent in Denmark. In particular, in Italy the guidelines and overall objectives of the Employment Strategy/Growth and Jobs Strategy (chiefly employability and adaptability) have been instrumental to the government's goals of reforming the labour market and adopting ALMPs, although the approach of the government has been subject to criticism for its political instrumentalism in the way it has used European targets. In the Czech Republic meeting the objectives of the EES was part of strategic convergence on the part of the government in the sense that compliance with the EES, at least in the initial pre-accession phase, was necessary to ensure EU membership rather than for problem solving in the area of employment. Denmark represents a different scenario in that it has always met the quantitative targets of high and full employment, including that of women. Moreover, its policies, such as its "flexicurity" model, have been used (together with that of the Netherlands) by the Commission to develop the European Union's model of "flexicurity". Hence it is not possible to establish whether the EES has had a clear cognitive impact on Denmark's labour market and employment measures.

The chapter showed that between 1998 and 2002 the EES helped to make the commitment to gender equality more visible by including equal opportunities between women and men as the then fourth pillar of the Employment Guidelines and by including gender mainstreaming as one of the guidelines of the EES (G 19). During this earlier period gender equality was on the agenda of both Italy's and Denmark's governments' agenda. However, the study showed that even though the EES includes significant learning-promoting mechanisms there is not enough comprehensive statistical data and information available to confirm that changes at national level are directly linked to the implementation of the EES. During the first years of implementation of the EES gender equality was not top of the agenda of the Czech Republic's government. This is explained in part by the legacy of the socialist regime and, linked to it, by an aversion to social intervention and in part by the restructuring and privatization processes which have brought about some significant social losses, including a rapid and spiralling increase in female unemployment.

Following the disappearance of the Equal Opportunities pillar and the subsequent removal of the gender-equality guideline Italy's, Denmark's and the Czech Republic's NAP and NRP Reports seem to have placed less emphasis on gender-equality measures, the

---

32 For a critique of the notion of modernization in labour law, see Sciarra (2007).

primary focus being adaptability and "flexicurity". The focus on ALMPs and "flexicurity" is not surprising. The reforms of the welfare state respond to the changes under way in (post)modern society and they aim at strengthening the ability of the welfare state to alleviate new social risks in conditions of permanent economic austerity (Sirovátka 2008). Substantive welfare state provisions as well as the governance of public policy are continually confronted with new challenges. Nevertheless, it remains unclear why the security element is still weak and why the gender dimension seems to have lost importance in governmental policies and measures, given the increased feminization of the labour market and the societal changes brought about by globalization and transnationalization processes which have led to a dual-earner family model in all three countries. At European level, gender mainstreaming and gender equality have lost visibility in the format of the new Integrated Guidelines. As stated by Fagan *et al.* (2006: 586) 'this new format has made it even more apparent how much political and capacity building is needed if gender equality is to be mainstreamed into employment policy as well as economic and social policies'. There is a need, therefore, for some reform of the Integrated Guidelines to reinforce the gender dimension of employment policies. At the same time, the current situation of gender equality and gender mainstreaming confirm the fact that problems concerning the implementation of concrete measures for ensuring the mainstreaming of gender issues and for promoting equality cannot be explained solely as a consequence of the redesign of the EES.[33] The comparative analysis of Italy's, Denmark's and the Czech Republic's labour markets, welfare and family structure showed that a combination of factors such as, for example, the economic and social situation, cultural and societal norms and governments' political will may be key determinants of either positive or negative developments in the field of gender equality.

This chapter showed that the EES and, in particular, the European gender-mainstreaming strategy within it, have achieved very little success in Italy and the Czech Republic, even at discourse level.[34] Denmark on the other hand has been implementing a gender-mainstreaming approach at governmental level since the year 2000, although as seen earlier, the government in power has reduced the use of gender mainstreaming.

While this situation may be ascribed in part to the peculiarities of each country and, more broadly, to the embedded character of the welfare state they represent, there are also other reasons which hold true. According to Fodor (2006: 11) the ambitions of the European Union in the area of gender equality are hardly radical, just as the socialist

33 In this register, for example, Mr Laurent Aujean posits that, because of the complexity of gender equality and the fact that progress in this area can be seen only in the long term, it is difficult for the Commission to establish when a recommendation should be made to a given Member State; for example, should it be made when gender statistics are available? But even then there are two sets of problems: first, their reliability and, second, the extent to which quantitative factors truly reflect positive change from the perspective of substantive gender equality. Interview with Laurent Aujean, Unit G/1, Equality between Men and Women, DG Employment, European Commission, Brussels, 4 December 2008.

34 Mr Paolo Sestito (Director of the Research Unit of the Bank of Italy and formerly Chief Economic Adviser to the Ministry of Labour and Social Affairs of Italy) argues that generally the EES has fostered the promotion of domestic processes that had already been launched during the 1990s prior to the creation of the EES. This is also confirmed by Mr Luciano Forlani, official of the Italian Ministry of Labour and Social Affairs, who at the time of writing the book is also a member of EMCO. Interview of 16 October 2008. While confirming the significance of the Employment Strategy at discourse level Mr Sestito posits, on a more critical note, that this has not always been beneficial. For example, the *ad hoc* committee that was set up at the end of the 1990s to monitor labour market trends in Italy had suggested the adoption of measures which addressed certain problems peculiar to the Italian labour market. They were not always considered to be in tune with the objectives of the EES and, therefore, had to be "adjusted" accordingly without taking into account whether they would still tackle the problems of the Italian labour market. Interview of 1 October 2008, Rome.

state's emancipation campaign fell far short of a true reorganization of gender roles or the division of labour between men and women. The stated goal of EC gender-equality policies is to include women into the labour market – without changing, however, the underpinning principles and philosophies of the labour market. In other words, without attempting to redefine our understanding of what it means to work or to have a career. These concepts are defined in a way that fits the life course of people who can devote their full time and energy to their career, typically men. Women, who are more likely than men to take care of others, do not really fit that mould. As a result, women cannot participate in the labour market on an equal footing with men (*idem*). If such is the case at European level, it is hardly surprising then that we find gender stereotyping in all of the three countries under analysis. Overall, gender inequality is still carved into the very structures of the labour market and EU policies which promote women's participation without changing those structures will not achieve substantive gender equality. In this context, the chapter has shown that the EES and equally the Lisbon Strategy with their focus on process rather than substance can achieve little.

Moreover, in terms of participatory democracy the chapter showed that only in Denmark do the social partners and NGOs play an active role in the definition and implementation of gender-equality measures. This has been facilitated by the country's industrial relations system and thus there is little or no evidence suggesting that the EES has promoted "bottom-to-top" and decentralized forms of policy making. Non-governmental actors have not seen their role increase in significance since the launch of the EES. They have little power to achieve any systematic enforcement of their political agenda. Hence the gender-mainstreaming strategy promoted at European level clearly falls short of its participatory element and it remains largely "top-down" driven.

Overall, the emergence of New Governance practices and processes in CEECs has been characterized by divergence from the old Member States (Bruszt 2008). In part this may be explained by the socialist legacy of centralized governmental action (Grzegorz Grosse and Kolarska-Bobińska 2008). On the other hand, the Copenhagen Criteria of EU accession encouraged those countries to build the institutions of a functioning domestic market order. This process, as we have seen, was largely about strengthening central state capacities to uphold economic freedoms and to administer and regulate domestic markets rather than about empowering non-state and sub-state actors with the capacity to participate in addressing social and economic problems or co-ordinate developmental planning (Bruszt 2002). More specifically, institutional divergence between old and new Member States has been primarily represented by stronger reliance on state action and hierarchy, with weak and fragmented local government. Moreover, Grzegorz Grosse and Kolarska-Bobińska (2008) argue that New Governance processes by relying to a large extent on informal co-ordination, communication and negotiations may run the risk of reinforcing certain pathological practices in public administrations in CEECs precisely because of their informal nature.

Hence, with its focus on process, broadly defined goals and basic guidelines to achieve them, OMC processes such as the EES and the Jobs and Growth Strategy do not seem to offer much hope from the perspective of strengthening the "European social model" and the substantiation of social rights. Moreover, the chapter has showed that the shift towards a "workfare" approach to social rights has been particularly detrimental to the security element of "flexicurity" and gender-equality rights.

7 An assessment of the first ten years of the European Employment Strategy

1 Introduction

This chapter provides a thorough and critical evaluation of the EES and, in particular, it brings together the theoretical and empirical findings of the book to assess the legitimacy and effectiveness of the Employment Strategy in the wider context of EU social governance. In particular, the chapter examines the main strengths and weaknesses of the EES and its implementation through the OMC within the economic constitution and the overarching economic objectives of the European Union. It then utilizes the governance model elaborated in Chapter 2 which aims at strengthening the relationship between New Governance, law and constitutionalism. It is posited that such a renewed relationship may help overcome the EES's regulatory deficiencies without incorporating it into the "command and control" rationale of the classical modes of governance within the Community Method. The application of the above hybrid governance model could also provide the conditions for solving some of the more complex problems concerning the European Union.

The chapter maintains that the EES has important functions of promotion and mediation at discourse and cognitive levels which are made operational through periodic monitoring, supervision and peer pressure and also by fostering an open-ended learning process via the exchange of best practice. However, the analysis also shows that the limitations of the EES are mostly to be associated with the intrinsic weaknesses of the Strategy as a non-binding co-ordination process which inhibits its ability to perform these functions effectively. Hence the claim put forward is that rather than attempting to change its structure and mode of operation, a way of improving its overall functioning, including its learning-producing capacities and participatory forms of governance, is by strengthening its relationship with EU law and constitutionalism.

The chapter, therefore, puts forward a twofold proposal. First, it suggests a strengthening of the role of both European and national parliaments in the setting of a meta-governance framework which would introduce more transparency and facilitate scrutiny of measures, be it political or judicial. Second, it suggests creating a stronger relationship between the EES and EC social policy through the adoption of Framework Directives on the basis of the information retrieved through the NRPs process and in accordance with basic social rights and social standards recognized in international and European social rights conventions.

The chapter is structured as follows. The first section analyzes the relationship between the EES, the EMU, the Internal Market, EC competition policy and the EC state aid regime and shows how the potential conflict with these other areas of EU law and policy may seriously undermine the effective operation of the EES. The chapter then proceeds to assessing the EES on the basis of the theoretical and empirical analysis undertaken in the previous chapters of the book on the basis of the governance model developed in Chapter 2. In so doing, it seeks to answer the question put forward at the end of Chapter 5, namely whether it is possible to identify a theory of governance, for example democratic experimentalism or directly deliberative polyarchy or reflexive harmonization, which may be apposite to describe the democratic functioning of OMC processes.

2 The relationship between the European Employment Strategy and the European Monetary Union, the Internal Market, EC competition policy and state aid

After its initial pioneering phase, the EES has now entered a period of consolidation. Its rapid development during ten years of implementation through the OMC into an institutionalized Community governance process, now part of the Lisbon Strategy, has proved it to be a valid tool for keeping employment and growth high on the agenda of both the European Union and the Member States. At the same time though its coexistence with other EU policies concerning the economic sphere of European integration, namely the EMU project, the Internal Market, EC competition policy and state aid, is not without problems and, as the ensuing analysis will show, they seriously undermine the effectiveness of the EES.

With regard to the EMU, the creation of a "euro zone" has entailed a reconfiguration of macroeconomic policy instruments available to Member States. As Begg (2002: 4) argues, 'the advent of monetary union reinforces the case for the EU level to play a more extensive role in employment policy, particularly in developing an overarching framework within which local actors can deal with employment problems'. In particular, increasing the free movement of goods, capital and labour reduces the legal restrictions for economic actors and national public expenditure to finance social security systems could be ineffective because of labour and capital mobility.

The promotion of ALMPs at national level is an important element of the strategy, especially with regard to employability and equal opportunities policies (Council of the European Union 2002).[1] The horizontal objective of lifelong learning clearly requires Member States to adopt ALMPs, since it calls for an increase in human resources investments, higher levels of participation in education and training and the provision of incentives to adopt employment-friendly tax policies. Because of the way the strategy has been conceived, that is, as a supply-side strategy, it must avoid any obstacles to the operation of the EMU. It therefore seems difficult to reject the argument that EU social policy, and in particular the EES, remain anchored and dependent to the objectives and requirements of the EMU project. The combined proviso of Articles 126 EC and 128(2) EC provides that national reports and national employment policies have to be consistent with the BEPGs, pursuant to Article 99(2) EC. In addition, whereas non-compliance with the obligations provided in Article 104(9) and (10) EC and in the SGP[2] entails the application of legal sanctions, violation of the Employment Guidelines, on the contrary, is not complemented with any legal sanctions. Moreover, the provisions on EMU do not take sufficiently into consideration the profound structural and economic problems of the

1 E.g. G 1, 2, 3, 4, 6 and 17.
2 See, further, Chapter 3.

Member States. Deakin and Reed (2000: 98) argue that stability rather than growth is the priority of the misnamed SGP. The ECB's main mandate is to secure price stability[3] even though Article 105(1) EC does provide that 'the ESCB shall support the general economic policies in the Community with a view of contributing to the achievement of the objectives of the Community as laid down in Article 2'. Moreover, the ECB does not have the dual mandate that the Federal Reserve has in the United States, which can also focus on unemployment if the economic trend so requires. In addition, the SGP forces Member States to reduce their public expenditure on social security and makes it harder to implement welfare state reforms because the national budget, being subject to constraints, cannot supply for transitions towards new labour market reforms (Begg 2002: 6). Hence, during a period of economic recession the implementation of the EES may be seriously undermined, given the constraints imposed on Member States' budgets by the Treaty provisions on EMU and by the SGP.

With regard to the Internal Market, Syrpis (2001) has effectively explained how situations of conflict may arise between the objectives of the Internal Market and those of the European Union's social policy regime. In so doing, Syrpis uses the ruling of the *Tobacco Advertising Directive* case,[4] to emphasize how tensions may arise between the legislature and the judiciary and between discourses of flexibility and harmonization. In this case the European Court implicitly held that the mere possibility that there may be differences between the laws of the Member States such as to affect trade between them is sufficient to call for Community competence under Article 95 EC. Syrpis also shows how the European Court has often limited Member States' autonomy in order to ensure the completion of the Internal Market.

Begg (2002: 3) maintains that from an economic perspective the need for employment policy decreases with higher levels of market integration since asymmetrical shocks may be hampered and fluctuations severely reduced. Moreover, financial market integration may reduce regional specific shocks as a result of portfolio diversification and cross-border credit. The United States is a case in point (Asdrubali *et al.* 1996; Melitz and Zumer 1999). The problem with regard to the European Union is that while the EMU reduces the exchange rate instability it does not solve the problem of country-specific shocks, but simply "reallocates" them. Furthermore, fostering more free movement of goods, capital and labour reduces economic actors' legal restrictions (Begg 2002: 4) and fiscal policies aimed at favouring social security systems could be ineffective because of labour and capital mobility.

The European Court's approach above can be seen also in relation to other cases. The European Court's case law has been incoherent, sometimes subjecting social policy and social rights to securing the functioning of the Internal Market, particularly in the area of collective action and collective bargaining. In the *Maurissen* case[5] the ECJ defined the freedom to join a trade union of Community officials as a 'general principle of labour law applicable within the Community legal order'.[6] On the contrary, in *Commission v. France* the Court subjected the right to collective action and freedom of association to the free

---

3 See Article 105 EC.
4 See Case C-376/98 *Germany v. European Parliament and Council* [2000] ECR I-8419.
5 See Joined Cases C-193/87 and C-194/87 *Henri Maurissen and European Public Service Union v. Court of Auditors of the European Communities* [1990] ECR I-114.
6 *Ibid.*, para. 20.

movement of goods.[7] In three Dutch cases[8] the ECJ stated that collective agreements which by virtue of their nature and purpose have social policy objectives do not fall within the scope of EC competition rules.[9] Thus the ECJ seems to have suggested that in some situations the social dimension *per se* might take priority over the economic dimension. However, a closer look reveals a different picture. In particular, the Court's interpretation of some Treaty provisions in the *Albany* case has been subject to criticism. Vousden (2000: 182) argues that 'the Court's exemption of the collective agreements from the scope of Article 81 EC (formerly Article 85 EC) was justified on the ground that the subject matter of such agreements – remuneration – made a direct contribution to the improvement of working conditions'. However, the reasoning did not clearly distinguish between national and European law or between national and European social partners. It also implied that collective agreements do not violate competition law if they are stipulated in the context of the traditional subject matter of collective bargaining, that is, wages and working conditions (*ibid.*: 189). This implies that national measures aimed at modernizing work organization outside these traditional patterns might fall foul of EC law (*ibid.*: 189–190). Thus not only is social policy *sensu lato* still subject to competition law (Hervey 2000), but some of the objectives of the EES, namely those concerning adaptability, may be seriously undermined. As observed in Chapter 4, while the European Court performed a balancing act between social policy and competition law objectives it refused to consider collective bargaining as the exercise of a fundamental social right forming part, as such, of the nucleus of minimum preconditions for an autonomous labour law system. Moreover, in the *Viking*,[10] *Laval*,[11] *Rüffert*[12] and *Commission v. Luxembourg*[13] cases the Court, using the market access approach, said that the collective and governmental action in these cases constituted "restriction" on free movement and so breached Articles 43 and 49 EC even though in *Viking* and *Laval* it had recognized that the right to strike was a fundamental right which formed an integral part of the general principles of Community law. It also seemed to suggest that the fundamental economic freedoms of the Treaty are superior to fundamental rights and are not just meant to prevent protectionist discrimination against foreign suppliers but, more broadly, to provide a bulwark against any government or trade union measures that might, in some way, impede the exercise of those freedoms.

The objectives of the EES may also potentially be in conflict with the European Union's state aid regime.[14] Article Article 87(1) EC (formerly 83(1) EC) prohibits nationally granted state aid. Articles 87(2) and 87(3) EC allow exemptions or derogations from paragraph 1. The exemptions listed in Article 87(2) EC are mandatory; they cover aid of a social nature granted to individuals, financial support in the event of natural disasters, and aid to parts of Germany affected by the division of that country. The exemptions listed in Article 87(3) EC, instead, are discretionary and they cover aid promoting economic development in

---

7 See Case C-265/95 [1997] ECR I-6959; see also Orlandini (2000).

8 See Joined Cases C-115/97 and C-117/97 *Brentjens' Handelsonderneming v. Stichting Bedrijfspensioenfonds voor de Handel in Bouwmaterialen* [1999] ECR I-6025; Case C-219/97 *Maatschappij Drijvende Bokken v. Stichting Pensioenfonds voor de Vervoer- en Havenbedrijven* [1999] ECR I-6121; Case C-67196 *Albany International v. Stichting Bedrijfspensioenfonds Texttielindustrie* [1999] ECR I-5751.

9 See para. 60, *Albany*; para. 57, *Brentjens'*; para. 47, *Drijvende Bokken*. See also Case C-222/98 *Van der Woude* [2000] ECR I-7111, para. 25.

10 Case C-438/05 *Viking Line v. ITF* (11 December 2007).

11 Case C-341/05 *Laval v. Svenska Byggnadsarbetareforbundet* (18 December 2007).

12 Case C-346/06 *Rüffert v. Land Niedersachsen* (3 April 2008).

13 Case C-319/06 *Commission v. Luxembourg* (19 June 2008).

14 See Articles 87–89 EC (ex-Articles 83–85 EC).

certain areas; aid for projects of a common European interest or to remedy a serious disturbance in a national economy; certain sectoral or regional aid; aid to promote cultural and heritage conservation; and any other aid specified by QMV of the Council on the basis of a proposal of the Commission.

The main objective of EC state aid is to reduce levels of national subsidy and avoid the damaging effects of excessive subsidy within the Internal Market. The Commission has significant discretion in taking state aid decisions (European Commission 1999b). In the preliminary investigation phase, the Commission bases its decisions on the "market investor principle" (Bernitsas 1993: 110–123), according to which the measure is not classified as being state aid when the state acts as a private investor. Assuming that state aid is said to exist, the decision as to whether to grant the exemption or not will be dependent on whether it falls under one of the exemption clauses provided by Article 87 EC. The ECJ has stated, however, that, where there are no doubts, state aid must not be approved.[15] In the second stage, once the preliminary investigation has been made, the criterion used by the Commission to formulate its decision is the "compensatory justification principle", which involves weighting the pros and the cons of an aid (European Commission 1981). More precisely, this principle involves assessing whether the contribution by the beneficiary of the aid to the achievement of the Community objectives is above the normal interplay of market forces. Because of the broad discretion given to the Commission, Cini (2000) argues that the regulation of state aid allows for the balancing of the effects of legal certainty against a more flexible approach.

Under the Integrated Guidelines (e.g. 17–19) Member States are called upon to adopt incentive measures in the form of tax breaks and subsidies to encourage firms to invest in training courses that will improve the skills of their employees. Aid can be designed to restructure an undertaking, to rescue an undertaking, or to help it with operating costs. In general terms, operating aid that relieves an undertaking of costs that it would have to bear in normal circumstances without any changes of a technical nature or in its structure is in most cases rejected by the Commission and the European Court,[16] unless it concerns specific regional or sectoral problems (European Commission 1998d). Article 87(3)(a) EC states that 'aid to promote the economic development of areas where the standard of living is abnormally low or where there is serious underemployment' may be considered compatible with the Common Market. The Commission and the ECJ both maintain that the seriousness of a regional problem must be judged in the Community context and not in the national context (European Commission 1998d).[17] Article 87(3)(c) EC provides that 'aid to facilitate the development of certain economic activities or of certain economic areas, where such aid does not adversely affect trading conditions to an extent contrary to the common interest' may be compatible with the Common Market. Craig and de Búrca (2002: 1150) maintain that this is the provision through which Member States can seek to justify aid to a particular depressed region as judged by national criteria. The European Court, however, has held that this national criterion still needs to be assessed in terms of the impact of aid on Community trade and sectors.[18] The criteria applied by the Commission when examining the compatibility of national regional aid with the Common Market

---

15 See Case C-198/91 *William Cook v. Commission* [1993] ECR I-2486, the "*Cook* case".
16 See Case T-459/93 *Vlaams Gewest v. Commission* [1998] ECR II-717.
17 See also Case 730/79 *Philip Morris Holland v. Commission* [1980] ECR 2671.
18 See Cases T-126–127/96 *BFM and EFIM v. Commission* [1998] ECR II-3437.

under Article 87(3)(a) and (c) EC have been codified in the 1998 guidelines on national regional aid (European Commission 1998d).

The aid normally does not qualify under Article 87(3) EC if it is not linked to initial investment, to job creation and/or to the restructuring of the activities of the undertaking concerned. The aim must be the development of a particular sector or region and not the individual undertaking. Incentives, which are not open to all firms, fall foul of Article 87 EC. The same approach is used for incentive measures that aim at providing employment aid or subsidies to enterprises to encourage them to recruit or to retain certain employees. Hence subsidizing only some firms may potentially distort or hinder competition (Article 87(1) EC). In addition, the advantages of the aid in terms of a less favoured region must outweigh the resulting distortions of competition

As Evans (1997: 324–328; see also Hancher *et al.* 1999) points out in the context of state aid, the Commission has evaluated in more positive terms certain types of training and retraining aid and employment aid schemes. Moreover, the Commission has also adopted various guidelines to help Member States identify forms of aid that will not be potentially prohibited by the Commission. In 2006 it simplified the approval of regional aid by adopting a block exemption Regulation for regional investment aid (European Commission 2006e). Member States no longer have to notify regional investment aid schemes to the Commission if they comply with the new Regional Aid Guidelines for 2007–2013 (European Commission 2006f) and the approved regional aid map for 2007–2013. In 2006 regional aid maps identifying the disadvantaged regions eligible for aid and the maximum aid intensities allowed in these regions were approved for eighteen Member States, indicating that the Commission is quite lenient in its application of the criteria for eligibility. Furthermore, new Risk Capital Guidelines (European Commission 2006g) have been adopted, allowing Member States to improve access to finance for SMEs. They cover risk capital measures for investment in SMEs in their early and expansion stages. These guidelines form an important part of the Commission's Lisbon Strategy (European Commission 2005b) as they assist SMEs, which are seen as central to the economy of most Member States in terms of spurring economic growth and creating lasting employment. In addition, the Commission adopted a new *de minimis* Regulation (European Commission 2006h) exempting small subsidies from the requirement to be cleared by the Commission in advance. Under the new Regulation, aid of up to €200,000 granted over three fiscal years will not be regarded as state aid.

The criterion used is whether the training or employment aid schemes have positive externalities. With regard to employment aid, the distinction, therefore, is "maintaining jobs" and "creating jobs", the latter being considered as having positive externalities because it promotes employment growth (European Commission 2006f). In this context, Ekengren and Jacobsson (2000) have analyzed a state aid case in Sweden concerning the request of the Commission to the Swedish government to end its subsidy of a temporary special reduction in the payroll fees scheme for engagement of long-term unemployment people which according to the Commission was unacceptable because it applied only to some private companies even though the subsidy concerned "job creation". This case clearly illustrates the potential clash between the Internal Market requirements and legitimate national employment measures.

The same considerations apply with regard to training aid (European Commission 2001f). Training aid is, in general, subject to a less strict approach because it is considered to have positive external effects for society as a whole and also because it enhances the competitiveness of the Community. On the basis of the principle of positive externalities, training aid is subdivided into "general training" and "specific training". The "intensity" of aid, that is, the 'gross aid amount expressed as a percentage of the project's eligible costs' foreseen by the Regulation, differs depending on whether it concerns "general training" or "specific training". The "intensity" of aid is higher in the case of "general training", that is, 50 per cent for large enterprises or 70 per cent for SMEs for general training; 25 per cent for large enterprises and 35 per cent for SMEs for specific training. Moreover, there is no exemption from notification at all for aid exceeding €1 million. When a "general training" aid scheme is permitted, the Regulation requires the firm concerned to invest also in the type of transferable skills which firms are usually reluctant to subsidize. This is explained by the fact that the latter 'provides qualifications, which are largely transferable to other firms or fields of work', while specific training is 'directly and principally applicable to the employee's present or future position in the assisted firm' and provides qualifications, which 'are not or are only to a limited extent transferable to other firms or field of work'.[19] Ball (2001) highlights a series of problems with the Regulation on training aid. First, the boundary between "general training" and "specific training" is difficult to establish. Second, it is not always the case that "general training" is preferable to "specific training". Third, the "positive externalities principle" and the focus on "general training" do not always take into account the interests and needs of the individual employees. The possibility for Member States to subsidize either employment aid directed towards "maintaining jobs" or towards "specific training" schemes may be limited by EC state aid provisions. At the eve of the 2001 Laeken Summit, German Chancellor Schröder, speaking at the opening of a car plant in Dresden, in one of the poorer East German *Länder*, highlighted the fact that the Commission's policy of limiting Member States' right to offer selective regional assistance to attract new business to poorer regions was "hard to understand" (Spinant 2001).

However, besides these problems, which cannot be brushed aside, the above analysis also seems to indicate a more positive scenario: that while potential clashes between the EES and EC state aid provisions could have been stronger in the first years of implementation of the Employment Strategy, when its orientation was clearly more socially driven, since its overhaul in 2003 and 2005 and the simplification introduced in the eligibility criteria for receiving state aid (as well as certain measures supporting SMEs), the potential conflict between the two policy areas is not so significant as it first may seem. In addition, the Employment Guidelines included in the Integrated Guidelines seem to orient national policies towards job creation rather than measures aimed at ensuring employment protection. Moreover, EC Institutions have become more aware of these potential conflicts (Ball 2001: 361–362; Pochet 1999). The Employment Guidelines have been adopted by a joint ECOFIN/Social Affairs Council for several years now. Already in 2002 the BEPGs emphasized the importance of investing part of public expenditure in structural reforms aimed at investing in research, development and growth (Council of the European Union 2002a). In addition, on the occasion of the Barcelona European Council (2002), Member States agreed that 'automatic stabilizers should be allowed to play symmetrically, both in upturns and in downturns, provided the 3 per cent of GDP limit is not breached in downturns. This means in particular that in expansionary phases growth dividends should be fully reaped.'

On a more critical note, however, the reduced "friction" between the EES and the EC state aid regime confirms the fact that the EES heralds a deregulatory agenda which bodes well for the overall competitiveness strategy of the European Union. The Lisbon Strategy

---

19 *Ibid.*, Article 2(d).

itself presents internal contradictions, as it aims at achieving a set of objectives that inherently clash with one another. On the one hand, there are a series of objectives aimed at transforming the European Union into the most dynamic knowledge-based economy in the world and aimed at ensuring a fully fledged Internal Market (and with it the liberalization projects of specific sectors of the market, notably energy, transport and public utilities). On the other hand, there are the strategic goals aimed at modernizing the "European social model" and at reaching full employment (although this objective has been set aside) and increased levels of social cohesion. Another potential conflict may arise between the objective of employment creation and that of modernizing the social protection systems of the Member States. Member States cannot at the same time reduce public deficits, keep the overall level of taxes stable, or decrease it in some cases, invest in long-term growth factors, such as, education, research, infrastructure, etc., and maintain the level of expenditure on social security. As explained at length in previous chapters of the book, this fundamental contradiction is inherent in how the Lisbon Strategy has been built, as it reconciles opposite ideological stances: deregulation *versus* social intervention. In its Resolution on the Commission's Communication entitled *A Concerted Strategy for Modernizing Social Protection* ETUC (2000) criticized the fact that the Employment Guidelines emphasized the reduction of social/tax contributions or non-wage-related costs without including alternative sources of funding for losses of financial resources.

It remains to be seen to what extent the foregoing potential conflicts between the objectives of the EES and those of EMU, the Internal Market, EC competition policy and state aid may undermine the Employment Strategy. The above analysis has showed, however, that social policy remains the Cinderella of European integration.

One possible scenario for avoiding this situation which I suggested elsewhere (Velluti 2003) could be by establishing a stronger relationship between soft co-ordination processes such as the EES and the more traditional instruments based on hard law used within the Community Method. In this context, the social partners could play a central role: with their participation in the decision-making process, pursuant to the provisions laid out in Title XI of the Treaty, they represent the link between the European level and the national and local levels and could thus monitor the effective implementation of EU law at the lower levels of policy making, including the sectoral and inter-sectoral levels. For instance, Framework Agreements signed by the European social partners have already been transformed into EU secondary law via a Decision of the Council.[20]

3 A critical evaluation of the strengths and weaknesses of the European Employment Strategy

The EES has contributed in a variety of different ways to the reconceptualization of EU social policy and to the development of a "European social model". In particular, it has brought employment to the forefront of European and national debates. The EES has also created a common integrated framework for structural reform which enables synergies to be achieved between a wide range of areas ranging from tax and social benefits to equal opportunities, training and education, lifelong learning and "flexicurity".

As shown in Chapter 6, policy co-ordination, peer review and the iterative process of the EES have helped to establish a platform at European level where Member States which

---

20 See Chapter 4.

belong to different welfare state clusters can discuss possible solutions to common shared problems in the employment field. Among the most salient features used in the EES there are what Jacobsson (2004) has defined as "discursive regulatory mechanisms" which although not unique to this method are herein employed systematically. In particular, the EES provides a common cognitive framework for understanding and describing problems in national labour markets and for identifying workable solutions which are adaptable to the different socio-economic context of different welfare systems. Thus concepts and categories developed in the context of the iterative process of the EES are increasingly used in national labour market policy discourse and have had at least a symbolic impact nationally (*ibid.*). Moreover, peer review and critique are now seen by the Member States as a legitimate exercise and have been institutionalized as a governance procedure to take place on a regular basis.[21] Similarly, Ashiagbor (2005) talks about the emergence of a common discourse among elite actors. She argues that we can identify a transfer effect generated by the EES via the OMC which although less coercive than the one resulting from traditional hard law measures may change policy discourse within Member States, altering the boundaries of what is considered an acceptable range of policy choices for Member States (Ashiagbor 2005: 233). In this regard, the EES may be defined as an autonomy-preserving policy instrument to address common "European" issues while at the same time respecting the diversity of Member States' industrial relations systems. The aim of Community intervention in this area 'is not to constrict actors within a prescriptive framework, but to add value by organizing them in order to achieve shared policy ends' (Régent 2003: 198). Embedded in a policy environment which has removed their control over traditional instruments of macroeconomic policy, the EES is an attempt to lower the willingness of national governments and politicians to condone high unemployment and inactivity, and strengthen their resolve to engage in reform (Visser, 2002). According to Visser, by focusing on the employability of the workers in combination with adaptability policies, supply-side egalitarianism, on which the EES is premised, would make *ex post* political redistribution less pressing (Visser, 2002). However, as explained below, the EES has fallen short of reaching these initial expectations.

The EES may also promote new objectives on the EU agenda. As seen in Chapter 4, previous EU social policy and legislation were oriented to labour market policies linked to the completion of the Internal Market and the creation of EMU without taking into account core issues of national social policies. On the contrary, the EES aims at addressing issues that directly affect national employment policies and industrial relations systems. This is explained by the fact that the more nationally sensitive a subject, and the more difficult to resolve at national level, the more likely are Member States to become involved in an EU co-ordination procedure. Particularly with the Lisbon Strategy, a policy paradigm emphasizing prevention, activation and lifelong learning has clearly been established. It follows that the legal significance of national reports lies in the *way* Member States interpret and use the concepts developed in the EES as well as how the Commission and the Council use the information and knowledge gathered, transforming them into standards and structural indicators which Member States then use to develop their labour and employment policies. In this context, therefore, the EES may be said to promote the creation of new employment and labour market paradigms. This has certainly been the case with the Czech Republic, which started changing its employment and labour market policies in accordance with the Employment Guidelines of the EES even before becoming

---

21   E.g. visit <http://hwww.mutual-learning-employment.net/>.

a member of the Union, through the JAP exercise as well as twinning programmes on equal opportunities and social dialogue. While this was part of a strategic convergence plan on the part of the Czech Republic to secure accession, it has also led to a change in the rationale and approach to labour market measures.

The EES has also fostered new institutional arrangements and a rethinking of national policy making. As shown in Chapter 6, the NAP/NRP process has entailed further co-operation between different administrations and the rationalization of employment and labour market policies, one important aspect being the increase in expenditure for employment-related policies. This has been the case of all three countries, namely Italy, Denmark and the Czech Republic, independently of the type of welfare state to which they belong and their economic and social situation. For example, in the context of the promotion of equal opportunities, in the year 2000 the Danish Ministry of Social Affairs started working, together with the National Association of Municipal Authorities and the National Union of Childcare and Youth Workers, in order to initiate a joint project for the improvement of child care facilities. Moreover, in areas that are covered by the Employment Guidelines the EES does not always demand convergence: many of the guidelines leave the states with a substantial level of discretion with regard to the ways of adopting the measures concerned. It may be argued, therefore, that the EES does aim at achieving legislative harmonization, but it is mostly convergence of results rather policies. In this regard, the EES presents the same intrinsic logic as a Directive.

The EES has also influenced the operation of the ESF. Since the launch of the EES, the European Commission has considered it necessary to ensure co-ordination between the EES and the ESF priorities as well as consistency of assistance from the Structural Funds with employment policy. The ESF not only represents a means of financial support for the EES but also shares a similar type of functional logic in that the ESF promotes and encourages partnerships at different levels and the exchange of ideas and best practice (Régent 2003: 202). The EES may be defined, therefore, as a process within the process, that is, a non-binding co-ordination process within the broader context of the Community Method.

The EES, however, has various shortcomings, some of which are inherent in its soft law nature. The existence of these weaknesses has seriously undermined the effectiveness of the EES. First, the very nature of the Employment Strategy as a non-binding legal instrument does not allow accurate assessment of the results achieved, given that national measures might not refer to the Employment Guidelines for their adoption and that many elements of the EES are already part of national policy programmes, as in the case of Denmark, or national reports merely reformulating national programmes. Second, the subordination of the implementation of the EES to the economic and political situation within the various Member States combined with its soft law nature does not guarantee its further development in moments of economic recession or political instability. For example, in Italy the Employment Strategy, while representing a major stimulus for the adoption of active and preventive measures and the creation of *ad hoc* committees,[22] has not contributed to solving the country's major structural problems. This is due to delays in the implementation or even in the non-implementation of some of the Employment Guidelines and to the form of regulation, which remains largely centralized in Italy, but also to the fact that the EES does not sufficiently take into account the Italian structural

---

22 For a detailed analysis of the most important institutional developments in Italy since 1997, both before and after the launch of the EES, see Ferrera and Gualmini (2002).

problems, which cannot be solved exclusively with supply-side policies but need to be complemented with demand-side policies that take into account the adoption of macro-economic policies.[23] The extent to which the political situation in a Member State may hamper further developments (independently of whether the EC measure in question is soft or hard) is illustrated by the Czech Republic. As seen in Chapter 6, at the time of writing the country is having significant problems in passing the Anti-discrimination Framework Act. Hence, while the JAP exercise and subsequently the NAP/NRP process may be said to have fostered new institutional arrangements with regard to gender equality, they have been unable to introduce change in the country's approach to this policy area following its transition to an open market economy.

In addition, developing a transnational system of target setting, benchmarking and peer review with limited enforcement powers may allow Member States to reduce the possibility of unexpected and unwanted consequences, that is, of real structural changes in the areas where the OMC is implemented (Chalmers and Lodge, 2003).

Another weakness of the EES is the paucity of specific procedural rules and detailed guidelines, the lack of clear information on the exercise of benchmarking, chiefly on how parameters and structural indicators are selected and applied, the absence of a clear definition of distribution of competence, particularly at the national level, and the absence of a rule of law approach which, combined with the lack of transparency, does not ensure accountability and judicial scrutiny. The main criticism voiced by many lawyers is that the EES adds confusion as to who should be held accountable as well as raising doubts about its participatory democracy element, given the limited and piecemeal involvement of certain actors and stakeholders of civil society. These new actors are for the most part excluded from the decision-making sphere and are given a more important role in the implementation side of policy making. In this sense, these actors may clearly be seen as being regulatory and legitimacy resources of the European Union. The whole process seems to be taking place between "elites for elites". Moreover, the top-down deliberative mode of governance – which the EES as well as the Lisbon Strategy essentially are – have been criticized for reducing associative pluralism and intra-organizational diversity, either by imposing an official policy paradigm, or by failing to co-opt in governance actors who do not comply or fit with it. In particular, with regard to participatory democracy and social partnership, these strategies do not provide the coherent institutional framework that can encourage decentralized self-regulation in an accountable and democratic way ensuring the participation of different actors, both state and non-state actors. Even where the implementation of the employment guidelines appear to be mostly influential, such as in the case of Denmark, the EES had little direct relation with decisions made within the domestic labour market policy process, and the apparent success of the EES was mainly due to similar objectives.

Moreover, the whole process has been mainly administered at ministerial level and in most countries parliamentary bodies have been excluded from the EES process without the possibility of any decision-making input in the preparation of national reports. Knowledge about the EES is generally not well diffused in national or sub-national labour market administrations or in civil society (Jacobsson and Vifell 2007). In particular, the involvement of social partners has been more formalistic and passive, that is, more a matter of information than real consultation or negotiation with the governments. The only

---

23 I am indebted to Dr Paolo Sestito for raising this point. Dr Sestito has been a member of the Italian Committee for the Drafting of the National Action Plan for Employment; see also Sestito (2002).

exception seems to be Denmark, where the social partners, particularly in the first phase of the EES, have been actively involved in the drafting of the national reports. Recent studies show that there is greater participation, although the degree of the social partners' contribution varies according to the area taken into consideration and also depending on which management or labour representatives have been involved in the process (Jacobsson and Vifell, 2007). However, on the whole, the role of the social partners in the EES remains unsatisfactory. Casey (2005) argues that the strategy's contribution to the development of a social partnership approach has been disappointing. In his study he explains how this approach has not succeeded in depoliticizing employment-related problems from national contingencies. Moreover, the EES illustrates the elitist nature of social partnership in practice by including certain organizations and excluding others which may have hindered necessary reformulations of employment policy.

Moreover, in relation to the EES's mode of operation, the OMC, Büchs (2007: 144–145) argues that the role of the OMC in national policy making is not democratically controlled. 'Government and opposition parties, social partners, NGOs and other political actors can and partially do refer to the OMC in order to strategically support their positions and demands by the OMC' (*ibid.*: 145). For example, unpopular decisions have been legitimized by the OMC in several Member States. The previous chapter documented that both Italy and the Czech Republic have used the EES to buttress their emphasis on labour market flexibility, especially the Italian government when it adopted the Biagi law, which simplified the rules on workers' dismissal and introduced many forms of atypical contracts that were not backed up by employment protection measures and the 2008 Green Paper on Welfare State Reform which has continued this process of flexibilization of the labour market.

This shift in emphasis has become more visible since the inclusion of the EES in the Lisbon Strategy, which particularly since its relaunch as "Lisbon II", focuses principally on growth, jobs (in numerical terms) and budget stability. 'The Lisbon Strategy has been reduced to an employment strategy and this employment strategy is itself limited to making labour markets more flexible and increasing labour supply' (Raveaud 2007: 429). Furthermore, in the context of the "flexicurity" debate, national governments have used the OMC in a rather unbalanced way favouring flexibility measures to the disadvantage of the security of the workers. In part this may be explained by the complexity of the flexicurity concept and in part by the fact that the concept itself has not been defined in clear terms by the European Commission. In addition, and linked to this, rather than promoting the "European social model" the evidence seems to indicate a rather different picture. In the difficult task of balancing *more* with *better* jobs the EES still remains anchored to increasing employment rates. The EES is still about 'increasing monetary incentives and developing the flexibility of labour contracts. Such orientations jeopardize other goals of the EES, such as gender equality and social inclusion' (*ibid.*: 430).

With regard to quality in relation to gender equality measures, the European Commission adopted a work–life balance package in 2008 with a focus on reconciling professional work with personal and family life. While the measures and legislative proposals are to be welcomed there is no reliance on a gender mainstreaming approach and they do little to tackle structural inequality. In essence they remain either gender neutral or they consider gender equality as being a "women's problem" doing little to emphasize the importance of ensuring substantive gender equality for the family as a whole. These measures, therefore, maintain the *status quo* and do not attempt to change the traditional approach to the gender contract or eliminate gender stereotyping. This combined with the focus on process rather than substance in the EES leaves ample discretion to the Member States as to the type of measures they can adopt. Hence, overall, 'instead of providing for its original goals of more and better jobs, eradicating poverty and more social equality, the OMC tends to assist Member States governments in adjusting their social systems to the prioritization of economic growth and international competitiveness' (Büchs (2007: 145)).

To sum up, there are several limitations to the operation of the EES, some of which are linked to the soft and non-binding nature of the OMC. From a legitimacy perspective, the most problematic aspect of the EES and its mode of operation, the OMC, is that its participatory element is weak. Hence the actors who participate, largely national civil servants, may not be held accountable by the electorate because the overall co-ordination process lacks transparency. This is particularly disconcerting given that national parliaments are not involved in the NRP process.

The above analysis clearly shows that the EES as it stands is far from ensuring input legitimacy (politics by the people) and, as a consequence, output legitimacy (politics for the people) as defined by Scharpf (1999). The problem with co-ordination processes such as the OMC is an excess focus on output legitimacy, that is, on whether the policies adopted coincide with the interests of the citizens affected by the measures and leaving aside the much more complex and controversial question of how to ensure input legitimacy. Achieving input legitimacy remains one of the most vexed and open questions of the European Union's regulatory system, affecting its very own existence. To some extent this is hardly surprising, given that it was initially created as an international economic organization and the shift towards developing a European common identity or "European demos" is relatively recent.

4 Strengthening the legitimacy and democratic quality of the European Employment Strategy

In Chapter 2 a theoretical model of co-regulation was put forward with the aim of reducing the putative weakness of New Governance for its lacking of accountability and judicial scrutiny. In particular, by strengthening the relationship between New Governance and EU constitutionalism social rights and labour standards could be built into the EES in order to counterbalance that weakness creating the basis for the justiciability of enacted measures. In this way a space for national diversity and experimentation would be preserved and the open method would be maintained intact without incorporating it into the "command and control" regulatory model of EU constitutionalism. It is posited that this could be achieved by strengthening the role of both the European and national parliaments and by strengthening the relationship between the EES and EC social policy. It is acknowledged at the outset that this proposal may find some opposition in some quarters or that it may be deemed unworkable. However, there is evidence suggesting that the hybrid model put forward is being implemented in practice in certain areas of EU law and policy (e.g. Trubek and Trubek 2007; Sabel and Zeitlin 2008).

This hybrid model – representing an ideal governance model – embraces a broad notion of democracy and it acknowledges the importance of state constitutionalism rather than transcending it while, at the same time, it acknowledges the challenges to the constitutional state as the primary unit of political authority and accepts the existence of a more heterarchical order. In this context, law's function is not solely prescriptive but also becomes facilitative and reconstitutive providing for a set of rules about the procedure, organization, and constitution of other social fields and subsystems. Both European and national parliaments could have a key role in setting a meta-governance frame defining objectives and procedures, monitoring progress towards agreed goals and revising the processes in light of the results achieved. Their involvement in New Governance, however, would require a transformation of their traditional role as legislators by passing framework legislation containing commitments to a broad set of goals such as OMC objectives, establishing administrative infrastructures to stimulate decentralized experimentation, monitor the efforts of local units to improve their performance against them, pool resulting information and set provisional standards in light of what they have learned; reviewing the results and revising framework objectives and administrative procedures accordingly (Zeitlin 2005: 224–225). This renewed role may give national legislators access to insights and tools for producing better legislation and provides them with grounds for criticizing governmental legislative and administrative measures (Duina and Raunio 2007; de Ruiter 2009). Moreover, this could generate what Sabel and Zeitlin (2008) have termed a "democratizing destabilization effect" and could also help to remove the primacy given to executive federalism which has empowered the governments and marginalized the European and national parliaments. In addition, both European and national courts would act both in their more traditional role as norm enforcers and in their renewed role as catalysts facilitating the creation of 'process values and legitimacy principles by the institutional actors responsible for norm elaboration within New Governance [. . .] providing an incentive structure for participation, transparency, principled decision making, and accountability which in turn shapes, directly and indirectly, the political and deliberative process' (Scott and Sturm 2007: 565). The governance model presented here has two dimensions – a national and a European dimension – which are strictly linked to one another.

On the national plane, the aim would be to combine mutual accountability with classical democratic and political accountability. National parliaments could set the meta-governance procedural rules and administrative tools that provide checks and balances ensuring *inter alia* for fair participation and for accountability in network forms of governance. National parliaments could also have the final say on policy outcomes and outputs, by being an effective locus of critical scrutiny over proposals formulated by governance networks, which have for their part the advantage of pooling expertise and of facilitating acceptance by stakeholders. The role of national parliaments could be strengthened by the creation of a "rule of reasons" provision which could serve as a basis for judicial review. Such a provision could require all committees, agencies, private standardization bodies and fixed actors within more informal regulatory networks to maintain and make public detailed records of the processes of decision making and give access to information and documents, thus ensuring transparency. In turn judicial review proceedings could be triggered by the standing of impartial bodies such as parliamentary committees rather than merely by individual *locus standi*.

This renewed concept of accountability would enable the more nebulous New Governance practices and processes to operate in a way which may be held more democratically accountable and responsive whilst ensuring governability, policy efficiency and remaining more representative of public needs and values. Moreover, this notion of accountability would not entail a return to the same substantive regulatory rationality of "command and control" of the classical forms of regulation. On the contrary, it would preserve and strengthen the structure and mechanisms of both classical and experimental forms of governance.

In this context law would retain an important and renewed role. As Walker observes:

> the very circumstances that challenge and dilute the problem-solving capacity and symbolic authority of law guarantee that it remains a precious currency. The

problems of co-ordination and legitimacy of the new flexible order are on such a scale that law, with its traditionally vast regulatory potential, will inevitably continue to be invoked as a means of containing and resolving crises. Moreover, as a deeply layered and richly resourced repository of traditional and cultural meanings, the legal form retains a "legitimacy credit" and a versatility even in the face of new and apparently discontinuous contexts of political organization and regulation.

(Walker 2000: 12)

On the European plane, the model's objective is to establish new bonds of association and political configuration in which New Governance and EU constitutionalism can happily coexist, thereby identifying the conditions necessary to assure and optimize effective voice and participation as well as ensuring the preservation and application of the rule of law and due process. In this context constitutionalism rather than representing a fixed legal framework provides the ground for a process of continuous renewal and dialogue in relation to a polity – the European Union – that is always in the course of negotiation and renegotiation.

The hybrid model of co-regulation proposed could be ensured through the development of Framework Directives such as the Water Framework Directive (WFD),[24] which represents 'one of the most significant examples of how a mixed system of New Governance and more traditional legal approaches creates a new type of law' (Trubek and Trubek 2007: 550). The WFD replaces more traditional types of Directives and combines 'classic top-down regulatory modes and legally binding requirements with decentralized, bottom-up, participatory and deliberative processes; iterative planning; horizontal networks; stakeholder participation; information pooling; sharing of best practice, and non-binding guidance' (*ibid.*).

The claim put forward henceforth is that the same type of hybrid form of governance could be developed in the area of employment. Specifically, the argument would run as follows. The Employment Strategy and the European Social Dialogue have both reached a period of consolidation. However, both processes, in spite of each representing a departure to some extent from the Community Method, have been operating in isolation. As explained in earlier parts of the book, each process has certain regulatory deficiencies which undermine its effective operation. Their input and output legitimacy could be strengthened by establishing a link between Title VIII and Title XI. Hence, rather than buttressing the dichotomy hard–soft law, the main objective is, on the contrary, to transcend the hard–soft law debate.

The Employment Guidelines cover policy areas which directly affect social rights. Although the guidelines do not have binding legal effects they may have nevertheless other legal effects such as creating legitimate expectations for the individuals, clarifying the content of certain hard law provisions, or structuring the discretion of certain institutions. As explained elsewhere (Velluti 2009) the chances of litigation arising from the Employment Guidelines is complex and in this context we can envisage two scenarios. In the case of legal disputes between Member States or between Member States and either the Commission or the Council or between the latter and the European Parliament, whether the ECJ will be able to consider the legality of New Governance processes is open to debate and lawyers are divided on the matter (e.g. Barbera, 2006; De Búrca, 2003; Hatzopoulos,

---

24 Council Directive 2000/60/EC; see further Holder and Scott (2006). For examples of other hybrid governance models, see Sabel and Zeitlin (2008).

2007; Strazzari, 2006). There are a series of legal and technical problems which will need to be taken into consideration should a case be brought before the European Court. There is also another scenario to be considered, as guidelines may lead to the adoption of binding measures at national level. In that case, both public and private applicants who feel that certain social rights may have been infringed by a domestic measure adopted pursuant to the Integrated Guidelines will need to follow the judicial rules of standing at national level. In the case of actions brought before national courts, the *Mangold* case seems to provide a possible new scenario for private litigants. As seen in Chapter 2, in *Mangold*,[25] a case concerning a horizontal dispute on age discrimination, the ECJ held that Directive 2000/ 78[26] embodied among others the principle of non-discrimination on grounds of age, which should be regarded as a general principle of Community law derived from international instruments and the constitutional traditions common to the Member States. In this way the European Court sidestepped once again the issue of horizontal direct effect of unimplemented Directives and enabled the German court to enforce this general principle of Community law which the Directive in question embodied. In particular, by adopting a teleological approach the European Court held that there is a prohibition on discrimination on grounds of age as a general principle of Community law independently of Directive 2000/78 which constitutes a part of the general principle of equal treatment as a fundamental right under Community law. The European Court seemed to be assuming that general principles of law are directly effective, advancing the proposition that they are capable of conferring substantive rights and imposing substantive obligations in legal relations between individuals. While it is difficult to predict what type of impact or influence *Mangold* will exert on how we conjure the legal effects of soft law in the wider context of enforcement of Community hard law measures, at the same time it cannot be denied that its implications for the interpretation of soft law by the ECJ may be very significant because this case tells us how far the ECJ is willing to go to ensure the respect of a general principle of constitutional value and essentially a fundamental right against the respect of other general principles of EC law, namely legal certainty and legitimate expectations. Thus in the light of *Mangold* the proposition that nothing could stop the ECJ in the future from ruling that a given Employment Guideline enshrines a general principle of constitutional value or a fundamental right on the basis of a combined reading of, for example, Article 13 EC and Article 21 or Article 23 of the Charter, while probably difficult to effect in practice, cannot be completely ruled out. It would also be a way of solving the question raised by the horizontal provisions of the Charter of whether measures adopted by the Member States in the context of OMC processes may be considered as being implementing measures of EU law.

In light of the above, and because of the impact that the Employment Guidelines (now part of the Integrated Guidelines) may have on social rights and the difficulty and complexity of guaranteeing judicial scrutiny either at European or national level, the proposal of linking the two processes may hold some value. This would transcend the hard–soft law debate and identify a hybrid theory which conjugates the strengths of both modes of policy making by ensuring transparency, democratic legitimacy, accountability and legal certainty and without entailing a systematic review of the EU institutional framework or the

---

25 Case C-144/04 *Werner Mangold v. Rüdiger Helm* [2005] ECR I-9981.
26 Directive 2000/78 of 27 November 2000 establishing a general framework for equal treatment in employment and occupation [2000] OJ L 303/16.

insertion of specific provisions in the Treaty, as suggested by some academics and working groups of the Convention on the Future of Europe.[27]

The difficulty in establishing a dialogical relationship between the EES and the European Social Dialogue is due to the intrinsic difference between Title VIII and XI. As seen in Chapter 5, whereas Title VIII may be said to embody a "vertical consolidation" of a number of years of political thinking initiated by the Commission and often endorsed by the Member States through soft law measures, Title XI on the contrary may be said to represent a "horizontal consolidation" of accepted judicial and political practice. The difference between the two titles illustrates the structural dichotomy between sensitive and less sensitive areas of Community intervention in EC social policy. It is also acknowledged that this proposal may be difficult to put in practice, *inter alia* because of the different industrial relations systems and the different role of the social partners therein. However, it is posited that a stronger relationship between New Governance practices and processes and the Community Method would be mutually beneficial to both modes of regulation. It would also guarantee the rule of law approach as well as ensuring overall a more effective system of EU governance. Specifically, Framework Directives could be adopted on the basis of the large amount of information that results from the NRPs process. This would allow both the Commission and the Council to identify common problems to most Member States. In addition, it would also be possible to subject default national legislation to judicial scrutiny and review and thus create legal rights that could be enforceable in national legal systems, chiefly through the principles of indirect effect, incidental horizontal direct effect and state liability. For example, the amendments introduced in the Italian Workers Statute, and in particular the changes made to Article 18,[28] with two national legislative Acts, Act 2003/30 and Act 2003/276, could be challenged on the ground that the government has failed to implement or has only partially implemented a Directive on work organization or a reinforced Directive on collective redundancies or, more broadly, a Directive on employment protection. These Directives could be adopted on the basis of information retrieved through the NRPs process as well as in accordance with basic social rights and social standards recognized in International and European social rights covenants. Hence, by establishing a dialogical relationship between Title VIII and XI and by transcending the hard–soft law debate, it could be possible to combine the strengths of both modes of policy making and improve the effectiveness of both processes, chiefly of the EES.

Some first attempts to link the EES to EC labour law[29] since the Treaty of Amsterdam have already been made, particularly in the area of Framework Directives. The study of EC Framework Agreements and Directives shows that the soft implementation of the Employment Strategy and EC labour (hard) law are reciprocally influenced and reinforce the protection of the rights recognized in the Directives. This dialectical relationship would create a solid EC social policy framework and greatly improve the effectiveness of the EES both at the implementation and enforcement levels of policy making. What follows is a series of Directives that have made explicit reference to the EES. These Directives confirm the fact that it is possible to create a dialogical link between the Employment Strategy and

---

27 An interesting proposal for reform has been made by the Committee on Employment and Social Affairs of the European Parliament, which suggested that the EES and more broadly the OMC should be integrated with the national policy-making procedure and in particular that NAPs should be adopted by the national parliament concerned on the basis of a government Bill (European Parliament 2002a).

28 See Chapter 6.

29 See Brunn (2001), who exhaustively illustrates and explains the relationship between the EES and EC labour law. Most of the examples have been reproduced in this section; see also Scharpf (2002).

EC social policy and that a way of improving the effectiveness of the EES could be by way of establishing a link between the latter and EC social policy.

In the Preamble to the European Framework Agreement on Part Time Work, which led to the adoption of the homonymous Directive (Council of the European Union 1997e), the European social partners stated:

> This framework agreement is *a contribution to the overall European strategy on employment.*[30] Part-time work has had an important impact on employment in recent years. For this reason, the parties to this agreement have given priority attention to this form of work. It is the intention of the parties to consider the need for similar agreements relating to other forms of work.

In the Preamble to the Framework Agreement on Fixed Term Work concluded by the European social partners which led to the homonymous Directive (Council of the European Union 1999) the following is stated:

> This framework agreement illustrates the role that the social partners can play in the European employment Strategy agreed at the 1997 Luxembourg extraordinary summit[31] and, following the framework agreement on part-time work, represents a further contribution towards achieving a better balance between flexibility in working time and security of workers.

Paragraph 6 of the Preamble to the Council Directive emphasizes the relevance of the Employment Strategy:

> The Council Resolution of 9 February 1999 on the 1999 Employment Guidelines invites the social partners at all appropriate levels to negotiate agreements to modernize the organization of work, including flexible working arrangements, with the aim of making undertakings productive and competitive and achieving the required balance between flexibility and security.

In the Fixed Term Directive there are also some provisions that take into consideration the Employment Strategy. Paragraph 2 of Clause 6 prescribes that, as far as possible, employers should facilitate access by fixed-term workers to appropriate training courses in order to improve their skills, career development and occupational mobility. In this clause there is an implicit reference to the Employability pillar of the EPGs. The foregoing Framework Agreements and Directives are particularly relevant with regard to the role of the social partners, who have a pivotal role in the modernization of work organization and in guaranteeing a proper balance between flexibility and security.

In addition, the Directive on race and ethnic discrimination (Council of the European Union 2000a) directly refers to the Employment Strategy as a valuable policy tool in the promotion of minority groups in the labour market. The Preamble to the Directive refers to the Employment Guidelines for the year 2000:[32] 'The 2000 Employment Policy

---

30 Emphasis added.
31 Emphasis added.
32 See recitals 8–9.

Guidelines agreed by the European Council in Helsinki, on 10 and 11 December 1999, stress the need to foster conditions for a socially inclusive labour market by formulating a coherent set of policies aimed at combating discrimination against groups such as ethnic minorities.'

The Employment Framework Directive (Council of the European Union 2000b) has a direct link to the Employment Strategy. Its Preamble states:[33]

> The EC Treaty includes among its objectives the promotion of co-ordination between employment policies of the Member States. To this end, a new employment chapter was incorporated in the EC Treaty as a means of developing a co-ordinated European strategy for employment to promote a skilled, trained and adaptable work force. The Employment Guidelines for 2000 agreed by the European Council at Helsinki on 10 and 11 December 1999 stress the need to foster a labour market favourable to social integration by formulating a coherent set of policies aimed at combating discrimination against groups such as persons with disability. They also emphasize the need to pay particular attention to supporting older workers, in order to increase participation in the labour force.

Paragraph 1 of Article 6 provides the following:

> 1. Notwithstanding Article 2(2) Member States may provide that differences of treatment on grounds of age shall not constitute discrimination, if, within the context of national law, they are objectively and reasonably justified by a legitimate aim, including legitimate employment policy, labour market and vocational training objectives, and if the means of achieving that aim are appropriate and necessary.

The reference to the Employment Strategy is made explicit in paragraph 25 of the Preamble:

> The prohibition of age discrimination is an essential part of meeting the aims set out in the Employment Guidelines and encouraging diversity in the work force. However, differences in treatment in connection with age may be justified under certain circumstances and therefore require specific provisions which may vary in accordance with the situation in Member States. It is therefore essential to distinguish between differences in treatment which are justified, in particular, by legitimate employment policy, labour market and vocational training objectives, and discrimination which must be prohibited.

The Parental Leave Directive (Council of the European Union 1996) implicitly refers to the Equal Opportunities pillar of the EPGs. The Preamble to the Directive states that the purpose of the Directive is to reconcile work and family life and to promote equal opportunities and treatment between women and men, which are all objectives of the fourth pillar of the EPGs.

The explicit or implicit reference to the EES in these Directives shows that it is possible to establish a mutually reinforcing relationship between new or experimental modes of

---

33 See recitals 7–8.

governance and the more traditional instruments of the Community Method without altering the nature of either modes of regulation. The Directives analyzed above emphasize the fact that it is possible to transcend the hard–soft law debate by creating a hybrid governance model. In this context a monitoring mechanism could also be created. In particular, the social partners at national, sectoral and enterprise levels and works councils could monitor the protection of social rights and report any complaints to their representatives at the European level, who could then bring actions before the European Courts.

With regard to the strengthening of the role of the social partners, the Report of the High Level Group *Industrial Relations and Change in the European Union* (2002) highlights the need to create a link between the policy objectives under Title VIII and XI and also the importance of broadening the spectrum of social partners involved in the EES and European Social Dialogue. It maintains that 'a new agenda for industrial relations should be developed at all levels in order to cope with some key priorities' and 'build on already emerging new practices' (*ibid.*: 5).[34] The High Level Group:

> acknowledging the diversity of national patterns of industrial relations, identifies some main trends: the renewal of sectoral bargaining, the decentralization at enterprise level and local level and the role of national pacts to deal with strategic issues. The relationship between social dialogue and civil dialogue are also highlighted.
>
> (*Ibid.*; and 29–30)

At the time, this new agenda was also considered important for the structural adaptation of accession countries. Research shows that there is not so much civic engagement in most of the new Member States, namely CEECs, and the social partners have had to rethink their own function.

The High Level Group suggests the setting up of a benchmarking process and OMC for industrial relations as a New Governance instrument, with the support of the European Monitoring Centre on Change (EMCC). The social partners are uniquely suited to the strengthening of social policy because of their knowledge of the factual basis of various social and employment and labour market issues (Fredman 1998: 410). The High Level Group also states that industrial relations can make an important contribution to "good governance",[35] promoting the implementation of the Lisbon Strategy and fostering modernization based on a new social contract, which includes, *inter alia*, national pacts, European Works Councils and the European sectoral social dialogue. The High Level Group report also suggests ways of developing this new agenda in practice, for example by establishing a relationship between:

- The different levels (European, national, local, enterprise), taking into account the distinction between sectoral and cross-industry industrial relations.
- Bipartite and tripartite processes.

---

34 The key priorities are: competitiveness and innovation with social cohesion, wage responsiveness, social inclusion and social protection, training and lifelong learning, working conditions and work organization, new forms of employment, working time management, reconciliation of work and family life.

35 The High Level Group (2002: 24) defines it as 'the way society organizes and rules itself in order to make and to implement choices'.

- Different procedures (consultation, concertation, collective bargaining, etc.) and instruments (agreements, guidelines, etc.).

In this context, the European Works Councils (EWCs) play an important role as they represent 'networks of employees' representatives across borders, where local representatives are likely to meet on a regular basis'. This may provide a basis for dialogue and co-ordination of bargaining. The High Level Group also suggests the creation of a dialectical and political relationship between the European social partners and the Council on a more regular basis. This would provide an additional incentive for national social partners to actively participate in the European Social Dialogue. In this regard, Bercusson (1996: 99) argues that 'given the existing links with Member States trade unions, it would strengthen the legitimacy of EU level trade union organizations if trade union rights formulated at EU level reinforced trade union representation over enterprise or workplace-based representation'. In this respect, Bercusson emphasizes the importance of the creation of the EWCs, which 'promote for the first time a transnational system of worker representation *based on the enterprise*' (*ibid.*).

The governance proposals made by the High Level Group confirms the existence of limitations in both the law and policy and the need to strengthen the link between "centre and periphery", here intended loosely as the relationship between state and non-state actors. Moreover, the underlying message of the report is that more experimental modes of governance are necessary to take into account worldwide socio-economic changes. Thus by using the High Level Group's report as a point of departure this chapter puts forward a rather schematic proposal on how to achieve a possible encounter between Title VIII and XI that could strengthen the legitimacy and effectiveness of the EES and of the European Social Dialogue.

To recap, this section offered a "practical" application of the theoretical model elaborated in Chapter 2 with the aim of improving both the legitimacy and democratic quality of EU action in the field of employment. From the perspective of the involvement of non-state actors the focus has been on the social partners. Another possible scenario could be the adoption of Framework Directives on the basis of Article 13 EC with the same logic and structure as the ones envisaged for a link between Title VIII and Title XI. In this case other non-state actors such as NGOs (for example women's lobby groups) could also be involved at national and local levels in ensuring the development of, *inter alia*, a gender-mainstreaming approach in the adoption and implementation of national policies. This proposal, however, would require further detailed analysis and for reasons of space it cannot be the subject of this book.

5 Conclusion

The chapter started by explaining the main contribution of the EES to EU social governance and, in particular, how it has enabled the "social" to remain top of the European Union's and Member States' agenda, providing a cognitive framework in the context of which shared employment-related problems may be discussed, common solutions may be identified and best practice may be exchanged. The chapter then examined two key sets of problems which are at the core of the EES's weak effectiveness and that affect the operation, legitimacy and democratic quality of the EES. First, it critically analyzed how the EES remains subjected to the overarching economic objectives of the European Union and, in particular, how its scope of action is limited by the priorities of the Internal Market, EMU, EC competition law and state aid. Because of the way the Employment Strategy has been conceived, namely, as a supply-side strategy, it must avoid any obstacles to the operation of the Internal Market and EMU. Second, the chapter unravelled the main limitations of the EES, some of which may be associated with its soft law nature, such as the absence of a rule of law approach, its lack of legal sanctions and hence its weak enforcement capacity and limited success in promoting lesson drawing and "bottom-to-top" forms of policy making and participatory forms of democracy. In this context, the analysis seems to confirm the fact that none of the theories of democratic governance may be apt in describing democracy in the EES and the OMC.

Hence, on the basis of the accountability model developed by Benz and Papadopoulos (2006) and Benz (2007), and the hybrid governance model elaborated in Chapter 2, this chapter put forward a proposal for strengthening the relationship between new or experimental modes of governance and law and constitutionalism. This hybrid model was applied to Title VIII and Title XI of the EC Treaty, although other possible encounters between New Governance and law and constitutionalism may be envisaged which could be the object of future research projects.

8 Conclusion

As the sixth phase of the European Union's social dimension, which started with the Treaty of Amsterdam, has reached a period of consolidation and, within it, the EES its cruising speed, the enthusiasm with which many have greeted the OMC, considered the '*primus inter pares* in the European Union's new armoury of governance' (Idema and Kelemen 2006: 108) is gradually waning and losing proselytes. At its inception, it was perceived as an innovatory form of co-ordination or as a valid alternative to the legal harmonization furthered by the classic Community Method owing to its alleged malleability, flexibility and openness (de la Rosa 2005: 621): necessary characteristics for ensuring, *inter alia*, the respect of diversity and participatory democracy which are invoked by advocates of a stronger Social Europe.

Since its official launch, European integration scholars have unveiled quite a different if not opposite scenario in relation to the OMC: centralized co-ordination, a certain degree of stability, little or no participation of national parliaments, local authorities and non-state actors, bureaucratic management, symbolic politics and political instrumentalism on the part of national governments with no effective policy learning or policy influence on domestic policy developments. The OMC also seems to be inadequate to the realities of CEECs, exacerbating some of their long-standing problems, particularly those within public administrations because of its informal nature. In addition, in most of these countries there is still little understanding of certain EU law concepts and principles and the OMC is inadequate for providing the necessary toolkit for enabling these CEECs to learn and apply such concepts and principles. This is particularly problematic in relation to gender equality, as the transition to an open-market economy has reinforced gender stereotypes and women's discrimination at work.

Moreover, besides reviving the political and academic debates about European social policy, the OMC has been unable to truly strengthen the European Union's social dimension. The "European social model" is being undermined, particularly since Lisbon II. Specifically, in relation to the EES, the competing visions that underpin it have resulted in an Employment Strategy 'which is itself an uneven synthesis of rival, yet overlapping, policy discourses' (Ashiagbor 2005: 301). A clear shift in emphasis is discernible whereby the social-democratic element of the strategy, focusing on employment protection and social protection, has had to give way to a deregulatory agenda centred on labour market "efficiency" and "flexibility". In this context, it has been easier to have political consensus on measures to tackle unemployment than on measures ensuring high levels of employment and social protection. The emphasis on flexibility in the "flexicurity" debate is a case in point. It is also problematic given that flexibility appears to be a useful piece of political rhetoric which Member States and the European Institutions may and have imbued with their own interpretation, as shown in Chapter 6. At present, the development of EU social policy rests firmly embedded in the project of the realization of the Single Market.

The OMC has also brought about new problems. As Büchs (2007: 156) explains, the European Union has become involved in policy making in areas covered by the OMC but it has not acquired the means to guarantee social provision and entitlements because the social policy areas to which the OMC is applied remain formally the domain of the Member States, thus illustrating how strong the intergovernmental dimension of the OMC is. However, at the same time, domestic policy (in terms of both the agenda setting and programme formulation) has been influenced at discourse level by the OMC. The fuzzy and blurred fusion of competences to which the OMC has led is problematic because it obscures real responsibilities to the public and citizens (*idem*). Moreover, the rather vague objectives and goals of the Lisbon Strategy have enabled Member States to make instrumental use of it, particularly for the enactment of unpopular legislation. Since the 1980s the promotion of a stronger Social Europe has been strictly linked to the normative aspiration of giving broader legitimacy to the project of European integration through a social component. However, the book shows that, in relation to its more or less explicit or purported aim of increasing the legitimacy of EU action, the OMC has had a boomerang effect, promoting or rather preserving the image of the European Union as a one-eyed man solely preoccupied with the pursuit of economic objectives and doing little to tackle social injustice and discrimination.

Be that as it may, the OMC has undoubtedly pushed 'the boundaries of our understanding of government–society–economy interactions' (Borrás and Greve 2004: 335), forcing us to rethink current political and legal structures and make sense of the variety and multifarious forms of policy making and to revisit current understandings of law and constitutionalism, their role and their adequacy in relation to worldwide socio-economic and societal changes brought about by globalization processes. More precisely, the study of new approaches to governance compels us to set aside a simplified or simplistic vision of law and legal structures pursuant to the binary logic which upholds the soft–hard law divide. The EES is illustrative. As the book has demonstrated, because of its iteration and cyclicality any rigid definition of the Employment Strategy as being either supranational or intergovernmental is reductive, although the latter element is very strong and, at times, it is the predominant one. Likewise, defining the EES as being an example of soft law is limitative and fails to capture the development of the strategy at the national level. It is precisely in this sense that Ashiagbor (2005) talks about 'soft harmonization through hard law'. While at the European level soft law has become the principal legal instrument for coercing Member States to tackle labour market regulation in line with European objectives, at national level Member States may implement European *soft* policies through *hard* law measures.

The EES should be praised for its attempt to establish a nexus between different EU policy areas by widening its scope of action, which goes beyond the field of social policy *stricto sensu* and to promote a rethinking of policy making. On the domestic plane, the EES has attempted to create a common, integrated framework for structural reform and to establish synergies between different policy areas such as labour market policy, tax and benefit systems, training and education and enterprise policy.

Situated in post-ontological studies which seek to explore the resulting political and legal systems of the European integration process, the book examined the creation and further development of the EES and its regulatory tool, the OMC, to better understand future directions and the agenda of EU social policy, addressing effectiveness and legitimacy questions of EU social governance. In so doing, it looked at the extent to which and in what way legal instruments and processes as well as constitutional values and norms are involved in the operation of new modes of governance and what role new approaches to regulation have within the more well defined structures of law and constitutionalism. It is in this context that the OMC, as explained in Chapters 5–7 of the book, has its most serious shortcomings. While its creation and further development represent an acknowledgement of the fact that rule formulation and settlement increasingly take place within new forms of transnational governance, little has been done to provide an adequate governance architecture to the new processes and actors involved in policy making. As explained in Chapter 2, law is faced with representing or managing difference in legal aspirations no less than with promoting similarity in legal experience. There is the need, therefore, to revisit the roles of law and constitutionalism both at European and national levels. This is necessary to capture the evolving nature of the European Union and to take into account, respect and legitimize the growing diversity of processes, practices and actors, thus promoting active Union citizenship and improving the quality of democracy. The book shows that the EES has scored poorly on this account and it has failed to have a transformative effect on law, be it national or European. Moreover, it has not introduced new paradigms that Member States have then introduced into their legal systems; rather, the findings of the book indicate that Member States have gradually been able to ensure that their domestic priorities would be reflected in the Employment and Integrated Guidelines. As explained in Chapter 4, one of the limitations of EU social policy is the emphasis placed on process rather than substance, and the very creation and further implementation of the EES with its lack of formal legal sanctions was meant to please those countries like the United Kingdom which are fierce opponents of any further expansion of Community social intervention, even though its proponents at the time truly believed that the EES represented a valid instrument for strengthening the social dimension of the European Union. The only exception to what is being said is represented by the CEECs. The analysis of the Czech Republic clearly indicates that there was a paradigm shift long before accession. However, this change in the socio-economic rationale underpinning labour market policies in the Czech Republic is explained by strategic convergence for ensuring membership in the European Union.

Against this backcloth, the book suggests establishing a dialogic relationship between new and experimentalist modes of regulation, law and constitutionalism, the premise being that in spite of their intrinsic differences they form part of the same *corpus unicum*. Such a relationship is configured as a hybrid governance model embracing a broad notion of democracy and seeking to conjugate hierarchical forms of regulation usually represented by state constitutionalism with heterarchical forms of governance represented by New Governance. Both European and national parliaments could have a key role in setting a meta-governance frame defining objectives and procedures, monitoring progress towards agreed goals and revising the processes in light of the results achieved. In this context, their traditional role as legislators would be necessarily transformed to enable them to accommodate New Governance processes. In a similar vein, law would also acquire a new role and in addition to being prescriptive it would also be reconstitutive. This new approach to governance combining new governance with law and constitutionalism is particularly important for substantive gender equality. As the comparative case study in Chapter 6 showed, while there is a substantial amount of legislation on gender equality at European level and, in most Member States, little has been done to date to address structural inequality and since the overhaul of the EES gender mainstreaming seems to have lost its momentum. Both European and national courts would also have a renewed role alongside their more traditional role as norm enforcers, by promoting principles and values concerning participation, transparency, principled decision making and accountability. In this context, judicial review proceedings could be triggered by the standing of impartial bodies such as parliamentary committees rather than merely by individual *locus standi* less likely to succeed given the multi-level and heterarchical setting of the EU system.

A revised notion of accountability could ensure a loose coupling of New Governance with democratically legitimate representative structures creating interfaces that can be beneficial for mutual learning. Hence, while departing from the classical concept of accountability, the proposed hybrid governance model would enable the more nebulous New Governance practices and processes to operate in a way which may be held more democratically accountable and responsive while ensuring governability and policy efficiency and remaining more representative of public needs and values. It is posited that it would also help to strengthen input legitimacy. This would be achieved without entailing a return to the same substantive regulatory rationality of "command and control" of the classical forms of regulation. On the contrary, it would preserve and strengthen the structure and mechanisms of both classical and experimental forms of governance.

With regard to output legitimacy, where the OMC has also equally scored poorly, the book has put forward a rather controversial proposal, namely to establish a link between Title VIII and Title XI. Some first attempts to link the EES with EC labour law since the Treaty of Amsterdam have already been made, chiefly through the adoption of Framework Directives. The Employment Strategy and EC labour law may reciprocally influence each other and reinforce the protection of the rights recognized in the Directives. Chapter 7 showed how this could be achieved by identifying a hybrid theory combining the strengths of both modes of policy making, thus ensuring more transparency, democratic legitimacy, accountability and legal certainty. The establishment of this relationship would not entail a systematic review of the European Union's institutional framework or the insertion of specific provisions in the Treaty. This dialogical link between New Governance and law could be ensured by adopting Framework Directives on the basis of the information that results from the NRP process. In this model the reliability of the information pooled together would be ensured by the involvement of national parliaments and/or local authorities and other stakeholders. This would allow both the Commission and the Council to identify problems common to most Member States. In addition, it would also be possible to subject default national legislation to judicial scrutiny. This would ensure a 'stronger and more stable normative anchorage of the OMC' (Giubboni 2006: 250) and the protection of social rights potentially enforceable in national legal systems. In this context constitutionalism rather than representing a fixed legal framework provides the ground for a process of continuous renewal and dialogue in relation to a polity – the European Union – that is always in the course of negotiation and renegotiation.

Appendix 1

Genesis and development of the European Employment Strategy: key European Council meetings

June 1993 Delors's White Paper on Growth, Competitiveness and Employment

- Consensus on employment as a common objective of the European Union and on establishing a common policy for employment.

December 1994 Essen European Council

- A strategy to tackle unemployment based on multilateral co-operation is adopted with the definition of five EU common priorities on employment and multilateral monitoring. The five policy priorities are:

  (a) Education.
  (b) Macroeconomic policy.
  (c) Labour markets.
  (d) Rationalization.
  (e) Social inclusion.

June 1995 Cannes European Council

- Member States agree to reinforce the multilateral strategy to improve its effectiveness.

December 1995 Madrid European Council

- Member States agree to focus national measures on various policy areas regarding long-term unemployment, the young and women, in order to improve the levels of employment.

March 1996 Turin European Council

- *Memorandum pour un Modèle social européen*, presented by the French government, clearly stated that employment was to be one of the main priorities of the European Union.

June 1996 Florence European Council

- Member States agree on implementing the Territorial Employment Pacts project launched by President of the Commission Santer in his Communication *A Confident Pact for Employment.*

December 1996 Dublin European Council

- Proposal to introduce common indicators and benchmarks to employ in the evaluation of the achievement of the common objectives.

June 1997 Amsterdam European Council

- The Treaty of Amsterdam introduces a new title in the EC Treaty, Title VIII on Employment, creating thus a legal framework for a European Strategy for Employment.

November 1997 Luxembourg European Council

- At this Extraordinary Meeting of the European Council on employment, also known as the Luxembourg process, Member States agree to fast-track the common strategy on employment formalized in Title VIII. Consensus is reached on the co-ordination of policies as opposed to a multilateral co-operation strategy.

June 1998 Cardiff European Council

- A major structural reform process is launched in order to strengthen labour and goods, services and capital markets.

December 1998 Vienna European Council

- The Council invites the Commission to prepare several communications for 1999 on subjects such as tax regimes, international financial markets, investment in infrastructure and in human capital, economic policy co-ordination mechanisms, mainstreaming of EU policies and elements for a European Employment Pact.

June 1999 Cologne European Council

- Launch of the 'Macroeconomic dialogue', i.e. regular meetings where representatives of ECOFIN and the Social Affairs Council, the Commission, the European Central Bank and the social partners meet to exchange information and to better co-ordinate wage developments, fiscal and monetary policies.

March 2000 Lisbon European Council

- The Open Method of Co-ordination is introduced as a new mode of governance to be employed in specific sensitive policy areas. It is based on management by objectives rather than management by regulation. This new form of policy-making complements the Community method.

- The overall goal of the European Union is to become 'the most competitive and dynamic knowledge-based economy in the world, capable of sustainable economic growth, with better and more jobs and greater social cohesion'. The Lisbon Strategy is launched.
- Consensus is reached on holding an annual European Council meeting every spring, aimed at monitoring the implementation of the overall strategy. In addition, Member States agree to shift the target from 'high levels of employment' to 'full levels of employment'. Quantified targets are introduced: 70 per cent employment for men and 60 per cent for women by 2010.

December 2000 Nice European Council

- Adoption of a Social Policy Agenda for 2000–2005 and declaration of a European Charter of Fundamental Rights.
- The Open Method of Co-ordination is applied also to social protection and social inclusion.

March 2001 Stockholm European Council

- Intermediate targets are agreed. These are 67 per cent for men and 57 per cent for women by 2005.

June 2001 Göteborg European Council

- A Sustainable Development Strategy is adopted as a follow-up to the Lisbon Strategy. An environmental dimension is thus included in the Open Method of Co-ordination.

December 2001 Laeken European Council

- The European Council welcomes the decision to create and institutionalize a European Social Affairs Summit, to be held before each spring European Council Summit.
- Member States agree on the importance of developing structural indicators, particularly on quality of work.

March 2002 Barcelona European Council

- First annual European Council meeting to monitor and assess the overall implementation of the Lisbon Strategy.
- Calls for a simplification of the Employment Strategy by reducing the number of guidelines and for aligning the time frame with the Lisbon deadline of 2010.

March 2003 Brussels European Council

- European Council endorsement of the streamlining process of the Broad Economic Policy guidelines and Employment Policy guidelines within a three-year perspective.

- European Council endorsement of the Employment Strategy's overarching objectives set out by the Council of Ministers: full employment, quality and productivity at work, cohesion and inclusive labour markets.
- Calls for the setting up of a European Employment Task Force headed by Wim Kok to carry out an independent examination of key employment-related policy challenges.

March 2004 Brussels European Council

- The European Council calls for a narrower focus of the Lisbon Agenda on sustainable growth and more and better jobs.
- Accordingly, the Employment Strategy's priorities are: adaptability, job creation, job quality and investing in human capital.
- In addressing the mid-term review of the Lisbon Strategy, the European Council invites the Commission to establish a high-level group headed by Wim Kok to carry out an independent review to contribute to this exercise.

March 2005 Brussels European Council

- Recognition of shortcomings and delays in achieving the goals of the Lisbon Strategy.
- Relaunch of the Lisbon Strategy with a renewed focus on growth and employment.
- "Vital strands" of the relaunch are: knowledge and innovation; research and development; environmental policy; to foster free movement of services; social cohesion and social inclusion.
- Improving the overall governance of the Lisbon Strategy.

Appendix 2

The iterative process of the European Employment Strategy (Article 128 EC)

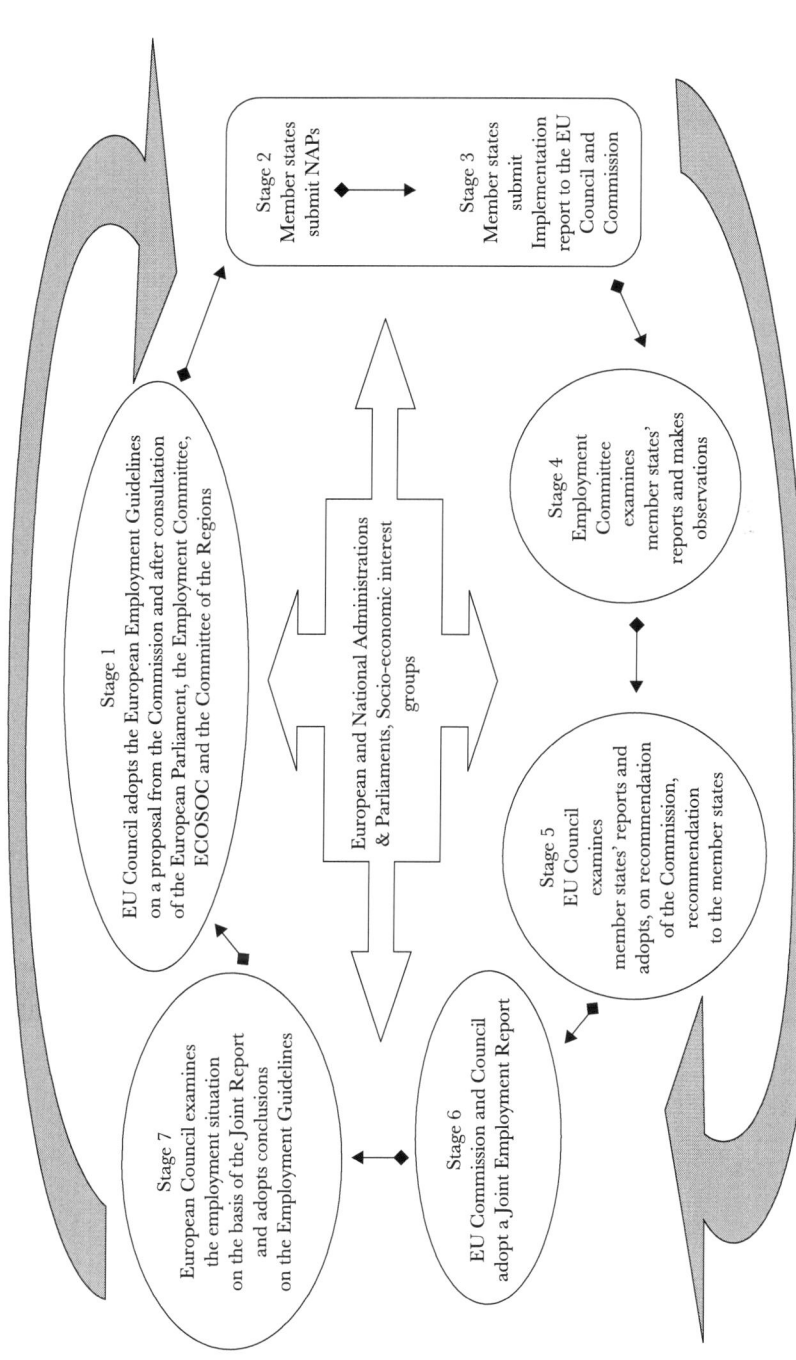

Stage 1
EU Council adopts the European Employment Guidelines on a proposal from the Commission and after consultation of the European Parliament, the Employment Committee, ECOSOC and the Committee of the Regions

Stage 2
Member states submit NAPs

Stage 3
Member states submit Implementation report to the EU Council and Commission

Stage 4
Employment Committee examines member states' reports and makes observations

Stage 5
EU Council examines member states' reports and adopts, on recommendation of the Commission, recommendation to the member states

Stage 6
EU Commission and Council adopt a Joint Employment Report

Stage 7
European Council examines the employment situation on the basis of the Joint Report and adopts conclusions on the Employment Guidelines

European and National Administrations & Parliaments, Socio-economic interest groups

Source: Meyer, Linsenmann and Wessels (2007), p. 19.

Appendix 3

Main co-ordination processes in fiscal, economic and employment policy

| Policy area | Hard co-ordination ←—————————→ Soft co-ordination | | |
	Fiscal policy	Macroeconomic policy mix	Employment policy
Instruments	Stability and Growth Pact (since 1997)	Broad Economic Policy Guidelines (since 1992)	Luxembourg process (since 1997)
Policy goals	Avoidance of negative externalities, especially free-riding of Member States in EMU	Sustainable and co-ordinated socio-economic policy making in EMU	Increasing employment levels through labour market reforms, active employment policy measures
Legal basis	Art. 104 EC, Protocol, Regulations 1466/97, 1467/97	Art. 99 EC, European Council of Helsinki 1999	Art. 128 EC, European Council of Luxembourg, 1997
Sanctions in cases of non-compliance	Peer pressure and negative publicity through individual recommendations and Option of the Council imposing financial fines in case of excessive budgetary deficits	Peer pressure and negative publicity through general and individual recommendations	Peer pressure and negative publicity through individual recommendations and benchmarking
Objectives, Guidelines and Benchmarks	Medium-term budgetary targets, national quantitative targets in stability/convergence programmes, quantitative thresholds	Depending on the policy area, qualitative guidelines and quantitative targets for EU and national levels, national reports	Qualitative guidelines and quantitative EU targets, common indicators, national action plans/national reform programmes, variable national benchmarks
Role of EU Commission and European Parliament	Monitoring of targets through DG Ecfin, Proposal for Decisions of ECOFIN Council by QMV	Monitoring of targets through DG Ecfin, Proposal for Decisions of ECOFIN Council by QMV, EP rights for *ex post* information	Monitoring of targets through DG Employment, Proposal for Decisions of Employment and Social Affairs Council by QMV, EP is being consulted
Procedures for voting and learning	Annual reporting and review cycles, QMV in Council on sanctions under the excessive deficit procedure	Annual reporting and review cycles	Annual reporting and review cycles, multilateral surveillance and partnering
Involvement of non-governmental actors	No, indirect through public sphere	No, indirect through macroeconomic dialogue and public sphere	Yes, social partners

Source: Meyer, Linsenmann and Wessels (2007: 14).

Appendix 4

The European Employment Strategy within the revised governance architecture of the Lisbon Strategy

10 Commission reviews implementation	**1** Strategic Report of the European Commission on economic and employment policy guidelines	**2** Spring European Council establishes political guidelines for the economic and employment strands of the strategy

3 In accordance with Articles 99 and 128 EC, the Council adopts a set of Integrated Guidelines

9 Member States submit single Annual Report setting out the measures taken to implement their national reform programme

4 Member States draw up national reform programmes after consulting all relevant stakeholders

4 The Commission presents a Community Lisbon Programme covering action to be taken at EC level

8 Adoption by Council of updated Integrated Guidelines package

5 Commission presents an Annual Progress Report, including draft joint employment report; proposals for update of Integrated Guidelines package

7 European Council reviews progress at spring Council and assesses Integrated Guidelines package

6 Various Council configurations discuss Annual Progress Report

Bibliography

Abbott, W. K. and Snidal, D. (2000), 'Hard and Soft Law in International Governance', *International Organization* 54(3): 421–456.

Adinolfi, A. (1998), 'Le innovazioni previste dal Trattato di Amsterdam in tema di politica sociale', *Diritto dell'Unione Europea*, Vols 2–3.

Ahern, A. (2001), 'Closed-door Democracy is not Worthy of Council of Ministers', *European Voice*, 28 June–4 July, p. 26.

Alston, P. and Weiler, J. (1999), 'An "Ever Closer Union" in Need of a Human Rights Policy: The European Union and Human Rights', in Alston, P., Bustelo, M. and Heenan, J. (eds), *The European Union and Human Rights* (Oxford: Oxford University Press), pp. 3–66.

Altomonte, C. and Nava, M. (2005), *Economics and Policies of an Enlarged Union* (Cheltenham: Elgar).

Amitsis, G., Berghman, J., Hemerijck, A., Sakellaropoulos, T., Stergiou, A. and Stevens, Y. (2003), 'Connecting Welfare Diversity within the European Social Model', Background Report for the International Conference of the Hellenic Presidency of the European Union, 'The Modernization of the European Social Model and EU Policies and Instruments', Ioannina, 21–22 May.

Andersen, G. E. (1999), *A Welfare State for the Twenty-first Century: Ageing Societies, Knowledge-based Economies, and the Sustainability of European Welfare States*, report prepared for the Portuguese Presidency of the European Union, spring 2000, second version, University of Trento, November.

Anderson, K. (2002), 'The Europeanization of Pension Arrangements: Convergence or Divergence?' in de la Porte, C. and Pochet, P. (eds), *Building Social Europe through the Open Method of Co-ordination* (Brussels: PIE/Peter Lang).

Andronico, A. and Lo Faro, A. (2005), 'Defining Problems: The Open Method of Coordination: Fundamental Rights and the Theory of Governance' in De Schutter, O. and Deakin, S. (eds), *Social Rights and Market Forces: Is the Open Coordination of Employment and Social Policies the Future of Social Europe?* (Brussels: Bruylant), pp. 41–96.

Appadurai, A. (1996), *Modernity at Large: Cultural Dimensions of Globalization* (Minneapolis MN: University of Minnesota Press).

Armstrong, K. (1998), 'Legal Integration: Theorizing the Legal Dimension of European Integration', *Journal of Common Market Studies* 36(2): 155–174.

Armstrong, K. (1999), 'Governance and the Single European Market' in Craig, P. and de Búrca, G. (eds), *The Evolution of EU Law* (Oxford: Oxford University Press), pp. 769–770.

Armstrong, K. (2002), 'Rediscovering Civil Society: The European Union and the White Paper on Governance', *European Law Journal* 8(1): 102–132.

Armstrong, K. (2002a), 'Mutual Recognition' in Barnard, C. and Scott, J. (eds), *The Law of the Single European Market: Unpacking the Premises* (Oxford: Hart), pp. 225–267.

Armstrong, K. (2008), 'Governance and Constitutionalism after Lisbon', *Journal of Common Market Studies* 46(2): 415–426.

Armstrong, K. and Bulmer, S. (1998), *The Governance of the Single European Market* (Manchester: Manchester University Press).

Armstrong, K. and Kilpatrick, C. (2007), 'Law, Governance, or New Governance? The Changing Open Method of Coordination', *Columbia Journal of European Law* 13(3): 649–677.

Arnold, C. (2001), 'The European Employment Strategy: Composite Factors leading to its Evolution', paper presented at the ECSA Conference, Madison WI, 31 May–2 June.

Arnull, A. (1990), 'The Legal Status of Recommendations', *European Law Review* 15(4): 318–321.

Arrigo G. (1998), *Il Diritto del Lavoro dell'Unione Europea*, Vol. I, *Principi, fonti, libera circolazione e sicurezza sociale dei lavoratori* (Turin: Giuffrè).

Arrowsmith, J., Sisson, K. and Marginson, P. (2004), 'What Can "Benchmarking" Offer the Open Method of Coordination?' *Journal of European Public Policy* 11(2): 311–328.

Asdrubali, P., Sorensen, B. and Yosha, O. (1996), 'Channels of Interstate Risk Sharing: United States, 1963–1990', *Quarterly Journal of Economics* 111: 1081–1110.

Ash, T. (2000), 'A Crazy Way to Run a Continent', *The Independent*, 11 December.

Artus, P. (1998), 'Un'armonia stonata se fatta di sola moneta', *La Repubblica, Affari e Finanza*, 4 May.

Ashiagbor, D. (2005), *The European Employment Strategy: Labour Market Regulation and New Governance* (Oxford: Oxford University Press).

Baldwin, R., Berglof, E., Giavazzi, F. and Widgren, M. (2001), *Nice Try: Should the Treaty of Nice be Ratified?* Monitoring European Integration 11, London: Centre for Economic Policy Research.

Ball, C. (1996), 'The Making of a Transnational Capitalist Society: The European Court of Justice, Social Policy, and Individual Rights under the European Community's Legal Order', *Harvard International Law Journal* 37(2): 307–388.

Ball, S. (2001), 'The European Employment Strategy: The Will but not the Way?' *Industrial Law Journal* 30(4): 353–376.

Bańkowski, Z. and Christodoulidis, E. (1998) 'The European Union as an Essentially Contested Project', *European Law Journal* 4(4): 341–354.

Barber, N. (2006), 'Legal Pluralism and the European Union', *European Law Journal* 12(3): 306–329.

Barbera, M. (1991), *Discriminazione ed uguaglianza nel rapporto di lavoro* (Milan: Giuffrè).

Barbera, M. (2002), 'Not the Same? The Judicial Role in the New Community Anti-discrimination Law Context', *Industrial Law Journal* 31(1): 82–91.

Barbera, M. (ed.) (2006), *Nuove forme di regolazione: il metodo aperto di coordinamento delle politiche sociali* (Milan: Giuffrè).

Barbier, C. (2004), 'Systems of Social Protection in Europe: Two Contrasted Paths to Activation, and maybe a Third' in Lind, J., Knudsen, H. and Joergensen, H. (eds), *Labour and Employment Regulations in Europe* (Brussels: Peter Lang), pp. 233–254.

Barnard, B. (1999), 'Euro Era Begins', *Europe: Magazine of the EU* 383, February.

Barnard, C. (1996), 'The External Dimension of Community Social Policy' in Emiliou, N. and O'Keeffe, D. (eds), *The European Union and World Trade Law: after the GATT Uruguay Round* (London: Wiley), pp. 149–164.

Barnard, C. (1999), 'EC "Social" Policy' in Craig, P. and de Búrca, G. (eds), *The Evolution of EU Law* (Oxford: Oxford University Press), pp. 481–516.

Barnard, C. (2000), 'Flexibility and Social Policy' in de Búrca, G. and Scott, J. (eds) (2000), *Constitutional Change in the EU: From Uniformity to Flexibility?* (Oxford: Hart), pp. 197–217.

Barnard, C. (2002), 'The Social Partners and the Governance Agenda', *European Law Journal* 8(1): 80–101.

Barnard, C. (2006), *EC Employment Law* (Oxford: Oxford University Press).

Barnard, C. (2009), 'Fifty Years of Avoiding Social Dumping? The EU's Economic and not so Economic Constitution' in Dougan, M. and Currie, S. (eds), *Fifty Years of the European Treaties: Looking Back and Thinking Forward* (Oxford: Hart), pp. 311–342.

Barnard, C. and Deakin, S. (2000), 'In Search of Coherence: Social Policy, the Single Market and Fundamental Rights', *Industrial Relations Journal* 31(4): 331–345.

Barnard C., and Deakin, S. (2001), 'Corporate Governance, European Governance and Social Rights', paper presented at 'Fundamental Social Rights: a Conference to mark the Fortieth Anniversary of the Introduction of a Course on Industrial Law (later called Labour Law), in Part II of the Cambridge Law Tripos', University of Cambridge, 21 July.

Barnard, C., Deakin, S. and Hobbs, R. (2001), 'Capabilities and Rights: An Emerging Agenda for Social Policy?' *Industrial Relations Journal* 32(5): 464–479.

Baroncelli, S. (2008), 'The EMU Model and its Aftermath: Back to Maastricht or Far from Maastricht?' in Baroncelli, S., Spagnolo, C. and Talani, L. (eds), *Back to Maastricht: Obstacles to Constitutional Reform within the EU Treaty* (Newcastle upon Tyne: Cambridge Scholars), pp. 121–154.

Barrell, R. (1992), *Economic Convergence and Monetary Union in Europe* (London: Sage).

Bavagos, C. and Martin, C. (2000), *Low Fertility, Families and Public Policies: Synthesis Report*, annual seminar, Austrian Institute of Family Studies, Seville, Spain, 15–16 September.

Beck, G. (2007), 'The State of EC Anti-sex Discrimination Law and the Judgment in Cadman, or, How the Legal can become the Political: Case Comment', *European Law Review* 32(4): 549–562.

Begg, I. (2002), 'EMU and Employment: Social models in the EMU: Convergence? Coexistence? The Role of Economic and Social Actors', 'One Europe or Several?' Working Paper 42/02, p. 3, <http://www.one-europe.ac.uk/pdf/w42begg.pdf>.

Bekker, S. (2007), 'Flexibility and Security in the Adaptability Pillar of the European Employment Strategy', Social Science Research Network, March, <http://ssrn.com/abstract=957769>.

Bellamy, R. and Castiglione, D. (1997), 'Building the Union: The Nature of Sovereignty in the Political Architecture of Europe', *Law and Philosophy* 16: 421–445.

Benz, A. (2007), 'Accountable Multilevel Governance by the Open Method of Coordination?' *European Law Journal* 13(4): 505–522.

Benz, A. and Eberlein B. (1998), 'Regions in European Governance: The Logic of Multi-level Inter-action', RSC Working Paper 98/31, <http://www.eui.eu/RSCAS//WP-Texts/98_31.html>.

Benz, A. and Papadopoulos, Y. (2006), 'Actors, Institutions and Democratic Governance: Comparing across Levels' in Benz, A. and Papadopoulos, Y. (eds), *Governance and Democracy: Comparing National, European and International Experiences* (London: Routledge), pp. 273–295.

Bercusson, B. (1990), 'The European Community's Charter of Fundamental Social Rights of Workers', *Modern Law Review* 53: 624–642.

Bercusson, B. (1994), 'The Dynamic of European Labour Law after Maastricht', *Industrial Law Journal* 23(1): 1–31.

Bercusson, B. (1996), *European Labour Law* (London: Butterworth).

Bercusson, B. (1999), 'Democratic Legitimacy and European Labour Law', *Industrial Law Journal*, 28(2):153–170.

Bercusson, B. (2001), 'A European Agenda?' in K. Ewing (ed.), *Employment Rights at Work* (London: Institute of Employment Rights).

Bercusson, B. (2009), *European Labour Law* (Cambridge: Cambridge University Press).

Bercusson, B. and Dickens, L. (1996), *Equal Opportunities and Collective Bargaining in Europe* 3 (Dublin: European Foundation for the Improvement of Living and Working Conditions; Luxembourg: OOPEC).

Bercusson, B. and Van Dijk, J. (1995), 'The implementation of the Protocol and Agreement on Social Policy of the Treaty of the European Union', *International Journal of Comparative Labour Law and Industrial Relations* 11(1): 3–30.

Bercusson, B. *et al.* (1997), 'A Manifesto for Social Europe', *European Law Journal* 3(2): 189–205.

Bermann, G. (2001), 'Law in an Enlarged European Union', *EUSA Review* 14(3): 1–5.

Bernard, N. (2000), 'Legitimising EU Law: Is the Social Dialogue the Way Forward? Some Reflections around the *UEAPME* Case' in Shaw, J. (ed.), *Social Law and Policy in an Evolving European Union* (Oxford: Hart).

Bernitsas, P. (1993), 'State Aids and Public Undertakings' in Harden, I. (ed.), *State Aid Control: Community Law and Policy* (Cologne: Bundesanzeiger), pp. 110–123.

Betten, L. (1998), 'The Democratic Deficit of the Participatory Democracy in Community Social Policy', *European Law Review* 23(1): 20–36.

Betten, L. and Shrubsall, V. (1998), 'The Concept of Positive Sex Discrimination in Community Law: Before and After the Treaty of Amsterdam', *International Journal of Comparative Labour Law and Industrial Relations* 14(1): 65–99.

Bettio, F. and Villa, P. (1996), 'A Mediterranean Perspective on the Breakdown of the Relationship between Participation and Fertility', Discussion Paper 5, University of Trento.

Beveridge, W. (1944), *Full Employment in a Free Society* (London: Allen & Unwin).

Biagi, M. (1998), 'The Implementation of the Amsterdam Treaty with regard to Employment: Coordination or Convergence?' *International Journal of Comparative Labour Law and Industrial Relations* 14(4): 325–336.

Biagi, M. (1998a), 'Lavoro, le promesse della ricetta Italia', *La Repubblica*, 3 June.

Biagi, M. (2000), 'The Impact of the European Employment Strategy on the Role of Labour Law and Industrial Relations', *International Journal of Comparative Labour Law and Industrial Relations* 16(2): 157–161.

Biagi, M. (2002), 'Quality in European Community Industrial Relations' in R. Blanpain (ed.), *The Evolving Employment Relationship and the New Economy* (The Hague: Kluwer).

Bignami, F. (2004), 'Three Generations of Participation Rights before the European Commission', *Law and Contemporary Problems* 68(1): 61–83.

Bíziková, L. *et al.* (2005), 'Gender Audit of the EU Pre-accession Funds, 1999–2004', Prague, <http://www.genderstudies.cz/en>.

Blanpain, R. (1998), 'Il Trattato di Amsterdam e oltre: la fine del modello sociale europeo?' *Diritto delle Relazioni Industriali* 1: 11–26.

Blanpain, R. (ed.) (2001), *Labour Law, Human Rights and Social Justice: Liber Amicorum in Honour of Ruth Ben-Israel* (The Hague: Kluwer).

Blanpain, R. and Colucci, M. (2000), *Il diritto comunitario del lavoro ed il suo impatto sull'ordinamento giuridico italiano* (Padua: CEDAM).

Blanpain, R. and Swiatkowski, A. (eds) (2009), *The Laval and Viking Cases: Freedom of Services and Establishment versus Industrial Conflict in the European Economic Area and Russia* (The Hague: Kluwer).

Blichner, L. and Molander, A. (2008), 'Mapping Juridification', *European Law Journal* 14(1): 36–54.

Blom J., Fitzpatrick, B., Gregory, J., Knegt, R. and O'Hare, U. (1995), *The Utilisation of Sex Equality Litigation Procedures in the Member States of the European Community: A Comparative Study*, V/782/96–EN, Brussels: European Commission.

Boeri, T. (1997), 'Learning from Transition Economies: Assessing Labour Market Policies across Central and Eastern Europe', *Journal of Comparative Economics* 25: 366–384.

Boeri, T. *et al.* (2000), 'The Concept and Measurement of European Labour Market Adaptability', paper presented at the Workshop 'Concepts and Measurement of European Labour Markets Flexibility/Adaptability Indices', Brussels, 26–27 October, <http://europa.eu.t_social/empl&esf/concepts_en.htm>.

Bogdandy, A. von (1999), 'The Legal Case for Unity: The European Union as a Single Organisation with a Single Legal System', *Common Market Law Review* 36(5): 887–910.

Bomberg, E. and Peterson, J. (2000), 'Policy Transfer and Europeanization: Passing the Heineken Test?' Queen's Papers on Europeanization 2/2000, Queen's University of Belfast.

Bonoli, G. (1997), 'Classifying Welfare States: a Two-dimensional Approach', *Journal of Social Policy* 26 (3): 351–372.

Borchardt, G. M. and Wellens, K. C. (1989), 'Soft Law in European Community Law' *European Law Review* 14(5), 267–321.

Bordogna, L. and Cella, G. (1999), 'Admission, Exclusion, Correction: The Changing Role of the State in Industrial Relations', *Transfer* 1–2: 14–33.

Borrás, S. and Greve, B. (2004), 'Concluding Remarks: New Method or Just Cheap Talk?' *Journal of European Public Policy* 11(2): 329–336.

Borrás, S. and Jacobsson, K. (2004), 'The Open Method of Coordination and New Governance Patterns in the European Union', *Journal of European Public Policy* 11(2): 185–208.

Bovens, M. (2007), 'Analysing and Assessing Accountability: A Conceptual Framework', *European Law Journal* 13(4): 447–468.

Brandsma, G., Curtin, D. and Meijer, A. (2008), 'How Transparent are EU "Comitology" Committees in Practice?' *European Law Journal* 14(6): 819–838.

Bredgaard, T. and Larsen, F. (eds) (2005), *Employment Policy from Different Angles* (Copenhagen: DJOF).

Britz, G. and Schimdt, M. (2000), 'The Institutionalized Participation of Management and Labour in the Community Law', *European Law Journal* 6(1): 45–71.

Brunn, N. (2001), 'The European Employment Strategy and the "Acquis Communautaire" on Labour Law', *International Journal of Comparative Labour Law and Industrial Relations* 17: 309–324.

Bruszt, L. (2002), 'Making Markets and Eastern Enlargement: Diverging Convergence?' *West European Politics* 25(2): 121–140.

Bruszt, L. (2008), 'Multilevel Governance: The Eastern Versions', NewGov Policy Brief 17, spring: Florence: European University Institute.

Büchs, M. (2007), *New Governance in European Social Policy: The Open Method of Coordination* (Basingstoke: Palgrave Macmillan).

Bulmer, S. and Padgett, S. (2005), 'Policy Transfer in the European Union: An Institutionalist Perspective', *British Journal of Political Science* 35(1): 103–126.

Burrows, N. and Robinson, M. (2007), 'An Assessment of the Recast of Community Equality Laws', *European Law Journal* 13(2): 186–203.

Buti, M., Eijffinger, S. and Franco, D. (2003), *Revisiting the Stability and Growth Pact: Grand Design or Internal Adjustment?* Economic Papers 180, Brussels: DG of Economic and Financial Affairs, European Economy, January.

Cafaro, S. (2003), 'La méthode ouverte de coordination: l'action communautaire et le rôle politique du Conseil européen', *Mélange en Hommage à Jean-Victor Louis*, Vol. II (Brussels: ULB).

Caporaso, J. (1996), 'The European Union and Forms of State: Westphalian, Regulatory or Postmodern?' *Journal of Common Market Studies* 34(1): 29–52.

Caracciolo di Torella, E (2007), 'The Principle of Equality, the Goods and Services Directive and Insurance: a Conceptual Approach', *Maastricht Journal of European and Comparative Law* 13: 339–350.

Carter, C. and Scott, A. (1998), 'Legitimacy and Governance beyond the European Nation State: Conceptualising Governance in the European Union', *European Law Journal* 4(4): 429–445.

Caruso, B. (1997), 'Il contratto collettivo europeo' II, *Lavoro, impresa e società* 322.

Casey, B. and Gold, M. (2005), 'Peer Review of Labour Market Programmes in the European Union: What can Countries Really Learn from One Another?' *Journal of European Public Policy* 12(1): 23–43.

Castle, S. and Grice, A. (2000), 'Radical Reform rejected for a Please-all Fudge', *The Independent*, 11 December.

Cecchini, P. (1988), *The European Challenge, 1992: The Benefits of a Single Market* (Aldershot: Gower).

Celin, M. (2003), 'The European Employment Strategy: the Right Answer for the Candidate Countries?' *Transfer* 9(1): 88–100.

Cerami, A. (2008), 'Central Europe in Transition: Emerging Models of Welfare and Social Assistance', MPRA Paper 8377, <http://mpra.ub.uni-muenchen.de/8377/>.

Chalmers, D. and Lodge, M. (2003), 'The Open Method of Co-ordination and the European Welfare State', ESRC Centre for Analysis of Risk and Regulation, Discussion Paper 11, London School of Economics and Political Science, June, <http://www.lse.ac.uk/collections/CARR/pdf/DPs/Disspaper11pdf>.

Chalmers, D. and Szyszczak, E.(1998), *European Union Law: Towards a European Polity*, Vol. II (Ashgate: Dartmouth).

Choluj, B. and Neusuess, C. (2004), 'EU enlargement in 2004: East–West priorities and perspectives from women inside and outside the European Union', unpublished paper, May.

Christensen, A. (2000), 'Structural Aspects of Anti-discriminatory Legislation and Processes of Normative Change', paper presented at the conference 'Legal Perspectives on Equal Treatment and Non-discrimination', Lund, Sweden, 7–8 December, pp. 1–25.

Cini, M. (2000), 'From Soft Law to Hard Law? Discretion and Rule-making in the Commission's State Aid Regime', RSC 2000/35.

Citi, M. and Rhodes, M. (2007), 'New Modes of Governance in the European Union: A Critical Survey and Analysis' in Jorgensen, K., Pollack, M. and Rosamond, B. (eds), *Handbook of European Union Politics* (London: Sage), pp. 463–482.

Clarke, S. (2001), 'Earnings of Men and Women in the EU: the Gap Narrowing But only Slowly', Statistics in Focus, EUROSTAT, Theme 3–5/2001.

Clarkson, S. (1997), 'Perché' no? Qualms about Currency Union from Over the Sea', Paper presented at the Workshop: *The Political and Institutional Deficits of the European Integration Process*, European University Institute, 30–31 May 1997.

Cohen, J. and Debonneuil, M. (2000), 'L'économie de la nouvelle économie' in Conseil d'Analyse Economique, Rapport 28, *Nouvelle économie*, Paris: Documentation française.

Cohen, J. and Sabel, C. F. (1997), 'Directly-deliberative Polyarchy', *European law Journal* 3(4): 313–342.

Cooper, I. (2009), 'Mapping the Overlapping Spheres: European Constitutionalism after the Treaty of Lisbon', paper presented for the EUSA Biannual Conference, Los Angeles CA, 23–25 April 2009.

Coppel, J. and O'Neill, A. (1992), 'The European Court of Justice: Taking Rights Seriously?' *Common Market Law Review* 29: 669–692.

Coriat, B. and Petit P. (1991), 'Deindustrialisation and Terziarization: Towards a New Economic Regime?' in Amin, A. and Dietrich, M. (eds), *Towards a New Europe?* (Aldershot: Edward Elgar), p. 18.

Coron, G. and Palier B. (2002), 'Changes in the Means of Financing Social Expenditure in France since 1945' in de la Porte, C. and Pochet, P. (eds), *Building Social Europe through the Open Method of Co-ordination* (Brussels: PIE/Peter Lang).

Costabile, L. (2004), 'Conclusions. Wage Moderation, Wage Differentials and the Evolution of the Employment Relation in Italy: A Critical Comment on the White Book of the Italian Ministry of Labour' in Antonelli, G. and De Liso, N. (eds), *European Economic Integration and Italian Labour Policies* (Aldershot: Ashgate), pp. 273–296.

Cotterell, R. (2007), 'Is it Bad to be Different? Comparative Law and the Appreciation of Diversity' in Orucu, E. and Nelsen, D. (eds), *Comparative Law: A Handbook* (Oxford: Hart), pp. 133–154.

Council of Europe (1998), *Gender Mainstreaming: Conceptual Framework, Methodology and Presentation of Good Practices, Final Report of the Activities of the Group of Specialists on Mainstreaming.* EG-S_MS(98)2 (Strasbourg: Council of Europe).

Craig, P. (1997), 'Democracy and Rule-Making Within the EC: An Empirical and Normative Assessment', *European Law Journal* 3(2): 105–130.

Craig P. (1999), 'The Nature of the Community: Integration, Democracy and Legitimacy' in Craig, P. and de Búrca, G. (eds), *The Evolution of EU Law* (Oxford University Press), pp. 1–53.

Craig, P. (2001), 'Constitutions, Constitutionalism and the European Union', *European Law Journal* 7(2): 125–150.

Craig, P. (2004), 'Competence: Clarity, Conferral, Containment and Consideration', *European Law Review* 29(3): 323–344.

Craig, P. (2008), 'The Treaty of Lisbon: Process, Architecture and Substance', *European Law Review* 33(2): 137–166.

Craig, P. and de Búrca, G. (1999), *The Evolution of EU Law* (Oxford: Oxford University Press).

Craig, P. and de Búrca, G. (2003), *EU Law: Text, Cases, and Materials* (Oxford: Oxford University Press).

Cram, L. (1997), *Policy-Making in the EU: Conceptual Lenses and the Integration Process* (London and New York: Routledge).

Cullen, H. and Campbell, E. (1999), 'The Future of Social Policy-Making in the European Union' in Craig, P. and Harlow, C. (eds), *Lawmaking in the European Union* (The Hague: Kluwer), pp. 262–283.

Currie, D. (1998), 'Does EMU Need Political Union?' *Prospect* 5, June.

Curtin, D. (1993), 'The Constitutional Structure of the Union: A Europe of Bits and Pieces', *Common Market Law Review* 30(1): 17–69.

Curtin, D. and Dekker, I. (1999), 'The EU as a "Layered" International Organisation: Institutional Unity in Disguise' in Craig, P. and de Búrca, G. (eds), *The Evolution of EU Law* (Oxford: Oxford University Press), pp. 83–186.

Czech Republic (1963), Civil Procedure Code (Act 99/1963), Prague: Czech Republic.

Czech Republic (1965), Labour Code (Act 65/1965), Prague: Ministry of Labour and Social Affairs of the Czech Republic.

Czech Republic (1991), Employment Act 1/1991, Prague: Ministry of Labour and Social Affairs of the Czech Republic.

Czech Republic (1991a), Act 9/1991 on Employment and the Competence of the state Administration Authorities of the Czech Republic, Ministry of Labour and Social Affairs of the Czech Republic.

Czech Republic (2000), Joint Assessment of the Employment Policy Priorities of the Czech Republic, <http://ec.europa.eu/employment_social/intcoop/news/assessment_en.pdf>.

Czech Republic (2001), Act 54/2001, Consolidated Act on Salary, Remuneration for Stand-by Work and Average Income, Prague: Ministry of Labour and Social Affairs of the Czech Republic.

Czech Republic (2002), Act 220/2002 amending Act 1/1991 on Employment and Act 9/1991 on Employment and Competence of the State Administration Authorities of the Czech Republic, Prague: Ministry of Labour and Social Affairs of the Czech Republic.

Czech Republic (2002a), Act 151/2002 amending certain Provisions in connection with the Enactment of the Rules of Administrative Procedure, effective as of 1 January 2003.

Czech Republic (2004), National Action Plan for Employment, 2004–2006, Ministry of Labour and Social Affairs of the Czech Republic.

Czech Republic (2004a), Employment Act 435/2004 of 13 May 2004, Prague: Ministry of Labour and Social Affairs of the Czech Republic.

Czech Republic (2005), *National Reform Programme of the Czech Republic, 2005–2008*, Prague: Ministry of Labour and Social Affairs of the Czech Republic, October.

Czech Republic (2006), Labour Code (Act 262/2006), Prague: Ministry of Labour and Social Affairs of the Czech Republic.

Czech Republic (2008), *National Reform Programme of the Czech Republic, 2008–2010*, October.

Czech Statistical Office, CSU (2009), 'Employment in Figures', <http://www.czech.cz>.

Dahl, R. (1982), *Dilemmas of Pluralist Democracy* (Hartford CT: Yale University Press).

D'Antona, M. (1994), 'Armonizzazione del diritto del lavoro e federalismo nell'Unione Europea', *Rivista Trimestrale di Diritto e Procedura Civile* 3: 695–717.

Dashwood, A. (2007–2008), '*Viking* and *Laval:* Issues of Horizontal Direct Effect', *Cambridge Yearbook of European Legal Studies* 10: 525–540.

Davies, G. (2005), ' "Any place I hang my hat"? or, Residence is the New Nationality', *European Law Journal* 11(1): 43–56.

Davies, G. (2006), 'Subsidiarity: The Wrong Idea, in the Wrong Place, at the Wrong Time', *Common Market Law Review*, 43(1): 63–84.

Davies, P. and Freedland, M. (1983), *Kahn-Freund's Labour Law and the Law* (London: Stevens).

Deakin, S. (2007–2008), 'Regulatory Competition after *Laval*', *Cambridge Yearbook of European Legal Studies* 10: 581–610.

Deakin, S. and Reed, H. (2000), 'The Contested Meaning of Labour Market Flexibility' in Shaw (ed.), *Social Law and Policy in an Evolving European Union* (Oxford: Hart).

de Búrca, G. (1995), 'The Language of Rights and European Integration' in Shaw, J. and More, G. (eds), *New Legal Dynamics of European Union* (Oxford: Clarendon Press), pp. 29 ff.

de Búrca, G. (1999), 'Reappraising Subsidiarity's Significance after Amsterdam', Jean Monnet Working Paper 7/99.

de Búrca G. (2000), 'Differentiation within the "Core"? The Case of the Internal Market' in de Búrca, G. and Scott, J. (eds), *Constitutional Change in the EU: From Uniformity to Flexibility?* (Oxford: Hart), pp. 133–171.

de Búrca, G. (2003), 'The Constitutional Challenge of New Governance in the European Union', *European Law Review* 28(6): 814–839.

de Búrca, G. and Scott, J. (eds) (2000), *Constitutional Change in the EU: From Uniformity to Flexibility?* (Oxford: Hart).

de Búrca, G. and Scott, J. (eds) (2006), *Law and New Governance in the EU and the US* (Oxford: Hart).

de Búrca, G. and Scott, J. (eds) (2007), 'Narrowing the Gap? Law and New Approaches to Governance in the European Union', *Columbia Journal of European Law*, special issue, 13(3).

de Búrca, G. (2008), 'New Modes of Governance and their Relevance for EU Law', NewGov Policy Brief 30, Florence: European University Institute.

de Grauwe, P. (1996), 'Monetary Union and Convergence Economics', *European Economic Review* 40: 1091–1101.

de Grauwe, P. (1997), *The Economics of Monetary Integration* (Oxford: Oxford University Press).

de Grauwe, P. (2002), 'Challenges for Monetary Policy in Euroland', *Journal of Common Market Studies* 40(4): 693–718.

de Grauwe, P. (2008), 'The EMU after Maastricht' in Baroncelli, S., Spagnolo, C. and Talani, L. (eds), *Back to Maastricht: Obstacles to Constitutional Reform within the EU Treaty* (Newcastle: Cambridge Scholars), pp. 266–281.

de la Porte, C. (2002), 'Is the Open Method of Coordination Appropriate for Organizing Activities at European Level in Sensitive Policy Areas?', *European Law Journal* 8(1): 38–58.

de la Porte, C., Pochet, P. and Room, G. (2001), 'Social Benchmarking, Policy Making and New Governance on the European Union', *Journal of European Social Policy* 11(4): 291–307.

de la Porte, C. and Deacon, B. (2002), 'Contracting Companies and Consultants: the EU and the Social Policy of Accession Countries', GASPP Occasional Paper 9/2002, <http://www.gasp.org>.

de la Porte, C. and Pochet, P. (2002), 'Supple Coordination at EU Level and Key Actors' Involvement' in de la Porte, C. and Pochet, P. (eds), *Building Social Europe through the Open Method of Co-ordination* (Brussels: PIE/Peter Lang).

de la Porte, C. and Nanz, P. (2004), 'The OMC: a Deliberative-democratic Mode of Governance? The Cases of Employment and Pensions', *Journal of European Public Policy* 11(2): 267–288.

de la Porte, C. (2008), 'The evolution and influence of the Open Method of Coordination: the cases of employment and social inclusion', Ph.D thesis (Florence: European University Institute).

de Munck, J. and Lenoble, J. (2001), 'Transformations in the Art of Governance' in de Schutter, O., Lebessis, N. and Paterson, J. (eds), *Governance in the European Union* (Luxembourg: OOPEC), pp. 29–51.

de Ruiter, R. (2009), 'Parliamentary Scrutiny of Methods of Open Coordination: The Involvement of the Dutch and British Parliaments in the EU Governance of the Knowledge-based Society', paper presented for the EUSA Biannual Conference, Los Angeles CA, 23–25 April.

de Schutter, O. (2002), 'Europe in Search of its Civil Society', *European Law Journal* 8(1): 198–217.

de Schutter, O. (2005), 'The Implementation of Fundamental Rights through the Open method of Coordination' in de Schutter, O. and Deakin, S. (eds), *Social Rights and Market Forces: Is the Open Coordination of Employment and Social Policies the Future of Social Europe?* (Bruxelles: Bruylant), pp. 279–343.

de Schutter, O. and Deakin, S. (eds) (2005), *Social Rights and Market Forces: Is the Open Coordination of Employment and Social Policies the Future of Social Europe?* (Bruxelles: Bruylant).

de Sousa Santos, B. (2002), *Toward a New Legal Common Sense: Law, Globalization, and Emancipation* (London: Butterworth).

de Witte, B. (1999), 'The Past and Future Role of the European Court of Justice in the Protection of Human Rights' in Alston, P., Bustelo, M. and Heenan, J. (eds), *The EU and Human Rights* (Oxford: Oxford University Press), pp. 859–897.

Degryse, C. and Pochet, P. (2000), *Social Developments in the European Union, 2000: Second Annual Report*, Brussels: OSE/ ETUI, November.

Degryse, C. and Pochet, P. (2001), *Social Developments in the European Union, 2000: Second Annual Report*, OSE, ETUI, Brussels, April, <http://www.ose.be/en/default.htm>.

Della Posta, P. (2008), 'The Long Road to EMU: Determinants and Theoretical Foundations of the EMS and EMU' in Baroncelli, S., Spagnolo, C. and Talani, L. (eds), *Back to Maastricht: Obstacles to Constitutional Reform within the EU Treaty* (Newcastle upon Tyne: Cambridge Scholars), pp. 220–241.

Delors, J. (1989), *Report on Economic and Monetary Union in the Community* ('Delors Committee') (Luxembourg: European Communities).

Denmark (1976), Equal Pay Act, Act 32/1976, <http://ligeuk.itide.dk/>.

Denmark (2000), Equal Opportunity Act, Act 388 of 30 May 2000, as amended by Section 4 of Act 440 of 7 June 2001, Act 146 of 25 March 2002, Section 2 of Act 373 of 6 June 2002 and Section 1 of Act 396 of 6 June 2002, <http://ligeuk.itide.dk/>.

Denmark (2001), Minister of Finance, *Agreement on Future Prosperity:* Welfare and Investments in the Future, <http://www.fm.dk>.

Denmark (2002), Danish National Institute of Social Research, Impact Evaluation of the European Employment Strategy, Denmark, Synthesis Report, February 2002, available on the web site of the European Commission Directorate General of Employment and Social affairs.

Denmark (2002a), The Danish Inter-ministerial Gender Mainstreaming Project Action Plan, 2002–2006, The New Gender Equality Strategy, <http://ligeuk.itide.dk/>.

Denmark (2003), 'NAP 2003. The Government: Denmark's National Action Plan for Employment, 2003', Copenhagen: Ministry of Employment.

Denmark (2003a), Act 756/2003 Respecting Equal Wages for Men and Women, Copenhagen: Ministry of Equal Opportunities.

Denmark (2005), Denmark's National Reform Programme. The Danish Reform Strategy. Contribution to EU's Growth and Employment Strategy (the Lisbon Strategy), Copenhagen: Ministry of Finance, October.

Denmark (2005a), *En ny chance til alle* (A new chance for everybody), May, <ec.europa.eu/ewsi/UDRW/images/items/docl_4298_420011852.pdf>.

Denmark (2006), An Agreement on Future Prosperity, Welfare and Investment in the Future (the Welfare Agreement), June, <www.fm.dk>.

Denmark (2006a), Act 562/2006 amending Act 756/2003 Respecting Equal Wages for Men and Women, Copenhagen: Ministry of Equal Opportunities.

Denmark (2007), The Danish Inter-ministerial Gender Mainstreaming Project Action Plan, 2007–2011, <http://ligeuk.itide.dk/files/PDF/Mainstreaming/mainhandlingsplan2007–2011eng.pdf>.

Denmark (2008), Denmark's National Reform Programme. The Danish Reform Strategy. Contribution to EU's Growth and Employment Strategy (the Lisbon Strategy), Copenhagen: Ministry of Finance, October.

Docksey, C. (1991), 'The Principle of Equality between Women and Men as a Fundamental Right under Community Law', *Industrial Law Journal* 20(4): 258–280.

Docksey, C. and Fitzpatrick, B. (1991), 'The Duty of National Courts to Interpret Provisions of National Law in Accordance with Community Law', *Industrial Law Journal* 20: 113.

Dolowitz, D. and Marsh, D. (2000), 'Learning from Abroad: The Role of Policy Transfer in Contemporary Policy-Making', *Governance* 13(1): 5–24.

Dorf, M. and Sabel, C. (1998), 'A Constitution of Democratic Experimentalism', *Columbia Law Review* 98(2): 267–243.

Dougan, M. (2000), 'Minimum Harmonization and the Internal Market', *Common Market Law Review* 37(4): 853–885.

Dougan, M. (2004), *National Remedies before the Court of Justice: Issues of Harmonization and Differentiation* (Oxford: Hart).

Dougan, M. (2006), ' "And some fell on stony ground . . ." A Critical Reading of G. Majone's Dilemma of European Integration', *European Law Review* 31: 865–878.

Dougan, M. (2008), 'The Treaty of Lisbon 2007: Winning Minds, Not Hearts', *Common Market Law Review* 45: 617–703.

Drywood, E. (2007), 'Giving with One Hand, Taking with the Other: Fundamental Rights, Children and the Family Reunification Decision', *European Law Review* 32(3): 396–407.

Duina, F. and Raunio, T. (2007), 'The Open Method of Coordination and National Parliaments: Further Marginalization or New Opportunities?' *Journal of European Public Policy* 14(4): 489–505.

Easterby Smith, M., Crossan, M. and Nicolini, D. (2000), 'Organisational Learning: Debates Past, Present and Future', *Journal of Management Studies* 37(5): 783–96.

Editorial (2003), 'Employment in the European Union Candidate Countries', *European Industrial Relations Review* 350: 22–27.

Editorial (2006), 'Horizontal Direct Effect: a Law of Diminishing Coherence?' *Common Market Law Review* 43: 1–8.

Editorial (2008), 'Direct Democracy and the European Union . . . is that a Threat or a Promise?', *Common Market Law Review* 45: 929–940.

EGGE (2009), *The National Reform Programmes 2008 and the Gender Aspects of the European Employment Strategy: Final Report*, Rome: Fondazione Giacomo Brodolini, March.

EGGSIE (2007), *Gender Mainstreaming of Employment Policies: A Comparative Review of Thirty European Countries*, Brussels: European Commission, Directorate General of Employment, Social Affairs and

Equal Opportunities, Unit G1, <http://ec.europa.eu/employment_social/gender_equality/docs/2007/gend_mainstr07_en.pdf>.

Ehlermann, C. D. (1984), 'How Flexible is Community Law? An Unusual Approach to the Concept of "Two Speeds" ', *Michigan Law Review* 82(1–2): 1274–1293.

Eichhorst, W., Kaufmann, O. and Konle Seidl, R. (eds) (2008), *Bringing the Jobless into Work? Experiences with Activation Schemes in Europe and the US* (Berlin: Springer).

Eiro (2001), 'Social Partners' Laeken Declaration', <http://www.eiro.eurofound.ie/2001/12/feature/EU0112262F.html>.

EIRR (1998), Repercussions of Vilvoorde closure (Implications for European social policy of Renault's failure to follow consultation requirements when making collective redundancies as result of closure of plant in Belgium), 289: 22–25.

Ekengren, M. and Jacobsson, K. (2000) 'Explaining the Consitutionalization of EU Governance: the Case of European Employment Co-operation', <URL:http://www.score.su.se/pdfs/2000–8.pdf>, pp. 13–14.

Ellis, E. (2005), *EU Anti-discrimination Law* (Oxford: Oxford University Press).

Ely, J. (1980), *Democracy and Distrust: A Theory of Judicial Review* (Cambridge MA: Harvard University Press).

Emerek, R. (2006), 'The Gender Pay Gap: The Danish Case. Thematic Report', European Commission's Expert Group on Gender, Social Inclusion and Employment Report for the Equal Opportunities Unit, Directorate-General Employment.

Engblom S. (2000), 'Equal Treatment of Employees and Self-employed Workers?' Paper presented at the conference 'Legal Perspectives on Equal Treatment and Non-discrimination', Lund, Sweden, 7–8 December.

Esping-Andersen, G. (1990), *The Three Worlds of Welfare Capitalism* (Cambridge: Polity Press).

Estella, A. (2002), *The EU Principle of Subsidiarity and its Critique* (Oxford: Oxford University Press).

Esty, C. D. (2006), 'Good Governance at the Supranational Scale: Globalizing Administrative Law', *Yale Law Journal* 115: 1490–1562.

ETUC (2000), Resolution on the 'EU Employment Guidelines 2001', 25–26 October, <http://www.etuc.org>.

ETUC (2000a), Resolution on the Commission's Communication entitled 'A Concerted Strategy for Modernizing Social Protection', <http://www.etuc.org/English/0003_Socialprotection.cfm?>. Lisbon, 21 and 22 March 2000>.

ETUC (2001), Luxembourg Process: ETUC Employment Fiches', <http://www.etuc.org>.

ETUC, CEEP, UNICE and UEAPME (2000), Joint Report 'Factors for success: a compendium of social partners' initiatives relating to the employment guidelines' in ETUC Resolution on the 'EU Employment Guidelines 2001', 25–26 October, <URL:http://www.etuc.org>.

EU NIEFR (2002), *EU Network of Independent Experts in Fundamental Rights Report on the Situation of Fundamental Rights in the European Union and its Member States in 2002*, <europa.eu.int/comm./justice_home/cfr_cdf/doc/rapport_2002_en.pdf>.

Evans, A. (1997), *EC Law of State Aid* (Oxford: Clarendon Press).

Everson, M. (1995), 'The Legacy of the Market Citizen' in Shaw, J. and More, G. (eds), *New Legal Dynamics of European Union* (Oxford: Oxford University Press), pp. 73–90.

Everson, M. (1998), 'Administering Europe', *Journal of Common Market Studies* 36(2): 195–215.

Everson, M. (1998a), 'Beyond the "Bundesverfassungsgericht:" On the Necessary Cunning of Constitutional Reasoning', *European Law Journal* 4(4): 389–410.

Fagan, C. *et al.* (2006), 'The Subordination of the Gender equality Objective: the National Reform Programmes and "Making Work Pay" Policies', *Industrial Relations Journal* 37(6): 571–592.

Falkner, G. (1999), *EU Social Policy in the 1990s* (London and New York: Routledge).

Fenger, H. (2007), 'Welfare Regimes in Central and Eastern Europe: Incorporating Post-communist Countries in a Welfare Regime Typology', *Contemporary Issues and Ideas in Social Sciences* 1–30, August.

Ferge, Z. (2001), 'European Integration and the Reform of Social Security in the Accession Countries', *Journal of European Social Quality* 3: 9–25.

Ferner, A. and Hyman, R. (1998), 'Introduction. Towards European Industrial Relations' in Ferner, A. and Hyman R. (eds), *Changing Industrial Relations in Europe* (Oxford: Blackwell), p. xvi.

Ferner A. (1991), *Changing Public Sector Industrial Relations in Europe*, Warwick Papers in Industrial Relations 37.

Ferrera, M. (1996), 'The "Southern" Model of Welfare in Social Europe', *Journal of European Social Policy* 6(1): 17–37.

Ferrera, M. *et al.* (2001) *The Future of Social Europe: Recasting Work and Welfare in the New Economy* (Oeiras, Portugal: Celta).

Ferrera, M. and Gualmini, E. (2002), 'La strategia europea sull'occupazione e la governance domestica del mercato del lavoro', paper presented for the 'ISFOL Project' (Istituto per lo Sviluppo della Funzione Professionale dei Lavoratori, 'Institute for the Improvement of the Professional Development of the Workers', Rome, February.

Fitzpatrick, B., Gregory, J. and Szyszczak, E. (1993), *Sex Equality Litigation in the Member States of the European Community: A Comparative Study*, V/407/94–EN (Brussels: European Commission).

Flek, V. and Večerník, J. (2005), 'The Labour Market in the Czech Republic: Trends, Policies, and Attitudes', *Czech Journal of Economics and Finance* 55: 5–24.

Foden, D. (1999), 'The Role of the Social Partners in the European Employment Strategy', *Transfer* 5(4): 215–245.

Fodor, E. (2006) 'Gender Mainstreaming and its Consequences in the European Union', *The Analyst: Central and Eastern European Review*, 7 January, <http://www.euractiv.com/29/images/Gender%20mainstreaming_apdf_tcm29–157876.pdf>.

Fredman, S. (1997), 'Labour Law in Flux: The Changing Composition of the Workforce', *Industrial Law Journal* 26(4): 337–352.

Fredman, S. (1998), 'Social Law in the European Union: the Impact of the Lawmaking Process' in Craig, P. and de Búrca, G. (eds), *Lawmaking in the European Union* (London: Kluwer), pp. 386–411.

Fredman, S. (1999), 'Social Law in the European Union: The Impact of the Lawmaking Process' in Craig, P. and Harlow, C. (eds), *Lawmaking in the European Union* (The Hague: Kluwer), pp. 386–411.

Fredman, S. (2004), 'Women at Work: The Broken Promise of Flexicurity', *Industrial Law Journal* 33(4): 299–319.

Freedland, M. (1996), 'Employment Policy' in Davies, P., Lyon-Caen, A., Sciarra, S. and Simitis, S. (eds), *European Community Labour Law: Principles and Perspectives. Liber Amicorum Lord Wedderburn of Charlton* (Oxford: Clarendon Press).

Freedland, M. (2003), *The Personal Employment Contract* (Oxford: Oxford University Press).

Friedman, L. (1975), *The Legal System: A Social Science Perspective* (New York: Russell Sage).

Fuszara, M. (2008), 'The OMC, Gender Policy and the Experience of Poland as a New Member State' in Beveridge, F. and Velluti, S. (eds), *Gender and the Open Method of Coordination: Perspectives on Law, Governance and Equality in the European Union* (Aldershot: Ashgate), pp. 103–117.

Garonna, P. (1998), 'Le "cento citta" ' in Europa: la classe dirigente locale nella competizione tra sistemi territoriali' in *Industria e Sindacato: Mensile dell'Associazione Sindacale Intersind*, July.

Gerstenberg, O. (1997), 'Law's Polyarchy: A Comment of Cohen and Sabel', *European Law Journal* 3(4): 343–358.

Giovannetti, G. and Marimon, R. (1995), *A Monetary Union for a Heterogeneous Europe*, EUI Working Paper, RSC No. 95/17.

Giubboni, S. (2006), *Social Rights and Market Freedom in the European Constitution: A Labour Law Perspective* (Cambridge: Cambridge University Press).

Goetschy, J. (1998), 'L'emploi et le social dans le traité d'Amsterdam: rattrapage, consolidation ou percée?' in Teló, M. and Magnette, P. (eds), *De Maastricht à Amsterdam: l'Europe et son nouveau traité* (Paris: Editions Complexe), pp. 139–163.

Goetschy, J. (1999), 'The European Employment Strategy: Genesis and Development', *European Journal of Industrial Relations* 5(2): 117–137.

Goetschy, J. (2000), 'The European Union and National Social Pacts: Employment and Social Protection put to the Test of Joint Regulation' in Fajertag, G. and Pochet, P. (eds), *Social Pacts in Europe: New Dynamics* (Brussels: OSE/ETUI).

Goetschy J. (2001), 'The European Employment Strategy from Amsterdam to Stockholm: Has it Reached its Cruising Speed Yet?' *Industrial Relations Journal* 32(5): 401–418.

Goetschy, J. (2001a), 'The Future of the European Employment Strategy' in Mückenberger *et al.* (eds), *Manifesto Social Europe* (Brussels: ETUI).

Goetschy, J. (2002), '2001–2002: Transition Years for Employment in Europe: EU Governance and National Diversity under Scrutiny', *Industrial Relations Journal* 33: 405–23.

Goetschy, J. (2003), 'The European Employment Strategy, Multi-level Governance and Policy Co-ordination: Past, Present and Future' in Zeitlin, J. and Trubek, D. (eds), *Governing Work and Welfare in a new Economy: European and American Experiments* (Oxford: Oxford University Press).

GOVECOR (2004), *EU Governance by Self-co-ordination? Towards a Collective 'gouvernement économique': Final Report*, <http://www.govecor.org>.

Grzegorz Grosse, T. and Kolarska-Bobińska, L. (2008), 'New Modes of Governance in New Member States', NewGov Policy Brief 25, spring, Florence: European University Institute.

Grant, W. and Keohane, O. (2005), 'Accountability and Abuse of Power in World Politics', *American Political Science Review* 99(1): 29–43.

Gualini, E. (2004), *Multi-level Governance and Institutional Change: The Europeanization of Regional Policy in Italy* (Aldershot: Ashgate).

Häberle, P. (1992), 'Verfassungsentwicklungen in Osteuropa. Aus der Sicht der Rechtsphilosophie und der Verfassungslehre', *Archiv des öffentlichen Rechts* 117: 170.

Hahn, H. (2002), 'The Stability Pact for European Monetary Union: Compliance with Deficit Limit as a Constant Legal Duty', *Common Market Law Review* 35: 77–100.

Haltern, U. (2002), 'Pathos and Patina: The Failure and Promise of Constitutionalism in the European Imagination', conWEB Paper 2002/6, Web Papers on Constitutionalism and Governance beyond the State, <www.bath.ac.uk/esml/conWEB>.

Hancher, L., Ottervanger, T. and Slot, P. J. (1999), *EC State Aids*, 2nd edn (London: Sweet & Maxwell).

Harlow, C. (2002), *Accountability in the European Union* (Oxford: Oxford University Press).

Harlow, C. and Rawlings, R. (2007), 'Promoting Accountability in Multilevel Governance: A Network Approach', *European Law Journal* 13(4): 542–562.

Hartwig, I. (2007), 'The European Employment Strategy and the Structural Funds: Spill-overs towards Communitarization?' in Linsenmann, I., Meyer, C. and Wessels, W. (eds), *Economic Government of the EU: A Balance Sheet of New Modes of Policy Coordination* (Basingstoke: Palgrave Macmillan), pp. 119–140.

Hassel, A. and Hoffmann, R. (2000), 'National Alliances for Jobs and Prospects for a European Employment Pact', DWP 2000.01.01 (E), ETUI, Brussels.

Hatzopoulos, V. (2005), 'A (More) Social Europe: A Political Crossroad or a Legal One-way? Dialogues between Luxembourg and Lisbon', *Common Market Law Review* 42: 1599–1635.

Hatzopoulos, V. (2007), 'Why the Open Method of Coordination is Bad for You: A Letter to the EU', *European Law Journal* 13(4): 309–342.

Hay, C., Watson, M. and Wincott, D. (1999), 'Globalisation, European Integration and the Persistence of European Social Models', POLSIS Working Paper 3/99, <www.bham.ac.uk/POLSIS/html>.

Hemerijck, A. and Visser, J. (2001), 'Learning and mimicking: how European welfare states reform', unpublished MS.

Henkin, L. (1968), *How Nations Behave: Law and Foreign Policy* (New York: Praeger).

Hepple, B. (1994), 'Green Paper. European Social Policy Options for the Union: Consultative Document. Communication by Mr Flynn, Commission of the European Communities, Directorate General of Employment, Industrial Relations and Social Affairs, Brussels, 17 November 1993', *Industrial Law Journal* 23(2): 180–183.

Hepple, B. (2001), 'The EU Charter of Fundamental Rights', *Industrial Law Journal* 30(2): 229.

Héritier, A. and Knill, C. (2000), 'Differential Responses to European Policies: A Comparison', Max Planck Projektgruppe Recht der Gemeinschaftsgüter, pre-print, Bonn.

Herod, A. (1998), 'Theorizing Trade Unions in Transition' in Pickles, J. and Smith, A. (eds), *Theorizing Transition: The Political Economy of Change in Central and Eastern Europe* (London: Routledge), pp. 197–217.

Hervey, T. (1998), *European Social Law and Policy* (London and New York: Longman).

Hervey, T. (2000), 'Social Solidarity: A Buttress against the Internal Market Law?' in Shaw, J. (ed.), *Social Law and Policy in an Evolving European Union* (Oxford: Hart), pp. 33–43.

High Level Group on Industrial Relations and Change in the European Union (2002), *Report*, European Commission, Directorate General of Employment and Social Affairs, Unit D1 (Luxembourg: OOPEC).

Hirst, P. (1994), *Associative Democracy* (Amherst MA: University of Massachusetts Press).

Hirst, P. (1997), *From Statism to Pluralism* (London: UCL Press).

Hodson, D. and Maher, I. (2000), 'Should We Mind the Gap? EMU and Consolidating Processes in Lisbon', *European Business Journal* 12(3): 140–145;

Hodson, D. and Maher, I. (2001), 'The Open Method as a New Mode of Governance: The Case of Soft Economic Policy Co-ordination', *Journal of Common Market Studies* 39(4): 719–746.

Hoffmann, J. and R. (2001), 'Globalisation, Risks and Opportunities for Labour Policy in Europe', DWP 97.04.01, ETUI, Brussels.

Holder, J. and Scott, J. (2006), 'Law and New Environmental Governance in the European Union' in de Búrca, G. and Scott, J. (eds), *Law and New Governance in the EU and the US* (Oxford: Hart), pp. 211–242.

Hood, C. (1986), 'The Hidden Public Sector: The "Quangocratization" of the World' in Kaufman, F.-X., Majone G. and Ostrom, V. (eds), *Guidance, Control and Evaluation in the Public Sector* (New York: de Gruyter).

Hood, C. (1991), 'Public Management for all Seasons', *Public Administration* 69: 3: 3–19.

Hooghe, L. and Marks, G. (2001), 'Types of Multi-level governance', *European Integration online Papers (EIOP)*, 5(11): 4–12, <http://eiop.or.at/eiop/texte/2001–011a.htm>.

House of Lords, European Union Committee (2008), 'The Treaty of Lisbon: an Impact Assessment', Tenth Report of Session 2007–2008, 13 March, <http://www.publications.parliament.uk/pa/ld200708/ldselect/ldeucom/62/62.pdf>.

Idema, T. and Kelemen, D. (2006), 'New Modes of Governance, the Open Method of Coordination and other Fashionable Red Herrings', *Perspectives on European Politics and Society* 7(1): 108–123.

Inman, R.P. and Rubinfield, D.L. (1994), 'The EMU and Fiscal Policy in the New European Community', *International Review of Law and Economics*, 14: 147–161.

International Labour Organization (ILO) (1956), 'Social Aspects of European Economic Co-operation: Report of a Group of Experts', *International Labour Review* 74: 99–123 (Ohlin Report).

International Labour Office (ILO) (1996), 'Full Employment: Still Feasible and Highly Desirable', press release, Geneva, 26 November.

International Labour Organization (ILO) (1999), Decent Work. Report of the Director General to the Eighty-seventh Session of the International Labour Conference, Geneva, June 2009, <www.ilo.org/public/english/standards/relm/ilc/ilc87/rep-i.htm>.

International Labour Organization (ILO) (2000), Maternity Protection 2000, News on Workers' Activities, <www.ilo.org/public/english/dialogue/actrav/genact/gender/mother/mater00.htm>.

Ippolito, F. (2007), *Fondamento, attuazione e controllo del principio di sussidiarietà nel diritto della Comunità e dell'Unione Europea* (Milan: Giuffrè).

Issing O. (2002), 'On Macroeconomic Policy Coordination in EMU', *Journal of Common Market Studies* 40(2): 345–358.

ISTAT (2005), Permanent Survey of the Labour Force, Third Quarter 2005.

Italy (1977), Legge 9 dicembre 1977, n. 903 'Parità di trattamento tra Uomini e Donne in materia di Lavoro', pubblicata nella *Gazzetta Ufficiale* n. 343 del 17 dicembre 1977.

Italy (1991), Legge 10 aprile 1991, n. 125 'azioni positive per la realizzazione della parita' uomo-donna nel lavoro', pubblicata nella *Gazzetta Ufficiale* n. 88 del 15 aprile 1991.

Italy (1997), Legge 24 giugno 1997, n. 196 'norme in materia di promozione dell'occupazione', pubblicata nella *Gazzetta Ufficiale* n. 154 del 4 luglio 1997 – Supplemento Ordinario n. 136.

Italy (1997a), Decreto del Presidente del Consiglio dei Ministri no. 405 del 28 Ottobre 1997 'regolamento recante istituzione ed organizzazione del Dipartimento per le Pari Opportunità nell'ambito della Presidenza del Consiglio dei Ministri', pubblicato nella *Gazzetta Ufficiale* n. 278 del 28 novembre 1997.

Italy (1998), Employment Action Plan, Italy, April, <http://europa.eu.int/comm/employment_social/naps/it_en.pdf>.

Italy (2000), Legge 8 marzo 2000, n. 53 'disposizioni per il sostegno della maternità e della paternità, per il diritto alla cura e alla formazione e per il coordinamento dei tempi delle città', pubblicata nella *Gazzetta Ufficiale* n. 60 del 13 marzo 2000.

Italy (2001), Ministero del Lavoro e delle politiche Sociali, 'Libro Bianco sul Mercato del Lavoro in Italia: proposte per una società attiva e per un lavoro di qualità', Rome, October.

Italy (2002), *Impact Evaluation of the European Employment Strategy, Italian Employment Policy in Recent Years: Impact Evaluation, Final Report, Draft*, <http://europa.eu.int/comm/employment_social/news/2002/may/eval_en.html>.

Italy (2003), Decreto Legislativo del 10 settembre 2003, n. 276 'attuazione delle deleghe in materia di occupazione e mercato del lavoro, di cui alla legge 14 febbraio 2003, n. 30', *Gazzetta Ufficiale* n. 235 del 9 ottobre 2003.

Italy (2003a), National Action Plan for Employment, Ministry of Labour and Social Affairs, Rome.

Italy (2004), Legge 23 agosto 2004, n. 243 'norme in materia pensionistica e deleghe al Governo nel settore della previdenza pubblica, per il sostegno alla previdenza complementare e all'occupazione stabile e per il riordino degli enti di previdenza ed assistenza obbligatoria', pubblicata nella *Gazzetta Ufficiale* n. 222 del 21 settembre 2004.

Italy (2005), Italy's Plan to relaunch the European Lisbon Strategy, Pico-piano per l'innovazione, la crescita e l'occupazione, Presidenza del Consiglio dei Ministri, Rome, 14 October.

Italy (2006), Decreto legislativo 11 aprile 2006, n. 198, 'Codice delle pari opportunità tra uomo e donna, a norma dell'articolo 6 della legge 28 novembre 2005, n. 246', pubblicato nella *Gazzetta Ufficiale* n. 125 del 31 Aprile 2006.

Italy (2008), National Reform Programme for 2008–2010, Interministerial Committee for EU Affairs, Department for EU Policies, Presidency of the Council of Ministers.

Italy (2008a), *The Good Life in Active Society*, Green Paper on the Future of the Welfare System, July, <www.lavoro.gov.it>.

Italy (2008b), Decreto Legge No. 137/2008, Disposizioni Urgenti in Materia di Istruzione e Università, GU, n. 204 del 1 Settembre 2008 (Gelmini Law).

Jachtenfuchs, M. (1995), 'Theoretical Perspectives on European Governance', *European Law Journal* 1(2): 115–133.

Jacobsson, K. (2004), 'Soft Regulation and the Subtle Transformation of States: The Case of EU Employment Policy', *Journal of European Social Policy* 14(4): 355–370.

Jacobsson, K. and Schmid, H. (2002), 'Real Integration or just Formal Adaptation? On the Implementation of the National Action Plans for Employment' in de la Porte, C. and Pochet, P. (eds), *Building Social Europe through the Open Method of Co-ordination* (Brussels: IE/Peter Lang), pp. 69–96.

Jacqueson, C. (2002), 'Union Citizenship and the Court of Justice: Something New under the Sun? Towards Social Citizenship', *European Law Review* 27(3): 260–281.

Jalušič, V. and Antić, M. (2000), 'Prospects for Gender Equality Policies in Central and Eastern Europe', SOCO Project Paper 70, Vienna.

Javaid, M. (2000), Employment Partner, DLA, London, chair of the workshop 'EU Anti-discrimination Directives: Implications and Developments' at the annual Oxford conference of the Industrial Law Society, 15–17 September, 'Employment Rights at the Turn of the Century', St Catherine's College, Oxford.

Jepsen, M. (2005), 'Towards a Gender Impact Analysis of Flexicurity' in Bredgaard, T. and Larsen, F. (eds), *Employment Policy from Different Angles* (Copenhagen:DJØf).

Jepsen, M. and Serrano Pascual, A. (2005), 'The European Social Model: An Exercise in Deconstruction', *Journal of European Social Policy* 15(3): 231–245.

Joerges, C. and Vos, E. (1999), 'Structures of Transnational Governance and their Legitimacy' in Vervaele, J. A. (ed.), Compliance and Enforcement of European Community Law (The Hague, London and Boston MA: Kluwer).

Joerges, C., Mény, Y. and Weiler, J. H. H. (eds) (2001), Mountain or Molehill? A Critical Appraisal of the Commission White Paper on Governance, New York University School of Law, Jean Monnet Series, <http://www.jeanmonnetprogram.org/papers/01/010601.html>.

Joerges, C. (2002), 'Deliberative Supranationalism: Two Defences', *European Law Journal* 8(1): 133–151.

Johansson, K. (1999), 'Tracing the Employment Title in the Amsterdam Treaty: Uncovering Transnational Coalitions', *Journal of European Public Policy* 6(1): 85–101.

Johnson, C. (1996), *In with the Euro, Out with the Pound: the Single Currency for Britain* (London: Penguin).

Jones, E. (2002), *The Politics of Economic and Monetary Union: Integration and Idiosyncrasy* (Lanham MD: Rowman & Littlefield).

Jones, E. L. (2002), 'Temporary Agency Labour: Back to Square One?' *Industrial Law Journal* 31(2): 183–190.

Junestav, M. (2002), 'Labour Cost Reduction, Taxes and Employment: The Swedish Case' in de la Porte, C. and Pochet, P. (eds), *Building Social Europe through the Open Method of Co-ordination* (Brussels: PIE/Peter Lang), pp. 137–176.

Kahn-Freund, O. (1960), 'Labour Law and Social Security' in Stein, E. and Nicholson, T. (eds), *American Enterprise in the European Common Market: A Legal Profile*, Vol. I (Ann Arbor MI: University of Michigan Press), pp. 297–458.

Kahn-Freund, O. (1979), *Labour Relations: Heritage and Adjustment* (Oxford: University Press).

Kasza, G. J. (2002), 'The Illusion of Welfare "Regimes" ', *Journal of Social Policy* 31(2): 271–287.

Keller, B. and Sörries, B. (1999), 'The New Social Dialogue: Old Wine in New Bottles?' *Journal of European Social Policy* 9: 111–125.

Keller, B. and Bansbach, M. (2000), 'Social Dialogues: An Interim Report on Recent Results and Prospects', *Industrial Relations Journal* 31: 291–307.

Kenner J. (1995), 'EC Labour Law: The Softly, Softly Approach', *International Journal of Comparative Labour and Law Industrial Relations* 11: 307–327.

Kenner, J. (1999) 'The EC Employment Title and the "Third Way": Making Soft Law Work?' *International Journal of Comparative Labour Law and Industrial Relations* 11(4): 307–326.

Kenner, J. (2000), *The Employment Title: Enhancing or Undermining EC Social Policy?* Panel 27, UACES conference, Budapest, April.

Kenner, J. (2001), 'The Charter of Fundamental Rights of the European Union: A Panacea for European Social Law?' Paper presented at the ECSA Seventh Biennial International Conference, Madison WI, 31 May–2 June.

Kenner, J. (2003), *EU Employment Law: From Rome to Amsterdam* (Oxford: Hart).

Kenner, J. (2009), 'New Frontiers in EU Labour Law: From Flexicurity to Flex-security' in Dougan, M. and Currie, S. (eds), *Fifty Years of the European Treaties: Looking Back and Thinking Forward* (Oxford: Hart), pp. 279–310.

Keune, M. (2003), 'Labour Market Flexibility in Central and Eastern Europe: an Analysis of Non-standard Employment and Working Time Arrangements in the Czech Republic and Hungary' in Wallace, C. (ed.), *Households, Work and Flexibility Survey, Comparative Volume 2* (Vienna: Institut für Höhere Studien/Institute of Advanced Studies).

Keune, M. (2008), 'Between Innovation and Ambiguity: The Role of Flexicurity in Labour Market Analysis and Policy-Making', Working Paper 4/2008, ETUI-REHS, 1–19.

Khol, H. and Platzer, H-W. (2003), 'Labour Relations in Central and Eastern Europe and the European Social Model', *Transfer* 1: 11–30.

Kilpatrick, C. (2001), 'Turning Remedies Around: A Sectoral Analysis of the Court of Justice' in de Búrca, G. and Weiler, J. (eds), *The European Court of Justice* (Oxford: Oxford University Press), pp. 143–176.

Kingsbury, B. (1998), ' "Indigenous Peoples" in International Law: A Constructivist Approach to the Asian Controversy', *American Journal of International Law* 92: 414–457.

Kingsbury, B., Krisch, N., Stewart, B. R. and Wiener, B. J. (2005), 'Foreword. Global Governance as Administration: National and Transnational Approaches to Global Administrative Law', *Law and Contemporary Problems* 68(1): 1–13.

Kjeldstad, R. (2001), 'Gender Policies and Gender Equality' in Kautto, M. *et al.* (eds), *Nordic Welfare States in the European Context* (London: Routledge).

Klabbers, J. (1994), 'Informal Instruments before the European Court of Justice', *Common Market Law Review* 31: 997–1023.

Klabbers, J. (1996), 'The Redundancy of Soft Law', *Nordic Journal of International Law* 65: 167–182.

Klabbers, J. (1998), 'The Undesirability of Soft Law', *Nordic Journal of International Law* 67: 381–391.

Knill, C. and Lehmkuhl, D. (1999), 'How Europe Matters: Different Mechanisms of Europeaniza-tion', *European Integration online Papers* (EIoP) 3(7): 1–20, <http://eiop.or.at/eiop/texte/1999–007a.htm>.

Knot, K., McDonald, D. and Swidersky, K. (1998), 'Policy Challenges for the Euro Area', *Finance and Development* 35(4): 4–8.

Knudsen, H. and Lind, J. (1999), 'The Implementation of EU Directives in National Systems: Lessons from the Danish Case', *Transfer* 1/2: 136–155.

Kohler-Koch, B. and Rittberger, B. (2006), 'Review Article. The "Governance Turn" in EU Studies', *Journal of Common Market Studies* 44: 27–49.

Kok, W. (2003), *Jobs, Jobs, Jobs: Creating More Employment in Europe*, Report of the Employment Task Force, chaired by Wim Kok, November (Luxembourg: OOPEC).

Kok, W. (2004), *Facing the Challenge: The Lisbon Strategy for Growth and Employment*, Report from the High Level Group (Luxembourg: OOPEC).

Koldinská, K. (2008), 'OMC in the Context of EU Gender Policy from the Point of View of New EU Member States' in Beveridge, F. and Velluti, S. (eds), *Gender and the Open Method of Coordination: Perspectives on Law, Governance and Equality in the European Union* (Aldershot: Ashgate), pp. 119–139.

Krisch, N. and Kingsbury, B. (2006), 'Introduction. Global Governance and Global Administrative Law in the International Legal Order', *European Journal of International Law* 17(1): 1–13.

Krugman, P. and Obstfeld, M. (1991), *Economia internazionale: teoria e politica economica*, Milan: Hoepli).

Kulachi, E. (2004), 'The Party of European Socialists and the Question of Unemployment' in Delwit, P., Kulachi, E. and Van de Walle, C. (eds), *The Europarties: Organization and Influence* (Brussels: Centre d'Etudes de la Vie Politique, Free University of Brussels), pp. 221–241.

Kvist, J. (1999), 'Welfare Reform in the Nordic Countries in the 1990s: Using Fuzzy-set Theory to Assess Conformity to Ideal Types', *Journal of European Social Policy* 9(3): 231–252.

Kvist, J. (2006), 'Diversity, Ideal Types and Fuzzy Sets in Comparative Welfare State Research' in Rihoux, B. and Grimm, H. (eds), *Innovative Comparative Methods for Policy Analysis: Beyond the Quantitative–Qualitative Divide* (New York: Springer), pp. 167–184.

Kuchařová, V. *et al.* (2007), 'Career, Families, Equal Opportunities: Studies on Women and Men in the Czech labour Market', Gender Studies, Prague, <http://www.genderstudies.cz/en>.

Ladeur, K-H. (1997), 'The Integration of Scientific and Technological Expertise into the Process of Standard-Setting according to German Law' in Joerges, C. *et al.* (eds), *Integrating Scientific Expertise into Regulatory Decision-Making* (Baden-Baden: Nomos), pp. 141–167.

Ladeur, K-H. (1997a), 'Towards a Legal Theory of Supranationality: The Viability of the Network Concept', *European Law Journal* 3(1): 33–54.

Ladeur, K-H. (1999), *The Theory of Autopoiesis as an Approach to a Better Understanding of Postmodern Law: From the Hierarchy of Norms to the Heterarchy of Changing Patterns of Legal Interrelationships*, EUI Working Paper LAW 99/3.

Ladeur, K.- H. (2008), ' "We, the European People . . ." Relâche?' *European Law Journal* 14(2): 147–167.

Ladrech, R. (1994), 'Europeanization of Domestic Politics and Institutions: The Case of France', *Journal of Common Market Studies* 32(1): 69–88.

Laffan, B. and Shaw, C (2005), Classifying and Mapping the Open Method of Coordination in Different Policy Areas, July, Project 02/D9, NEWGOV, New Modes of Governance Project, Project CITI-CT-2004–506392, <http://eucenter.wisc.edu/OMC /Papers/IaffanShaw.pdf>.

Lafoucrière, C. (2000), *The European Employment Strategy: The Third Pillar, Adaptability*, ETUI Working Paper, DWP 2000.01.03.

Larsen, F. (2005), 'Active Labour Market Policy in Denmark as an Example of Transitional Labour Market and Flexicurity Arrangements. What can be Learnt?' in Bredgaard, T. and Larsen, F. (eds), *Employment Policy from Different Angles* (Copenhagen: DJØf).

Lastra, R-M. (1992), 'The Independence of the European System of Central Banks', *Harvard Journal of International Law* 33(2): 479–519.

Latta, M. (2000), 'Side-streaming Gender? The Potential and Pitfalls of the European Ideology on Mainstreaming Gender Issues', *Transfer* 6(2): 290–320.

Le Cacheux, J. (2007), 'To Coordinate or not to Coordinate: An Economist's Perspective on the

Rationale for Fiscal Policy Coordination in the Euro Zone' in Linsenmann, I., Meyer, C. and Wessels, W. (eds), *Economic Government of the EU: A Balance Sheet of New Modes of Policy Coordination* (Basingstoke: Palgrave Macmillan), pp. 37–52.

Le Cacheux, J. and Touya, F. (2007), 'The Dismal Record of the Stability and Growth Pact' in Linsenmann, I., Meyer, C. and Wessels, W. (eds), *Economic Government of the EU. A Balance Sheet of New Modes of Policy Coordination* (Basingstoke: Palgrave Macmillan), pp. 72–90.

Lebessis, N. and Paterson, J. (2001), 'Developing New Modes of Governance' in De Schutter, O., Lebessis, N. and Paterson, J. (eds), *Governance in the European Union* (Luxembourg: OOPEC).

Leibfried, S. (1992), 'Towards a European Welfare State? On Integrating Poverty Regimes into the European Community' in Ferge, Z. and Kolberg, J. E. (eds), *Social Policy in a Changing Europe* (Frankfurt: Campus).

Leibfried, S. and Pierson, P. (1996), 'Social Policy' in Wallace H. and Wallace W. (eds), *Policy-Making in the European Union* (Oxford: Oxford University Press).

Lenaerts, K. and Foubert, P. (2001), 'Social Rights in the Case Law of the European Court of Justice: The Impact of the Charter of Fundamental Rights of the European Union on Standing Case Law', *Legal Issues of Economic Integration* 28(3): 267–296.

Lindbeck, A. and Snower, D. (1988), *The Insider–Outsider Theory of Employment and Unemployment* (Cambridge MA: MIT Press).

Linsenmann, I. (2007), 'Towards a Horizontal Fusion of Governing Structures? Coordination of Coordination Processes through the Broad Economic Policy Guidelines' in Linsenmann, I., Meyer, C. and Wessels, W. (eds), *Economic Government of the EU: A Balance Sheet of New Modes of Policy Coordination* (Basingstoke: Palgrave Macmillan), pp. 141–162.

Lobel, O. (2004), 'The Renew Deal: The Fall of Regulation and the Rise of Governance in Contemporary Legal Thought', *Minnesota Law Review* 89: 342–470.

LO (2003), Resolution on Equal Opportunities in the Trade Union Movement, adopted at LO's thirty-fifth ordinary Congress, <http://www.lo.dk/upload/LO/Documents/E/equal.PDF>.

LO (2005), LO's Equal Opportunities Accounts for 2005, <http://www.lo.dk/upload/LO/Documents/2/2007%200301%201301%20%20Ligestillingsrapport_3738.pdf>.

Lo Faro, A. (2000), *Regulating Social Europe: Reality and Myth of Collective Bargaining in the EC Legal Order* (Oxford: Hart).

Lo Faro, A. (2002), 'Fairness at Work? The Italian White Paper on Labour Market Reform', *Industrial Law Journal* 31(2): 190–198.

Lord, C. (2000), 'Legitimacy, Democracy and the EU: When Abstract Questions become Practical Policy Problem', Policy Paper 03/00, <http://www.one-europe.ac.uk>.

Louis, J. V. (2006), 'The Review of the Stability and Growth Pact', *Common Market Law Review* 43(1): 85–106.

Luciani, M. (2000), 'Diritti sociali e integrazione europea' in Associazione Italiana dei Costituzionalisti, *Annuario 1999: la Costituzione Europea*, Atti del XIV Convegno Annuale, Perugia, 7–9 October 1999, Padua, pp. 507 ff.

MacCormick, N. (1999), *Questioning Sovereignty: Law, State, and Nation in the European Commonwealth* (Oxford: Oxford University Press).

Madsen, P. K. (2006), 'Flexicurity: A New Perspective on Labour Markets and Welfare States in Europe: The Case of Denmark', Danish National Centre for Labour Market Research (CARMA), University of Aalborg.

Madsen, M. R. *et al.* (2008), 'General Introduction. Paradoxes of European Legal Integration' in Petersen, A. *et al.* (eds), *Paradoxes of European Legal Integration* (Aldershot: Ashgate).

Maher, I. (2004), 'Economic Policy Coordination and the European Court: Excessive Deficits and ECOFIN Discretion', *European Law Review* 29(6): 831–841.

Mailand, M. (2006), *Coalitions and Policy Coordination: Revision and Impact of the European Employment Strategy* (Copenhagen: DJØF).

Majone, G. (1993), 'The European Community between Social Policy and Social Regulation', *Journal of Common Market Studies* 31: 153–170.

Majone, G. (2002), 'Delegation of Regulatory Powers in a Mixed Polity', *European Law Journal* 8(3): 319–339.

Majone, G. (2008), 'Unity in Diversity: European Integration and the Enlargement Process', *European Law Review* 33(4): 457–481.

Majone, G. and Wildavsky, A. (1979), 'Implementation as Evolution' in Pressmann, J. and Wildavsky, A. (eds), *Implementation* (Berkeley CA: University of California Press), pp. 163–180.

Mancini, G. F. (1989), 'The Making of a Constitution for Europe', *Common Market Law Review* 26: 595–614.

Marcussen, M. (2002), 'Multilateral Surveillance and the OECD: Playing the Idea Game' in Armingeon, K. and Beyeler, M. (eds), *OECD Surveillance and the Welfare State* (Aldershot: Edward Elgar).

Mariucci, L. (2002), 'La forza di un pensiero debole: una critica del Libro Bianco del lavoro', *Lavoro e Diritto* 1: 3.

Marks, G., Hooghe, L. and Blank, K. (1996), 'European Integration from the 1980s: State-centric v. Multiple-level Governance', *Journal of Common Market Studies* 34(3): 341–378.

Marsden, D. (1997), 'Public Service Pay Reforms in European Countries: European Review of Labour and Research' *Transfer* 3(1): 62–85.

Marshall, T. H. (1975), *Social Policy* (London: Hutchinson).

Martin, A. (1999), 'Wage Bargaining under EMU: Europeanization, Renationalization or Americanization?' DWP 99.01.03, ETUI, Brussels.

Martin, A. (2004), 'The EMU Macroeconomic Policy Regime and the European Social Model' in Martin, A. and Ross, G. (eds), *Euros and Europeans: Monetary Integration and the European Model of Society* (Cambridge: Cambridge University Press), pp. 20–50.

Martin, A. and Ross, G. (2004), 'Introduction: EMU and the European Social Model' in Martin, A. and Ross, G. (eds), *Euros and Europeans: Monetary Integration and the European Model of Society* (Cambridge: Cambridge University Press), pp. 1–19.

Martin, B. (1997), 'Reform of Public Management: A Relevant Question for Unions in the Public Sector?', DWP 97.05.01, ETUI, Brussels.

Martin, S. and Pearce, G. (1999), 'Differentiated Multi-level Governance? The Response of British Sub-national Governments to European Integration', *Regional and Federal Studies* 32(9): 32–52.

Mastronardi, F. (1998), 'Un territorio per l'Europa: la valorizzazione della dimensione locale nell'Unione Europea', *Industria e Sindacati*, December.

Masson, P. (2000), 'Fiscal Policy and Growth in the Context of European Integration', IMF Working Paper, WP/00/133, 3–31.

Mayer, O. (1895), *Deutsches Verwaltungsrecht*, vol. I (Duncker & Humblot, Leipzig), pp. 64 *et seq.*

McKinnon, R. (1963), 'Optimum Currency Areas' *American Economic Review* 717.

McWilliams, A. and Siegel, D. (2001), 'Corporate Social Responsibility: a theory of the firm perspective', *Academy of Management Review* 26(1): 117–127.

Meenan, H. (2007), 'Equality Law in an Enlarged European Union: Understanding the Article 13 Directives' (Cambridge: Cambridge University Press).

Melitz, J. and Zumer, F. (1999), 'Inter-regional and International Risk Sharing and Lessons for EMU', *Carnegie Rochester Conference Series on Public Policy* 51: 149–188.

Merry, S. E. (2003), 'Human Rights Law and the Demonization of Culture (and Anthropology along the Way)', *Polar: Political and Legal Anthropology Review* 26(1): 55–77.

Meulders, D. and Plasman, R. (1997), 'European Economic Policies and Social Quality' in Beck W., van der Maesen, L. and Walker A. (eds), *The Social Quality of Europe* (The Hague, London and Boston MA: Kluwer), pp. 31–33.

Meyer, C. and Kunstein, T. (2007), 'Towards a *grand débat européen* on Economic Governance? Publicised Discourses as Indicators for the Performance and Evolution of Policy Coordination Modes' in Linsenmann, I., Meyer, C. and Wessels, W. (eds), *Economic Government of the EU: A Balance Sheet of New Modes of Policy Coordination* (Basingstoke: Palgrave Macmillan), pp. 187–210.

Meyer, O., Linsenmann, I. and Wessels, W. (2007), 'Evolution towards a European Economic Government? Research Design and Theoretical Expectations' in Linsenmann, I., Meyer, C. and Wessels, W. (eds), *Economic Government of the EU: A Balance Sheet of New Modes of Policy Coordination* (Basingstoke: Palgrave Macmillan), pp. 11–52.

Micklewright, J. and Stewart, K. (2000), 'Child Well-being in the EU – and Enlargement to the East',

Innocenti Working Papers, Economic and Social Policy Series 75, UNICEF, Innocenti Research Centre, Florence.

Milman-Sivan, M. (2009), 'Representativity, Civil Society and the EU Social Dialogue: Lessons from the International Labor Organization', *Indiana Journal of Global Legal Studies* 16(1): 311–337.

Muir, E. (2006), Case comment. 'Enhancing the Effects of Community Law on National Employment Policies: the Mangold Case', *European Law Review* 31(6): 879–891.

Mulgan, R. (2000), 'Accountability: An Ever-expanding Concept?' *Public Administration* 78(3): 555–573.

Mundell, R. (1961), 'A Theory of Optimal Currency Area', *American Economic Review* 51: 657–665.

Navarro, L. (2001), 'As the Euro Prepares for Take-off: a Critical Review of the First Three Years of EMU', *Groupement d'Etudes et de Recherches Notre Europe*, Working Paper 9.

Negrelli, S. (2000), 'Social Pacts in Italy and Europe: Similar Strategies and Structures; Different Models and National Stories' in Fajertag, G. and Pochet, P. (eds), *Social Pacts in Europe: New Dynamics* (Brussels: ETUI).

Nelken, D. (2004), 'Using the Concept of Legal Culture', *Australian Journal of Legal Philosophy* 29: 1–28.

Nelken, D. (2008), 'Normalizing Time: European Integration and Court Delays in Italy' in Petersen, A. *et al.* (eds), *Paradoxes of European Legal Integration* (Aldershot: Ashgate), pp. 299–324.

Nickell, S. (2000), 'Comments on the Concept and Measurement of European Labour Market Adaptability', paper, Brussels, 26–27 October, at:<http://europa.eu.int/comm/employment_social/empl&esf/concepts_en.htm>.

Nicolaïdis, K. (2007), 'Trusting the Poles? Constructing Europe through Mutual Recognition', *Journal of European Public Policy* 14(5): 682–698.

Nielsen, R. and Szyszczak, E. (1997), *The Social Dimension of the European Union* (Copenhagen: Handelshøjskolens Forlag).

Nielsen, R. (2000), *EC Labour Law* (Copenhagen: DJØF).

Nielsen, R. *et al.* (2002), 'Implementation of EC Directives in Denmark', *International Journal of Comparative Labour Law and Industrial Relations* 18(4): 459–478.

Noaksson, N. and Jacobsson, K. (2003), 'The Production of Ideas and Expert Knowledge in OECD: The OECD Jobs Strategy in Contrast with the EU Employment Strategy', SCORE Working Paper 2003–7, <http://www.score.su.se/pdfs/2003–7.pdf>.

Novitz, T. (2007–2008), 'A Human Rights Analysis of the Viking and Laval Judgments', *Cambridge Yearbook of European Legal Studies* 10: 541–562.

OECD (1994), *The OECD Jobs Study*, Part I and Part II (Paris: OECD).

OECD (1995), *Review of the Labour Market in the Czech Republic* (Paris: OECD).

OECD (1997), *Employment Perspective*, <www.oecd.org/eco/Eo.htm>.

OECD (1998), *Employment Outlook*, <www.oecd.org/eco/out/Eo.htm>.

OECD (1998a), *The OECD Jobs Strategy: Progress Report on Implementation of Country-specific Recommendations*, Economics Department Working Paper 196.

O'Keeffe, D. and Bavasso, A. (1998), 'Fundamental Rights and the European Citizen' in M. La Torre (ed.), *European Citizenship: An Institutional Challenge* (The Hague, London and Boston MA: Kluwer.

Olsen J. P. (2002), 'Reforming European Institutions of Governance', *Journal of Common Market Studies* 40(4): 581–602.

Orenstein, M. (1995), 'Transitional Social Policy in the Czech Republic and Poland', *Czech Sociological Review* 3(2): 179–196.

Orlandini, G. (2000), 'The Free Movement of Goods as a Possible "Community" Limitation on Industrial Conflict', *European Law Journal* 6(4): 341–362.

Ost, D. (2000), 'Illusory Corporatism in Eastern Europe: Neoliberal Tripartism and Post-communist Class Identities', *Politics and Society* 28: 503–530.

Oxenstierna, S. (1990), *From Labour Shortage to Unemployment? The Soviet Labour Market in the 1980s* (Stockholm: Universitet Stockholm).

Padoa-Scioppa, A. (2001), 'Una costituzione per l'Europa', *Il Mulino*, 1/2001, pp. 48–55.

Padoa Schioppa, T. (1994), *The Road to Monetary Union in Europe: The Emperor, the Kings and the Genies* (Oxford: Clarendon Press).

Papadopoulos, Y. (2007), 'Problems of Democratic Accountability in Network and Multilevel Governance', *European Law Journal* 13(4): 469–486.

Paterman, C. (1970), *Participation and Democratic Theory* (Cambridge: Cambridge University Press).

Pech, L. (2009), 'The Rule of Law as a Constitutional Principle of the European Union', paper presented for the EUSA biannual conference, Los Angeles CA, 23–25 April.

Peerenboom, R. (2009), 'The Future of the Rule of Law: Challenges and Prospects for the Field', *Hague Journal on the Rule of Law* 1: 1–10.

Pernice, I. (1999), 'Multi-level Constitutionalism and the Treaty of Amsterdam: European Constitution Making Revised?' *Common Market Law Review* 36: 703–750.

Pernice, I. (2001), 'Rethinking the Methods of Dividing and Controlling the Competencies of the Union', October, <http://europa.eu.int/comm/governance/index_en.htm>.

Peters, A. (1996), 'The Many Meanings of Equality and Positive Action in Favour of Women under European Community Law: A Conceptual Analysis', *European Law Journal* 2(2): 177–196.

Peters, A. (2005), 'Global Constitutionalism Revisited: Why Obey International Law?' *International Legal Theory* 11: 39.

Petersen, A. *et al.* (eds) (2008), *Paradoxes of European Legal Integration* (Aldershot: Ashgate).

Petite, M. (1998), 'The Treaty of Amsterdam', Jean Monnet Working Paper, <www.law.harvard.edu/programs/JeanMonnet/papers/98/98–2–html>.

Philippopoulos-Mihalopoulos, A. (2008), 'When "No" means "Yes": A Constitution for Europe and the Limits of Ignorance' in Petersen, A. *et al.* (eds), *Paradoxes of European Legal Integration* (Aldershot: Ashgate), pp. 29–44.

Pieterse, J. N. (1995), 'Globalization as Hybridation' in Featherstone, M. *et al.* (eds), *Global Modernities* (London: Sage).

Pisani-Ferry, P. (2000), *Plein emploi* (Paris: Documentation française).

Pisani-Ferry, J. and Sapir, A. (2006), 'Last Exit to Lisbon', Bruegel policy brief 2006/02, March, <http://www.bruegel.org/index.php?pid=73>.

Plant, R. (1998), 'The Third Way', Friedrich-Robert-Stiftung, Working Paper 5/98.

Pochet, P. (1999), 'The New Employment Chapter of the Amsterdam Treaty', *Journal of European Social Policy* 9(3): 271–278.

Poiares Maduro, M. (1998), *We, the Court: The European Court of Justice and the European Economic Constitution* (Oxford: Hart).

Poiares Maduro, M. (2000), 'Europe's Social Self: "The Sickness unto Death" ' in Shaw, J. (ed.), *Social Law and Policy in an Evolving European Union* (Oxford, Hart).

Poiares Maduro, M. (2003), 'Europe and the Constitution: What if This is as Good as it Gets?' in Weiler, J. H. H. and Wind, M. (eds), *European Constitutionalism beyond the State* (Cambridge: Cambridge University Press), pp. 74–102.

Poiares Maduro, M. (2007), 'So Close and yet so Far: The Paradoxes of Mutual Recognition', *Journal of European Public Policy* 14(5): 814–825.

Puhani, P. A. (1999), *Labour Mobility: An Adjustment Mechanism in Euroland?* ZEW Discussion Paper 99.

Radaelli, C. (2000), 'Policy Transfer in the European Union: Institutional Isomorphism as a Source of Legitimacy', *Governance* 13(1): 25–43.

Radaelli, C. (2000a), 'Whither Europeanization? Concept Stretching and Substantive Change', *European Integration online Papers* (EIoP), 4(8): 1–28, <http://eiop.or.at/eiop/texte/2000-008a.htm>.

Radaelli, C. (2004), 'Europeanization: Solution or problem?' *European Integration online Papers* (EIoP), 8(16): 1–26, <http://eiop.or.at/eiop/texte/2004-016a.htm>.

Ragin, C. (2000), *Fuzzy-set Social Science* (Chicago and London: University of Chicago Press).

Rampini, F. (2000), *New Economy: una rivoluzione in corso* (Rome and Bari: Laterza).

Rampini, F. (1998), 'L'Europa accusa', *La Repubblica*, 30 May.

Raunio, T. (2006), 'Does OMC Really Benefit National Parliaments?' *European Law Journal* 12(1): 130–131.

Raveaud, G. (2007), 'The European Employment Strategy: Towards More and Better Jobs?' *Journal of Common Market Studies* 45(2): 411–434.

Regalia, I. (2003), 'Decentralising Employment Protection in Europe: Territorial Pacts and Beyond' in Zeitlin, J. and Trubek, D. M. (eds), *Governing Work and Welfare in a new Economy: European and American Experiments* (Oxford: Oxford University Press), pp. 154–181.

Régent, S. (2002), 'The Open Method of Coordination: A Supranational Form of Governance' ILO, pp. 3–6.

Régent, S. (2003), 'The Open Method of Coordination: A New Supranational Form of Governance?' *European Law Journal* 9(2): 190–214.

Reich, N. (2001), 'Union Citizenship: Metaphor or Source of Rights?' *European Law Journal* 7(1): 4–23.

Rhodes, M. (1995), 'A Regulatory Conundrum: Industrial Relations and the Social Dimension' in Leibfried, S. and Pierson, P. (eds), *European Social Policy: Between Fragmentation and Integration* (Washington DC: Brookings Institution).

Rhodes, M. (2005), 'Employment Policy: Between Efficacy and Experimentation', in Wallace, H., Wallace, W. and Pollack, M. (eds), *Policy-making in the European Union* (Oxford: Oxford University Press), pp. 279–304.

Röben, V. (2003) 'Constitutionalism of Inverse Hierarchy: the Case of the European Union', *Jean Monnet Working Paper* 8/03, New York School of Law, <www.jeanmonnetprogram.org/papers/03/030801.pdf>.

Roberts, I. and Springer, B. (2001), *Social Policy in the European Union: Between Harmonization and National Autonomy* (Boulder CO and London: Lynne Rienner).

Rodrigues João, M. (2001), 'The Open Method of Co-ordination as a New Governance Tool' in Telò, M., *l'evoluzione della governance europea*, special issue of *Europa/Europe* (Rome), 2–3 2001: 96–107.

Rodriguez-Piñero Royo, M. C. (2000), 'Flexibility and European Law: A Labour Lawyer's View' in G. de Burca and J. Scott (eds), *Constitutional Change in the EU: From Uniformity to Flexibility* (Oxford: Hart).

Rolstadås, A. (ed.) (1995), *Performance Management: A Business Process Benchmarking Approach* (London: Chapman & Hall).

Rometsch, D. and Wessels, W. (1996), *The EU and Member States: Towards Institutional fusion?* (Manchester: Manchester University Press).

Rönmar, M. (2000), 'The Right to Direct and Allocate Work: From Employer Prerogatives to Object-ive Grounds?' Paper presented at the conference 'Legal Perspectives on Equal Treatment and Non-discrimination', Lund, Sweden, 7–8 December.

Rönnmar, M. (2007–2008), 'Free Movement of Services versus National Labour Law and Industrial Relations Systems: Understanding the Laval Case from a Swedish and Nordic Perspective', *Cambridge Yearbook of European Legal Studies* 10: 493–524.

Rosenau, J. (1999), 'A Transformed Observer in a Transforming World', *Studia Diplomatica* 1/2: 5.

Rosenfeld, M. (1994), 'Modern Constitutionalism as Interplay between Identity and Diversity' in Rosenfeld, M. (ed.), *Constitutionalism, Identity, Difference and Legitimacy: Theoretical Perspectives* (Durham NC and London: Duke University Press), pp. 3–38.

Rubery, J. *et al.* (1999), *Women's employment in Europe: Trends and Prospects* (London and New York: Routledge).

Rubery, J., Grimshaw, D., Fagan, C., Figueiredo, H. and Smith, M. (2003), 'Gender Equality Still on the European Agenda – But For How Long?' *Industrial Relations Journal* 34(5): 477–497.

Rusciano, M. (1996), 'Quale diritto del lavoro per il futuro', *Lavoro Italia* 9: 5.

Ryan, B. (2000), 'The Private Enforcement of European Union Labour Law' in Kilpatrick, C., Novitz, T. and Skidmore, P. (eds), *The Future of Remedies in Europe* (Oxford: Hart), pp. 141–163.

Sabel, C. F. and Simon, W. (2006), 'Epilogue: Accountability without Sovereignty' in de Búrca, G. and Scott, J. (eds), *Law and New Governance in the EU and the US* (Oxford: Hart), pp. 395–411.

Sabel, C. F. and Zeitlin, J. (2003), 'Active Welfare, Experimental Governance, Pragmatic Consti-tutionalism: The New Transformation of Europe', paper presented at the Workshop 'Opening the Open Method of Coordination', European University Institute, Florence, 4–5 July.

Sabel, C. F. and Zeitlin, J. (2008), 'Learning from Difference: The New Architecture of Experimentalist Governance in the EU', *European Law Journal* 14(3): 271–327.

Saint-Arnaud, S., and Bernard, P. (2003), 'Convergence or Resilience? A Hierarchical Cluster Analysis of the Welfare Regimes in Advanced Countries', *Current Sociology* 51(5): 499–527.

Salais, R. (2001), 'Europe and the Politics of Capabilities: Stakes and Routes', *European Trade Union Yearbook*, Brussels: ETUI, pp. 271–293.

Sand, I. J. (1998), 'Understanding the New Forms of Governance: Mutually Interdependent, Reflexive, Destabilised and Competing Institutions', *European Law Journal* 4(3): 271–293.

Santer, J. (1996), Speech delivered by President Jacques Santer at the Tripartite Conference on Growth and Employment, Rome, 14 June, *EU Bull.*, Suppl. 4/96: 9–10.

Sapir, A. *et al.* (2004), *An Agenda for a Growing Europe. The Sapir Report* (New York: Oxford University Press).

Saxonberg, S. and Sirovátka, T. (2009), 'Neo-liberalism by Decay? The Evolution of the Czech Welfare State', *Social Policy and Administration* 43(2): 186–203.

Sbragia, A. M. (2002), 'The Dilemma of Governance with Government', Jean Monnet Working Paper 3/02, New York Law School, <http://www.jeanmonnetprogram.org/papers/02/020301.pdf>, 1–15.

Sbragia, A. (2004), 'Shaping a Polity in an Economic and Monetary Union: the EU in Comparative Perspective' in Martin, A. and Ross, G. (eds), *Euros and Europeans: Monetary Integration and the European Model of Society* (Cambridge: Cambridge University Press), pp. 51–75.

Schadler, S. *et al.* (2005) 'Adopting the Euro in Central Europe', IMF Occasional Paper 234, Washington DC: International Monetary Fund.

Scharpf, F. W. (2001), 'European Governance: Common Concerns versus the Challenge of Diversity', MPIfG Working Paper 01/6, Cologne: Max Planck Institute for the Study of Societies.

Scharpf, F. (2002), 'The European Social Model: Coping with the Challenges of Diversity', *Journal of Common Market Studies* 40(4): 654–655.

Scheinin, M. (1995), 'Economic and Social Rights as Legal Rights' in Eide, A., Krause, C. and Rosas, A. (eds), *Economic, Social and Cultural Rights: A Textbook* (Dordrecht: Nijhoff).

Schelkle, W. (2007/2008), 'How Effective are new Approaches to Economic Governance? The Relaunched Lisbon Strategy and the Revised Pact', NewGov Policy Brief 5, winter, Florence: European University Institute.

Schiek, D. (2002), 'A New Framework on Equal Treatment of Persons in EC Law?' *European Law Journal* 8(2): 290–314.

Schiek, D. (2006), 'The ECJ Decision in Mangold: A Further Twist on Effects of Directives and Constitutional Relevance of Community Equality Legislation', *Industrial Law Journal* 35(3): 329–341.

Schiek, D., Waddington, L. and Bell, M. (eds) (2007), *Materials, Cases and Text on National, Supranational and International Non-discrimination Law* (Oxford: Hart).

Schier, D. (2000), 'Positive Action before the European Court of Justice: New Conceptions of Equality in Community Law? From Kalanke and Marschall to Badeck', *International Journal of Comparative Labour Law and Industrial Relations* 16(3): 251–275.

Schimdt, M. (1999), 'Representativity: A Claim Not Satisfied: The Social Partners' Role in the EC Law-making Procedure for Social Policy', *International Journal of Comparative Labour Law and Industrial Relations*, 15(3): 259–267.

Schmid, G. (1995), 'Is Full Employment Still Possible? Transitional Labour Markets as a New Strategy of Labour Market Policies', *Economic and Industrial Democracy* 16: 429–456

Schmid, G. (2008), *Full Employment in Europe: Managing Labour Market Transitions and Risks* (Cheltenham: Edward Elgar).

Schmidt, S. (2007), 'Mutual Recognition as a New Mode of Governance', *Journal of European Public Policy* 14(5): 667–681.

Schuman, R. (1991), in 'Quelle Europe?', quoted in Heilbron Price, D., *New Cold War or Common European Home? The Question of the Millennium*, p. 12, <http://www.schuman.org/Berlin.htm>.

Schüttpelz, A. (2005), 'The Europeanization of Employment Policy in the Czech Republic', paper prepared for the ESPAnet Conference, University of Fribourg, Switzerland, 22–24 September, <http://eucenter.wisc.edu/OMC/Papers/Enlargement/schuettpelz.pdf>.

Schusterschitz, G. and Kotz, S. (2007), 'The Comitology Reform of 2006 increasing the Powers of the European Parliament without Changing the Treaties', *European Constitutional Law Review* 3: 68–90.

Sciarra, S. (1995), 'European Social Policy and Labour Law: Challenges and Perspectives' in *Collected Courses of the Academy of European Law*, Vol. IV, Book 1 (The Hague: Nijhoff), p. 64.

Sciarra, S. (1995a), 'Social Values and the Multiple Sources of European Social Law', *European Law Journal* 1(1): 60–83.

Sciarra, S. (1999), 'From Strasbourg to Amsterdam: Prospects for the Convergence of European Social Rights Policy' in Alston, P. *et al.* (eds), *The European Union and Human Rights* (Oxford: Oxford University Press).

Sciarra, S. (1999a), 'The Employment Title in the Amsterdam Treaty: A Multi-language Legal Discourse' in O'Keeffe, D. and Twomey, P. (eds), *The Treaty of Amsterdam* (Oxford: Hart), pp. 157–170.

Sciarra, S. (2000), 'Global or Renationalised? Past and Future of European Labour Law' in Snyder, F. (ed.), *The Europeanisation of Law* (Oxford: Hart), pp. 269–292.

Sciarra, S. (ed.) (2001), *Labour Law in the Courts: National Judges and the European Court of Justice* (Oxford: Hart).

Sciarra S. (2002), 'Market Freedom and Fundamental Social Rights' in Hepple, B. (ed.), *Social and Labour Rights in a Global Context* (Cambridge: Cambridge University Press), pp. 95–121.

Sciarra, S. (2005), 'Fundamental Labour Rights after the Lisbon Agenda' in de Búrca, G. and de Witte, B. (eds), *Social Rights in Europe* (Oxford: Oxford University Press), pp. 199–215.

Sciarra, S. (2007), 'EU Commission's Green Paper "Modernizing Labour Law to Meet the Challenges of the Twenty-first Century', *Industrial Law Journal* 36: 375–382.

Sciarra, S. (2007–2008), 'Viking and Laval: Collective Labour Rights and Market Freedoms in the Enlarged EU', *Cambridge Yearbook of European Legal Studies* 10: 563–580.

Scott, C. (2000), 'Accountability in the Regulatory State', *Journal of Law and Society* 27(1): 38–60.

Scott, J. (1998), 'Law, Legitimacy and EC Governance: Prospects for "Partnership" ', *Journal of Common Market Studies* 36(2): 175–194.

Scott, J. and Trubek, D. (2002), 'Mind the Gap: Law and New Approaches to Governance in the European Union', *European Law Journal* 8(1): 1–18.

Scott, J. and Sturm, S. (2007), 'Courts as Catalysts: Rethinking the Judicial Role in New Governance' in de Búrca, G. and Scott, J. (eds), 'Narrowing the Gap? Law and New Approaches to Governance in the European Union', *Columbia Journal of European Law*, special issue, 13(3): 565–594.

Senden, L. (2004), *Soft Law in European Community Law* (Oxford: Hart).

Serrano Pascual, A. (2007), 'Activation Regimes in Europe: A Clustering Exercise' in Serrano Pascual, A. and Magnusson, L. (eds), *Reshaping Welfare States and Activation Regimes in Europe* (Brussels: Peter Lang).

Sestito, P. (2002), *Il mercato del lavoro in Italia* (Rome and Bari: Laterza).

Shaw, J. (1994), 'Twin-track Social Europe: The Inside Track' in O' Keefe, D. and Twomey, P. (eds), *Legal Issues of the Maastricht Treaty* (Chichester: Wiley), pp. 295–311.

Shaw, J. (1996), 'European Union Legal Studies in Crisis? Towards a New Dynamic', *Oxford Journal of Legal Studies* 16(2): 231–253.

Shaw, J. (1999), 'Postnational Constitutionalism in the European Union', *Journal of European Public Policy* 6: 579.

Shaw, J. (2000), 'Constitutionalism and Flexibility in the EU: Developing a Relational Approach' in de Búrca, G. and Scott, J. (eds), *Constitutional Change in the EU: From Uniformity to Flexibility?* (Oxford: Hart), pp. 331–358.

Shaw, J. (2001), 'Gender and the Court of Justice' in de Búrca, G. and Weiler, J. (eds), *The European Court of Justice* (Oxford: Oxford University Press), pp. 87–142.

Shaw, J. and Wiener, A. (2000), 'The Paradox of the European Polity' in Green Cowles, M. and Smith, M. (eds), *The State of the European Union*, Vol. 5, *Risks, Reform, Resistance and Revival* (Oxford: Oxford University Press).

Siaroff, A. (1994), 'Work, Welfare and Gender Equality: a New Typology' in Sainsbury, D. (ed.), *Gendering Welfare States* (London: Sage).

Siedentopf, H. and Hauschild, C. (1988), 'Comparative Conclusions' in Siedentopf, H. and Ziller, J. (eds), *Making European Policies Work*, Vol. 1 (London: Sage).

Silvia, S. J. (1991), 'The Social Charter of the European Community: A Defeat for European Labor', *Industrial and Labour Relations Review* 44(4): 626–643.

Sirovátka, T. (2008), 'Activation Policies under Conditions of weak Governance: Czech and Slovak Cases Compared', *Central European Journal of Public Policy* 2(1): 4–29.

Sisson, K. and Marginson, P. (2001), ' "Soft Regulation": Travesty of the Real Thing or New Dimension?' ESRC Working Paper 32/01.

Skidmore, P. (2001), 'EC Framework Directive on Equal Treatment in Employment: Towards a Comprehensive Community Anti-discrimination Policy?' *Industrial Law Journal* 30(1): 126–132.

Slaughter, A-M., Tulumello, A. and Wood, S. (1998), 'International Law and International Relations Theory: A New Generation of Interdisciplinary Scholarship', *American Journal of International Law* 92: 367–397.

Smismans, S. (2004), 'EU Employment Policy: Decentralization or Centralization through the Open Method of Coordination', EUI Working Paper LAW 2004/1.

Smismans, S. (2005), 'Reflexive Law in Support of Directly Deliberative Polyarchy: Reflexive-Deliberative Polyarchy as a Normative Frame for the OMC' in De Schutter, O. and Deakin, S. (eds), *Social Rights and Market Forces: Is the Open Coordination of Employment and Social Policies the Future of Social Europe?* (Brussels: Bruylant), pp. 99–144.

Smismans, S. (2005a), 'How to be Fundamental with Soft Procedures? The Open Method of Coordination and Fundamental Social Rights' in de Búrca, G. and de Witte, B. (eds) *Social Rights in Europe* (Oxford: Oxford University Press), pp. 217–238.

Smismans, S. (2007), 'New Governance: The Solution for Active European Citizenship, or the End of Citizenship?' *Columbia Journal of European Law* 13(3): 595–622.

Smismans, S. (2007a), 'The European Social Dialogue between Constitution and Labour Law', *European Law Review* 32(3): 341–364.

Smismans, S. (2008), 'The European Social Dialogue in the Shadow of Hierarchy', *Journal of Public Policy* 28(1): 161–180.

Smismans, S. (2008a), 'Multi-level Governance and the OMC: Inclusion, Subsidiarity and the Coordination of Coordination' in Committee of the Regions, *The Contributions to the 2008 Ateliers* (Brussels: Forward Studies/Cellule de Prospective, Committee of the Regions), pp. 171–177.

Smith, M. (1998), 'Sign of Progress in EU Campaign for more Jobs', *Financial Times*, 12 June.

Smuraglia, C. (1996), 'On the Current State of Implementation of Law No. 125 of 10 April 1991, containing Provisions concerning Positive Action for the Achievement of Equal Opportunities between Women and Men in Employment', *Rivista Italiana sul Diritto del Lavoro* 3: 112.

Snyder, F. (1993), 'The Effectiveness of European Community Law: Institutions, Processes, Tools and Techniques', *Modern Law Review* 56: 19–54.

Snyder, F. (1995), 'The Effectiveness of European Community Law: Institutions, Processes, Tools and Techniques' in Daintith, T. (ed.), *Implementing EC Law in the United Kingdom: Structures for Indirect Rule* (Chichester: Wiley).

Snyder, F. (1998), *EMU Revisited: Are we Making a Constitution? What Constitution are we Making?* EUI Working Paper LAW 98/6.

Snyder, F. (1999), *Global Economic Networks and Global Legal Pluralism*, EUI Working Paper LAW 99/6.

Snyder, F. (1999), *Globalisation and Europeanization as Friends and Rivals: European Union Law in Global Economic Networks*, EUI Working Paper LAW 99/8.

Snyder, F. (2000), 'Introduction' in Snyder, F. (ed.), *The Europeanization of Law* (Oxford: Hart).

Sol, E., Westerveld, M. (eds) (2005), *Contractualism in Employment Services: A new Form of Welfare State Governance* (The Hague: Kluwer).

Sousa Santos, B. (1992), 'State, Law and Community in the World System: an Introduction', *Social and Legal Studies* 1: 133–172.

Spaak, P-H. (1956), *Intergovernmental Committee on European Integration*, the Brussels Report on the General Common Market (Spaak Report), June.

Spaventa, E. (2009), 'Federalization versus Centralization: Tensions in Fundamental Rights Discourse in the EU' in Dougan, M. and Currie, S. (eds), *Fifty Years of the European Treaties: Looking Back and Thinking Forward* (Oxford: Hart), pp. 343–364.

Special issue (1999), 'The Cologne Process', *International Journal of Comparative Labour Law and Industrial Relations* 15(2): 137–160.

Spinant, D. (2001), 'Schröder Urges EU Reforms, Hits EU State Aid Rules', Eurobserver D., <http://euobserver.com/front_print.phtml?article_id=4534>.

Stalford, H., Currie, S. and Velluti, S. (eds) (2009), *Gender and Migration in Twenty-first Century Europe* (Aldershot: Ashgate).

Ştefan, O. A. (2008), 'European Competition Soft Law in European Courts: A Matter of Hard Principles?' *European Law Journal* 14(6): 753–772.

Stewart, B. R. (1986), 'Reconstitutive Law', *Modern Law Review* 46: 86.

Stokke, T. A. (1999), 'Collective Bargaining and State Intervention in the Scandinavian Countries', *Transfer* 1/2: 156–174.

Stournaras, Y. (1999), *The Converging Greek Economy: Developments, Policies, and Prospects*, Document of the Ministry of the National Economy, October, <http://www.hri.org, p. 1>.

Streeck, W. (1995), 'From Market-Making to State-Building: Reflections on the Political Economy of European Social Policy' in Leibfried, S. and Pierson, P. (eds), *European Social Policy: Between Fragmentation and Integration* (Washington DC: Brookings Institution).

Streeck, W. (1999), 'Competitive Solidarity: Rethinking the "European Social Model" ', Cologne: Max Planck Institute for the Study of Societies (MPIfG).

Streeck, W. (2000), 'Competitive Solidarity: Rethinking the "European Social Model" ' in Hinrichs, K. *et al.* (eds), *Kontingenz und Krise. Institutionenpolitik in kapitalistischen und postsozialistischen Gesellschaften* (Frankfurt: Campus).

Supiot, A. (1999), *Au-delà de l'emploi: transformation du travail et devenir du droit du travail en Europe* (Paris: Flammarion).

Supiot, A. (2000), 'The Dogmatic Foundations of the Market', *Industrial Law Journal* 29(4): 321–346.

Svensson, L. E. O. (1997), 'Inflation Forecast Targeting: Implementing and Monitoring Inflation Targets', *European Economic Review* 41: 1111–1146.

Symposium (2002), 'New Forms of Governance: Ceding Public Power to Private Actors', *UCLA Law Review* 49(6): 1687.

Syrpis, P. (2001), 'Smoke without Fire: The Social Policy Agenda and the Internal Market', *Industrial Law Journal* 30(3): 271–288.

Syrpis, P. (2002), 'Legitimising European Governance: Taking Subsidiarity Seriously within the Open Method of Co-ordination', EUI Working Paper LAW 2002/10.

Syrpis, P. (2007), *EU Intervention in Domestic Labour Law* (Oxford: Oxford University Press).

Syrpis, P. (2008), 'The Treaty of Lisbon: Much Ado . . . But about What?' *Industrial Law Journal* 37(3): 219–235.

Swank, D. (2002), *Global Capital, Political Institutions and Policy Change in Developed Welfare States* (Cambridge: Cambridge University Press).

Sweden, Government Offices of (2009), Work Programme for the Swedish Presidency of the EU, 1 July–31 December, <http://www.sweden.gov.se/sb/d/11312>.

Swyngedouw, E. (1992), 'The Mammon Quest: "Glocalisation", Interspatial Competition and the Monetary Order: The Construction of New Scales' in Dunford, M. and Kaflakis, M. (eds), *Cities and Regions in the New Europe* (London: Belhaven Press).

Szelewa, D. and Polakowski, M. P. (2008), 'Who Cares? Changing Patterns of Childcare in Central and Eastern Europe', *Journal of European Social Policy* 18(2): 115–131.

Szyszczak, E. (2000), *EC Labour Law* (London and New York: Longman).

Szyszczak, E. (2000a), 'The Evolving European Employment Strategy', in Shaw, J. (ed.), *Social Law and Policy in an Evolving European Law* (Oxford: Hart), pp. 197–220.

Szyszczak, E. (2001), 'III. Social Policy', *International Comparative Law Quarterly* 50: 175–186.

Szyszczak, E. (2001a), 'The New Paradigm for Social Policy: a Virtuous Circle?' *Common Market Law Review* 38: 1125–1170.

Szyszczak, E. (2002), 'Social Policy in the post-Nice Era' in Arnull, A. and Wincott, D. (eds), *Accountability and Legitimacy in the European Union* (Oxford: Oxford University Press).

Szyszczak, E. (2002a), 'Golden Shares and Market Governance', *Legal Issues of Economic Integration* 29(3): 255–284.

Szyszczak, E. (2006), 'Experimental Governance: The Open Method of Coordination', *European Law Journal* 12(4): 486–502.

Tavlas, G. (1993), 'The "New" Theory of Optimum Currency Areas', *World Economy* 16: 663.

Taylor, C. (1995), 'EMU 2000? Prospects for European Monetary Union', Chatham House Papers, London: RIIA.

Teague, P. (1998), 'Monetary Union and Social Europe', *Journal of European Social Policy* 8 (2): 117–137.

Teague, P. (2001), 'Deliberative Governance and EU Social Policy', *European Journal of Industrial Relations* 7(1): 7–26.

Telò, M. (2001), 'Governance and Government in the European Union: The Open Method of Co-ordination' in Rodriguez M. J. (ed.), *The New Knowledge Economy in Europe* (Cheltenham: Edward Elgar).

Teubner, G. (1988), 'Introduction to Autopoietic Law' in Teubner, G. (ed.), *Autopoietic Law: A New Approach to Law and Society* (Berlin and New York: de Gruyter), p. 1.

Teubner, G. (1989), 'How the Law Thinks: Towards a Constructivist Epistemology of Law', *Law and Society Review* 23(5): 727–757.

Teubner, G. (1993), *Law as an Autopoietic System* (Oxford: Oxford University Press).

Teubner, G. (1998), 'Legal Irritants: Good Faith in British Law, or, How Unifying Law Ends up in New Divergences', *Modern Law Review* 61: 11–32.

Thym, D. (2006), 'The Political Character of Supranational Differentiation', *European Law Review* 31(6): 781–799.

Toth, A. G. (1994), 'Is Subsidiarity Justiciable?' *European Law Review* 19(3): 268–285.

Treib, O., Bähr, H. and Fakner, G. (2005), 'Modes of Governance: A Note towards Conceptual Clarification', European Governance Papers, EUROGOV 2/2005.

Tronti, L. (ed.) (1998), *Benchmarking Employment Performance and Labour Market Policies: Final Report, 1997* (Berlin: Institute of Applied Socio-economics, IAS).

Trubek, D. and Mosher, J. (2003), 'New Governance, Employment Policy and the European Social Model' in Zeitlin, G. and Trubek, D. (eds), *Governing Work and Welfare in a New Economy: European and American Experiments* (Oxford: Oxford University Press), pp. 30 *ff.*

Trubek, D. and Trubek, L. (2007), 'New Governance and Legal Regulation: Complementarity, Rivalry and Transformation' in de Búrca, G. and Scott, J. (eds), 'Narrowing the Gap? Law and New Approaches to Governance in the European Union', *Columbia Journal of European Law*, special issue, 13(3): 539–564.

Tsakatika, M. (2007), 'A Parliamentary Dimension for EU Soft Governance', *Journal of European Integration* 29(5): 549–564.

Tsoukalis, L. (1996), 'Economic and Monetary Union' in Wallace, H. and Wallace, W. (eds), *Policy-Making in the European Union* (Oxford: Oxford University Press), p. 280.

Tully, J. (2002), 'The Unfreedom of the Moderns in Comparison to their Ideals of Constitutionalism and Democracy', *Modern Law Review* 65(2): 204–228.

Tuytschaever, F. (2000), 'EMU and the Catch 22 of the EU Constitution-making' in de Búrca, G. and Scott, J. (eds), *Constitutional Change in the EU: From Uniformity to Flexibility* (Oxford: Hart), pp. 173–196.

Twining, W. (2008), 'Surface Law' in Petersen, A. *et al.* (eds), *Paradoxes of European Legal Integration* (Aldershot: Ashgate), pp. 157–183.

UNESCAP (2009), 'What is Good Governance?' <http://www.unescap.org/pdd/prs/ProjectActivities/Ongoing/gg/governance.asp>.

Usher, J. (1998), 'Economic and Monetary Union: A Model for Flexibility?' *Cambridge Yearbook of European Legal Studies* 1: 39.

Valenduc, G. and Vendramin, P. (2001), 'Telework: from Distance Working to new Forms of Flexible Work Organisation', *Transfer* 2: 244–257.

van Berkel, R. and Valkenburg, B. (eds) (2007), *Making it Personal: Individualising Activation Services in the EU* (Bristol: Policy Press).

Vandenbroucke, F. (2001), 'Open Coordination on Pensions and the Future of Europe's Social Model', closing address to the conference 'Towards a New Architecture for Social Protection in Europe', Leuven, 19–20 October.

Vaughan-Whitehead, D. (2000), 'New Hidden Borders: Economic and Social Gaps in an Enlarged European Union', Robert Schuman Policy Paper 2000/29, EUI, June.

Vaughan-Whitehead, D. (2003), *EU Enlargement versus Social Europe? The Uncertain Future of the European Social Model* (Cheltenham: Edward Elgar).

Večerník, J. (2001), 'Labour Market Flexibility and Employment Security: The Czech Republic', Employment Paper 2001/27, Geneva: ILO.

Velluti, S. (2003), 'Towards the Constitutionalisation of New Forms of Governance: A Revised Institutional Framework for the European Employment Strategy', *Yearbook of European Law* 22: 353–405.

Velluti, S. (2007), 'What European Union Strategy for Integrating Migrants? The Role of OMC Soft Mechanisms in the Development of an EU Immigration Policy', *European Journal of Migration and Law* 9: 53–82.

Velluti, S. (2008), 'Promotion of Gender Equality at the Workplace: Gender Mainstreaming and Collective Bargaining in Italy', *Feminist Legal Studies* 16(2): 195–214.

Veneziani, B. (1999), 'The Intervention of the Law to regulate Collective Bargaining and Trade Union Representation Rights in European Countries: Recent Trends and Problems', *Transfer* 5(1–2): 100–135.

Verloo, M. (2005), 'Mainstreaming Gender Equality in Europe: A Frame Analysis Approach', special issue, 'Differences in the Framing of Gender Inequality as a Policy Problem across Europe', *Greek Review of Social Research* 117(B1): 11–34.

Vervaele, J. A. (1999), 'Transnational Cooperation of Enforcement Authorities in the Community Area' in Vervaele, J. A. (ed.), *Compliance and Enforcement of European Community Law* (The Hague, London and Boston MA: Kluwer).

Vigneau, K., Ahlberg, B., Bercusson B. and Bruun N. (eds) (1999), *Fixed-term Work in the EU: A European Agreement against Discrimination and Abuse* (Stockholm: National Institute for Working Life and the Swedish Trade Unions).

Villa, P. (2005), 'EGGSIE: Assessment of the 2004 National Action Plans for Employment from a gender perspective, Italy', <http://ec.europa.eu/employment_social/gender_equality/docs/2005/italy-napemp_en.pdf>.

Visser, J. (2002), 'Is the European Employment Strategy the Answer?', paper prepared for the NIG Workshop 'Governability in Post-industrial Societies: The European Experience', Utrecht School of Governance, 26–27 April.

Vousden, S. (2000), 'Albany, Market Law and Social Exclusion', *Industrial Law Journal* 29: 181–191.

Walker, N. (1998), 'Sovereignty and Differentiated Integration in the European Union', *European Law Journal* 4(4): 355–388.

Walker, N. (1999), 'Flexibility within a Metaconstitutional Frame: Reflections on the Future of Legal Authority in Europe', Harvard Jean Monnet Working Paper 12/99, Harvard Law School, <www.jeanmonnetprogram.org/papers/99/991201.html>, pp. 1–44.

Walker, N. (2000), 'Flexibility within a Metaconstitutional Frame: Reflections on the Future of Legal Authority in Europe' in de Búrca, G. and Scott, J. (eds), *Constitutional Change in the EU: From Uniformity to Flexibility?* (Oxford: Hart), pp. 9–30.

Walker, N. (2002), 'The Idea of Constitutional Pluralism', *Modern Law Review* 65: 318.

Walker, N. (2003), 'Postnational Constitutionalism and the Problem of Translation' in Weiler, J. H. H. and Wind, M. (eds), *European Constitutionalism: Beyond the State* (Cambridge: Cambridge University Press), pp. 27–54.

Walker, N. (2006), 'EU Constitutionalism and New Governance' in de Búrca, G. and Scott, J. (eds) (2006), *Law and New Governance in the EU and the US* (Oxford: Hart), pp. 15–36.

Walker, N. (2009), 'The Rule of Law and the EU: Necessity's Mixed Virtue' in Palombella, G. and Walker, N. (eds), *Relocating the Rule of Law* (Oxford: Hart), pp. 119–138.

Wallace, H. (1998), 'Differentiated Integration' in Dinan, D. (ed.), *Encyclopedia of the European Union* (Boulder CO: Lynne Rienner), p. 137.

Wallace, H. and Wallace, W. (1996), *Policy-Making in the European Union* (Oxford: Oxford University Press).

Wälti, S. and Kübler, D. (2003), ' "New Governance" and Associative Pluralism: The Case of Drug Policy in Swiss Cities', *Policy Studies Journal* 31(4): 499–525.

Watson, P. (1993), 'Social Policy after Maastricht', *Common Market Law Review* 30(3): 481–513.

Weatherill, S. and Beaumont, P. (1999), *EU Law*, 3rd edn (London: Penguin).

Weddenburn, K. W. (1995), *Labour Law and Freedom: Further Essays in Labour Law* (London: Lawrence & Wishart).

Weiler, J. (1991), 'The Transformation of Europe', *Yale Law Journal* 100: 2403–2483.

Weiler, J. (1999), 'European Democracy and its Critics: Polity and System' in *The Constitution of Europe* (Cambridge: Cambridge University Press).

Weiler, J. (2002), 'A Constitution for Europe? Some Hard Choices', *Journal of Common Market Studies* 40(4): 563–580.

Weiler, J. (1995), 'The State *über alles*: Demos, Telos and the German Maastricht Decision' in Due, O., Lutter, M. and Schwarze, J. (eds), *Festschrift für Ulrich Everling* (Baden-Baden: Nomos).

Weiler, J. (1999), 'European Democracy and its Critics: Polity and System' in *The Constitution of Europe* (Cambridge: Cambridge University Press).

Weiler, J. H. H. (1993), 'Journey to an Unknown Destination: A Retrospective and Prospective of the European Court of Justice in the Arena of Political Integration', *Journal of Common Market Studies* 31(4): 417–446.

Weiler, J. H. H. (1994), 'A Quiet Revolution: The European Court of Justice and its Interlocutors', *Comparative Political Studies* 26(4): 510–534.

Weiler, J. H. H. (1999), 'European Models: Polity, People and System' in Craig, P. and Harlow, C. (eds), *Lawmaking in the European Union* (The Hague: Kluwer), pp. 3–31.

Weiler, J. H. H. (1981), 'The Community System: the Dual Character of Supranationalism', *Yearbook of European Law* 1: 268–306.

Weiler, J. H. H. (1995), 'Does Europe need a Constitution? Reflections on Demos, Telos and the German Maastricht Decision', *European Law Journal* 1(3): 219–258.

Weiler, J. H. H. (1996), 'European Citizenship and Human Rights' in Winter, J. *et al.* (eds), *Reforming the Treaty on European Union* (The Hague: Kluwer).

Weiler, J. H. H. (2002), 'A Constitution for Europe: Some Hard Choices', *Journal of Common Market Studies* 40(4): 563–580.

Weiler, J. H. H., Haltern, U. R. and Mayer, F. C. (1995), 'European Democracy and its Critique', *West European Politics* 18(3): 4–39.

Weiler, J. H. H. and Wind, M. (2003), 'Introduction. European Constitutionalism beyond the State' in Weiler, J. H. H. and Wind, M. (eds), *European Constitutionalism beyond the State* (Cambridge: Cambridge University Press), pp. 1–4.

Weiss, M. (1992), 'The Significance of Maastricht for European Social Policy', *International Journal of Comparative Labour Law and Industrial Relations* 8(1): 3–14.

Wellens, K. C. and Borchardt, G. M. (1989), 'Soft Law in European Community Law', *European Law Review* 14(5): 267–321.

Wendon, B. (1998), 'The Commission and European Union Social Policy' in Sykes, R. and Alcock, P. (eds), *Developments in European Social Policy: Convergence and Diversity* (Bristol: Policy Press).

Wiener, A. (1998), 'The Embedded *Acquis Communautaire*: Transmission Belt and Prism of New Governance', RSC Working Paper 98/35.

Wiener, A. (1998), 'The Developing Practice of "European Citizenship" ' in M. La Torre (ed.), *European Citizenship: An Institutional Challenge* (The Hague, London and Boston MA: Kluwer).

Wiener, A. (2007), 'Contested Meanings of Norms: A Research Framework', *Comparative European Politics* 5: 1–17.

Wiener, A. and Della Sala, V. (1997), 'Constitution-Making and Citizenship Practice: Bridging the Democracy Gap in the EU?' *Journal of Common Market Studies* 35(4): 595–614.

Wilthagen, T., Tros, F. and van Lieshout, H. (2004), 'Towards "Flexicurity"? Balancing Flexibility and Security in EU Member States', *European Journal of Social Security* 6(2): 113–136.

Winkler, B. (1995), 'Towards a Strategic View on EMU: A Critical Survey', EUI Working Paper RSC 95/18, p. 11 n. 24.

Wincott, D. (1995), 'The Role of Law or the Rule of the Court of Justice? An Institutional Account of Judicial Politics in the European Community', *Journal of European Public Policy* 2(4): 583.

Wyatt, D. (2003), 'Subsidiarity: Is it too Vague to be Effective as a Legal Principle?' in Nicolaidis, K. and Weatherill, S. (eds), *National Models and the Constitution of the European Union* (Oxford: Oxford University Press/European Studies at Oxford/Whose Europe?), pp. 86–97, <http://denning.law.ox.ac.uk/iecl/pdfs/whoseeurope.pdf>.

Yataganas, X. A. (2001), 'The Treaty of Nice: The Sharing of Power and the Institutional Balance in the European Union: A Continental Perspective', *European Law Journal* 7(3): 255.

Zagrebelsky, G. (1922), *Il diritto mite: legge, diritti, giustizia* (Turin: Einaudi).

Zeitlin, J. (2005), 'Social Europe and Experimentalist Governance: Towards a New Constitutional Compromise?' in de Búrca, G. (ed.), *EU Law and the Welfare State: In Search of Solidarity* (Oxford: Oxford University Press), pp. 213–241.

Zeitlin, J. and Trubek, D. M. (2003), *Governing Work and Welfare in a new Economy: European and American Experiments* (Oxford: Oxford University Press).

Zeitlin, J. and Pochet, P. with Magnusson, L. (eds) (2005), *The Open Method of Coordination in Action: The European Employment and Social Inclusion Strategies* (Brussels: PIE/Peter Lang).

Web sites

http://www.connex-network.org

http://www.cordis.europa.eu/eesd/ka4/home.html

http://ec.europa.eu/regional_policy/innovation/innovating/pacts/en/index.html

http://ec.europa.eu/growthandjobs/national-dimension/member-states-2005–2008–reports/index_en.htm

http://ec.europa.eu/growthandjobs/european-dimension/index_en.htm

http://epp.eurostat.ec.europa.eu/portal/page/portal/structural_indicators/introduction

http://eucenter.wisc.edu/OMC

http://www.eu-newgov.org

http://www.eurocities.org

http://europa.eu.int/comm/enlargement/pas/phare/intro.htm

http://europa.eu.int/comm/enlargement/pas/europe_agr.htm

http://www.majorcities.org/pics/medien/1_1102506953/BETUING.pdf

http://www.mutual-learning-employment.net/

http://www.oecd.org/

http://www.sustainable-cities.eu/

http://www.tesoro.it/Euro/comitato.htm

Index